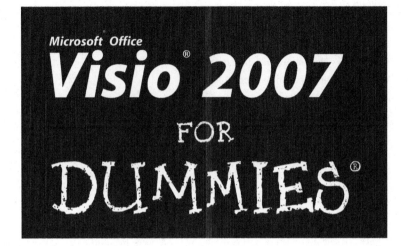

Microsoft Office
Visio® 2007
FOR
DUMMIES®

by John Paul Mueller and Debbie Walkowski

BICENTENNIAL

1807

WILEY

2007

BICENTENNIAL

Wiley Publishing, Inc.

Visio® 2007 For Dummies®

Published by
Wiley Publishing, Inc.
111 River Street
Hoboken, NJ 07030-5774

www.wiley.com

Copyright © 2007 by Wiley Publishing, Inc., Indianapolis, Indiana

Published by Wiley Publishing, Inc., Indianapolis, Indiana

Published simultaneously in Canada

WILEY

About the Authors

John Mueller is a freelance author and technical editor. He has writing in his blood, having produced 70 books and over 300 articles to date. The topics range from networking to artificial intelligence and from database management to heads-down programming. Some of his current books include a Windows power optimization book, a book on .NET security, and books on Amazon Web Services, Google Web Services, and eBay Web Services. His technical editing skills have helped more than 51 authors refine the content of their manuscripts. John has provided technical editing services to both *Data Based Advisor* and *Coast Compute* magazines. He's also contributed articles to magazines like *DevSource*, *InformIT*, *Informant*, *DevX*, *SQL Server Professional*, *Visual C++ Developer*, *Hard Core Visual Basic*, *asp.netPRO*, *Software Test and Performance*, and *Visual Basic Developer*.

When John isn't working at the computer, you can find him in his workshop. He's an avid woodworker and candle maker. On any given afternoon, you can find him working at a lathe or putting the finishing touches on a bookcase. He also likes making glycerin soap and candles, which comes in handy for gift baskets. You can reach John on the Internet at JMueller@mwt.net. John is also setting up a Web site at http://www.mwt.net/~jmueller/; feel free to look and make suggestions on how he can improve it. Check out his weekly blog at http://www.amazon.com/gp/blog/id/AQOA2QP4X1YWP.

Debbie Walkowski has worked in the computer industry for more than 20 years in a variety of positions from sales and marketing to teaching and training. For the last 14 years, she has made writing her primary focus. Her company, the Writing Works, specializes in writing computer self-help books and providing writing services to companies such as Microsoft Corporation, Hewlett-Packard (formerly Digital Equipment Corporation), and AT&T Wireless Communications. She has authored 18 books on popular computer software, including Microsoft Office, Microsoft Works, Microsoft PowerPoint, Microsoft Excel, Microsoft Project, Microsoft Windows, Visio, Quicken, WordPerfect, and Lotus 1-2-3.

Dedication

This book is dedicated to those purveyors of the medicinal latte, Muhammad and Marilyn Kharbush.

Author's Acknowledgments

From John Mueller: Thanks to my wife, Rebecca, for working with me to get this book completed. I really don't know what I would have done without her help in researching and compiling some of the information that appears in this book. She also did a fine job of proofreading my rough draft and page-proofing the result. She also had to do without my help in the garden this summer, which made things mighty tough on her.

Russ Mullen deserves thanks for his technical edit of this book. He greatly added to the accuracy and depth of the material you see here. Russ is always providing me with great URLs for new products and ideas. I really appreciated Russ' input on several of the new Visio 2007 features. They were helpful in rounding out the information you find in this book.

Matt Wagner, my agent, deserves credit for helping me get the contract in the first place and taking care of all the details that most authors don't really consider. I always appreciate his assistance. It's good to know that someone wants to help.

A number of people read all or part of this book to help me refine the approach, test the examples, and generally provide input that every reader wishes they could have. These unpaid volunteers helped in ways too numerous to mention here. I especially appreciate the efforts of Eva Beattie who read the entire book and selflessly devoted herself to this project. Members of various newsgroups and the support staff from Microsoft were instrumental in helping me overcome obstacles. A number of other people helped me in ways too numerous to mention.

Finally, I would like to thank Kyle Looper, Nicole Sholly, John Edwards, Jennifer Theriot, and the rest of the editorial and production staff for their assistance in bringing this book to print. It's always nice to work with such a great group of professionals.

Publisher's Acknowledgments

We're proud of this book; please send us your comments through our online registration form located at www.dummies.com/register/.

Some of the people who helped bring this book to market include the following:

Acquisitions, Editorial, and Media Development

Project Editor: Nicole Sholly

Acquisitions Editor: Kyle Looper

Copy Editor: John Edwards

Technical Editor: Russ Mullen

Editorial Manager: Kevin Kirschner

Media Development Specialists: Angela Denny, Kate Jenkins, Steven Kudirka, Kit Malone

Media Development Coordinator: Laura Atkinson

Media Project Supervisor: Laura Moss

Media Development Manager: Laura VanWinkle

Editorial Assistant: Amanda Foxworth

Sr. Editorial Assistant: Cherie Case

Cartoons: Rich Tennant (www.the5thwave.com)

Composition Services

Project Coordinator: Erin Smith

Layout and Graphics: Lavonne Cook, Stephanie D. Jumper, Clint Lahnen, Barbara Moore, Barry Offringa, Lynsey Osborn, Heather Ryan, Julie Trippetti

Proofreaders: Kevin Broccoli, Jessica Kramer, Christy Pingleton

Indexer: Techbooks

Publishing and Editorial for Technology Dummies

Richard Swadley, Vice President and Executive Group Publisher

Andy Cummings, Vice President and Publisher

Mary Bednarek, Executive Acquisitions Director

Mary C. Corder, Editorial Director

Publishing for Consumer Dummies

Diane Graves Steele, Vice President and Publisher

Joyce Pepple, Acquisitions Director

Composition Services

Gerry Fahey, Vice President of Production Services

Debbie Stailey, Director of Composition Services

Contents at a Glance

Table of Contents

Introduction

*V*isio is one of the most flexible and easy-to-use drawing products around. Yet, its ease of use doesn't mean that this product lacks functionality. You can draw anything of just about any complexity you want. The whole focus of Visio is getting your ideas down on electronic paper as quickly as possible. Using this program means that you can think about your ideas, rather than how to perform the next task. *Visio 2007 For Dummies* introduces you to this very exciting drawing program and demonstrates the ever-growing number of features it provides.

Of course, you don't have to use all of these features. *Visio 2007 For Dummies* is structured like Visio — you can use as little or as much of the book as you want to achieve your level of comfort with Visio. If your only goal is to sketch out a few ideas using something better than a napkin, the first two parts of the book are all you need.

One of the most exciting things about Visio 2007 is that you gain access to a number of new productivity features. Instead of wasting time formatting shapes one at a time, you can use themes to format an entire drawing with one click. If that sounds interesting, you'll find the whole scoop in this book. Likewise, if you're tired of having to update the data in a drawing manually every time you open one, check out the new Data Link feature. This feature makes it possible to track changes to a system quickly and easily. Analysts will love the new PivotDiagram feature. You can drill down as far as necessary to see the interactions in your data when using Visio. These are just a few of the new features you'll find in this book.

About This Book

This book is for anyone who has an idea that he or she wants to put down on paper. It doesn't matter who you are; somewhere, someone has a template you can use to start drawing quickly and has a set of stencils with shapes for your particular trade. The number of templates and stencils that Visio provides is nothing short of amazing (read about them in Chapter 2). However, these templates and stencils are just the tip of the iceberg. Visio is all about you. Instead of forcing you to jump through hoops, Visio helps you get that idea down on paper. This book is your guide to all of the cool features that Visio provides. If you want to get started creating drawings for your ideas quickly, this is the book to get.

With this in mind, *Visio 2007 For Dummies* is designed to make you productive as quickly as possible. You find basic, useful information that helps you accomplish your goals. You find real-world examples and figures that *show* you how to do something rather than just *tell* you. You find concise step-by-step instructions for accomplishing specific tasks rather than a lot of rambling text that fills space and means nothing to you.

This book doesn't provide everything to everyone. For example, even though Visio supports Visual Basic for Applications (VBA) so you can write programs to make it do even more, this book doesn't discuss VBA. *Visio 2007 For Dummies* focuses on user tasks; it makes you more productive, fast.

Conventions Used in This Book

Here's a summary of the conventions used in this book:

- When directions indicate that you type something, for example, "Enter **13** in the size box," the characters you type appear in bold.

- When you are to *click* something, that means to click your left mouse button. *Right-clicking* is — you guessed it — clicking the right mouse button. (These terms assume that you are using the mouse with your right hand.)

- When you *drag* something, you click and hold the left mouse button as you move the mouse. Release the mouse button when you're finished dragging.

- The term *shortcut menu* refers to the pop-up menu that appears when you right-click something on the screen. (Shortcut menus are not available for all elements in a drawing.)

- You can select commands using toolbar buttons, menu commands, or the Alt key. Because toolbar buttons are by far the fastest method, these buttons are always listed along with the menu command. (When toolbar buttons aren't available, only the menu command is shown.) A menu command is specified by writing, for example, *Choose File➪Save*, which means click the File menu to open it and then choose the Save option.

What You're Not to Read

If you're new to Visio and just want to know enough to create simple drawings or diagrams, you can safely skip Part IV. That section takes you deeper into customizing Visio and using some of its advanced features. Clearly, not every reader will become devoted to discovering advanced features. Browse through Part III for any features that you might find useful and have the time to work through. Also, glance through Part V, which contains many interesting tips, tricks, and trivia that you might find very useful.

On the other hand, if you've used Visio before, you can safely skip Parts I and II, which offer basic getting-up-and-running information.

Foolish Assumptions

You probably have a reasonable working knowledge of Microsoft Windows and have at least some idea of what you want to draw. For this reason, Chapter 1 doesn't spend any of your valuable time describing how to find your way around Windows or how to work with dialog boxes. If you need to review these concepts, see *Windows Vista For Dummies,* by Andy Rathbone (published by Wiley).

Although Chapter 2 does provide a basic overview of all of the templates available in Visio, this book doesn't tell you when you need to use the Unified Modeling Language (UML) Model Diagram template. If you don't already know what the UML Model Diagram does, you can safely skip that description. None of the examples in the book focus on a particular kind of diagram except when you need a specific diagram type to accomplish a particular task in the more advanced sections. In short, all of the procedures and techniques work for all diagram types unless the book specifically mentions that you must use a particular diagram type.

How This Book Is Organized

Visio 2007 For Dummies is organized into five distinct parts. Use the parts to guide you to where you want to go on your Visio journey. You don't need to read the chapters in order. The book is designed so that you can skip around to suit your needs.

Part 1: Starting with Visio 2007 Basics

Part I lays the groundwork for your success with Visio. Every software program has its unique personality; Visio is no exception. Here you find conceptual information about Visio, get the Visio terminology down, discover how to recognize and work with what's on the screen, start Visio, save and open files, and print drawings.

Part II: Creating Visio Drawings

Part II is for those in a hurry because it teaches you the basics of creating a *simple* drawing. You find out about the basic elements of a Visio drawing and discover how to implement those elements in your drawing. You'll also discover how to add and manipulate text, as well as how to work with margins and tabs, indentation, alignment, spacing, and more. You see how to use and manipulate a drawing's connectors, the lines that connect one shape to another. (They're more than just simple lines, as you'll soon discover.)

Part III: Taking Your Drawings to the Next Level

In Part III, you move into the intermediate features of Visio. You find out how to place shapes precisely on a drawing, create your own shapes, enhance and manipulate shapes, perform complex tasks with connectors, and work with pages and layers.

Part IV: Advancing Your Knowledge of Visio

Certainly not every user needs to pursue Part IV! Here you find out how to create custom templates and themes, how to store data in shapes and report on that data, and how to protect your shapes and drawings from inadvertent changes. You also see how to use Visio drawings with other programs and how to save files for publishing on the Web. Most importantly, this is the part that helps you discover the new Data Link and PivotDiagram functionality that Visio provides.

Part V: The Part of Tens

One of the most useful sections of every *For Dummies* book, "The Part of Tens" is a collection of a variety of information. In *Visio 2007 For Dummies,* you find ten "how to" pointers for useful tasks and ten pointers to online resources for Visio.

About the Web Site

This book contains a wealth of drawing examples, a few themes, some stencils, and other helpful Visio drawing information. Trying to replicate what you see in the book precisely could be time consuming and wholly unnecessary since the work is already done. Consequently, you'll find all of the art in this book on the Dummies Web site at www.dummies.com/go/visiofd2007. All you need to do is download it, locate the chapter you're working with, and open the drawing you want to use. The drawings all have names that make their purpose quite clear. Using the Web site content will help you discover Visio with greater ease without having to worry about becoming an artist to do it.

Icons Used in This Book

The following icons are used in this text to call attention to specific types of information.

The Tip icon indicates information that's likely to save you time or information that will make you say to yourself, "Wow, I never knew that!" Be sure to read this stuff.

Wherever a Technical Stuff icon occurs, you'll find a discussion of something that's bogged down in technical jargon. Generally, you can skip these paragraphs because they contain advanced information. However, more experienced readers will want to read this material because it provides essential information for advancing your skill further.

Definitely pay attention to the Warning icons. They're designed to warn you of impending doom or, at the very least, a possible problem you'd just as soon avoid.

Remember icons are designed as a gentle nudge rather than a blatant slam to the head. In other words, "Remember this — it may be important to you some day."

This icon draws attention to the slick new improvements in Visio 2007. Chapter 1 provides an overview of these new features. However, Microsoft improved Visio 2007 in a considerable number of ways, so it's important to look for these icons when you're upgrading from an earlier version of Visio.

Where to Go from Here

If you've never used Visio before, definitely start with Part I! Work your way through Part II as well, but don't feel that you must go beyond this point. If you've used Visio before, you might get crazy and start with Part V, skim Parts I and II, and go directly to Parts III and IV to look for any features you might not be familiar with. Whether you are a beginner or an experienced Visio user, be sure to look through Part V for answers, tips, and pointers to Visio-related Web sites.

Chapter 1

Visio 101

Close your eyes for a minute and picture the amount of visual information that comes to you on any given day. Magazines, newspapers, reports, television programs, and presentations illustrate a great deal of information in the form of charts, tables, graphs, diagrams, and technical drawings. These graphical elements often convey ideas far more quickly and clearly than long, boring paragraphs. You don't typically think of charts, diagrams, and graphs as *art,* but they are graphical, and this is where Visio comes in.

Although Visio is easy to use, you can benefit from a bit of explanation before you jump right in creating drawings. In this chapter, you become familiar with what you see on the Visio screen and find out how Visio works conceptually.

Getting the Scoop on Visio

In simple terms, Visio is a diagramming tool for anyone who needs to create drawings, even self-confirmed nonartists. Although many people view Visio as a *drawing* tool, it isn't one, because it requires no artistic ability. It's more accurate to say that Visio is a *diagramming* tool. That's reassuring because even in highly analytical, non-art-related careers, you may need to create a chart, diagram, or drawing! If the suggestion of drawing *anything* strikes terror in your heart, Visio can help.

Visio's grab bag of icons — or *shapes,* as Visio calls them — represents all sorts of things from computer network components, to office furniture, to boxes on an organization chart or a flow chart, to electrical switches and relays. Even programmers can use Visio to create diagrams that represent application elements and then use that content to create the application. You simply drag the shapes that you want into the drawing window, and arrange and connect them the way that you want. You can add text and other graphical elements wherever you like.

Comparing Visio products

Over the years, Visio has been available in several different flavors — Standard, Professional, Technical, and Enterprise — plus you could find advanced developer's tools in Visual Studio .NET and advanced network diagramming tools in Visio Enterprise Network Tools. Whew! All these versions became confusing and overwhelming to the average user, so Microsoft decided to simplify things and produce just two editions of Visio: Standard and Professional. The same "engine" drives both, but the audience for each is slightly different and the types of charts and diagrams you can create address different needs:

- ✔ **Visio Standard:** Designed for business professionals, this edition gives all kinds of businesspeople — from product managers to financial analysts to sales and marketing professionals — the ability to create business-related charts and diagrams that illustrate business processes, marketing trends, organizations, project schedules, and so on. However, just about anyone can make use of this version. For example, an office manager could use this version to show the office arrangement in a building or the structure of an organization. It's important to not limit yourself; Visio can help you diagram just about anything you can imagine as long as the diagram doesn't require the precise measurements normally provided by a computer-aided design (CAD) program.

- ✔ **Visio Professional:** Designed for technical users, this edition includes everything that Visio Standard includes and more. Network managers and designers, electrical engineers, IT managers, facilities planners, Internet specialists, Web designers and administrators, and software developers can use Visio Professional to create charts and diagrams that illustrate a wide variety of technical concepts and processes. The professional version also contains a number of database features that you can use to import data from other applications. For example, you could import information from Access and use it to create a special diagram.

So, how do you know which Visio is right for you? If you're involved in networks, IT, Internet or Web design, electrical engineering, architecture facilities planning and management, or software development, Visio Professional is the edition to use because it provides all the shapes and symbols you need to create simple or complex diagrams. If you're not involved in any of these fields but are a business professional involved in company sales, profits, marketing, or managing projects, Visio Standard is right for you. It includes all the shapes you need to create business-related charts, diagrams, and drawings, without cluttering your screen with shapes you'll never use (such as a proximity limit switch or a guided light transmitter).

It's easy to get lost when you look at all of the diagrams that Visio can create. Many people get started using Visio for simple needs. For example, just about everyone needs a calendar from time to time. With Visio, you can create a custom calendar to meet any need. You can also use it to create directional maps to show someone how to get from the airport to your company. When working with Visio, it's best to start simple and work your way up to the complex diagrams used by various professionals.

A quick peek at some Visio features

Visio is often a misunderstood product, especially by those who've never used it. Some people limit Visio to drawing organizational charts, but it can do considerably more. The following list describes some of the tasks you can perform with Visio:

- **Printing what you want:** Even though creating a diagram in Visio is relatively easy, you still need to show other people the graphical representation of your ideas. Fortunately, Visio provides extensive printing capabilities, which means you get just the output you need. (See Chapter 3 for more information on printing everything from a simple calendar to complex floor diagrams.)

- **Diagrams without drawing:** Visio provides a wealth of shapes that you can use to create diagrams of any type. All you do is place the shape where you want to see it on-screen; no drawing is required! (See Chapter 2 for more information on using shapes to create any diagram type.)

- **Customize shapes easily:** One of the best features of Visio is that you can use it to customize shapes in a number of ways. You can add text, modify the size of the shape, change its appearance, and connect shapes. No matter what your skill level or how you use Visio, you can create professional-looking results with a few clicks. (See Chapters 5 through 7 for details on customizing shapes simply. Chapter 8 describes how you can create your own shapes when the defaults don't work. Chapters 9 through 12 show how to manipulate shapes in various ways.)

- **See only the data you need:** Data overload is a condition where you become overwhelmed by the very data that you're supposed to use to complete tasks. Layering in Visio helps you reduce complexity by letting you see only the layer of data you actually need. All of the data is still there, but you only access it when you actually need it. (See Chapter 10 for ideas on how you can use layering to manage your data efficiently.)

✔ **Make your diagrams a group activity:** The ability to comment on ideas in a group is essential in business today. The diagrams that you create are ideas only they're in graphical, rather than textual, format. Visio helps you make the diagrams you create a group activity by providing a number of ways to add comments and revisions. (See Chapter 13 for more information on working with comments and the Visio review features.)

✔ **Report on data:** Wouldn't it be great if you could store data in a drawing and then report on that data? With Visio, you can. Suppose you draw an office layout plan that includes cubicle walls, fixtures, office furniture, and telephone and computer equipment. You can store each piece of furniture and office equipment with data such as its inventory number, owner, and current location. From this drawing, you can generate property, inventory, and location reports. (See Chapter 12 for more information on storing and reporting on data in shapes.)

✔ **Use the drill-down feature:** Jump quickly from an overview drawing to a detailed drawing and back again. For example, you can draw an overview map of a worldwide computer network and double-click the name of a city to see a drawing of that city's computer network. This drill-down feature is possible because Visio lets you define a shape's behavior when you double-click it. (See Chapter 12 for more information.)

✔ **Generate drawings from data:** In contrast to the previous point, wouldn't it be great to be able to generate drawings from existing data? Again, with Visio, you can. Suppose you have employee data (name, title, department, reporting manager, and so on) stored in a text or spreadsheet file. You can generate an organization chart automatically from this data using Visio. (See Chapter 14 for more information on using external data in Visio.)

✔ **Use hyperlinks:** Often, you can't convey in a single drawing all the information necessary to make your point. You might want to refer the reader to a separate drawing, a Web site, or another document with related information. With Visio, you can add hyperlinks to a drawing or shape. This is an invaluable feature for pulling pieces of information together to present a comprehensive picture. (See Chapter 14 for tips on using hyperlinks in diagrams.)

Visio actually provides support for eight categories of drawings. You can create everything from business charts to software and database diagrams. The "Understanding the Visio Drawing Categories" section of Chapter 2 provides a description of each of these drawing categories so that you have a better idea of precisely what Visio can do for you.

What's new in Visio 2007?

Visio 2007 has a lot to offer. With each update, Visio improves the functionality you need to create diagrams quickly. The emphasis in this update is efficiency — helping you get more done with fewer errors and in less time. The following list provides you with an overview of the major feature changes in Visio 2007. You'll see these features described in more detail throughout the book.

- **Starting quickly with improved templates:** Visio 2007 supports fewer template categories and the category names now make more sense. You actually have access to more templates, but Microsoft has organized them better. In addition, the template examples are larger with clear text descriptions, so you have a better idea of how to use a particular template. A recent template list tells you which templates you use most often and makes these templates easier to access. The Professional edition also includes sample diagrams and data sources that you can use as examples of how to retrieve data from your own data sources.

- **Improving drawing appearance with themes:** You have probably seen the effect of themes in Windows. A theme in Visio is the same concept. You use themes to give your diagrams a particular appearance. Using themes helps ensure that your diagrams have a pleasing appearance and are easy to see.

- **Automatically connecting shapes:** Visio now makes it easier to create great-looking drawings with greater ease by creating the connections you need automatically and aligning new drawing elements. You can connect drawing elements when you drag the shape onto the form. However, when you decide to make the connection later, all you need to do is point at the two connectors that you want to connect. You'll discover more about these fast connection techniques in Chapter 6.

- **Sharing diagrams with other Office applications:** Keeping others informed about your ideas is essential. This feature relies on SharePoint server to make it easier to share data in various ways. For example, you can generate a Visio pivotdiagram from within Microsoft Project and place it on SharePoint server for comment by other collaborators. You can also attach Visio diagrams to e-mail created in Outlook. Other people can see the diagrams even if they don't have Visio installed.

- **Saving data using the XPS file format:** A problem with custom data formats is that it isn't easy to move the data to other locations. The XML Paper Specification (XPS) file format provides a standard method of saving your data in a form that other applications can use. You can effectively use the data in any application that supports XML.

  ✔ **Improving efficiency with smaller diagrams:** Other people don't always need every piece of information in a diagram. For example, you might have unused master shapes or comments that other people don't need to see. Visio makes it easier to clean up your diagrams before you send them to someone else. In addition to presenting a cleaner form, your diagram will also consume less space, making it more efficient for data transfers and local storage.

One of the ways you can determine whether you need Visio Professional edition is by the features it provides. The following list describes a number of special features that the Professional edition provides. These aren't the only differences, but they're significant reasons for choosing the Professional edition over the Standard edition.

  ✔ **New templates and shapes:** The Professional edition of Visio comes with a number of new templates and shapes that make it easier to display complex data on-screen. The PivotDiagram, Value Stream Map, and Information Technology Infrastructure Library (ITIL) templates help you model complex data in new ways. In addition, the new Work Flow shapes that are part of the Work Flow Diagram template help you model dynamic workflows that better match how people in your company perform tasks. Workflows model business processes of all types, which includes everything from the steps to produce a product to the events that occur when you receive a customer order.

  ✔ **Using data from other sources in diagrams:** You already have a vast store of data to use in creating diagrams. The problem is that this data isn't in graphical format, making it very difficult to understand. Visio now makes it easy to create a connection to that data so that the information you already have appears in the diagrams you create. Because of the connection between your diagram and the data source, any changes in the data automatically appear in the diagram. A new Data Selector Wizard helps you create the data connection to data in other applications such as Access, SQL Server, and Excel (in addition to a number of non-Microsoft products).

  ✔ **Seeing data in the Data Graphics task pane:** Getting data from an external data source is only part of the process. Although plain text is fine for a report, you might want to dress it up a bit for your diagram. The Data Graphics task pane helps you turn plain text into something that will dazzle those around you.

  ✔ **Viewing complex data using a pivotdiagram:** A *pivotdiagram* is a collection of shapes in a treelike structure that helps you present complex data in a less confusing manner. Using a pivotdiagram helps you analyze the data, drill down into it, and display it from various perspectives.

Familiarizing Yourself with Visio Lingo

Like all software programs, Visio uses a particular terminology. You need to be familiar with the following terms before you begin creating diagrams and drawings:

- **Drag and drop:** The method Visio uses to create drawings. What are you dragging and where are you dropping it, you ask? You drag shapes and you drop them onto a drawing page.

- **Shape:** Probably the most important element in Visio. A *shape* represents an object of nearly any conceivable kind, such as a piece of office furniture in an office-layout diagram, a road sign in a directional map, a server in a network diagram, a box on an organization chart, or a bar on a comparison chart. Visio contains literally thousands of shapes. You can draw and save your own shapes as described in Chapter 8.

- **Master shape:** A shape that you see on a stencil. When you drag a shape onto the drawing page, you're copying a *master shape* onto your drawing page, making it just one *instance* of that shape. Visio makes the distinction between master shapes and instances of shapes. The only time this distinction is important is when you begin modifying Visio to meet specific needs by creating your own shapes.

- **Stencil:** A tool Visio uses to organize shapes so that you can find the one you're looking for. A *stencil* is nothing more than a collection of related shapes. If you want to create a cubicle-layout diagram for your office, for example, you use the cubicles stencil, which includes shapes such as workstations, posts, panels, work surfaces, storage units, and file cabinets. Stencils are displayed in the Shapes pane on the left side of the screen so that the shapes are always available while you're working.

- **Template:** A collection of stencils in addition to predefined document settings. A *template* is essentially a model for creating a particular type of drawing. A template defines certain characteristics of the drawing so that the drawing is consistent. For example, when you use a Visio template for a specific type of drawing, Visio automatically opens one or more appropriate stencils, defines the page size and scale of your drawing, and defines appropriate styles for things such as text, fills, and lines. You can change any of these elements, but the point of using a template is to maintain consistency throughout the drawing.

- **Connector:** A line that connects one shape to another. Perhaps the most common example of a connector is in an organization chart. The lines that connect the president to various groups in an organization and the lines that run through an organization are connectors. Chapter 6 describes connectors in detail.

Understanding the Vista Difference

Visio operates a little differently from a visual and security perspective under Vista than it does under earlier versions of Windows, such as Windows XP. In fact, you don't get to see all of the functionality that Visio can provide unless you use it under Vista. The best way to describe these differences is to group them into two categories: graphical (what you can see) and security (the protection Visio provides).

In addition to Visio-specific changes, Vista also requires a change in how you perform some Visio-related tasks. For example, when you want to work with a printer in Vista, you must locate it within the Control Panel. It's easy to find the Vista specifics in the Visio help file. Simply type Vista in the Search field of the Visio Help file and click Search. The following sections describe the Visio-specific differences in Vista.

The graphical interface difference

Vista sports the new Aero Glass visual interface. This new interface offers some efficiencies not found in older versions of Windows and, of course, it provides a healthy dose of eye candy. The big thing to remember is that Vista doesn't affect the actual functionality of Visio. All of the features (the techniques you use to perform a task) work the same under Windows XP as they do under Vista.

You do receive some additional benefits from using Vista. Graphics do appear faster on-screen and you'll notice that Vista does tend to make the graphics look better. For example, the fonts are easier to read and the lines used to create a diagram look crisper. Even though this might seem like a small benefit for Visio users who work in Vista, the effects can reduce eyestrain and help you avoid mistakes that you might otherwise make. Vista makes it less likely that you'll encounter errors such as connections where you didn't think any existed.

Helpful user interface changes

Vista also promises to be a less painful experience for users. For example, normally when you apply a patch and the system has to reboot, you have to restart your applications, locate your position, and only then start work again. It's a waste of time and effort. Vista provides a new feature called Freeze Dry that remembers program settings such as window size, window position, and even cursor position. After a system reboots, Vista automatically resets your Office application to its previous state for you.

You may have run into problems accessing information on international Web sites in the past. Vista now supports the special characters used by these Web sites so that your Visio experience can include data from these sites. In addition, Vista provides full Internet Protocol Version 6 (IPv6) support. This means that your copy of Visio is ready to work with the additional Web addresses that IPv6 provides.

All Office products now use the Vista Save, Open, and Insert common dialog boxes, which means that you gain full access to the Vista functionality. The Vista functionality includes the ability to organize your files with greater ease and to search for documents based on metadata as well as regular content. For example, you can search for a Visio document based on the author or the comments you provide.

A very useful feature for Visio users is the ability to store a thumbnail of your diagram. Instead of looking one document at a time for a particular diagram, you can simply view the thumbnails. This feature makes it considerably easier to locate a particular diagram. Even when several diagrams look similar, you can usually reduce the number of diagrams you have to check.

Office also emphasizes reliability under Vista. If Office or Vista detects that a certain operation could cause the operating system to crash, Office will stop the operation and tell you about the problem, rather than attempting to perform the operation as it did in the past. Generally, this feature means that you'll not only see fewer crashes, but you'll also encounter a reduced risk of data loss.

Understanding the security features

The biggest reason to use Vista is the security features. It's a lot easier to protect the data in your diagrams under Vista and you'll find that the security is very reliable. In addition, many of the security features work automatically. You don't have to remember to change a setting to protect the data, in many cases, because Vista does it for you — at least from an operating system level. The following sections describe a few other security changes for Visio users under Vista.

Defining the difference between users and administrators

One of the most difficult changes that users will encounter under Vista is that it differentiates between users and administrators. In addition, every account works in user mode most of the time. Consequently, activities that might have worked fine in the past may not work under Vista. For example, you'll find that you need to give yourself permission to access your data directory. Although this sounds very odd, it does help protect your data. No one gains access to your data unless you specifically give him rights to do so.

Digitally signing your macros

You'll probably find that those macros you relied on in previous versions of Visio no longer work. That's because most people don't sign their macros. In order to use macros successfully in many cases, you must digitally sign the file that contains them. Since Microsoft is making this particular feature more robust as it introduces new versions of Office and Windows, it's probably a good time to start signing your macros now.

In addition to macros, you'll find that Vista makes it more difficult to perform some tasks using Explorer or typing from the command line. For example, you must have administrative privileges to perform tasks such as deleting a file. These changes work along with the macro protection to make it less likely that an errant macro will destroy your data. If your macro performs any command line tasks, such as deleting a file, it also requires the correct privileges. The bottom line is that no matter how you try to perform some tasks, Vista won't let you unless you have the correct rights. Many macros will simply stop working as currently written.

This book doesn't discuss how to create or use macros. A book such as *VBA For Dummies,* 5th Edition (published by Wiley) provides complete coverage of this topic.

Relying on trusted locations

Vista is also quite fussy about where you store your data. Trying to open a file on a network drive or store data on a network drive will normally meet with a number of permission requests. Generally, you must have administrative privileges or specific rights on the network drive to use it. In this case, however, you can get around the problem by setting Visio to use trusted locations. See the "Saving Drawings" section of Chapter 2 for more details on using trusted locations.

Jumping Head First into Visio

The best way to get started with Visio is to open a new drawing page, so you can cruise around the screen and get a feel for what's there. Then, in Chapter 2, you create a drawing.

To start Visio, choose Start⇨Programs⇨Microsoft Office⇨Microsoft Office Visio 2007. Visio displays the window shown in Figure 1-1.

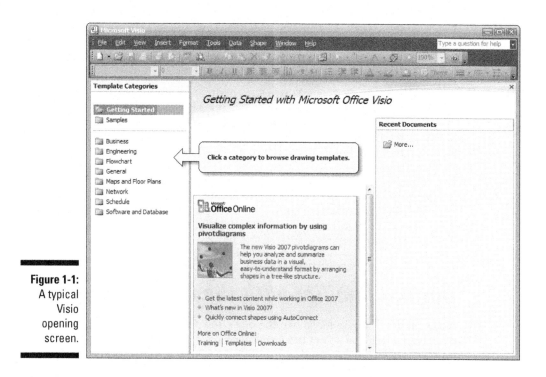

Figure 1-1:
A typical
Visio
opening
screen.

Visio divides the application functionality into several areas. At the top are the toolbars and menus you use when working with Visio. Most of the toolbar entries are grayed out because you haven't selected a template yet. The rest of the book describes these entries. Along the left side of the display, you see several entries that control the appearance of the right side of Visio. For example, when you select Getting Started, you see topics that help you begin using Visio. The following list describes these entries:

- ✔ **Getting Started:** This entry displays two panes. The center pane contains information on how to get started using Visio. You can obtain information about training, templates, and downloading, in addition to the latest news about Visio. The right pane contains a list of your current projects. Simply click the project to open it.

- ✔ **Samples:** If you're wondering how to use a particular diagram template or simply don't want to start from scratch, select the Samples entry. This entry also displays two panes on the right side. The center pane contains a list of the samples that Microsoft has provided. The sample entry contains a basic view of the template type and the sample name. The right pane contains a detailed view of the selected sample. The diagram is bigger and more detailed. You'll also see a write-up about the sample. To use the sample, select the US Units or Metric option, and click Open Sample Data.

✔ **Category**: The Category list shows eight items. These items represent the diagram types including Business, Engineering, Flowchart, General, Maps and Floor Plans, Network, Schedule, and Software and Database. Selecting a particular category displays a list of associated templates in the center pane. For example, when you select the Business category, you see Brainstorming Diagram, Organizational Chart, and PivotDiagram as templates. Below these templates is a list of other templates that you might want to see when looking for business diagrams, even though Microsoft hasn't placed them in this category. Select a particular template and you'll see a larger, more detailed picture of it along with a two- or three-sentence description. To create a new drawing based on a template, choose the template, select the US Units or Metric option, and click Create.

Getting familiar with the Visio screen

A typical Visio screen looks like the one shown in Figure 1-2. This screen is displayed when you select the General category and the Basic Diagram (US units) template. In this section, you look at what's going on in this window.

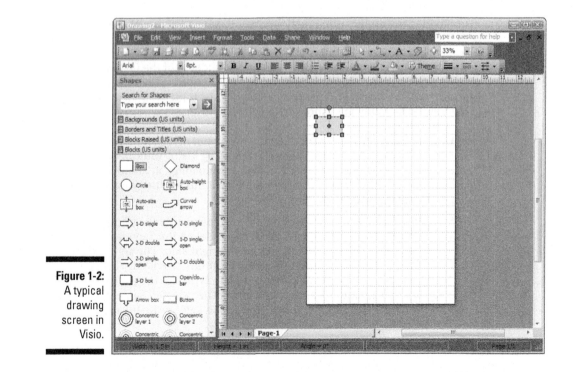

Figure 1-2:
A typical drawing screen in Visio.

The display contains the same menu, Standard toolbar, and Formatting toolbar as before, but the entries are active now. The left side of the display contains the Shapes window, while the right side contains the Drawing window.

The Shapes window contains the list of shapes that you can use. In this case, the drawing is using the Box shape. The shapes appear within stencils. This example uses the Blocks (US Units) stencil.

The Drawing window contains the area where you create a diagram. You see rulers across the top and left side of this window that help you position and size shapes. The drawing area looks like graph paper. You can use the lines to position shapes, as shown in Figure 1-2.

Checking out the menus

Visio's menu bar contains some typical menus found in almost every Windows application (such as File, Edit, Format, and Help). Even so, it's important to review each menu for commands that you may not expect. The following list describes commands unique to Visio (even though some of the menus might look familiar):

- ✔ **Tools:** On this menu, you find all kinds of tools for working with Visio shapes, the Visio drawing page, and the drawing itself. There are tools for setting Visio's color palette, rulers, grids, and so on. You also find the standard Microsoft options such as Spelling, Track Markup, Customize, and Options.

- ✔ **Data:** The Data menu only appears when you use the Professional edition. It contains entries that help you obtain data from other sources and create reports.

- ✔ **Shape:** The Shape menu contains commands for grouping, rotating, flipping, and aligning, as well as commands for choosing a drawing's color scheme. You also find commands for changing the stacking order of shapes and doing some creative things such as fragmenting and intersecting shapes. (See Chapter 8 for details.)

  The options on the Shape menu change depending on the type of drawing you're creating.

For certain types of drawings, Visio adds an additional menu to the menu bar. For example, when you create a Gantt chart using the Gantt Chart template in the Schedule category, Visio adds a Gantt Chart menu just after the Shape menu and before the Window menu (see Figure 1-3). On the Gantt Chart menu, you find commands specific to creating Gantt charts, such as adding and deleting tasks, linking tasks, and setting working hours. As soon as you close the drawing, the menu option disappears.

| File Edit View Insert Format Tools Data Shape Gantt Chart Window Help | Type a question for help |

Working with toolbars

Visio has a dozen or so toolbars, two of which are displayed automatically
when you start the program. The two default toolbars are Standard and
Formatting. You can hide either of these, and you can display additional toolbars as well.

After you begin to recognize the toolbar buttons, it's much faster to click a
button than to select a menu command. Many of these buttons appear on the
Cheat Sheet at the beginning of this book.

To hide or display toolbars, right-click anywhere in the toolbar area. On the
shortcut menu that appears, click a toolbar name. Toolbars that have a check
mark next to them are displayed; all others are hidden (see Figure 1-4).

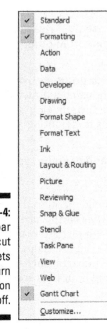

All Visio toolbars can be docked at different locations on the screen. Just grab the vertical bar at the left end of any toolbar and drag it to a new location on the screen. A moved toolbar automatically becomes its own window, and you can position it anywhere you like on the screen by dragging its title bar.

If you're a toolbar fanatic, you might want to customize the toolbars by adding buttons you use most often and deleting buttons you never use. You can also choose any buttons you want and create a new toolbar.

Creating a toolbar

To create a custom toolbar, follow these steps:

1. **Choose View⊏⟩Toolbars⊏⟩Customize.**

   Visio displays the Customize dialog box.

2. **On the Toolbars tab, click the New button.**

   Visio displays the New Toolbar dialog box.

3. **In the Toolbar Name field, type a name (see Figure 1-5), and then click the OK button.**

   Visio adds the new name to the list of toolbars and displays a new, blank toolbar on the screen. (It's small, but it's there!)

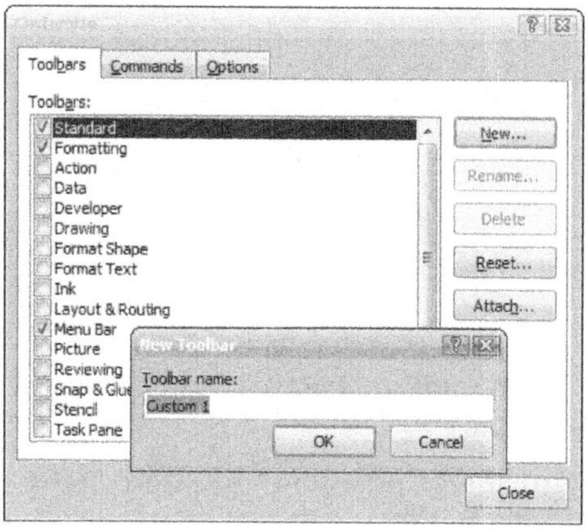

Figure 1-5: You can add and delete toolbar buttons or create a custom toolbar.

4. **If you want to add buttons to the new toolbar, drag and drop the new blank toolbar into the toolbar area, and then follow the steps in the next section, "Modifying a toolbar."**

5. **Click Close to close the Customize dialog box.**

Modifying a toolbar

If you just want to add a button here or there, consider modifying an existing toolbar rather than creating a new one. However, in many cases, it's a good idea to create your own custom toolbar so that you can see everything you want without having to worry about someone changing the toolbar back to a default state later. Use the following steps to modify any toolbar:

1. **Display the toolbar that you want to change.**

   To do so, right-click the toolbar area and select the toolbar.

2. **Right-click the toolbar and choose Customize.**

   Visio displays the Customize dialog box.

3. **Click the Commands tab.**

   Categories are on the left and commands are on the right, as shown in Figure 1-6.

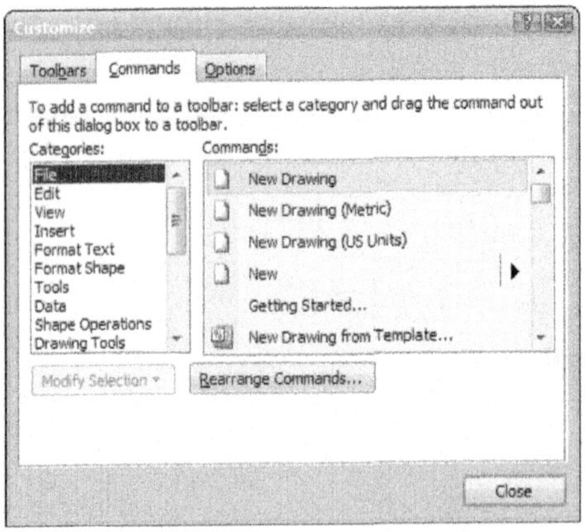

Figure 1-6:
Choose a toolbar on the left and buttons on the right.

4. **Click a category on the left, and then scroll through the list of commands (buttons) on the right.**

5. **Drag the button from the dialog box to the location on the toolbar where you want to add the button.**

   When you release the mouse button, the new button becomes part of the existing toolbar at the point where you dropped it.

Deleting a button from a toolbar

Sometimes you end up with buttons you don't really want on a toolbar. The following steps tell how to remove a button from a toolbar:

1. **Display the toolbar that you want to change.**

2. **Right-click the toolbar and choose Customize.**

   Visio displays the Customize dialog box.

3. **Drag the button that you want to delete off the toolbar.**

   If you want to delete additional buttons, repeat this step.

4. **Click the Close button to close the Customize dialog box.**

Getting Help When You Need It

Visio makes it easy to obtain help about any topic. Microsoft has centralized help in Visio 2007 and made it easier to use. The following sections describe the two forms of help that Visio provides.

Using general help

Visio presents help using a separate window. You can display this window by clicking the question mark (?) in any dialog box and pointing to any control. Visio displays the Help window with the information for that control displayed. If you want help on a general topic, choose the Help➪Microsoft Office Visio Help command. You see a general listing of Visio help as shown in Figure 1-7.

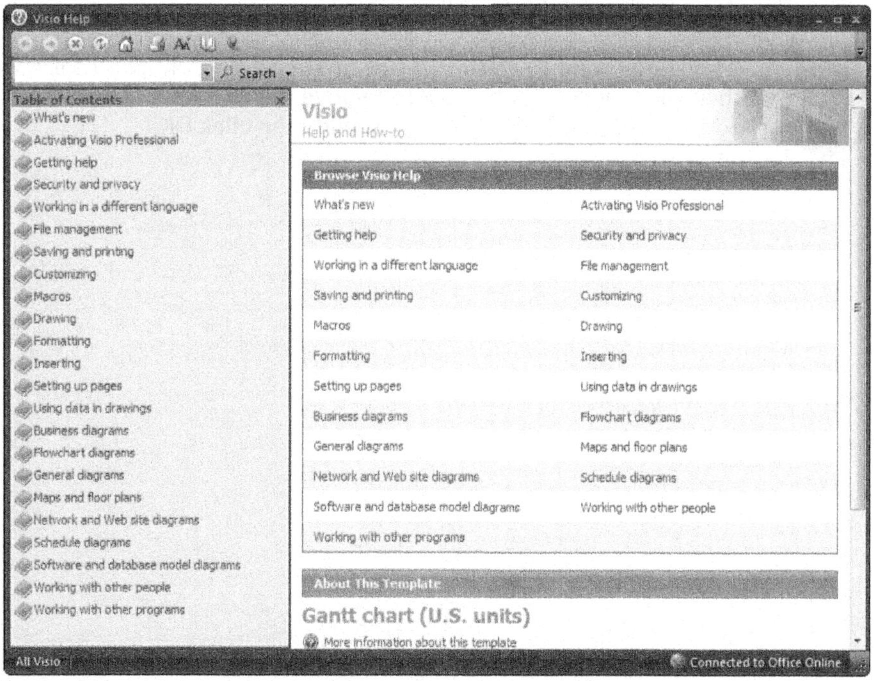

Figure 1-7: The general help topics help you find the information you need quickly.

If you don't see the help you want, type a search term in the Type Words to Search For field and click Search. For example, if you want to learn more about the Vista differences for Visio, type **Vista** and click Search. Help displays all of the entries associated with Vista in the right pane.

Sometimes Help returns too much information. You can limit the scope of a search by clicking the down arrow next to the Search button. The context menu contains a list of places that you can search. For example, you might choose to search just the Visio Templates, rather than All Visio (the default).

You may not have any search terms in mind when you begin your search. Perhaps you're just looking to see what Visio offers. In this case, you can use the Table of Contents list in the left pane of the Help window. Click a book icon to open that particular topic. You can drill down through the topics to find the information you need.

Don't forget ToolTips

Like most Windows programs, Visio also uses ToolTips. When you point to a button on a toolbar and *hover* over it (pause without clicking), a tip pops up to tell you the name of the button. This is especially helpful when you're learning Visio.

Visio expanded the concept of ToolTips to its stencils. When you hover over a stencil shape, a tip pops up and gives the name of the shape and a description, as shown in Figure 1-8.

If you don't want to view ToolTips or stencil tips, choose Tools➪Options, and then click the View tab. Click to remove the check mark from Toolbar ScreenTips and Other ScreenTips, and then click OK.

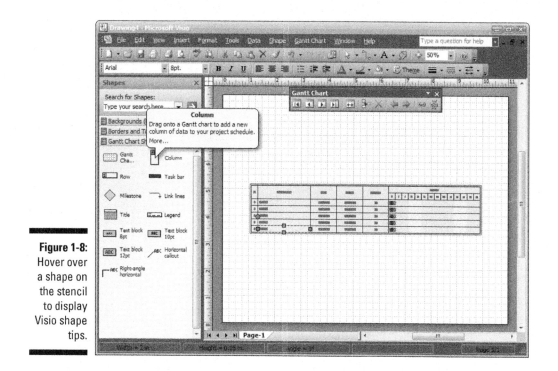

Figure 1-8:
Hover over
a shape on
the stencil
to display
Visio shape
tips.

Closing Visio

When you're ready to close Visio, choose File➪Exit. If you haven't recently
saved all open files, Visio prompts you to do so for each file. Choose Yes to
save or Cancel to return to Visio without saving the drawing.

Chapter 2

Creating and Saving a Simple Visio Drawing

*V*isio provides many ways to create diagrams of all types. However, as with anything else, it pays to begin simply and move on to topics that are more complex later. In this chapter, you find out the standard way to create a simple drawing, bring shapes in, and move around on the screen. More importantly, you discover more about the kinds of diagrams you can create. You also discover how to create drawings using different methods and how to save a drawing and reopen it later.

Creating a Drawing the Standard Way

You can create a diagram using several methods in Visio. This chapter reviews several techniques that you can use, but begins with the standard technique that you'll use most often. Visio makes the standard way as easy as possible by guiding you through the choices. The following steps describe the standard method for creating a diagram:

1. **Choose Start➪Programs➪Microsoft Office➪Microsoft Office Visio 2007 if Visio isn't already running.**

   You see the opening Visio window, as shown in Figure 2-1.

2. **Click a category on the left side of the window (the example uses the Schedule category).**

   Visio displays a sample of the types of drawings, diagrams, or charts available in that category. Use the scroll bar, if necessary, to display all available templates.

3. **Click a template (the example uses the Calendar template).**

   Visio shows details about the template you selected.

4. **Choose a Measurement Units option, and then click Create.**

   Visio creates a new drawing page. One or more stencils open automatically on the left side of the screen.

Now that you have a new diagram to use, try dragging one of the shapes from the Shape window to the Drawing window. The example uses the Month shape found in the Calendar Shapes (US Units) stencil. You may see a Configure dialog box when you drag and drop the shape. For example, the Month shape asks which month and year you want to use, as shown in Figure 2-2.

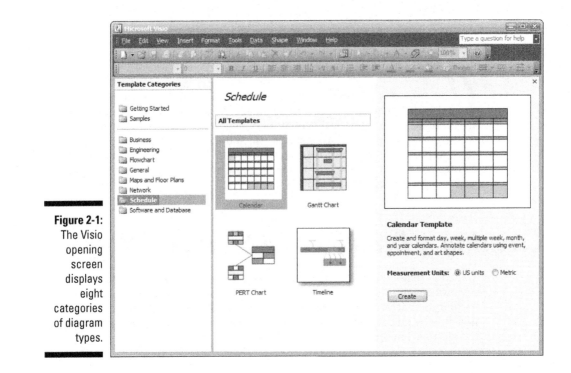

Figure 2-1:
The Visio opening screen displays eight categories of diagram types.

Figure 2-2:
Shapes may
require
configura-
tion
information
before you
can use
them.

After you answer any configuration questions, Visio displays the shape
on-screen. Figure 2-3 shows a typical example of a calendar. You use other
shapes in the Calendar Shapes (US Units) stencil to add important dates to
this calendar. Notice that the mouse pointer on the screen is an arrow. Visio
automatically selects the Pointer Tool on the Standard toolbar when you
start a new drawing. You discover more about using this tool later in the
chapter.

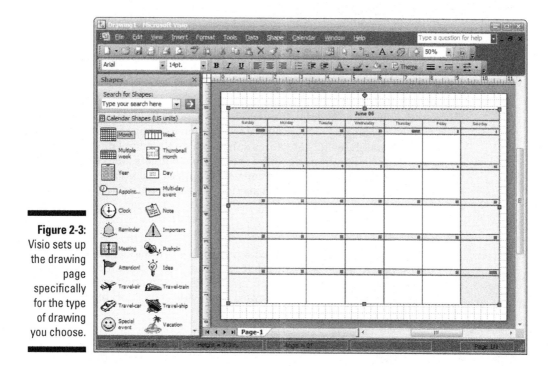

Figure 2-3:
Visio sets up
the drawing
page
specifically
for the type
of drawing
you choose.

Where's the template?

You might think of a template as a visible form with blanks or boxes that you fill in with information. In Visio, a *template* determines how Visio sets up a diagram and what stencils it provides. For example, if you choose Charts and Graphs as your template (from the Business category), Visio automatically performs the following tasks (in no particular order):

✔ Opens three stencils (Backgrounds, Borders and Titles, and Charting Shapes) on the screen. These can appear in any order.

✔ Sets the drawing page size to 8½ x 11, the page orientation to Portrait, and the drawing scale to 1:1.

✔ Chooses an appropriate font, point size, and color.

✔ Chooses a variety of other settings such as line color and width, shadow position, text alignment, and bullet or numbering style.

Understanding the Visio Drawing Categories

Visio provides a vast array of templates, and you can download more templates as you need them. In fact, you can create your own template when you don't find a template you can use anywhere else. The point is that there are many templates to consider.

To make the choice of template easier, Visio organizes them in categories. You choose the category you want to use and then a template within that category. Unfortunately, using categories can also hide the template you really need. The following sections describe the various templates and tell you where to find them. The associated categories appear in parentheses behind the template name. You can use this section as a guide to finding just the template you need.

Active Directory (Network)

The main purpose of the Active Directory template is to model an Active Directory setup. It includes shapes that represent Active Directory objects such as domains, servers, and computers. However, you don't need to limit this template to Active Directory because it provides considerable flexibility in designing other kinds of diagrams.

The Active Directory Objects stencil includes standard security shapes such as groups and users. In addition, the Exchange Objects stencil contains mail, Post Office Protocol (POP), and Network News Transfer Protocol (NNTP) shapes you can use to model everything from an Exchange server setup to any common mail server. Chapter 4 describes how to locate stencils based on a shape you remember or by loading the entire stencil.

If you regularly work with Active Directory, you might want to check out *Windows Server 2003 For Dummies,* by Ed Tittle and James Michael Steward (published by Wiley). Of course, this book discusses a lot more than just Active Directory. You'll find out all of the details about Windows Server 2003. Find out more about this book at `http://www.dummies.com/WileyCDA/ DummiesTitle/productCd-0764516337.html`.

Audit Diagram (Business)

The Audit Diagram template provides a means to diagram any auditing process including any type of accounting or financial management task. Many of the shapes are the same as those used for a flowchart. Of course, the meanings are different in this context. If you're new to the document Six Sigma strategy, you can find some basic answers at `http://www.isixsigma.com/library/ content/six-sigma-newbie.asp`. The ISO Standards Web site, at `http:// www.praxiom.com/`, describes the International Standards Organization (ISO) 9000 standard.

This template also includes two stencils that come in handy for dressing up any diagram. The first is the Backgrounds stencil that contains an assortment of background images for your diagram. The second is the Borders and Titles stencil that contains shapes you can use to add pizzazz to any diagram. A third stencil, Arrow Shapes, appears as part of a number of templates. It contains basic arrow shapes that you can use to show some type of flow between two objects. You shouldn't confuse the arrow shapes with an actual connection, however. The arrow shapes help you show flow, while the connections show actual relations between objects.

Basic Diagram (General)

Use this template for any general diagram. It includes basic shapes that you can use to create any simple diagram. A good basic rule of thumb for this particular template is that it comes in handy when one of the specific templates won't do the job. Visio doesn't include any templates for creating a basic poster. You can choose to use one of the marketing-related templates to create a poster, but in some cases, the basic diagram offers you a little added flexibility. Visio offers a vast array of special-purpose templates and you should always use them whenever possible, but the Basic Diagram template lets you think outside the box to create other diagrams that Microsoft didn't consider.

This template includes the Basic Shapes stencil, which contains shapes that come in handy for everything from creating a poster to adding emphasis to any other diagram. For example, instead of placing plain text in a particular diagram, place it within a star. The added emphasis draws the viewer's attention to that area of the diagram and helps you make your point with greater ease.

Basic Electrical (Engineering)

The Basic Electrical template helps you create diagrams that include switches, relays, and other electrical and electronics components. This template differs from other electrical diagrams that Visio provides in that the symbols are both standardized and relatively simple. For example, you might use this diagram to show how to connect a system to a surge suppressor, but you wouldn't use it to create the motherboard for your next computer. You can actually use this template to create simple component diagrams, such as a stereo setup, or combine it with a floor plan to show the location of PA components in an auditorium. The electrical symbols are sufficiently complex that you could show how the electrical power will run through a building or display the connections required for a motor. Special shapes, such as radiation, can help you create diagrams of alternative energy electrical setups, such as a solar panel.

Many people tinker with electronics and end up with some useful and interesting home additions as a result. If you like to tinker, check out *Electronics For Dummies,* by Gordon McComb and Earl Boysen. This book covers all of the basics, including techniques for creating your own schematics. Find out more about this book at `http://www.dummies.com/WileyCDA/DummiesTitle/productCd-0764576607.html`. If you run out of ideas on your own, you might want to check out *Electronics Projects For Dummies,* by Earl Boysen and Nancy Muir (both books are published by Wiley). This book contains a wealth of interesting electronics projects and discusses topics such as safe component handling. Find out more about this book at `http://www.dummies.com/WileyCDA/DummiesTitle/productCd-0470009683.html`.

Basic Flowchart (Business, Flowchart, and General)

The reason this template appears in so many categories is that it's extremely flexible and useful. The Basic Flowchart shows the path information, ideas, work, or any other tangible or intangible flow can take between one point and another. Even though the basic flowchart shapes haven't changed in many years, the way that people use them to convey ideas has changed considerably.

Basic Network Diagram (Network)

The Basic Network Diagram lets you show the logical layout of your network, rather than the physical layout. The diagram can include everything from firewalls and servers to PCs and users. In fact, you'll find a wealth of peripheral devices listed, so you should be able to model anything that a modern network might have attached.

This template includes two specialized templates. The first, Computers and Monitors, contains all of the shapes normally associated with users on a network, except for the actual user. The second, Network and Peripherals, includes all of the shapes normally associated with network infrastructure, including servers. This stencil also includes a User shape you can use to identify users on the network. A special Legend shape automatically tracks any shapes you add to the diagram. Consequently, the resulting diagram automatically tracks the number of users, computers, servers, routers, hubs, firewalls, printers, and other equipment connected to your network.

If you want to know more about networking, especially for your home network, check out *Home Networking For Dummies, 3rd Edition* by Kathy Ivens (published by Wiley). This book provides all of the details, including answering the question of whether you need a home network at all. Find out more about this book at `http://www.dummies.com/WileyCDA/DummiesTitle/ productCd-0764588494.html`.

Block Diagram (General)

Block diagrams present abstract ideas in ways that most people can understand by relying on blocks of various shapes. An entire process, piece of software, idea, concept, or strategy can appear as a single block. Sometimes an important subcomponent appears as a block within a block. The purpose of this template is to help you express complex ideas that may not have a physical representation. By adding arrows, you can show a flow between the various elements and make it easier for others to understand the inner workings of even the most abstract processes.

The template comes with both 2D (Blocks) and 3D (Raised Blocks) stencils, so you can create a flat presentation or one with a three-dimensional appearance. The shapes include basic squares, circles, and frames, along with an assortment of arrows and nonstandard shapes such as corners.

Block Diagram with Perspective (General)

The Block Diagram with Perspective template is a specialized form of the Block Diagram template. It incorporates a vanishing point — the point at which things disappear from view because they're too far away. Think of a series of buildings. As the buildings get farther away, they appear smaller, not because they are smaller, but because your perspective of them changes. This block diagram incorporates the same idea so that you can create visualizations where the 3-D provided by the diagram depends on the placement of the vanishing point.

Brainstorming (Business)

This template helps you create diagrams that describe the thought processes used in your organization. You can use it to define planning, problem-solving, decision-making, and brainstorming processes. The interesting thing about this diagram is that it actually helps you create an outline you can use in other applications such as PowerPoint by helping you to organize your thoughts. You can create a list of topics you want to discuss, move these ideas around, and provide as much or as little detail as you want.

Calendar (Schedule)

The Calendar template lets you create calendars of every shape and size. The associated Calendar Shapes stencil includes shapes for month, day, and year calendars, plus a wide range of add-ons, such as smiley faces and meeting entries. The Calendar Shapes stencil is actually underutilized in many cases. For example, you could place date calendars on a flowchart to show the dates when a particular phase of a project must complete. A calendar placed directly on any planning diagram will let you keep dates in perspective. In fact, if you couple the calendar shape with your personal schedule, you can ensure the resulting diagram won't have any personal conflicts.

Cause and Effect Diagram (Business)

You might know this template by other names including Ishikawa, fishbone, and root cause analysis diagram. Kaoru Ishikawa originally created this diagram to show the causes of a particular event. The diagram helps with critical thinking, so you can use it anywhere a causal relationship exists. The more fleshed out your fish becomes, the greater the depth of the brainstorming you have done to understand all of the causes of a particular effect. You can discover more about this diagram at `http://mot.vuse.vanderbilt.edu/mt322/Ishikawa.htm`.

Charts and Graphs (Business)

This template contains a special stencil, Charting Shapes, that helps you draw just about any chart or graph imaginable and in considerable detail. You'll find all of the usual variations of the bar, pie, and line graph, including 3-D versions of each. In addition, you have access to various grids and chart and graph additions. For example, you can add annotations to the charts and graphs. Because you can easily include data from multiple sources, this particular template is often more flexible than equivalent charting and graphing in a spreadsheet. The ability to add various diagrams into the chart or graph takes this template well outside the range of most spreadsheets. Unfortunately, you won't find some of the most complex analysis graphs offered, so the flexibility comes at the price of analysis power in some cases.

Many of the Visio templates (including Charts and Graphics, Gantt Chart, and Organization Chart) let you use external sources for the data you want to display. Chapter 14 describes how to use external data to create diagrams with less effort.

Circuits and Logic (Engineering)

The Circuits and Logic template helps you create relatively complex circuit diagrams for any use. You can create both analog and digital circuitry using the Analog and Digital Logic, Integrated Circuit Components, Terminals and Connectors, and Transmission Paths stencils. This is a good tool for playing with an idea, fleshing out a concept, or discussing a technical issue with someone else. Hobbyists may find that this template provides all they need to create basic circuitry. Not only does it include standard circuitry, including a number of standard Integrated Component (IC) shapes, but it also includes all of the standard hardware, such as microphone jacks.

COM and OLE (Software and Database)

The COM and OLE template helps you describe software interfaces. You can actually use this template for far more than Component Object Model (COM) and Object Linking and Embedding (OLE) programming. For example, you could easily use it to describe the interfaces provided by any application language, including newer languages such as C# or Java. The COM and OLE stencil is deceptively simple. It includes shapes, such as an object hierarchy, and both standard and weak references. In short, anyone who works with objects can probably use this diagram to present interface information.

Conceptual Web Site (Network and Software and Database)

The Conceptual Web Site template helps you create the overall structure of a Web site. The Conceptual Web Site Shapes stencil includes all of the shapes you might expect, including Web pages, home pages, pop-ups, forms, and major site objects. The Web Site Map Shapes stencil includes shapes for major object types, including Word documents, audio files, JavaScript, and File Transfer Protocol (FTP) connections, among others. By combining these two stencils, you can create a comprehensive Web site design.

This template also includes the Callouts stencil that lets you annotate any diagram. Not only will you find the standard arrows combined with text, but you'll also find bracketed text, yellow sticky notes, and even files. You can even create your own personalized stamp to place on the final diagram. Any diagram can benefit from this particular stencil because there are few times when you don't require some type of diagram annotation (even if you don't leave the annotation in place on the final diagram).

Cross-Functional Flowchart (Business and Flowchart)

The essential purpose of this template is to help you diagram the relationship between a business process and the responsible party. Visio supports both horizontal and vertical cross-functional flowcharts. The orientation option you choose often depends on personal taste, rather than a strict requirement or guideline. You can also choose the number of bands that appears in the diagram when you create it. The best practice is to create enough bands to hold each step of the process you want to document. Visio does place a limit of five bands on this template, but you can add additional bands after you create the drawing. Visio also lets you use external data to create this flowchart.

Data Flow Diagram (Business and Flowchart)

Use the Data Flow Diagram template to describe data processes. You can use this diagram to assist in data analysis or show the flow of information for a process. The Data Flow Diagram Shapes stencil includes shapes for entities, states, and data processes. In general, you'll use this template to diagram the actions within a data flow, rather than the static state of a database.

Data Flow Model Diagram (Software and Database)

Don't confuse the Data Flow Model Diagram with the Data Flow Diagram template. The Data Flow Model Diagram uses the Gane-Sarson Data Flow Diagram (DFD) notation. The Gane-Sarson stencil consists of four simple shapes that help you describe processes, interfaces, data stores, and data flows. You can find more information about this particular modeling technique at `http://www.agilemodeling.com/artifacts/dataFlowDiagram.htm`. The tutorial, at `http://www.smartdraw.com/tutorials/software-dfd/dfd.htm`, shows how to draw a DFD.

Database Model Diagram (Software and Database)

The Database Model Diagram template helps you design and implement database structures. You can use both Entity-Relationship (ER) and Integrated Definition for Data Modeling (IDEF1X) notation when creating the diagram. Unlike many of the other diagrams that Visio supports, this template includes a special window that displays the database properties. When you create an entity such as a table, the additional window helps you define the table properties. The template includes the Entity Relationship stencil for use with ER diagrams and the Object Relational stencil for use with IDEF1X diagrams. The University of Texas Web site, at `http://www.utexas.edu/its/windows/database/datamodeling/dm/erintro.html`, describes the ER notation in detail. The Essential Strategies Web site, at `http://www.essentialstrategies.com/publications/modeling/idef1x.htm`, describes the IDEF1X notation in detail.

One of the more interesting features of this template is that you can use it to reverse-engineer existing databases. Simply choose the Database⇨Reverse Engineer command to display the Reverse Engineer Wizard. Follow the prompts to create a connection to the database of choice and Visio does all of the work required to build a model of your database. Generally, you'll find that the model is complete and only requires minor changes to create a complete view of your database. Not only can you work with Access, dBase, and SQL Server as data sources, but you can also model any Open DataBase Connectivity (ODBC) source (or create a new one) and Excel data files as well. Visio also includes sample database files you can use for experimentation.

Visio can also use existing drawings created by other products. Use the options on the Database⇨Import menu to import data from products that produce ERwin ERX files or VisioModeler IMD files.

After you finish a database model, you can export the results to a database using the Export to Database add-on found on the Tools⇨Add Ons⇨Visio Extras menu. (Don't confuse the Export to Database add-on with the

Database Export Wizard, which exports shape data to a table in an ODBC-compliant database.) You can use Visio as the design tool for your database, export the results, and then test the results using the Database Management System (DBMS) of your choice.

Detailed Network Diagram (Network)

The Detailed Network Diagram template is an extension of the Basic Network Diagram template. You use the Basic Network Diagram template to create an overview of complex networks; the Detailed Network Diagram template helps you create a machine-by-machine view of the network. For example, instead of simply saying that a particular machine acts as a server, you'd use a special symbol that signifies the server type, such as an FTP server.

The Detailed Network Diagram template includes a number of additional stencils. The Annotation stencil includes various callout types including round, oval, and square. It also contains directional arrows, break lines, references, section indicators, and drawing scales. The Detailed Network Diagram stencil includes shapes for devices such as radio towers, satellites, and an Extensible Markup Language (XML) Web service. You'll find physical location shapes, such as towns and cities, in the Network Locations stencil. The Network Symbols stencil includes router, bridge, Wide-Area Network (WAN), lock, and key shapes (among others). Finally, you can find specific machine types, such as a directory server, on the Servers stencil.

Directional Map (Maps and Floor Plans)

Imagine being able to create a truly functional and descriptive map without the usual problems in getting it drawn. If you've ever gotten lost after following a map on a napkin, you can appreciate the benefits of the Directional Map template. This template includes a wealth of stencils to make it easy to create a directional map with all of the extras. For example, the Landmark Shapes stencil includes easily recognizable shapes such as a barn, gas station, and airport. The Metro Shapes stencil contains shapes that help you build the metro line path to the destination. Use the Recreation Shapes stencil to include signposts that reflect local recreational activities, such as fishing and horseback riding. The Transportation Shapes stencil includes shapes that look like familiar road signs, such as school zone and stop signs. You build the actual map using the shapes on the Road Shapes stencil that includes roads of various types.

The stencils included with the Directional Map template all work exceptionally well with other templates. For example, when creating a floor plan, you can include external elements from the Landmark Shapes stencil. A detailed network diagram could include impediments to future upgrades such as trees (also found on the Landmark Shapes stencil) or roads (found on the Road Shapes stencil).

Directional Map 3D (Maps and Floor Plans)

The Directional Map 3D template is a simplified three-dimensional version of the Directional Map template. You use it to create a map with a 3D appearance. This template doesn't include all of the helpful stencils that the Directional Map template includes. In general, you'll find that this particular template is better suited to local needs, rather than across a city. What this template lacks in flexibility, it makes up in appearance, however.

Electrical and Telecom Plan (Maps and Floor Plans)

The Electrical and Telecom Plan helps you design the electrical layout of any location (generally a building). It includes a special Electrical and Telecom stencil that you use to place shapes, such as receptacles, ceiling fans, and lights, on the floor plan you create. Anyone can use this template to create a diagram that specifies how you want the electrical features of a room laid out. You don't actually create a wiring diagram; the electrician will do that. Consequently, whether you want some new outlets in your home or office, you can use this template to show the electrician where to place them.

This template includes the Drawing Tool Shapes stencil. This stencil is helpful when you need to measure something (it actually has a tape-measure shape that measures distance for you). You can also use the shapes to create exact angles, boxes of a specific size, circles, arcs, polygons, and any other geometric shape you need. The whole idea is to help you create diagrams with the required level of precision without having to worry about doing the work yourself.

As with all of the floor plan diagrams, this template also includes a stencil that helps you create the building. The Walls, Shell, and Structure stencil includes wall shapes of various kinds, and you can even create some rooms using a room shape instead of individual walls. You'll also find window and door shapes of various types, so that the building you create looks just like the real thing. All of the shapes in this stencil include automatic dimensioning so that you can make the rooms the correct size without a lot of extra work.

Enterprise Application (Software and Database)

As applications grow in size, you need to consider the physical layout of the application, as well as the underlying code design. For example, you might need to set up a server farm to run your database. An application might require a special server to provide external client support. The Enterprise Application template includes a single stencil, Enterprise Application, which helps you define the physical layout of an application. The stencil includes basic shapes for servers, workstations, users, and software elements such as interfaces.

EPC Diagram (Business)

Use the Event-driven Process Chain (EPC) Diagram template to model business processing relying on the SAP R/3 model. The diagram helps you describe the sequence of events and functions in a business process. The template provides access to a number of standard stencils and one special stencil, EPC Diagram Shapes. The EPC Diagram Shapes stencil includes event, function, process, and decision shapes. You can discover more about EPC diagrams at `http://paginas.terra.com.br/negocios/processos2002/epc_e_eepc.htm`.

Express-G (Software and Database)

Use the Express-G template to create entity- and schema-level diagrams of a database that rely on the Express-G notation method. The resulting diagrams adhere to the Standard for Exchange of Product (STEP) model data specification. You generally use this kind of diagram for large database designs. The associated Express-G stencil includes shapes for entities, relationships, cardinality, structure, and schema. You can discover more about the Express-G notation at `http://archives.si2.org/si2_publications/htmlSpecs/DR/part3.fm4.html`. The Web site, at `http://www.isr.umd.edu/Labs/CIM/ospam/node3.html`, tells you more about the STEP specification. You can obtain STEP-related tools from a number of places, but the best place to look is the National Institute of Standards and Technology (NIST) Web site, at `http://www.mel.nist.gov/msid/msidprod.htm`.

Fault Tree Analysis Diagram (Business)

Use this template to document business processes in a form that adheres to the document Six Sigma and ISO 9000 standard (see the "Audit Diagram (Business)" section, earlier in this chapter, for additional details). The special stencil for this template, Fault Tree Analysis Shapes, includes logic shapes that help you define the fault path for any process. Essentially, you use this template to compute the reliability of any given process by reviewing the potential failure modes. You can discover more about this diagramming technique at `http://www.weibull.com/basics/fault-tree/index.htm`.

Floor Plan (Maps and Floor Plans)

Sometimes you need a specialized floor plan a visitor can use or just to track resources in your organization. The Floor Plan template provides access to many of the same stencils that the specialized floor plan templates include. For example, you'll find the Electrical and Telecom stencil that the Electrical and Telecom Plan template uses. However, the purpose of this template differs from other templates because you use it to acquaint others with a particular business layout.

The highlight of this particular floor plan is the Points of Interest stencil, which includes shapes that identify particular areas of interest in your building. Some shapes identify large areas such as conference rooms, while others identify particular pieces of equipment, such as a copier. The whole idea is to help someone get around in your building without expending a lot of excess effort. Most of the shapes allow for customization. For example, the Conference Room shape includes properties for the number of people the room holds and the name of the room (making it easier for people to locate a particular conference room).

Fluid Power (Engineering)

Use the Fluid Power template to model both hydraulic and pneumatic systems. This template helps you describe anything that transfers gases or liquids from one location to another. The Fluid Power - Equipment stencil includes shapes of physical devices such as separators, pumps, actuators, and filters. The Fluid Power - Valve Assembly stencil includes valve representations and components (such as springs). The Fluid Power - Valves stencil contains shapes that represent complete valves. Finally, the Connectors stencil contains the shapes you use to make connections between the various fluid system components.

Gantt Chart (Schedule)

Just about everyone uses a Gantt chart at one time or another to define a timeline, manage projects and tasks, create an agenda, or set goals. When you select the Gantt Chart template, Visio asks you to provide information about it using the Gantt Chart Options dialog box. You need to specify information such as the number of tasks, the starting and ending day of the project, time units, and duration. The Format tab of the Gantt Chart Options dialog box contains options that let you set the starting and ending symbols for each task, labels, summary bar shapes, and milestone shape.

The template includes the Gantt Chart Shapes stencil that includes shapes for adding new tasks, defining additional columns, adding a title and legend, and providing annotation. You can annotate the actual bars or provide callouts to the Gantt chart elements. This template also exposes the Gantt Chart toolbar that helps you move around in the Gantt chart, add or delete tasks, and link or unlink tasks.

Home Plan (Maps and Floor Plans)

The Home Plan template is the counterpart of the Floor Plan template. You use the Floor Plan template for business needs and the Home Plan template for home needs. Like the Floor Plan template, the Home Plan template includes a wealth of stencils that help you define elements of your home. For example, you use the Appliances stencil to define the location of applications such as a stove or refrigerator. The Bath and Kitchen Plan stencil contains shapes for fixed elements such as bathtubs and sinks. You'll even find a number of sink types; it's possible to differentiate between a standard and pedestal sink. The Furniture and Garden Accessories stencils help you further define the layout of your home. In addition to these custom stencils, you'll find all of the standard floor plan stencils so that you can add walls, electrical elements, and annotations to your home floor plan.

HVAC Control Logic Diagram (Maps and Floor Plans)

The Heating, Ventilation, and Air Conditioning (HVAC) Control Logic Diagram template helps you describe the location of the devices that provide HVAC control within a building. The HVAC Controls stencil contains shapes that help you define control locations such as smoke detectors, thermostats, and timers. The HVAC Controls Equipment stencil helps you describe the locations of devices such as fans, filters, valves, and ducts.

HVAC Plan (Maps and Floor Plans)

The HVAC Control Logic Diagram template provides an overview of an installation, while the HVAC Plan provides specifics. Consequently, you'll find many of the same features in this template as you do in the HVAC Control Logic Diagram template. In addition to these basic features, you'll find stencils that help you describe details. For example, the HVAC Ductwork stencil helps you show the actual duct runs in a building. The Registers, Grills, and Diffusers stencil makes it possible to show the locations of inputs and outputs to the system. Most communities have standards that you must follow when submitting an HVAC plan. For example, visit `http://www.energy.ca.gov/efficiency/qualityhomes/procedures.html` for a detailed look at one standard.

IDEF0 Diagram (Flowchart)

The Integrated Definition for Function Modeling (IDEF0) Diagram helps you model the decisions, actions, and activities of an organization. The model is hierarchical, so you begin with a basic assumption and move into the details as the diagram progresses. For example, you could use this diagram to perform a benefits analysis. The IDEF0 stencil contains all of the common shapes used to create this diagram type. You can discover how to create an IDEF0 diagram of your own at `http://www.idef.com/idef0.html`.

Industrial Control Systems (Engineering)

The Industrial Control Systems template helps you document industrial power systems. The associated stencils include a wide range of electrical and electronic elements. For example, the Fundamental Items stencil includes electronic items such as resistors, capacitors, and inductors. The Rotating Equip and Mech Functions stencil includes complete motors and motor components such as fields. You'll also find stencils that include shapes for switches, relays, terminals, connectors, transformers, windings, and transmission paths.

This diagram won't provide you with a parts list or other data normally associated with CAD packages. You use it for descriptive or initial design purposes, rather than for specific information. Most of the shapes don't provide any special data, but some do. It's possible to define the specifics of a rotating machine, but not a switch. None of the shapes includes manufacturer or part information.

ITIL Diagram (Business)

The Information Technology Infrastructure Library (ITIL) Diagram template helps you diagram best practices for management of Information Technology (IT) service processes. Because of the way you use this diagram, you'll find a diverse set of stencils that are associated with other diagram types. For example, you'll find the Basic Flowchart Shapes stencil. The special ITIL Shapes stencil contains shapes that help you tie all of these elements together into a comprehensive document. You can discover more about ITIL diagramming techniques at `http://www.itil.org.uk/`. Get help with your ITIL diagram on The Itil Community Forum, at `http://www.itilcommunity.com/`.

Jackson (Software and Database)

The Jackson template helps you create application designs based on the Jackson methodology. This technique relies on a hierarchical structure of processes and procedures. The Jackson stencil contains all of the essential elements that you'll need to create this diagram. You can find out more about the author of this methodology at `http://mcs.open.ac.uk/mj665/`. The Web site at `http://cisx2.uma.maine.edu/NickTemp/JSP&JSDLec/jsd.html` tells you how to create a diagram using the Jackson methodology.

LDAP Directory (Network)

The Lightweight Directory Access Protocol (LDAP) Directory template helps you document directory services such as Active Directory. The LDAP Objects stencil contains a complete list of directory services objects starting with organization and moving down into individual objects, such as applications and users. You can discover more about LDAP diagrams at `http://www.ust.hk/itsc/ldap/understand.html`.

Marketing Charts and Diagrams (Business)

While you use the Charts and Graphs template to show static data, the Marketing Charts and Diagrams template helps you depict live or predicted data. For example, you can use this template to perform a "what if" analysis on data to determine the best way to achieve a specific result. You can also use this template to perform process diagramming, benchmark simulation, sales pyramids, and other forms of analysis. Although this template includes the same Charting Shapes stencil used by the Charts and Graphs template, you'll likely use the other stencils to perform much of the work in this template. For example, the Marketing Diagrams stencil includes several forms of the matrix shape. After you perform any required analysis, you can use the shapes on the Marketing Shapes stencil to dress up the output of your diagram.

Office Layout (Maps and Floor Plans)

The Office Layout template has several uses. You could focus on an individual office or use this template to generate the floor plan for an entire office area. It's even possible to focus on a particular area with special needs. The stencils let you include everything someone would find in an office, from the wastepaper baskets to the desk. The Office Equipment stencil includes shapes for common items such as copiers. You use the Cubicles stencil to create offices that rely on removable walls and the Walls, Doors, and Windows stencil to create offices that have fixed walls.

Organization Chart (Business)

You use this template to show a hierarchical organization of something. Although the template assumes that you'll show the organization of your company, you can use this template to show the organization of anything. For example, you could use it to describe the organization of a Web site. The only criterion for using this diagram is that you have a starting point and elements that branch out from that starting point.

ORM Diagram (Software and Database)

The Object Role Model (ORM) Diagram template helps you model object-oriented application designs. This is one of several agile methods of designing applications. The ORM Diagram stencil includes all of the required shapes for this diagramming strategy, including entities, values, constraints, and connectors. Although the Unified Modeling Language (UML) (see the "UML Model Diagram (Software and Database)" section, later in this chapter, for details) is strong on modeling a specific approach to a problem, ORM is strong in analysis. It helps groups understand a particular software model faster and promotes faster changes. Given the right tools, you can derive a UML diagram from an ORM diagram, but ORM diagrams can require more time and patience to design correctly. You can discover more about this method of designing applications at `http://www.orm.net/`. The ORM tutorial, at `http://osm7.cs.byu.edu/OSA/orm.html`, describes how to create ORM diagrams.

UML isn't as complex as some people want to make you believe. The trick is to find an easy-to-use guide and discover how to use UML correctly so that you can obtain maximum benefit from it. *UML 2 For Dummies,* by Michael Jesse Chonoles and James A. Schardt (published by Wiley) provides everything you need to get a good start. Find out more about this book at `http://www.dummies.com/WileyCDA/DummiesTitle/productCd-0764526146.html`.

Part and Assembly Drawing (Engineering)

The Part and Assembly Drawing template helps you create rough drawings of machine tools and other mechanical devices. The device need not be complex. You could use this template to create something like a fancy doorknob or a new type of clothes hanger. The stencils include drawing primitives, such as circles and squares, that you'll find in the Drawing Tool Shapes stencil.

Fortunately, you don't have to draw everything from scratch. For example, you'll find a number of screws, bolts, and other fasteners in the Fasteners 1 and Fasteners 2 stencils. The Springs and Bearings stencil helps you add these complex parts to your diagram without hours of drawing. You can even show welds by using the shapes in the Welding Symbols template.

The Title Block stencil helps you create a title block for your diagram with a single shape. Many people associate title blocks with mechanical drawings, but they also come in handy for other kinds of diagrams because they let you track revisions for that particular diagram. You may want to include a title block with all of your diagrams to make the revision information easier to find and see.

PERT Chart (Schedule)

The Program Evaluation Review Technique (PERT) Chart template helps you diagram workflows, milestones, schedules, timetables, critical paths, and other planning requirements for a project. The PERT Chart Diagram stencil includes two task shapes, connectors, a legend, a summary, and callouts. You can discover more about PERT charts at `http://www.netmba.com/operations/project/pert/`.

Piping and Instrumentation Diagram (Engineering)

The Piping and Instrumentation Diagram (PID) template helps you describe a complex piping system. The piping system can carry anything from gases to the heaviest liquid. The template includes all of the pipes, devices, valves, instrumentation, and other elements of a complex system. This template has a significant number of stencils, all of which address a particular piping system element such as valves. In fact, the template includes an entire stencil devoted to the topic of heat exchangers. Unlike many of the templates, the Process Annotations stencil includes shapes that will list valve, pipeline, equipment, and instrumentation requirements for the given diagram. You can discover more about the PID and see a sample diagram at `http://www.engineeringtoolbox.com/p&id-piping-instrumentation-diagram-d_466.html`.

PivotDiagram (Business)

The PivotDiagram template accepts data from any of a number of data sources including Excel, Access, SQL Server, SharePoint Server, Object Linking and Embedding Database (OLEDB), and Open DataBase Connectivity (ODBC). After you have the data imported, you can add PivotNode shapes and manipulate the data in various ways to create the output you need. For example, you could create a pivotdiagram that shows how many times you received income from an account and the sum of the income for that particular account. Pivotdiagrams can also perform comparisons of data from multiple sources.

Plant Layout (Maps and Floor Plans)

While the Floor Plan template helps you create general floor plans for office space and other nonmanufacturing buildings, the Plant Layout template concentrates on various types of manufacturing. You can use this template to create any type of manufacturing space.

In addition to the standard floor plan stencils, you'll find that this template includes several manufacturing-specific stencils. The Shop Floor - Machines and Equipment stencil contains an array of manufacturing-specific machines such as welders, drill presses, and milling machines. The Shop Floor - Storage and Distribution stencil includes shapes for forklifts, racks, rollers, and cranes. Finally, the Warehouse - Shipping and Receiving stencil includes a number of shapes for loading and unloading goods such as dockside cranes and loading bays.

You may run out of vehicle types to use with some of the diagrams that Visio provides. Fortunately, the Plant Layout template contains a wealth of them in the Vehicles stencil. This stencil includes everything from a compact car to a fire truck.

Plumbing and Piping Plan (Maps and Floor Plans)

You use the Plumbing and Piping Plan to create a detailed diagram of the plumbing infrastructure for any building. The template helps you show waste-water disposal, as well as hot- and cold-water supplies. The various stencils include a vast array of piping types and valves. The Plumbing stencil includes all of the usual plumbing fixtures. However, you might find that you need to augment the list of plumbing fixtures from the Bath and Kitchen Plan stencil included as part of the Home Plan template. For example, the Plumbing stencil includes just one sink, while the Bath and Kitchen Plan stencil includes several designs.

Process Flow Diagram (Engineering)

The Process Flow Diagram (PFD) helps you describe the relationship between elements of a piping system. In fact, you'll often see it referenced alongside a PID (see the "Piping and Instrumentation Diagram (Engineering)" section, earlier in this chapter, for details). This template has a significant number of stencils, all of which address a particular piping system element such as valves. In fact, the template includes an entire stencil devoted to the topic of heat exchangers. Unlike many of the templates, the Process Annotations stencil includes shapes that will list valve, pipeline, equipment, and instrumentation requirements for the given diagram. You can discover more about the PFD at `http://www.engineeringtoolbox.com/pfd-process-flow-diagram-d_465.html` and see an example diagram at `http://www.osha.gov/OshStd_gif/Process.gif`.

Program Structure (Software and Database)

You use the Program Structure template to create application structural diagrams, flowcharts, and memory diagrams. The Memory Objects stencil includes a number of memory structure shapes, including arrays, stacks, variables, and pointers. The Language Level Shapes template includes shapes for functions, conditional invocation, lexical inclusion, various kinds of flow, and other language-specific requirements. This template doesn't produce a diagram that follows any specific design convention such as UML or ORM.

Rack Diagram (Network)

The Rack Diagram template helps you visualize the layout of equipment in a rack. Rather than physically moving the equipment around to achieve an optimal layout, you can use this template to design one. The Free-standing Rack Equipment stencil includes monitors, servers, printers, and other freestanding shapes. The Network Room Elements template includes essential room features such as doors, windows, and tables. The Rack-mounted Equipment stencil includes the rack, server, RAID array, patch panel, shelf, and other rack elements.

Reflected Ceiling Plan (Maps and Floor Plans)

Most commercial buildings use ceiling tiles with an open space above for everything from lighting to plumbing and network cabling. This template helps you create a diagram that defines the layout of the ceiling area so you can avoid conflicts and document where all of those elements go. The stencils include all of the normal floor plan additions. In addition, the Registers, Grills, and Diffusers template contains special shapes for all of the items that normally appear in place or as part of a ceiling tile.

ROOM (Software and Database)

Real-time systems have special requirements and need a special modeling system to ensure that the application meets these requirements. The Real-time Object Oriented Modeling (ROOM) language template helps you model the special needs of real-time systems. The ROOM stencil includes all of the shapes required to create a ROOM diagram including actor, state, port, transition, and binding elements. You can discover more about creating your own ROOM diagrams at `http://www.smartdraw.com/tutorials/software-room/room.htm`.

SDL Diagram (Flowchart)

The Specification and Description Language (SDL) template helps you create object-oriented designs for communications and telecommunications systems and networks. In addition to the normal flowchart stencils, this template includes a special SDL Diagram Shapes stencil. You'll find that the SDL Diagram Shapes includes all of the Consultative Committee for International Telegraphy and Telephony (CCITT)–recommended features such as procedures, requests, and decisions. You'll find a full tutorial on SDL at `http://www.sdl-forum.org/sdl88tutorial/index.html`.

Security and Access Plan (Maps and Floor Plans)

Anyone can use the Security and Access Plan template to create a security plan for any environment. The template includes all of the usual floor plan stencils. In addition, it contains three special templates that contain the latest security devices. The Alarm and Access Control stencil includes shapes for card readers, biometric access, keypads, and other access control devices. The Initiation and Annunciation stencil includes shapes such as printers, audio devices, two-way radios, and document destroyers. The Video Surveillance stencil includes detectors such as cameras, glass-break detectors, recorders, and security windows. Unlike many of the shapes that Visio provides, these shapes accept a considerable amount of data. Not only can you choose device type and technology, but you can also include physical elements such as the location height on a wall.

Site Plan (Maps and Floor Plans)

Unlike many of the other plans that Visio supports, the Site Plan template doesn't concentrate on the inside of something; instead, it focuses on the outside. You use this template to create the layout of a series of buildings on a plot of land or even the layout of your own home. This template lets you create plat maps and design parks.

The template includes many of the same stencils as a standard plan; however, it includes many special stencils as well. The Garden Accessories stencil helps you design garden features, as well as physical features, such as fences, walkways, and patios. The Irrigation stencil helps you design an irrigation system to keep everything watered. Use the Parking and Roads stencil to create parking areas and the roads leading to them. Finally, the Sports Fields and Recreation stencil includes everything from swimming pools to tennis courts. This template also includes the Points of Interest and Vehicles stencils included with other templates.

The Site Plan template includes two stencils that come in handy for other plans, even inside plans at times. It's easy to add vegetation to your diagram using the trees, shrubs, and plants on the Planting stencil. The Site Accessories stencil includes shapes for picnic tables, lights, Dumpsters, and other outdoor items that sometimes appear inside as well.

Space Plan (Maps and Floor Plans)

You might find the Space Plan confusing at first because it bears similarities to the Floor Plan, Home Plan, and Office Layout templates. However, these other plans help you design an initial layout; they represent a static presentation of the ideal condition of a particular office or home space. The Space Plan is more dynamic. It helps you present the actual day-to-day configuration of a space. For this reason, the template even includes people so that you can show how specific people will utilize a particular space.

This template begins by asking you to supply a floor plan. The floor plan can appear as a JPG, GIF, Visio drawing, or CAD drawing (DXF or DWG format). You can also choose None as an option, but choosing this option defeats the purpose of using the template. After you obtain a floor plan, the template asks you to supply a room list. You can use an existing spreadsheet, create a new spreadsheet, or manually enter the room information.

After you have the floor plan imported, you can add furniture to it using the shapes on the Office Furniture stencil. Use the Cubicles stencil to add partitions to the plan. The Office Equipment stencil includes shapes for items such as PCs, copiers, projectors, and telephone jacks. The Resources stencil includes a person shape, as well as a number of reports. For example, you'll find a Move Report shape that helps you document moves from one location to another. All of the shapes in this template include data entries that help you track resources. For example, a Sofa shape includes the ID (identifier), width, depth, name, department, asset number, serial number, product description, purchase date, and product number (among other items). Consequently, you can use this template to help manage an office and note changes in configuration as needed.

Don't get the idea that this template only works well for offices. It also works well in the home environment. For example, you can use this template to perform "what if" scenarios for moving items around without the backbreaking work of actually performing the task. This template provides an ideal way to perform redecoration and keep track of your assets for insurance purposes.

Systems (Engineering)

The Systems template differs from the Basic Electrical, Circuits and Logic, and Industrial Control Systems templates by helping you annotate and document a design. While the other templates help you create a particular design, the Systems template helps you document the design in such a way that other people can easily understand it. Think of this template as helping you create an overview of an entire system where details aren't quite as important as seeing the project as a whole.

The stencils for the template focus on the overview. For example, in the Composite Assemblies stencil, you find shapes for an entire amplifier, rather than the components used to build the amplifier. The Maps and Charts stencil includes shapes for items such as a radio station, telegraph repeater, geothermal station, and switching station. This particular template includes too many stencils to list here, but what you'll find mainly are telecommunications, radio, electrical, and electronic shapes, with a few plant and power/water shapes mixed in for good measure.

Timeline (Schedule)

The Timeline stencil helps you create an overview of the detailed scheduling information provided by detailed scheduling aids such as the Gantt chart.

You can create a single timeline that shows where a project should be on a given date. The special Timeline stencil includes shapes for five timeline types (block, line, rule, cylindrical, and divided), milestones, and intervals. You can use the Today Marker shape to show the current date. Finally, the Expanded Timeline shape helps you show some details for a particular time-line section.

TQM Diagram (Business)

Use the Total Quality Management (TQM) Diagram template to create cause-and-effect, top-down, and cross-functional process flow diagrams in a form that adheres to the document Six Sigma and ISO 9000 standard (see the "Audit Diagram (Business)" section, earlier in this chapter, for additional details). You can obtain an overview of TQM at `http://www.isixsigma.com/me/tqm/`. The essential goal for TQM is to ensure that products consistently meet or exceed customer expectations (something that is easier said than done). The special stencil for this template, TQM Diagram Shapes, includes logic shapes that help you define the failure modes and process flow for any product development scenario. You can see an example of this diagramming technique at `http://home.att.net/~iso9k1/tqm/tqm.html#Planning%20a%20Change`.

UML Model Diagram (Software and Database)

The Unified Modeling Language (UML) Model Diagram template helps you create a software design that includes not only the actual software, but also demonstrates how the user interacts with the software and considers the sequence of events that will normally occur in a given usage (case). Because UML covers so much ground, this template includes a special Model Explorer that helps you choose elements of the particular model you want to create. Right-clicking a particular folder displays a context menu that contains a list of the elements you can create. For example, when you right click the Top Package folder, you can choose to create any of the diagrams that UML supports. The various stencils provide shapes that help you model application activity, collaboration, component, deployment, sequence, state, structure, and uses. You can discover more about UML at `http://www.uml.org/`. A UML tutorial appears at `http://pigseye.kennesaw.edu/~dbraun/csis4650/A&D/UML_tutorial/`.

Value Stream Map (Business)

You can use the Value Stream Map template to document the flow of information and material in a lean manufacturing process. The special Value Stream Map Shapes stencil supplied with this template includes shapes for inventory, processes, various kanbans, load leveling, and directional arrows. (Just in case you're wondering, kanban is a Japanese word that means *instruction card*. Kanbans are manual pull devices that move parts from one department to another. In addition, the kanban reorders products based on minimum/ maximum inventory levels.) You can find details about this mapping technique along with a sample diagram (see bottom of Web page) at http:// www.strategosinc.com/vsm2.htm.

Web Site Map (Network and Software and Database)

Use the Web Site Map template to map the pages on a Web site of any kind and in any location (even local drives). The template begins by displaying a Generate Site Map dialog box where you enter the URL for the Web site. Click Settings to define how Visio generates the site map. For example, you can change the depth of search that Visio uses to locate new pages. After you click OK, you can get a cup of coffee as Visio leisurely generates the site map. The special Web Site Map Shapes stencil includes shapes you can use to create new pages or add special symbols to existing pages.

The interesting part about this particular template is that it works just fine on Web sites you don't know, so you can create a map of Web sites that don't include site maps. Even when the Web site includes a site map, you can use this template to create a personalized version with symbols indicating areas of special interest. Consequently, anyone who uses Web sites can benefit from this template; it's not just for developers.

Windows XP User Interface (Software and Database)

If you're a developer, you might wonder why you would create a user interface using Visio, rather than your development environment. Users already realize that Visio gives them the power to define the user interface they want, rather than what the developer thinks they need. Visio provides a means of communication between users and developers that lets everyone work together to create an interface using a tool that everyone understands. The Windows XP User Interface template helps you design interfaces that truly meet everyone's needs.

The stencils included with this template include everything from simple controls to complete dialog boxes. The Common Controls stencil contains all of the controls that you commonly see, including text boxes, labels, and mouse pointers with ToolTips attached. The Icons stencil includes a meager list of the most common icons associated with Windows, such as My Computer and the Recycle Bin. You'll likely need to augment these icons with a few of your own. The Toolbars and Menus stencil includes individual menu and toolbar items, as well as special icons to dress up the appearance of the menu or toolbar. The Wizards stencil includes a complete series of standard wizard dialog boxes. Finally, the Windows and Dialogs stencil includes complete windows and dialog boxes, as well as components you can use to augment a particular design.

Work Flow Diagram (Business and Flowchart)

Use the Work Flow Diagram to document information flow, business process automation, business process reengineering, accounting, management, and human resources in a form that adheres to the document Six Sigma and ISO 9000 standard (see the "Audit Diagram (Business)" section, earlier in this chapter, for additional details). Some references also refer to a workflow diagram as a Business Process Management (BPM) diagram. The stencils included with this template help you model departments, workflow objects, and workflow steps. You can see practical examples of workflow diagrams at `http://www.deas.harvard.edu/courses/es96/spring1995/end_process/images/marr_wilson_2.gif` and `http://www.allergysa.org/flowdiag.htm`. The Web site at `http://www.smartdraw.com/tutorials/bpm/bpm10.htm` provides a workflow tutorial.

Working with Stencils

When you choose a drawing category and template, Visio automatically opens the stencils you commonly use to create your drawing. The "Understanding the Visio Drawing Categories" section, earlier in this chapter, provides suggestions of other stencils you might want to use with particular templates. Sometimes it's helpful to close templates you no longer need to avoid clutter. The following sections describe how to work with Visio stencils.

Moving and arranging stencils

Most templates automatically open more than one stencil. Figure 2-4 illustrates the nine stencils that open automatically when you select the Part and Assembly Template of the Engineering category.

The default docking location for stencils is the Shapes pane, on the left side of the screen. Stencils are stacked atop one another with just the title bar showing. As you open additional stencils, Visio adds them to the stack. This stacking arrangement saves space for the drawing area.

You can change the docking location to the top, bottom, or right side of the screen. A fourth option is to float a stencil so that it appears in a separate window with its own Close and Minimize buttons. This option lets you place the stencil anywhere you want on the screen, move it, resize it, and minimize it.

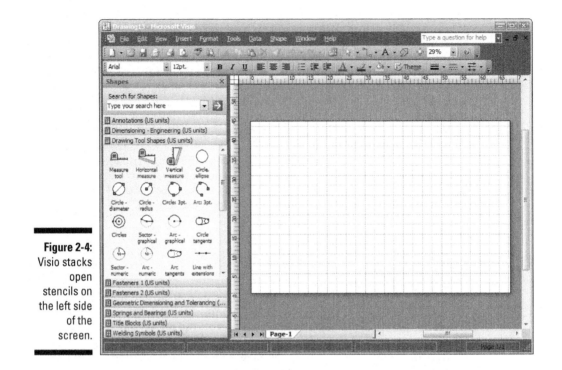

Figure 2-4:
Visio stacks
open
stencils on
the left side
of the
screen.

To reposition a stencil, click the title bar and drag the stencil to another location on the screen. The stencil docks itself depending on where you release the mouse button. For example, if you drag the stencil to the bottom of the drawing area, the stencil docks itself there. If you drag it to the top of the drawing area, it docks there. If you want a stencil on the right side of your screen, first close the Help pane, and then drag the stencil there. If you drag a stencil anywhere else on the screen, it floats in its own separate window.

Closing stencils

To close a stencil displayed in the stack in the Shapes pane, right-click its title bar and choose Close. The title bar of a floating stencil or a stencil docked somewhere other than in the Shapes pane contains an *X*. Click the *X* to close the stencil.

Opening additional stencils

If you want to use a shape that's not available in any of the open stencils, you can open additional stencils. In fact, you can open as many stencils as you have room for on your screen.

If you're not sure which stencil you need to open, check out the "Finding the Shapes You Want" section in Chapter 4, where you find out how to search for shapes. Use the following steps to open a new stencil after you create a diagram:

1. **Choose File⇨Shapes.**

   A list of drawing categories appears. This list mirrors the category list that appears when you start Visio. Each category has a right-pointing arrow.

2. **Point to the category you want.**

   A list of all the templates in that category appears.

3. **Point to the template you want.**

   A list of all of the stencils for that template appears.

4. **Click a stencil name.**

   Visio opens the stencil and displays it on the left side of the screen.

A step-by-step method for creating drawings

You've seen it before. The okay-what-do-I-do-now? stare that creeps across someone's face when he or she starts a new program. As they say, it always pays to have a plan. At least with a plan, you can *pretend* you know what you're doing!

Use this checklist whenever you create a drawing using a template:

- ✔ Know what kind of drawing you want to create so that you can choose an appropriate drawing category.

- ✔ Start a new drawing by choosing a template in that category.

- ✔ Open any additional stencils that you may want to use (see the nearby section "Opening additional stencils" in this chapter).

- ✔ If you want your drawing to have multiple pages, add them now (see Chapter 9).

- ✔ Drag and drop shapes from the stencil onto the drawing (see Chapter 4).

- ✔ Connect the shapes (see Chapter 6).

- ✔ Add text to the drawing (see Chapter 5).

- ✔ Apply a color scheme to the drawing (see Chapter 4).

- ✔ Save the drawing.

- ✔ Print your drawing (see Chapter 3).

The process can be far more involved than this. You can create background pages, add layers, incorporate hyperlinks, insert objects from other programs, and so on. However, this is the basic process you follow each time you create a drawing. Refer to this list until you're more comfortable working with Visio.

Selecting a Pointer Tool Button

Before you can place or select shapes in a drawing, click the Pointer Tool button on the Standard toolbar, as shown in Figure 2-5. Fortunately, Visio selects the Pointer Tool for you automatically when you start Visio.

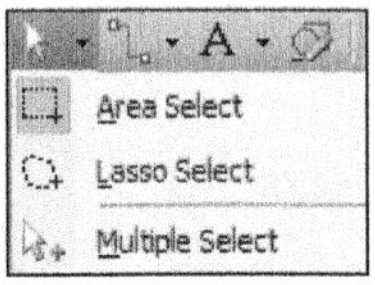

Figure 2-5:
The Pointer Tool has three variations.

In the drawing area, the pointer is a simple white arrow just like the one used in many other software programs. Visio calls this standard Pointer Tool *Area Select.* The Pointer Tool has two other variations:

- ✔ **Lasso Select:** This lets you select shapes by drawing a lasso around them. You use this setting most often when your drawing is dense with shapes and you want to select specific shapes in an area.

- ✔ **Multiple Select:** This setting causes the mouse to add to your selection each time you click a shape.

To choose the Lasso Select or Multiple Select button, click the down arrow next to the Pointer Tool, and then click the variation of the tool that you want.

Unfortunately, the mouse pointer on your screen doesn't change to reflect the type of Pointer Tool you select. You can only tell which Pointer Tool is selected by the behavior of the pointer after you start using it. Later in this chapter, you use these pointers to select multiple shapes. For now, continue using the standard Area Select tool.

Working with Shapes

Shapes are the essence of all Visio drawings. The first thing you do to create a drawing is to add shapes. Later you can add connectors, text, and other elements to the drawing.

Adding a shape to a drawing

The diagrams you create are composed of shapes. To add a new shape to a diagram, point to a shape in the stencil, click and hold down the left mouse button, and then drag the shape into the drawing area. Release the mouse button when the shape is where you want it. Remember to drag the shape from the stencil to the drawing area.

You can drag a shape into a drawing as many times as you want — the master shape stays on the stencil. As you drag a shape into your drawing area, you see an outline of the shape on the screen. When you release the mouse button, the actual shape appears in your drawing and remains selected (Visio displays green handles on the outside of the shape) until you click a blank area of the drawing page.

You can also drag a whole bunch of shapes into a drawing at once. Suppose you're creating a directional map and you know you want to use these shapes from the Landmark Shapes stencil: airport, townhouse, ferry, river, hospital, and sports stadium. Hold down the Shift key as you click each shape. In the stencil, each shape you click remains highlighted. When you select the last shape, release the Shift key and drag the shapes into the drawing. Visio stacks the shapes on top of each other (slightly staggered so that you can see each one). Now you can arrange them however you like.

Selecting a shape

Selecting a shape in a drawing is even easier than dragging it onto a drawing — just click the shape. When you select a shape, its green selection frame and handles become visible (see Figure 2-6). You need to select a shape before you can move it, copy it, delete it, or change it in any other way. Notice in Figure 2-6 that selecting a shape doesn't automatically select the shapes outside of it or shapes that it contains. In this case, selecting the desk doesn't select the room or the PC.

A shape displays different types of selection handles depending on the tool you use to select the shape. You find out more about controlling, working with, and manipulating shapes in Chapter 4.

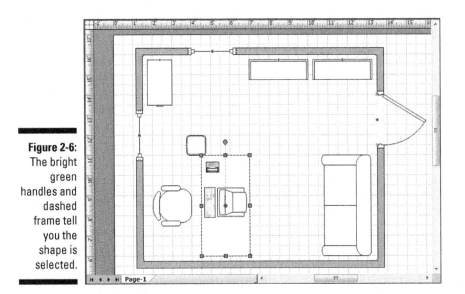

Figure 2-6:
The bright
green
handles and
dashed
frame tell
you the
shape is
selected.

Selecting more than one shape at a time

Sometimes you may want to perform the same task (such as moving, copy-ing, rotating, or flipping) on several shapes at a time. You can use one of the following four methods to select multiple shapes:

✔ **Use the Area Select Pointer Tool button and hold down the Shift key as you click each shape that you want to select.** As you select shapes, they're enclosed in a *selection box* (a green dotted rectangle). Green han-dles appear at the corners of the selection box. Visio outlines all of the selected shapes in magenta (the first one in a bolder outline).

✔ **Use the Area Select Pointer Tool button and drag a selection box around multiple shapes.** Just drag the mouse around the shapes that you want to select, and then release the mouse button. You must fully enclose all the shapes that you want to select; if you cut across a shape, it isn't selected.

✔ **Use the Lasso Select Pointer Tool button and click and drag the mouse pointer around the shapes you want to select.** As you drag, a lasso on the screen follows your path. As soon as you release the mouse button, Visio encloses the selected shapes in a rectangle.

✔ **Use the Multiple Select Pointer Tool button and click each shape that you want to add to the current selection.** (You don't need to hold the Shift key or do any dragging with this option.) Visio changes the Pointer Tool button to show a plus sign when you select this feature. When you're finished, you need to remember to turn off this pointer by select-ing it a second time. Otherwise, Visio continues selecting shapes every time you click one!

If you select multiple shapes and then decide to exclude one of them, you can deselect it without deselecting all the shapes. Hold down the Shift key and click the shape you want to remove. You can tell that you successfully deselected the shape because the selection box shrinks to *exclude* the shape. To deselect all selected shapes, click any blank area of the drawing or press Esc. To select all shapes in a drawing quickly, press Ctrl+A or choose Edit➪Select All.

Navigating through a Drawing

Often drawings contain multiple pages, and you need to be able to move from one page to another quickly. The drawing shown in Figure 2-7 contains four pages. The name of each page appears on a tab at the bottom of the drawing window on the navigation bar. To move from one page to another, just click the page tab. Visio highlights the tab for the page you select.

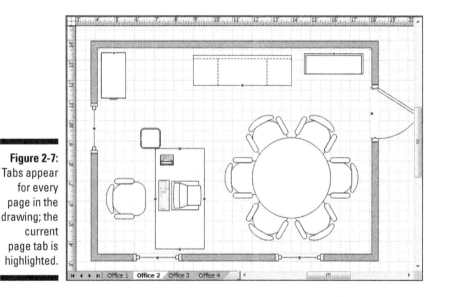

Figure 2-7:
Tabs appear for every page in the drawing; the current page tab is highlighted.

If the navigation bar isn't wide enough to display all the page names, put your mouse pointer over the right end of the navigation bar until the pointer changes to a double-headed arrow. Now you can drag the navigation bar to the right until it displays all the page tabs in your drawing. (This shortens your scroll bar, but you can still scroll.)

Zeroing In on a Drawing

As you work on a drawing, it's nice to be able to zoom in on a particular area. Visio gives you several options for zooming in and out.

Using the Zoom button

The typical way to adjust your view of a drawing is to use the Zoom button on the Standard toolbar. Next to the Zoom button (the one that displays a percentage) is a drop-down arrow. When you click this arrow, a list of percentages (50%, 75%, 100%, 150%, 200%, and 400%) is displayed, along with three other options (see Figure 2-8).

Figure 2-8:
The Zoom button offers preset zoom percentages and other options.

Just click the percentage you want, type a percentage, or click one of the following options:

- ✓ **Last:** Returns to the last percentage used
- ✓ **Width:** Displays the width of the page
- ✓ **Page:** Displays the entire page

These options appear also in the View menu under Zoom, but using the Zoom toolbar button is faster.

One way to zoom — and by far, the fastest — is to hold down the Ctrl key and use the scroll wheel on the mouse. Scrolling forward (away from you) zooms in; scrolling backward (toward you) zooms out. Of course, this method requires a scroll wheel on your mouse. If your mouse doesn't have one, you can zoom using Ctrl+Shift. When you press and hold these keys, the mouse pointer changes to a magnifying glass with a plus sign. Click the left mouse button to zoom in; click the right mouse button to zoom out. To zoom back out again to display the entire drawing, press Ctrl+W.

When you're zoomed in close, you can *pan* (move right, left, up, or down) through a drawing by using the scroll bars.

Using the Pan & Zoom window

When you're working on an enormous drawing, it's easy to lose your bearings when you zoom in on a specific area. Using the scroll bars to pan through a drawing can get cumbersome. A great way to keep your perspective on a drawing and navigate at the same time is to use the Pan & Zoom window, shown in Figure 2-9.

This tiny window gives you a full-page view of your drawing; a zoom box marks the area you're currently zoomed in on. You can use the zoom box simply to keep an eye on the area you're working in, or you can move it to a different location in the drawing. Follow these steps to experiment with the Pan & Zoom window:

1. **Choose View⇨Pan & Zoom Window.**

   Visio displays the Pan & Zoom window. The red rectangle outlines the area of the drawing you're currently viewing.

2. **To zoom in on a different area of the drawing:**

   a. **Place the mouse pointer over the red rectangle until the pointer changes to a four-headed arrow.**

   b. **Drag the red rectangle to a new location in the drawing.**

3. **To move to a different location in the drawing, point anywhere outside the red rectangle and drag the mouse.**

   A new rectangle is drawn automatically and Visio shifts your view of the drawing.

4. **To resize the red rectangle (which changes the size of the area you view in the drawing):**

   a. **Move the mouse pointer over the red rectangle until the mouse pointer changes to a two-headed arrow.**

   b. **Click and drag the mouse in any direction to resize the rectangle.**

   Visio automatically shifts your view of the drawing to the boundaries defined by the red rectangle.

Like other windows, you can make the Pan & Zoom window a floating window by dragging it anywhere on the screen, or you can dock it along any edge of the drawing area just by dragging it. Clicking the *X* closes the window. Click the thumbtack and you can hide the window until you need it. Move the mouse over the title bar and the entire Pan & Zoom window appears again. Most of the optional windows that Visio provides have these features.

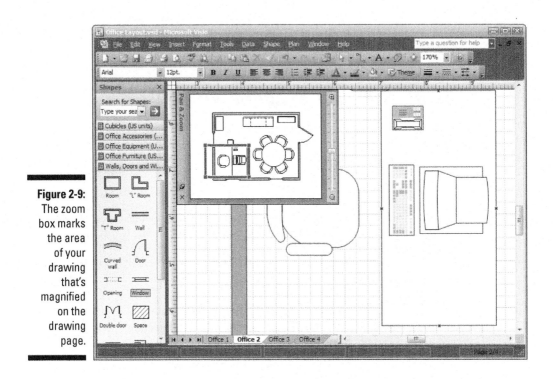

Figure 2-9:
The zoom box marks the area of your drawing that's magnified on the drawing page.

Using Drawing Explorer

Drawing Explorer is like central database administration for your drawing. It keeps track of a truckload of drawing data (some you might think trivial!), such as the following:

- Number and name of the foreground and background pages
- Order of the pages
- Shapes used on a specific drawing page
- Layers used on a specific drawing page
- Styles used throughout the drawing
- Master shapes used throughout the drawing
- Fill pattern, line pattern, and line ends used in the drawing

Why would you possibly care about this kind of information? For some drawings, you may not care and won't even bother to open Drawing Explorer. However, as drawing complexity and the number of pages in a drawing increase, you need tools to help manage the drawing. Drawing Explorer helps you locate important bits of information without expending a lot of energy looking at each shape in a drawing one page at a time.

To open Drawing Explorer, choose View⇨Drawing Explorer. Drawing Explorer displays information about a drawing in a hierarchical format. It's modeled after Windows Explorer, which uses a tree structure, folder and document icons, and the – and + symbols to indicate whether a folder is empty. In Figure 2-10, the first line in the Drawing Explorer window displays the path name for the drawing. Below the path name are various folders, beginning with Foreground Pages. Office 1 contains the Shapes folder, which is open. The list of shapes appears within the Shapes folder. When you expand a particular shape, you can see its properties.

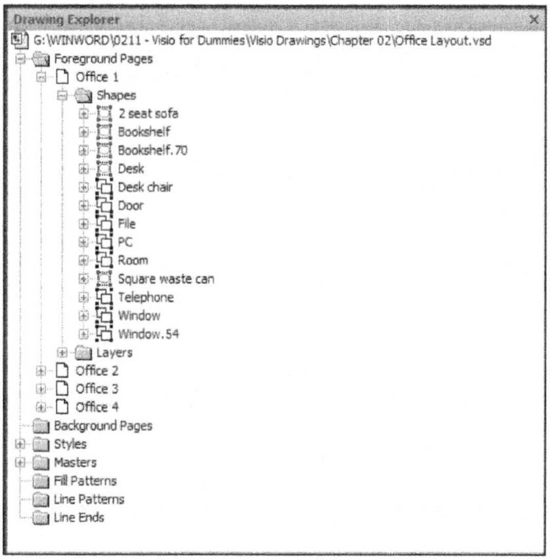

Figure 2-10: Drawing Explorer displays a wealth of information about your drawing in a hierarchical format.

```
Drawing Explorer                                          ×
  G:\WINWORD\0211 - Visio for Dummies\Visio Drawings\Chapter 02\Office Layout.vsd
  Foreground Pages
    Office 1
      Shapes
        2 seat sofa
        Bookshelf
        Bookshelf.70
        Desk
        Desk chair
        Door
        File
        PC
        Room
        Square waste can
        Telephone
        Window
        Window.54
      Layers
    Office 2
    Office 3
    Office 4
  Background Pages
  Styles
  Masters
  Fill Patterns
  Line Patterns
  Line Ends
```

Notice the icon next to each shape entry. The icon indicates the kind of information the shape supports. The icon next to 2 seat sofa tells you that it only supports a list of layers, while the icon next to Desk chair tells you that this shape supports both shapes and layers.

You can right-click any folder or folder entry to display a context menu. The options available on the menu are unique to the item you click. For instance, if you right-click the Foreground Pages folder, the context menu lets you insert or reorder pages.

The best way to find out about Drawing Explorer is to play with it: open and close folders and right-click everything. You'll soon become familiar with the type of information that's available and your options for using it.

Saving Drawings

When you've spent a lot of time creating a drawing, the last thing you want to do is lose it! You should save a drawing as soon as you create it and continue saving it every few minutes (or at least every time you add anything significant to it). Of course, we all get busy. The best way to ensure you don't lose your valuable drawing is to tell Visio to save it for you. The "Setting up AutoSave" section, later in this chapter, describes this technique in detail.

Saving a drawing the first time

The first time you save a drawing, Visio displays the Save As dialog box. Follow these steps to save your drawing:

1. **Choose File⇨Save.**

   Visio displays the Save As dialog box.

2. **Choose a folder to use to store your drawing.**

   If necessary, use the icons on the left or click the drop-down arrow on the Save In box to navigate to the folder where you want to save your drawing. When working with Vista, click Browse Folders to provide a graphical display of folders on your system.

3. **In the File Name field, type a name for your drawing.**

4. **In the Save As Type field, select Drawing from the list if it's not already selected.**

   For information on the different file types, see the "Saving a drawing in another file format" section, later in this chapter.

5. **Click Save.**

   Visio saves your file and keeps your drawing on the screen.

Setting up AutoSave

In most cases, you'll want to set Visio up to save files automatically for you. *This is not a substitute for saving files yourself!* However, in the event of a power failure (or a clumsy coworker kicking out your power cord), AutoSave allows you to recover a file in the state in which it was last saved. Here's how to set up a time interval for saving files:

1. **Choose Tools⇨Options.**

   You see the Options dialog box.

2. **Click the Save/Open tab.**

   Visio displays the Options dialog box, shown in Figure 2-11.

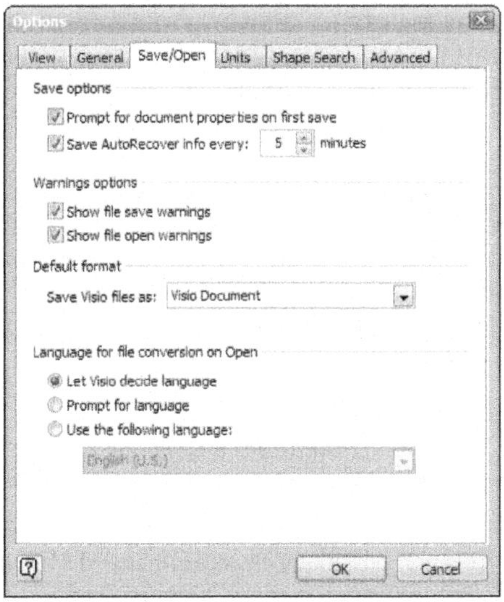

Figure 2-11:
You can specify the time interval for auto-saving.

3. **Select the Save AutoRecover Info Every option. Use the up or down arrow to select a time interval.**

4. **Click OK.**

   Visio begins saving your document automatically.

The interval you choose for automatically saving your document depends on the importance of the diagram and the kind of device you're using. Saving the diagram every 5 minutes on a laptop will drain the battery quite quickly because the hard drive never shuts down. However, you want to save the diagram often enough to ensure you can recover it quickly. Desktop users should consider intervals of 5 minutes, while laptop users might want to work as long as 15 minutes on the road.

Saving a drawing as a template

It's also possible to save a Visio drawing as a template. Many corporations find it useful to create and save custom templates because they can incorporate their company logos and other company-specific information. See Chapter 11 for more information about creating and saving custom templates.

Saving a drawing in another file format

In Visio, you have many options for saving drawings in different file formats. Don't let the humongous list of file types intimidate you. Many of these you'll never use, but it's nice to know that they're available should you ever find the need.

Visio defaults to the Drawing file type, which is the type you'll use most often. You can also save a Visio drawing as a Visio 2002 file type, if necessary, but you can't save a drawing in an earlier version of Visio (such as Visio 5). The following file formats are supported by Visio 2007 (Microsoft may offer the Portable Document Format (PDF) as an add-on):

Drawing	AutoCAD Drawing
Stencil	AutoCAD Interchange
Template	Web Page
XML Drawing	Compressed Enhanced Metafile (EMZ)
XML Stencil	Enhanced Metafile (EMF)
XML Template	Graphic Interchange Format (GIF)
Visio 2002 Drawing	JPEG File Interchange Format (JPG)
Visio 2002 Stencil	Portable Network Graphics (PNG)
Visio 2002 Template	Tagged Image File Format (TIFF and TIF)
Scalable Vector Graphics (SVG)	Windows Bitmap (BMP) and Device Independent Bitmap (DIB)
Scalable Vector Graphics Compressed	Windows Metafile (WMF)
XML Paper Specification (XPS) Document	

Using a Visio Wizard to Create a Drawing

Most programs use only one standard way to create a new document, but Visio gives you several options. This section describes one method that relies on a wizard. You can also create a drawing at any time after Visio is running by choosing File⇨New⇨Choose Category⇨Choose Template. Visio creates a new drawing page and opens the appropriate stencils.

If you've used other Microsoft programs, you're probably familiar with wizards. If not, a *wizard* is a tool that guides you through the steps you need to perform a task quickly and easily. Applications normally supply wizards to help you perform complicated tasks and don't supply them to perform all tasks. In Visio, they help you create specific kinds of drawings.

Visio 2007 reduces the complexity of using wizards. Unlike previous versions of Visio, you'll find all of the wizards in one place. To use a wizard, choose Tools⇨Add-Ons⇨Choose a Category⇨Choose a Wizard. The wizards have the same name as the diagram you want to create with the word *wizard* added. For example, when you want to create an Organization Chart, select the Organization Chart Wizard.

Opening Drawings

After you've created and saved some Visio drawings, you need to know how to reopen them. You can open drawings saved in the current version of Visio or a previous version of Visio, and you can open and work on more than one drawing at a time. If Visio is already running, you can use the File⇨Open command to open a file of any type, including the workspace files used by previous versions of Visio. Navigate to the location you used to store your diagram and select it. Click Open to open the diagram. You can use Ctrl+Click and Shift+Click to select multiple drawing files. Any drawing you open remains open until you close it, even if you open another drawing.

When you open a drawing created by an earlier version of Visio, Visio converts it to the latest format. When the drawing contains stencils or other features that the current version of Visio doesn't support, the application tells you about the problem. Normally, you'll need to find an alternative stencil or shape to fulfill the need. Fortunately, this problem doesn't occur very often.

You can also open other file types by selecting the type to the right of the File Name field. Visio supports the drawing, stencil, template, workspace, SVG, AutoCAD, EMZ, EMF, GIF, JPG, PNG, TIF, TIFF, BMP, DIB, and WMF file formats.

Chapter 3

Printing Visio Drawings

. . . .

In This Chapter

▶ Discovering how Visio "thinks" about printing

▶ Adjusting the orientation and page size

▶ Looking at your drawing before you print

▶ Printing your drawing

▶ Adding headers, footers, and gridlines

▶ Printing part of a drawing

▶ Reducing and enlarging your drawing

▶ Using online printing for custom or large tasks

▶ Marking shapes you don't want to print

▶ Printing comments

▶ Printing backgrounds and layers

. . . .

*F*or the most part, printing in Visio is a breeze — not much different from printing from any other Windows application. If your drawing doesn't vary from the template, without any major changes to the page size or orientation, you can often just click Print and get exactly the results you expect. However, sometimes your drawings won't be this straightforward. What if your drawing is larger than the paper? What if it's small and you want it to fill the page? What if your drawing is wider than it is tall, and it won't fit on standard paper? In this chapter, you find the answers to these questions and discover what you need to know to print all kinds of drawings (or selected portions of drawings) successfully.

Understanding How Visio Prints

The most important concept to keep in mind when printing with Visio is that the printer paper size and the drawing page size are independent of one another. The *printer paper size* refers to the paper you use in your printer. The *drawing page size* refers to the paper you see represented in white (usually shown with gridlines) in the drawing window on the screen.

Most of us use printers that handle 8½-by-11-inch or 8½-by-14-inch paper. Sometimes the printer may handle tabloid-size paper (11 by 17 inches). And if you work in an architectural firm, an engineering lab, a graphics design firm, or a large corporation with vast resources, you might have access to a plotter as well, which prints on large rolls of paper up to 60 inches wide. The truth is, it doesn't matter what your printing resources are. Visio can print your drawing no matter what size paper your printer handles.

When you use a Visio template to create a drawing, it sets up your drawing page size and printer paper size so that they match. Depending on the type of drawing you're creating, it might set up the page in *portrait* mode (taller than it is wide) or *landscape* mode (wider than it is tall). Visio matches the drawing page size to the printer paper size and keeps the drawing page size that way unless you do something to change it. It's okay to change it! (Visio wants to work the way you work, not force you to conform to inflexible rules.) You just need to know how it will affect your printing if you do.

Preparing to Print

Before you print any drawing, you should do the following:

- ✔ Check to see whether the printer paper size and the drawing page size are different
- ✔ Center your drawing
- ✔ Use Print Preview to get a look at how your drawing will print

In this section, you find out more about the importance of each of these steps and how to do each one. (You could try skipping these steps, but if you do, you'll just be wasting paper!)

Checking the printer paper and drawing page sizes

To compare the printer paper size and the drawing page size, choose File➪Page Setup to display the Page Setup dialog box, shown in Figure 3-1. This dialog box lets you make any necessary changes to the printer paper size and the drawing page size.

The Print Setup tab is where you make changes to the printer paper size. To make changes to the drawing page size, you use the Page Size tab. (For now, you can ignore the rest of the tabs in this dialog box.)

Figure 3-1: Here, you see the drawing paper size and printer page size together.

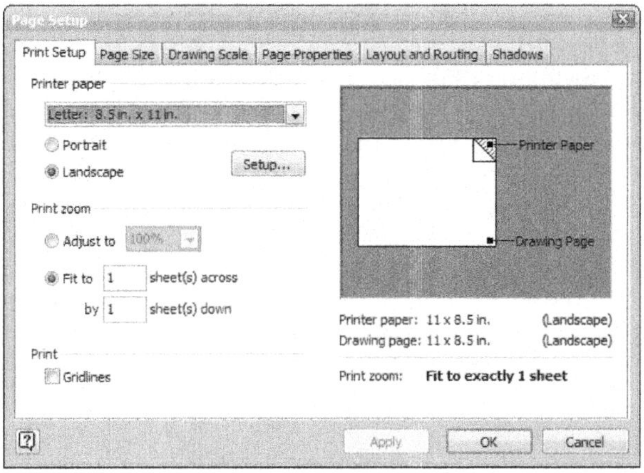

The terrific feature of this dialog box is the illustration on the right, which appears in both the Print Setup tab and the Page Size tab. The illustration shows you a picture of both the printer paper size and the drawing page size on top of one another, so you can tell immediately how things are lining up.

Figure 3-1 shows a drawing in which the printer paper size and the drawing page size line up perfectly in landscape mode (the default setting for many templates). You don't need to do anything special to print successfully except preview your drawing, as you see later in this chapter.

But what if you go to print your drawing and the Page Setup illustration looks like the one in Figure 3-2? The printer paper size and drawing page size don't line up. You know you need to do some adjusting before you print, but what do you change?

Figure 3-2: A discrepancy between the printer paper size and drawing page size.

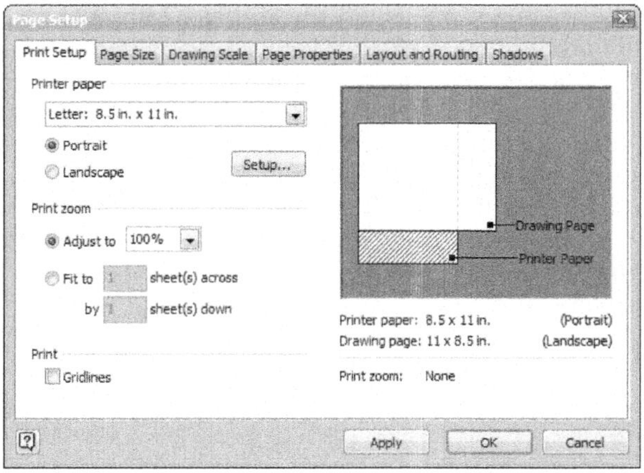

The illustration shows you that your drawing paper is in landscape mode and your printer is set to print in portrait mode. This means that if you have any shapes in your drawing that fall *outside* the area shown by the printer paper, they won't print. (Even if you don't have shapes outside the printer paper area, your drawing won't appear centered neatly on the page.)

In this example, the problem is one of orientation and is easy to solve: Change either the printer paper orientation to match your drawing (refer to Figure 3-2) or change the drawing page orientation to match the paper (refer to Figure 3-3). Your choice depends on the content of your drawing and how you want it displayed. Whichever you choose, the goal is to have the orientation and size of the paper match the orientation and size of the drawing page.

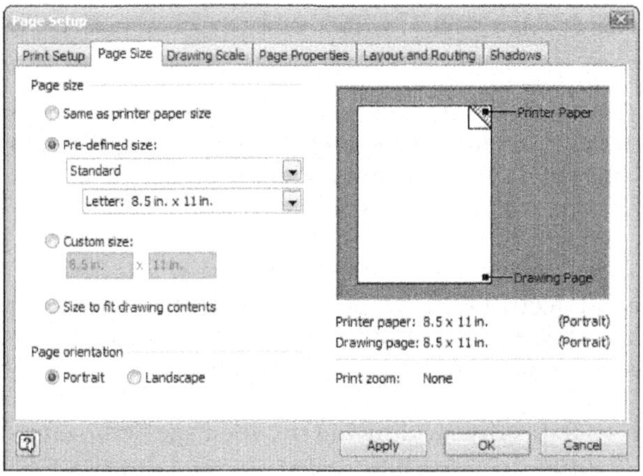

Figure 3-3:
The Page Size tab also has a setting for page orientation.

Page Setup

Print Setup | Page Size | Drawing Scale | Page Properties | Layout and Routing | Shadows

Page size

○ Same as printer paper size

◉ Pre-defined size:
Standard
Letter: 8.5 in. x 11 in.

○ Custom size:
8.5 in. x 11 in.

○ Size to fit drawing contents

Page orientation
◉ Portrait ○ Landscape

Printer Paper

Drawing Page

Printer paper: 8.5 x 11 in. (Portrait)
Drawing page: 8.5 x 11 in. (Portrait)

Print zoom: None

Apply | OK | Cancel

Even with the page orientation and size set correctly, the printed version of your diagram may not contain all of the shapes. Every printer has a printing margin; usually between ¼ and ½ inch. Visio automatically sets this value for you based on the printer you select, but you can change the setting by clicking Setup on the Print Setup tab of the Page Setup dialog box. The Print Setup dialog box shown in Figure 3-4 contains the margin and other settings for your printer. (Notice that this dialog box also contains check boxes to center small drawings on the printed page, even when you don't center them in your diagram.) When a shape falls within this margin, Visio won't output the shape, even though the shape should theoretically fit on the paper. That's one of many reasons that you should always preview your diagram using the technique described in the next section of this chapter.

Previewing your drawing

You should always preview your drawing after checking the page and paper
setups. Why? Because the Print Setup and Page Size dialog boxes show you
how the printer paper size and drawing page size compare to one another;
they don't show you anything about the drawing itself and where the shapes
are located. Print Preview gives you a preview of the actual drawing. You can
display the print preview screen by clicking the Print Preview button on the
Standard toolbar or by choosing File⇨Print Preview.

Your goal in Print Preview is to see that all shapes fall inside the wide gray
border around the edge of the paper, which indicates the drawing's margins.
These page margins are visible only in Print Preview — another good reason
to check here before printing! Any shape that falls across the margin lines
won't print correctly. The drawing shown in Figure 3-5 is ready to print. You
can see that the page is set to print in landscape mode and that all the
shapes fall within the page margins.

If your drawing's shapes fall across page margins, you can try several options.
You can print on larger paper, adjust the placement of the shapes in the drawing, tile the drawing, or reduce the size of the drawing to fit the paper. Tiling
and reducing the drawing are discussed later in this chapter in the "Printing
oversized drawings" section. Refer to Chapter 4 for information about moving
shapes in a drawing. To print on larger paper, refer to the preceding section. If
the shapes are only a little into the margin area, you can try adjusting the margins using the Print Setup dialog box shown in Figure 3-4. However, the margins usually reflect physical limitations of the printer and the shapes might
not print even with the adjustments (or they might look faded).

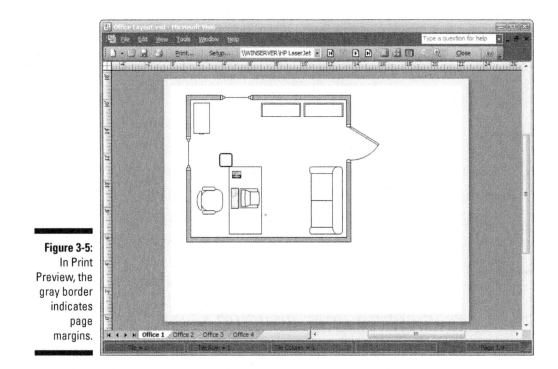

Figure 3-5:
In Print Preview, the gray border indicates page margins.

A clear view in Print Preview

If you've never used Print Preview before, here are a few tips. Notice in Figure 3-5 that Print Preview has its own toolbar. The first four buttons — New, Open, Save, and Print Page — also appear on the Standard toolbar. The remaining buttons are described in Table 3-1. You can use these buttons to change your view of Print Preview. Click Close when you want to return to your drawing in Visio.

Table 3-1	Print Preview Toolbar Buttons	
Button	*Name*	*What It Does*
Print...	Print	Displays the Print dialog box
Setup...	Setup	Displays the Page Setup dialog box

Button	Name	What It Does
\\WINSERVER\HP LaserJet	Current Printer	Displays the current printer and lets you choose a different one
	First Tile	Displays the first tile (if you selected the Single Tile option)
	Previous Tile	Displays the tile before the one currently displayed (if you selected the Single Tile option)
	Next Tile	Displays the tile after the one currently displayed (if you selected the Single Tile option)
	Last Tile	Displays the last tile (if you selected the Single Tile option)
	Single Tile	Displays a single tile in a tiled drawing
	Whole Page	Displays all the tiles in a tiled drawing
	Current View	Displays only the area of the drawing that was displayed before you chose Print Preview
	Zoom Out	Reduces your view in the print preview window (you can see more of the drawing)
	Zoom In	Magnifies your view in the print preview window (you see less of the drawing)
Close	Close	Closes the print preview window and returns to the normal drawing view
	Microsoft Office Visio Help	Changes the mouse pointer to a question mark and displays help on the item you click

Printing Your Drawing

When you've checked the settings for the printer paper size and the drawing page size, and you've centered and previewed your drawing, you're ready to print. Always save your drawing before you print it to ensure that any changes you make to the contents and setup appear in the output. With your file open, follow these steps:

1. **Choose File⇨Print.**

   The Print dialog box appears, as shown in Figure 3-6.

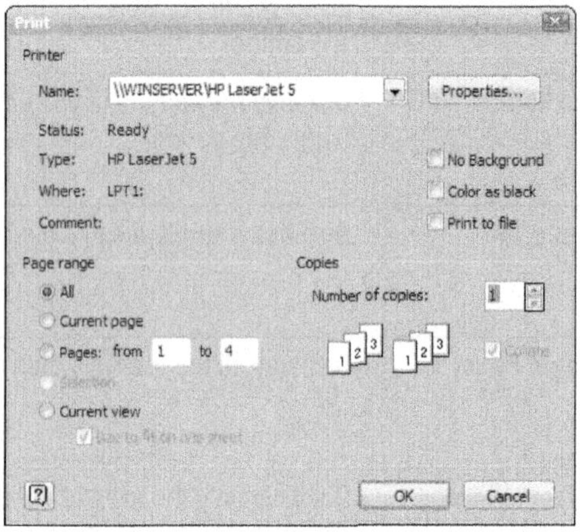

Figure 3-6:
Specify the printer settings, pages to print, and number of copies.

2. **Choose the printer you want to use if more than one is available.**

3. **If you want to check the settings for your printer:**

   a. **Click Properties.**

   b. **Adjust the printer settings as you normally do.**

   c. **Click OK to return to the Print dialog box.**

4. **In the Page Range section, choose All, Current Page, or Selection, or specify a range of pages by typing page numbers.**

   You can specify a range of pages only if the drawing has more than one page. Similarly, you can specify to print the selection only if you make a selection before displaying the Print dialog box.

5. **Specify the number of copies you want to print.**

6. **Click OK.**

Some Windows applications give you the option of printing a group of selected pages, such as 2, 4, and 7. Visio doesn't provide this option. To print a group of selected pages, you need to print each page individually in the Pages: From option. For example, to print pages 2 and 4, you would type 2 and 2 in the Pages: From option, click OK to print that page, type 4 and 4 in the Pages: From option, and click OK.

Now that you know the basics of printing, the following sections look at some special considerations for printing, such as centering a drawing, including headers or footers in a drawing, printing gridlines, and printing partial drawings. These are common tasks, but they require a little extra effort to set up.

Adding Headers and Footers to a Drawing

A *header* refers to text that appears at the top of each page of a drawing; a *footer* is text that appears at the bottom of each page. Headers and footers are optional. If you decide to add them to a drawing, you can include text such as a title, a file name, a date, or automatic page numbers. You decide where you want them to appear in the header or footer area: at the left margin, centered, or at the right margin.

You only need to set the header and footer once per drawing. Headers and footers apply to every page in a drawing.

A header can include the time, date, file name, page name, or page number in addition to any information you want to include, such as a company name. The time, date, file name, page name, and page number are automatic entries that you select from a list; you must type in other supplementary information as needed. The header and footer are blank when you create the diagram. You can insert the following items:

- ✔ Page name
- ✔ Page number
- ✔ Total printed pages
- ✔ Current time
- ✔ Current date (short)
- ✔ Current date (long)
- ✔ File name

✔ File extension

✔ File name and extension

When you choose one of these items, Visio enters a formatting code in the dialog box, such as &t for the current time. Don't let this throw you; Visio inserts the correct information automatically when you print the drawing. Note that you can use more than one of these items for each location in the header or footer. For example, if you want a centered header to include the page number, page name, and file name, click all three options in the Header Center box. Just be sure to add spaces between each entry. The following steps tell you how to add a header or footer to your diagram:

1. **Choose View⇨Header and Footer.**

   The Header and Footer dialog box appears.

2. **In the appropriate Header or Footer text box (Left, Center, Right), type the information that you want to appear, such as "Company Confidential."**

   If you want Visio to automatically insert the date, time, file name, or other information, click the right arrow at the end of the Left, Center, or Right text box (see Figure 3-7) and then click the option you want. If you're inserting more than one option, add appropriate punctuation and spacing.

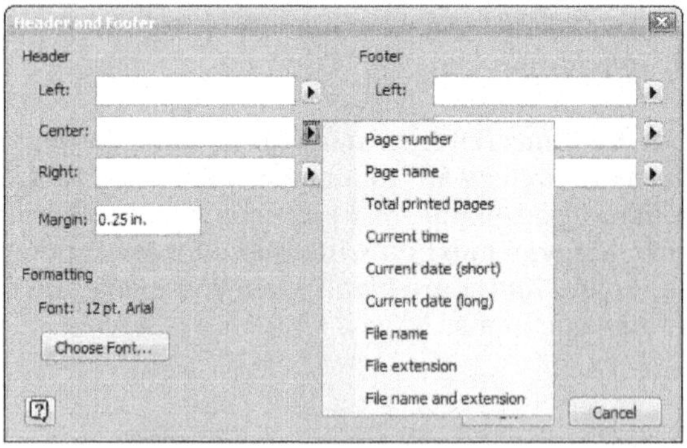

Figure 3-7:
The Header and Footer dialog box makes it easy to enter titles or special text such as the date or file name.

Header		Footer	
Left:	▶	Left:	▶
Center:	▶	Page number	▶
Right:	▶	Page name	▶
Margin: 0.25 in.		Total printed pages	
Formatting		Current time	
Font: 12 pt. Arial		Current date (short)	
Choose Font...		Current date (long)	
		File name	
⑦		File extension	
		File name and extension	Cancel

You can enter as many characters as will fill one line. (The exact number depends on the font size you choose in Step 4.) If you enter more characters than will fit across the page, the characters overtype at the right margin.

3. **In the Margin boxes, type a size for the header margin and footer margin, if you want.**

   You shouldn't need to adjust margins unless you want an extra-wide margin.

The margin setting for a header is the distance from the top of the header text to the top edge of the page. For a footer, it's the distance from the bottom of the footer text to the bottom edge of the page. Unlike in other programs, Visio headers and footers don't print inside the page margin area; they print inside the drawing area.

4. **To format the header and footer text:**

   a. **Click Choose Font.**

      The Choose Font dialog box appears, as shown in Figure 3-8.

   b. **Choose a font, size, style, special effects, and color for the header and footer text.**

      Formatting applies to all header and footer text; you can't format each one individually.

   c. **Click OK to close the Choose Font dialog box.**

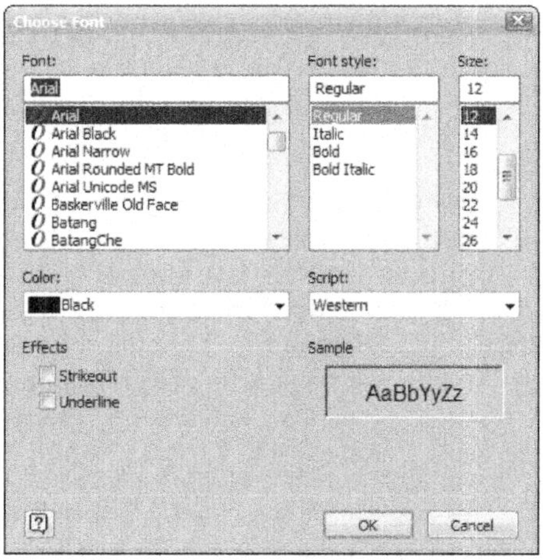

Figure 3-8:
Choose a font, size, style, and color for header and footer text.

5. **Click OK to close the Page Setup dialog box.**

Click Print Preview on the Standard toolbar or choose File⇨Print Preview to see how your header and footer text will look when you print your drawing. (Header and footer text is only visible in Print Preview or on the printed drawing.)

In a tiled drawing (one that's printed across several sheets of paper), Visio prints headers and footers on each sheet. You may want to put header and footer information on a background page (a separate page that works as an underlay) instead. For details about creating background pages, see Chapter 9. For information about tiling a drawing, see the "Printing oversized drawings" section, later in this chapter.

Printing Gridlines

You often need to print gridlines as part of your diagram. Any diagram that relies on specific measurements, where you might have to rely on the diagram as a source of measurement, will probably require gridlines. For example, a Floor Plan template may not require gridlines when you use it to place office equipment and assign places to people in your organization. It does require gridlines when you use the diagram to place receptacles or other nonmovable equipment. Someone will have to measure the location of the receptacle. If the diagram is off due to problems with printing, then you might not see the receptacle in the right place. The gridlines reduce the risk of an errant measurement. To print gridlines, follow these steps:

1. **Choose File➪Page Setup.**

   The Page Setup dialog box appears.

2. **Click the Print Setup tab if it isn't already selected (refer to Figure 3-1).**

3. **In the Print area near the bottom of the dialog box, click the Gridlines option.**

4. **Click OK.**

Visio isn't a CAD application. Consequently, you should always include a note that the drawing isn't to scale when you think someone might try to take measurements directly from a printout. Instead, you should use gridlines for rough measurements and actual dimensions for more precise measurements. For example, the Walls, Shell, and Structure stencil includes the Room Measurement shape that you can use to display the actual dimensions of a room.

Printing Part of a Drawing

It's nice to know that you can always print a portion of a drawing if you need to. Maybe your drawing includes a lot of shapes and you want to print only a few of them. In some cases, you may want to print a portion of your drawing when the remainder is still in flux. You can choose the shapes you want to print and prevent the others from printing by not selecting them. Use these steps:

1. **Select only the shapes that you want to print by clicking them or using the other selection techniques described in Chapter 2.**

2. **Choose File➪Page Setup to check your drawing's paper size and orientation, and then click OK.**

3. **Choose File⇨Print.**

   Visio displays the Print dialog box.

4. **Choose the printer settings as you normally do.**

5. **In the Page range area, click Selection.**

6. **Click OK.**

   Visio prints only the shapes you select.

Visio normally won't center the shapes on-screen when you choose only a few shapes. You'll see that Visio prints the drawing starting from the upper-left corner as if you didn't request centering.

Reducing and Enlarging Printed Drawings

When you create an *oversized drawing* (one that's larger than the paper in your printer), you can see right away in Print Preview that the drawing won't print on a single sheet of paper. It might make sense to *tile* the drawing (that is, print it across several sheets of paper). But if you need the drawing to print on one page, another option is to change the print scale. Changing the *print scale* lets you print the drawing at a smaller percentage of its original size. It's like creating a reduced copy of a drawing on a copy machine.

Conversely, when a drawing is too small, you can enlarge the print scale and make the drawing easier to read when you print it.

Note that print scale is different from the drawing scale. *Print scale* is simply a percentage of the original drawing size. *Drawing scale* expresses a relationship between the size of real-world objects and the size at which they're shown in a drawing. You find out how to change the drawing scale in Chapter 7.

Although Visio will let you cram an entire house plan onto an 8½-by-11-inch sheet of paper, it generally doesn't make sense to do so. The details will suffer when you try to shrink the drawing that much. You might find that the writing is nearly impossible to read and that some smaller shapes disappear. Change the print scale of your diagram with care.

Altering the print scale of a drawing

Changing the print scale makes it possible to place more information on one sheet of paper. The following steps describe how to change the print scale of a drawing:

1. **Choose File➪Page Setup.**

   The Print Setup tab of the Page Setup dialog box appears, as shown in Figure 3-1.

2. **Select the Adjust To option in the Print Zoom area.**

   Enter a number smaller than 100 percent to reduce the printed size of the drawing, or a number greater than 100 percent to increase the printed size of the drawing.

3. **Click OK to close the Page Setup dialog box.**

4. **Choose Print➪Preview or click Print Preview on the Standard toolbar.**

   Make sure your drawing fits on the drawing page.

5. **Repeat Steps 1 to 4 as necessary to adjust the drawing.**

You may expect your drawing to change on the screen, but it doesn't. This is because you've altered the *print* scale, not the *drawing* scale. Again, as when you reduce or enlarge a page on a photocopier, the size of the original doesn't change; only the copied result changes. If you need to print the drawing at regular scale, follow the previous steps to change the percentage back to 100 before you print again.

Printing oversized drawings

Suppose you create a very large drawing, say 2½ feet wide by 3 feet high. If you have a plotter, printing the drawing is a breeze. Just enter the page size and drawing size in the Page Setup dialog box as described earlier in this chapter, preview the drawing, and then print.

However, you may not have access to a plotter and want to print the drawing at actual size. For example, you want to use the drawing in a presentation for a large audience. Another option for printing an oversized drawing is to print it on separate sheets of paper and tape or paste the sheets together. This is called *tiling* a drawing. Using the following steps, you specify exactly how many sheets of paper you want your drawing to fit on:

1. **Choose File➪Page Setup.**

   The Print Setup tab of the Page Setup dialog box appears.

2. **In the Print Zoom area, click the Fit To option and then enter the number of sheets across and the number of sheets down.**

3. **Click OK.**

To view exactly how your drawing will be tiled when printed, click Print Preview on the Standard toolbar, or choose File➪Print Preview. The gray lines in the print preview screen represent the borders between pages. Another way to view tiles while you're working is to choose View➪Page Breaks. This option displays the same page borders right on the drawing page so you can make adjustments as you work without switching to Print Preview.

Fitting the drawing on the number of pages you specify affects the printed copy but not the scale of the drawing. To "untile" a large drawing, return to the Page Setup dialog box and reset the zoom percentage to 100%.

Depending on your printer's physical limitations, the printer margins you set in Visio, and how Visio tiles the drawing, you might not get perfect results. You may notice small differences in the way lines align in the output, and some shapes may have a small gap. Generally, you can overcome this problem by using different tiling criteria and changing the print scale slightly. Look at the tiling lines in Print Preview and try to avoid having a line go directly through a shape.

Using online printing services

Changing the print scale of a diagram works in some cases and tiling works in others, but these options don't always work as well as you'd like them to. In this case, you might consider using other alternatives such as online printing. Many of these online printing services, such as PrintingForLess.com (`http://www.printingforless.com/`) and FedEx/Kinkos (`http://www.fedex.com/us/officeprint/main/`) make it very easy to send your diagram for professional printing using the same File➪Print command that you normally use. The only difference is that the output won't appear at your local printer. Here are some advantages of using online printing:

- ✔ You can generally use any size paper; check with the online printing service for potential limits.

- ✔ The resulting output is professional looking. In many cases, you have a choice of color printing, professional binding, and even paper type.

- ✔ Local printing limitations don't matter. Your diagram prints at the higher speed of a professional printing service, rather than facing the constraints of a local printer.

- ✔ It's possible to print in one location and send the output to another in many cases. Consequently, you can print the presentation for your next meeting and have it sent directly to the meeting place — no more lugging boxes of printouts around.

- ✔ You don't have to worry about running out of the one printing supply you really need.

Online printing isn't for everyone. Make sure you carefully check the credentials of the company you want to use to ensure they can meet your expectations. If you want color printing on glossy paper, you have to make sure the online service actually supports it. In addition, you don't want to send your secret documents to an online printer. It's unlikely that the printer will seek out the competition and give it full details of your next product, but you never know. A more likely scenario is that a mistake occurs at the printer and the printer accidentally ships your order to the competition. It has happened in the past.

Printing to scale

Although Visio isn't a CAD application, it does have the precision required to print to scale as long as you take the required precautions. It's probably not a good idea to use Visio for critical drawings; don't design a pacemaker or artificial heart using Visio. However, it does work fine for many less critical applications, such as floor plans.

Most of the diagrams you can create with Visio don't have a scale. If you're creating a flow chart, you don't have to worry about printing to scale; this section isn't for you. Only when you need to consider physical entities do you need to think about printing to scale.

When you do need to print to scale, make sure you have a printer that can handle the entire diagram without tiling or rely on an online printing service. Tiling makes it impossible to ensure the accuracy of the output, as do low-quality printers.

Assuming that you do have the equipment required to print large output, you need to ensure that Visio is set up to output the diagram at the appropriate scale. The following steps tell you how to check the drawing scale of a diagram (Chapter 7 provides you with all of the details for setting this important page feature):

1. **Choose File⇨Page Setup.**

   The Print Setup tab of the Page Setup dialog box appears.

2. **Select the Drawing Scale tab of the Page Setup dialog box.**

   You see the drawing scale features shown in Figure 3-9. Notice that this diagram is set to use an architectural scale. The scale you use must match the requirements for the particular diagram.

3. **Verify that the scale settings are correct or change them as described in Chapter 7.**

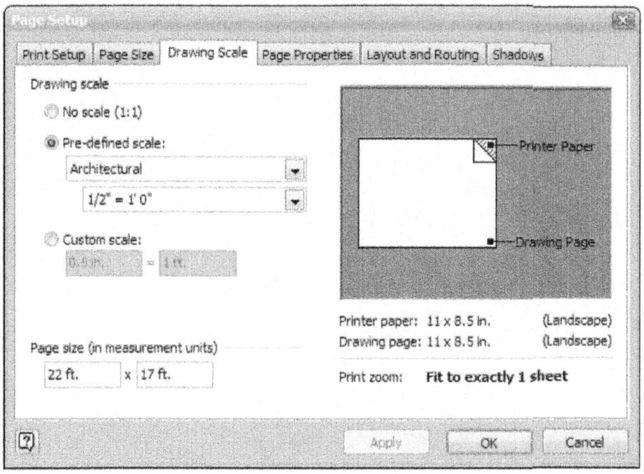

Figure 3-9:
Verify the
drawing
scale is
correct
before you
print.

4. **Click OK.**

   Visio sets the drawing scale for this drawing.

5. **Check your drawing notes to ensure you have indicated the drawing scale on the drawing so that the measurement prints with the diagram.**

6. **Print the diagram as usual.**

Setting Shapes Not to Print

Sometimes it's just as important *not* to print a shape or shapes as it is to print others. For example, if you're printing an office layout plan, your employees are interested in seeing the cubicle layout but don't need to see the wiring components. In some cases, information on a diagram is still confidential. You may have named a new department head in your company but you don't want your employees to see the name of the new boss on the organization chart yet. Maybe you're planning office space but aren't sure some of the office furniture you've ordered will be available. These are all cases when you might want to set a specific shape or shapes to not print in your drawing. The following steps tell you how to set a shape not to print:

1. **Right-click the shape you want to set for nonprinting and choose Format➪Behavior.**

   The Behavior dialog box appears.

2. **Select the Behavior tab (see Figure 3-10).**

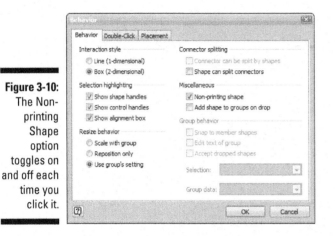

Behavior

Figure 3-10:
The Non-printing
Shape
option
toggles on
and off each
time you
click it.

3. **In the Miscellaneous section, click the Non-printing Shape option.**

4. **Click OK.**

To make sure that the shape is set to not print, click Print Preview on the Standard toolbar or choose File➪Print Preview. The shape should not appear on the print preview screen. When you print the drawing, the shape will not print. To make the shape print again, follow the previous set of steps and click to deselect the Non-printing Shape option in Step 3.

Printing Reviewers' Comments

Visio incorporates some advanced reviewing and markup features. (See Chapter 13 to find out about annotating and reviewing Visio drawings.) When you've asked one or more people to review a drawing for you, it's nice to be able to print the drawing showing their comments. To do this, follow these steps:

1. **Choose View➪Markup to display reviewers' marks on the drawing.**

2. **Choose View➪Task Pane.**

3. **Select Reviewing from the Other Task Panes list box in the Task pane.**

   The pane to the right of the drawing window summarizes the reviewers' comments, as shown in Figure 3-11. Notice that the comment has the reviewer's initials and a number assigned to it. The location of this comment on the diagram has the same identifier attached to it. Any added shapes appear as overlays as shown in the figure. You can select one, some, or all of the reviewer changes to the diagram.

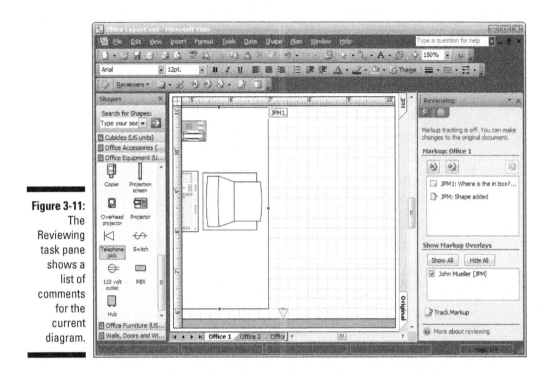

Figure 3-11:
The
Reviewing
task pane
shows a
list of
comments
for the
current
diagram.

4. **In the Show Markup Overlays section of the pane, click Show All.**

   Visio selects all of the reviewer shape additions and deletions for the diagram.

5. **Choose File⇨Print Preview to preview the drawing.**

6. **Choose File⇨Print.**

   The Print dialog box appears.

7. **Choose print settings as you normally do, and then click Print.**

   Visio prints your drawing showing all reviewers' comments. To return to printing the drawing without reviewers' comments, choose View⇨Markup again to deselect this option.

Printing a Background Separately

Visio lets you create backgrounds for the pages in your drawings. A background is assigned to and appears behind a page in the drawing. To find out more about creating and using backgrounds, see Chapter 9.

If your drawing contains a background page, you might find it useful to print the background separately from the rest of the drawing. This is an easy task because the background is stored as a separate page in a drawing. Follow these steps:

1. **Click the Background tab at the bottom of the drawing window to make it the current page.**

2. **Choose File⇨Print Preview to preview the drawing.**

3. **Choose File⇨Print.**

   The Print dialog box appears.

4. **Click the Current page option, and then click OK.**

   Only the background page prints.

Printing Layers Separately

Visio lets you place shapes on separate layers in a drawing. There are many circumstances where it makes sense to print layers separately. For example, in a drawing that depicts a building or a home plan, only the plumber cares about seeing the pipe layout and only the electrical team cares about seeing the wiring and telecom layout. If you place these components on individual layers, you can print the layers separately. For details on creating layers and printing them separately, see Chapter 10.

Part I

Starting with Visio 2007 Basics

The 5th Wave · By Rich Tennant

"Okay, well, I think we all get the gist of where Jerry was going with the site map."

In this part . . .

*V*isio is an amazing program! If you can imagine it, you can probably sketch it using Visio. Many people use Visio as their only drawing application because it does provide great output, but many others use it for sketching their ideas and sharing them with others. In some respects, Visio is a tool for showing your dreams to others.

Other drawing applications help you create graphics. Visio, however, is a different animal. It's not really a drawing program, and it's certainly not a Computer-Aided Design (CAD) program. In this part, you understand what Visio is and what it does, you discover how to "speak" and "think" Visio, you negotiate your way around the screen, and you find out how to get help when you need it. You also print a drawing, something you'll no doubt find useful if you want to be productive!

This part of the book also provides a complete listing of the templates that Visio provides so that you better understand what comes in the package. Of course, you can always add to these basic templates. Look at the Visio offerings as a place to start.

Chapter 4

Discovering What Visio Shapes Are All About

Shapes are the most important elements of Visio; they're the building blocks you use to create diagrams, drawings, charts, and graphs. Regardless of the type of drawing you create — a flowchart, a network diagram, an architectural drawing, a project timeline — you create each drawing by using shapes. Visio includes many types of shapes that not only *look* different but also *behave* differently. In this chapter, you discover many different types of shapes, what makes them different, and how to work with them in your drawings and diagrams.

Performing tasks quickly and efficiently is important to everyone. Some people work better with a mouse, others the keyboard. The important issue is to use whichever input device works best for you. Although this chapter emphasizes keyboard input, you'll find that every command also has a menu and some-times a toolbar equivalent. In some cases, you can issue the required command by right-clicking the object and choosing the correct option from the context menu. You can combine input techniques by becoming familiar with the input device of your choice. Many people associate context menus with the mouse, but most keyboards include a context menu button between the right-side Ctrl and Alt keys. In short, you can do things your way; the procedures in the chapter only illustrate one method in most cases.

Discovering What's in a Shape

If you think you may not have enough shapes to choose from when you're building your drawings, think again. Visio includes thousands of shapes!

Shapes are stored in *stencils,* which are normally collections of related shapes displayed in their own window on your Visio screen. Stencils can have other themes, too, such as most commonly used shapes or shapes that you normally require for a specific task. You'll create most drawings by using the shapes that Visio supplies, but you can create and store your own shapes as well. Chapter 8 covers creating and storing shapes.

A shape can be as simple as a single line or as complex as an industry-specific network component for a computer system. Unlike clip art, shapes have certain "smart" characteristics or *properties.* For instance, if you add text to a shape and then resize the shape, the text reformats automatically to the new size. Shapes with glued connectors (like the lines that connect boxes on an organization chart or flowchart) stay connected when you move them. A pie chart isn't just a pie chart. You decide the number of slices it should have, and when you want to adjust percentages, the shape adjusts automatically. Figure 4-1 shows a pie chart and its associated properties.

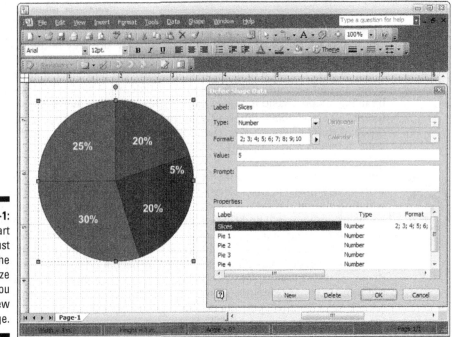

Figure 4-1:
Pie-chart slices adjust to the proper size when you enter a new percentage.

You can control a particular aspect of a shape, such as the angle and direction of the vanishing point of a three-dimensional shape like a cube. (The *vanishing point* is the point at which parallel lines of a three-dimensional object appear to converge.) You can store data (for example, inventory numbers, service dates, or serial numbers) with a shape and generate reports from the stored data. (For more information about storing data in shapes, see Chapter 12.) If you're a software developer creating a custom Visio solution, you can program specific behavior into shapes. You can see why Visio shapes are called *SmartShapes.* Many have built-in brainy behavior.

Examining open and closed shapes

You can classify shapes as either *open* or *closed,* as shown in Figure 4-2. An open shape is one in which the endpoints aren't connected, such as a line, an arc, or a freeform shape. A closed shape is a fully connected object such as a square or circle. Figure 4-2 also shows that you can access all of these shapes using the Drawing toolbar (right-click the toolbar area and choose Drawing from the context menu).

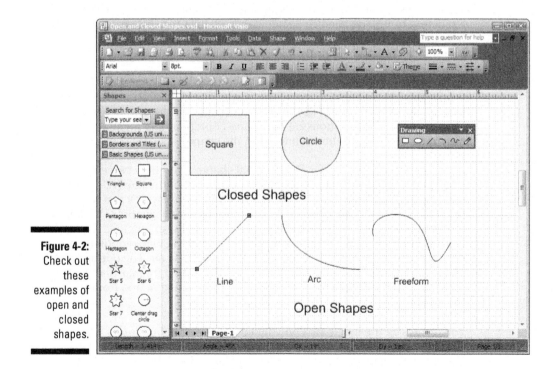

Figure 4-2:
Check out these examples of open and closed shapes.

What difference does it make whether a shape is open or closed? You can fill a closed shape with a color or a pattern. You can't fill an open shape, but you can add endpoints such as arrowheads and other symbols.

Comparing one- and two-dimensional shapes

All Visio shapes are either one-dimensional (lines and text) or two-dimensional (squares and circles). The three-dimensional shapes, such as those used for the Directional Map 3D template, only simulate the third dimension; you can't actually access the *z* axis normally associated with a true three-dimensional shape. Two-dimensional shapes have length and height. When you select a two-dimensional shape with the Pointer Tool, you can see its selection frame and selection handles (see Figure 4-1). At the top of the shape, you can see the rotation handle, which appears as a circle instead of a square.

The *selection frame* is a green dotted line that fully encloses a shape. *Selection handles* are green squares that appear at the corners and sides of a frame. (Later you see that handles can look different when you select a shape using a different tool.) The handles enable you to change the shape's length and height. Even a nonrectangular shape (such as a pie chart) displays a rectangular frame with side and corner handles when you select the shape.

The rotation handle is a green circle that appears outside of the selection frame. Move this handle to rotate the shape. The shape rotates in 15-degree increments. A bull's-eye in the shape's center shows the center of rotation. You can also use the options on the Shape⇨Rotate or Flip menu to perform rough (90-degree) rotational changes to the shape.

A line is an example of a one-dimensional shape. It has only two *endpoints* — small green boxes — that are visible when you select the line (refer to Figure 4-2). The beginning point — that is, the point from which you begin drawing — contains an *x;* the endpoint contains a plus symbol (+). Unlike a two-dimensional shape, a one-dimensional shape doesn't include a rotational handle. You change the rotation by moving one of the two endpoints or by selecting an option from the Shape⇨Rotate or Flip menu. The options on the Shape⇨Rotate or Flip menu also appear on the Action toolbar that you can display by right-clicking the toolbar area and choosing Action from the context menu.

You can resize the length of a one-dimensional shape, but not its height; a one-dimensional shape has no height. (A line has *thickness,* which you can alter by using a formatting command. Thickness isn't the same as height.) Other forms of one-dimensional shapes include arcs and freeform shapes. You might consider an arc a two-dimensional shape, but it lacks an inside area. When you select an arc, it has a starting point, an endpoint, and a handle in the middle that you can use to change the arc's size, but there isn't any depth adjustment. The middle handle is a *control handle* and it helps you control the amount of bend in the arc.

You see a shape's handles only when the shape is selected. The type of handle you see depends on the tool that you use to select the shape. You see more examples of shape handles throughout this chapter.

Displaying all of the shape handles

Arcs and freeform shapes have additional handles that only appear under certain circumstances. Choose Tools⇨Options to display the Options dialog box. Select the General tab shown in Figure 4-3. Select the Show More Shape Handles on Hover option and click OK. You can now see the additional handles when you hover the mouse over the object.

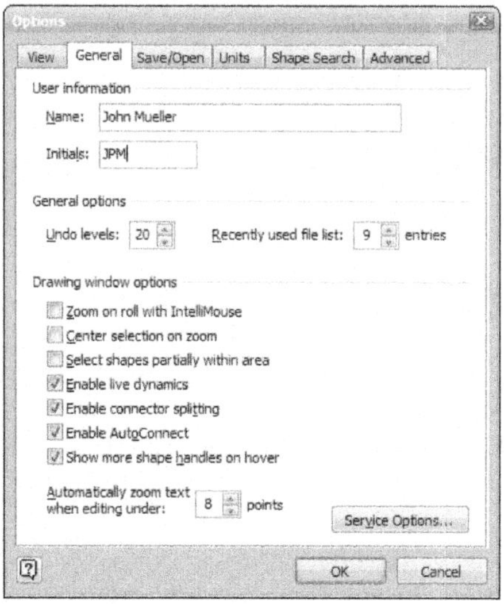

Figure 4-3:
Set Visio to display all of the handles available for a particular shape.

The extra handles help you bend an arc or freeform shape. You can see them best when viewing a freeform shape, as shown in Figure 4-4. Notice that these handles have a diamond-shaped end. When you hover the mouse over them, the ToolTip tells you that the handle lets you bend the shape in question. See the "Controlling Shapes" section, later in this chapter, to find out more about working with control handles on other types of shapes.

You see the extra handles associated with arcs and freeform shapes only when you set Visio to use the extra handles and when you hover the mouse over the shape. Simply selecting the shape won't display the additional handles.

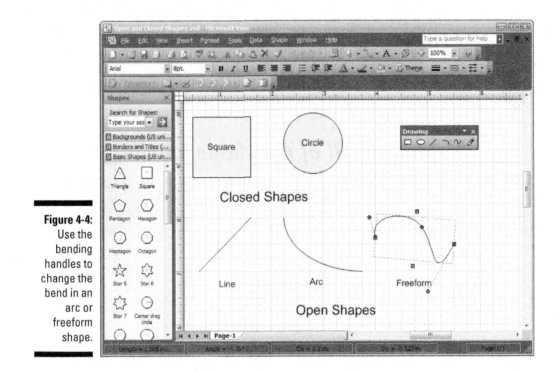

Figure 4-4:
Use the
bending
handles to
change the
bend in an
arc or
freeform
shape.

Working with Shapes

After you have shapes in your drawing, you'll want to do all kinds of things to them, such as moving, copying, pasting, deleting, and resizing. These are some of the most common tasks you do with shapes that don't involve altering the shape itself. Table 4-1 shows some toolbar buttons you use to work with shapes.

Table 4-1	Standard Toolbar Buttons for Working with Shapes	
Button	*Name*	*What It Does*
	Cut	Removes the selected shape from the drawing and makes it available for pasting.
	Copy	Saves a copy of the selected shape and makes it available for pasting.
	Paste	Places the selection that you cut or copied into the drawing.
	Delete	Removes the selected shape without making it available for pasting.

Button	Name	What It Does
	Format Painter	"Picks up" the formatting of a selected shape and makes it available to apply to another shape.
	Shapes	Displays a list of the Visio categories. You can follow the categories to a templates submenu and finally a list of stencils for that template. Click on the stencil entry to add it to the list of open stencils.

REMEMBER

To drag a shape, you have to click the shape with the left mouse button and hold the button down as you move the shape.

Visio used to contain a Stamp button on the Standard toolbar. The Stamp button places the selected shape into the drawing whenever you click it (rather than dragging a shape repeatedly from the stencil). You might wonder where this button has gone in Visio 2007. Unfortunately, you won't find this particular button, and your only alternative is to continuously drag and drop the shapes you need onto the design area.

Moving shapes

After you have shapes in your drawing, you'll move them around a lot until you get them exactly where you want them. Moving a shape is simple: Just drag the shape wherever you want it. As you drag a shape, watch the vertical and horizontal rulers. The shape's top, middle, and bottom points are indicated on the ruler by faint dotted lines. If you want to place a shape 3 inches from the top border of your drawing and 2 inches from the left border, for example, you can see exactly where the shape is aligned by watching the indicators on the ruler.

TIP

You can restrict the movement of a shape by holding down the Shift key as you drag the shape. If you drag the shape horizontally, it moves only to the right and left and keeps its vertical position. If you drag the shape vertically, it moves up and down and keeps its horizontal position.

See Chapter 7 for additional information on how to snap shapes into alignment by using rulers, a grid, and alignment commands that can make the placement of your shapes more exact.

If you want to move a shape from one drawing to another, you have to cut it and paste it. Cutting removes the shape from the current drawing and places it on the Windows Clipboard. Pasting places a copy of the shape in the location you choose. The techniques for cutting a shape are similar to those discussed in the "Deleting shapes" section, later in this chapter, and include

- ✔ Pressing Ctrl+X
- ✔ Clicking Cut on the Standard toolbar
- ✔ Choosing Edit➪Cut

Never press Delete to cut a shape. The methods for pasting a shape appear in the "Copying and pasting shapes" section, later in this chapter. It doesn't matter whether you copy or cut the shape to place it on the Clipboard; you can paste as many copies as desired.

Nudging shapes

Sometimes a mouse can be a clumsy instrument to use. What if you need to move a shape exactly $\frac{1}{32}$ of an inch? It's just not going to happen with a mouse! Visio lets you nudge shapes. *Nudging* is essentially bumping a selected shape by using the arrow keys on the keyboard. When you nudge a shape, the shape moves in tiny increments, usually to the nearest ruler subdivision. Variables such as the ruler scale, grid, and zoom percentage can determine how much the shape moves. Try this quick and easy way to reposition shapes:

1. **Click the shape that you want to nudge.**

2. **Position the shape by pressing the up-, down-, right-, or left-arrow key repeatedly.**

3. **When your shape is positioned where you want it, click anywhere on the drawing page to deselect the shape.**

If you want to nudge several shapes at the same time, hold down the Shift key as you select the shapes you want and then use the arrow keys to nudge the selected shapes as a unit.

Copying and pasting shapes

Copying and pasting shapes are things you do often when creating a drawing. If you know you want to use a shape more than once, you could drag the shape from the stencil into the drawing each time you want to use it. But wouldn't it be better to drag just one instance of the shape into your drawing, make any necessary changes to it (such as changing its size, color, fill, or text), and then copy it to other places in the drawing? When you're modifying the shape, it's easier to copy the shape from one place in the drawing to another, rather than to start all over again from the stencil.

You can copy and paste a shape in a single step. Hold down the Ctrl key, drag the shape you want to copy, and then release the mouse button in the new location. As soon as you press Ctrl, you see a plus symbol attached to the mouse pointer. This tells you Visio will _add_ (or copy) the shape rather than move it. Presto! You've copied and pasted all in one simple step.

If you're using a lot of the same shape in your drawing, another quick way to copy and paste in a single step is to select the shape and then press Ctrl+D (short for Edit➪Duplicate). Visio pastes the copy of the shape to the right and slightly below the original shape. Now you can move it wherever you want.

If you prefer the two-step method for copying and pasting, here are the different ways to copy a shape after you select it:

✔ Press Ctrl+C

✔ Right-click the shape and choose Copy from the pop-up menu

✔ Click Copy on the Standard toolbar

✔ Choose Edit➪Copy

All of these methods place a copy of the shape (or shapes) on the Windows Clipboard. To paste the shape in a new location, do one of the following:

✔ Press Ctrl+V

✔ Right-click a blank area of the drawing page and choose Paste from the pop-up menu (the shape or text most recently copied is pasted)

✔ Click Paste on the Standard toolbar

✔ Choose Edit➪Paste

You can continue to paste multiple copies of the shape until you use a copy command again to copy a different shape to the Clipboard.

Sizing up your shapes

In many cases, you'll want to resize shapes for your drawings. Visio makes resizing simple. Use the following steps to adjust the size of shapes:

1. **Select the shape with the Pointer Tool.**

2. **Do one of the following:**

   • Drag a side handle to change the shape's width.

   • Drag a top or bottom handle to change the shape's height.

• Drag a corner handle to change the height and width at the same time. Visio maintains the shape's height-to-width proportions when you drag at the corner.

3. **Release the mouse button when the shape is the size that you want.**

If your shape contains text, the text reformats automatically as you resize the shape. (See Chapter 5 to find out how to enter text in shapes.)

These steps may seem to imply that all shapes are parallelograms. They're not, but remember that every two-dimensional shape has a rectangular frame, which *is* a parallelogram, so that the shape can be resized in width, height, or both proportionally.

If you want a shape to be a specific size, for example, 2 by 1½ inches, watch the status bar at the bottom of the screen as you resize the shape. The status bar displays the shape's height and width as you move the mouse.

You can also use Visio's Size & Position window to specify the size and location of a shape in a drawing. To display this window, choose View⇨Size & Position Window (see Figure 4-5). Type the height and width you want for your shape and then press Enter. To close the window, click the Close button in the window's title bar.

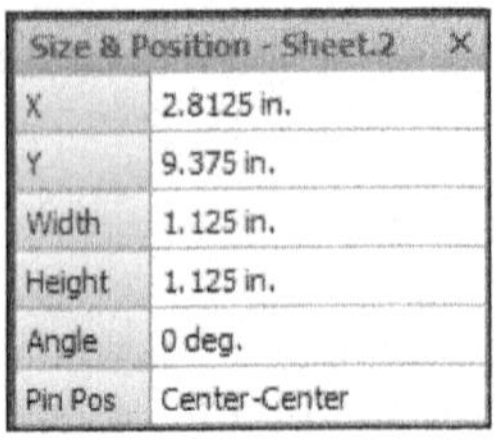

Figure 4-5:
Use the Size & Position window to enter the exact size or location for a shape.

Size & Position - Sheet.2	✕
X	2.8125 in.
Y	9.375 in.
Width	1.125 in.
Height	1.125 in.
Angle	0 deg.
Pin Pos	Center-Center

Like other windows, you can make the Size & Position window a floating window by dragging it anywhere on the screen. Or you can dock it along any edge of the drawing area just by dragging it.

You can also use the Size & Position window to position the shape accurately by changing the *x* and *y* properties. The angle property lets you change the orientation of the shape on-screen. Instead of using 15-degree increments, you can use any increment you want. The Pin Pos property lets you change the position of the bull's-eye in the center of the shape. The placement of this feature determines how the various handles work.

Deleting shapes

Deleting a shape from a drawing doesn't necessarily mean that the shape is actually gone. Generally, Visio places the shape on the Windows Clipboard. The only exception to this rule is when you press the Delete key (even then, you can recover the shape by clicking Undo). You can delete a shape in one of four ways by selecting the shape and then doing one of the following:

- ✔ Pressing the Delete key
- ✔ Pressing Ctrl+X
- ✔ Clicking Cut on the Standard toolbar
- ✔ Choosing Edit⇨Cut

Pressing the Delete key is the easiest way to delete a shape. However, if you think you may want to bring the shape back again, use Ctrl+X or Cut instead. That way, the shape is stored on the Clipboard so that you can paste it in the drawing again (as long as you paste it before you cut anything else).

You can use the same method to delete more than one shape at a time. Select all the shapes you want to delete (either click them or draw a selection box around them) and then choose one of the four delete options. (Refer to Chapter 2 to find out how to select multiple shapes at once.)

If you delete something by mistake, you can choose Edit⇨Undo, press Ctrl+Z, or click Undo to bring it back. By default, Visio has 20 levels of Undo, so you can undo up to the last 20 commands that you performed. If you think you want more, you can set up to 99 levels of Undo! Choose Tools⇨Options, click the General tab, and type a number in the Undo Levels box. Increasing the number of undo levels does increase Visio's memory requirement, so you should add undo levels with care.

Controlling Shapes

You already know that when you select a shape using the Pointer Tool, the shape displays selection handles, which are small green squares on the shape's rectangular frame. These usually appear at the four corners and the sides of a shape's frame.

Selection handles allow you to resize a shape, but you might want to make other changes. For example, you might want to change the width of bars in a bar chart or the magnitude of a curve. Or you might want to change the vanishing point for a three-dimensional cube. You can't use selection handles to accomplish any of these tasks, but Visio provides different types of handles, points, and vertices that allow you to make these kinds of changes to a shape, as shown in Table 4-2. In this section, you find out how to use these handles, points, and vertices to change different aspects of a shape.

Table 4-2		Handles, Points, and Vertices Used for Controlling a Shape	
Shape	*Color*	*Name*	*What It Does*
◈	Yellow	Control handle	Varies depending on the type of shape. It might adjust the direction an arrow points or the width of bars in a bar chart.
■	Green	Selection handle	Changes the height or width of a shape.
⬢	Green	Control point	Changes the curve or symmetry of a line segment.
●	Green	Rotation handle	Rotates a shape to a different angle.
⬢	Green	Eccentricity handle	Adjusts the magnitude and angle of an arc.
✦	Green	Vertex	Changes the point at which two line segments meet.
▼	Blue	Automatic connection point	Marks a location where you can create a connection between two shapes automatically. Visio places a red square around the destination shape.
✳	Blue	Connection point	Marks the location where you can glue a shape.

Note: When a handle or point appears in gray on the screen, it's locked and can't be changed.

Not all shapes contain all the handles and points shown in Table 4-2! For example, control handles appear on some shapes and often apply to an aspect of the entire shape, whereas control points appear only on part of a shape, such as lines, line segments, arcs, and freeform curves. Some shapes might not include eccentricity handles. Don't panic if you can't find a handle or point when you're expecting one. If it's not there, it's not necessary.

Adjusting shapes using control handles

When you select a shape, the control handles — if the shape has any — appear somewhere on or near the shape and help you to control some aspect of the shape. Every shape's control handles have a purpose. The purpose varies depending on the shape. To discover the purpose of a shape's control handles, select the shape, and then hover the mouse over the control point to display the tip for the control handle.

Figure 4-6 shows an example of a bar chart. The yellow diamonds are control handles. The control handle near the bottom allows you to adjust the width of the bars; the control handle near the top allows you to adjust the overall height of the bars. Notice how Visio tells you about the purpose of yellow diamonds by using a ToolTip. In addition, Visio changes the cursor shape to indicate the task that you'll perform with it.

Figure 4-6:
When selected, this bar-chart shape displays control handles that let you alter the dimensions of the bars.

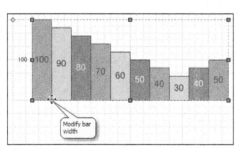

The Vanishing-Point control handle for the shapes in Figure 4-7 has a different function. In this 3-D block diagram, the Vanishing Point control handle defines the orientation of the three-dimensional effect for all shapes in the drawing. You can change the depth of the three-dimensional effect by right-clicking the shape and choosing Set Depth from the context menu. As shown in the figure, all of the shapes use a common vanishing point that appears as a gray diamond surrounded by a black square and labeled as V.P.

In addition to the single vanishing point that affects all of the shapes, each 3-D shape in the drawing has its own control handle that lets you change the shape's individual vanishing point. To change the vanishing point for a single shape, select the shape with the Pointer Tool. Notice that the Vanishing Point control handle color changes to red. Drag the vanishing point to a new location. When you release the Vanishing Point control handle, the diamond turns yellow. Figure 4-8 shows a typical example of a shape that has a different vanishing point than the other shapes in a drawing.

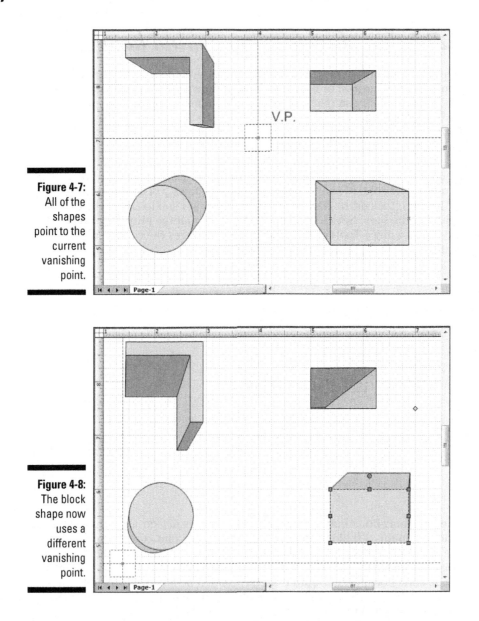

Figure 4-7:
All of the
shapes
point to the
current
vanishing
point.

Figure 4-8:
The block
shape now
uses a
different
vanishing
point.

Adjusting a shape's control handle is simple. Select the shape using the Pointer Tool, and then hover the mouse over the control handle until the ToolTip appears. The ToolTip might say something like "Adjust Corner Rounding" or "Adjust Pie Slice." Drag the control handle until you get the result you want — that's all there is to it!

Adjusting shapes using control points

Control *points* (as opposed to control *handles*) appear on lines, line segments, arcs, and freeform curves. (These elements might be freestanding or part of a more complex shape.) A control point lets you control the shape of a line, an arc, or a curve. (When you hover over a control point, the tip says "Bend Shape.") Another way to describe the function of control points is to say that they let you control the shape of a shape. For example, when you want to make a straight-sided rectangle look like a bulging rectangle, you drag a control point on the rectangle's line segments. Think of a control point as a rubber-band point.

To work with a shape's control points, you can select the shape using the Line, Arc, Freeform, or Pencil Tool button on the Drawing toolbar. (If the Drawing toolbar isn't displayed, right-click in the toolbar area and select the Drawing toolbar from the pop-up menu.) Table 4-3 describes these tools. You can also select the shape using the Pointer Tool when you have the Show More Shape Handles on Hover option selected (see the "Displaying all of the shape handles" section, earlier in this chapter, for details). When you select a shape using one of these tools, Visio first displays the shape's control points and vertices. Then, a split-second later, Visio displays the selection frame and handles.

Table 4-3	Drawing Toolbar Tools for Displaying a Shape's Vertices and Control Points	
Button	**Name**	**What It Does**
	Line Tool	Lets you draw a line
	Arc Tool	Lets you draw an arc
	Freeform Tool	Lets you draw "freeform" in any direction
	Pencil Tool	Lets you draw lines, arcs, or circles, depending on how you move the mouse

To adjust a control point, choose one of the drawing tools from Table 4-3 or the Pointer Tool, and then select the shape. Visio displays the control points as green circles with an *X* inside (refer to Table 4-2). When you click a control point to select it, the point turns magenta until you release the mouse button in its new position. Figure 4-9 shows how a pentagon shape looks before and after its control points are moved.

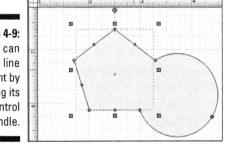

Figure 4-9:
You can curve a line segment by dragging its control handle.

Shaping corners

Just as control points enable you to bend line segments, *vertices* let you reshape the angle at which line segments meet. You can display a shape's vertices (green diamond-shaped points) by selecting a shape with any of the drawing tools shown in Table 4-3 or the Pointer Tool when you have the Show More Shape Handles on Hover option selected.

Hover over a vertex and the tip says "Adjust Corner." When you click on a vertex to select it, it turns magenta. After you have selected the vertex, you can drag it in any direction, changing the length and angle of the lines that form the vertex. If you want to alter a leg of a star, for example, drag the vertex (see Figure 4-10). To find out how to add or delete vertices, see Chapter 8.

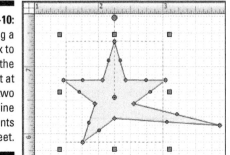

Figure 4-10:
Drag a vertex to adjust the point at which two line segments meet.

Visio seldom displays vertices on shapes that you drag into a drawing from a stencil. That's because many Visio shapes are complex enough that moving a vertex may destroy the shape. However, you can always display vertices on shapes that you draw. See Chapter 8 for information about drawing your own shapes.

Rotating shapes into place

Many Visio shapes can be rotated so that you can place them at the angle you prefer. To display a shape's rotation handle, you don't need to select the shape using a drawing tool; the Pointer Tool works just fine. The round, green *rotation handle* usually appears outside the perimeter of the selection frame and selection handles. When you point to the rotation handle, the mouse pointer changes to a single curved arrow. When you hover the mouse over the rotation handle, the ToolTip says "Rotate Shape."

Every rotation handle has an accompanying *center of rotation* pin, marking the point around which the shape rotates. The center of rotation pin is a small green circle with a plus symbol.

To rotate a shape, drag a rotation handle using a circular motion. The mouse pointer changes to a rotation pointer (four arrows in a circular shape), and you see an outline of the frame as you rotate it around the center of rotation. A shape's rotation pin is usually located in the center of the shape, but you can move it. If you want to rotate a rectangle around its lower-right corner, for example, drag the center of rotation pin to the lower-right corner of the rectangle and then rotate the shape. (Check out Chapter 8 for more details on rotating shapes.)

Modifying arcs using eccentricity handles

In simple terms, an elliptical shape is an oval. In Visio, an elliptical shape can also be *part* of an oval, as in an oval-shaped arc. All elliptical shapes in Visio have *eccentricity handles,* which help you adjust their *off-centeredness* or *eccentricity.* For example, if you draw an arc, you use the eccentricity handles to change the angle at which the arc sits relative to its endpoints.

Eccentricity handles are visible only when you select a shape using the Pencil Tool or the Pointer Tool when you have the Show More Shape Handles on Hover option selected. First, you see the arc's control point, a small green circle with an *x* in it. As soon as you click the control point, it turns magenta and Visio displays the shape's eccentricity handles joined to the control point by a green dotted line. The eccentricity handles are also green circles with an *x* inside. The dotted line represents the angle at which the curve sits relative to the curve's endpoints (see Figure 4-11).

Figure 4-11:
Eccentricity
handles let
you change
the angle
and
"centered
ness" of an
arc or
freeform
curve.

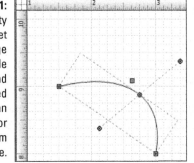

To change the magnitude of an arc, click the control point at the top of the arc and drag it in any direction. If you want the arc to angle differently, drag either eccentricity handle up or down. When you select an eccentricity handle, the handle color changes to magenta. To change an arc's eccentricity (in effect, its "bend" point), drag either eccentricity handle closer to or farther from the control point. (The closer the eccentricity handles are to the control point, the more circular the arc becomes.) The best way to figure out how to work with eccentricity handles is to play with them!

Using connection points

Connection points are the places on a shape where you can manually create a connection to another shape. The connections can appear as straight lines, right angles, or curves in most cases. For example, the boxes in an organization chart have connection points where the lines connect to the boxes. (Note that not all shapes have connection points.)

You can display connection points by choosing View⇨Connection Points. These small, blue *X*s can appear almost anywhere on a shape — but usually appear at corners, midpoints of lines, or centers of shapes, as shown in Figure 4-12. Notice that the figure shows three of the connectors in use for each shape and that each connection shows a different connection type (straight, right angle, and curved).

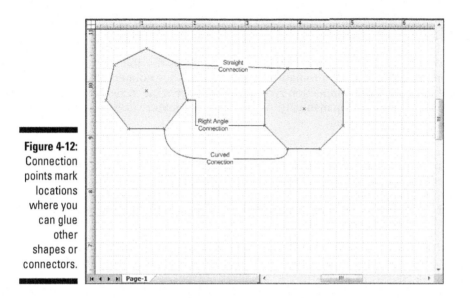

Figure 4-12:
Connection
points mark
locations
where you
can glue
other
shapes or
connectors.

To create a connection, select the Connector Tool. Draw a line between the
two connections that you want to use.

All connectors let you add text to the connection. Double-click the connection
and Visio displays a text box where you can type the text associated with a particular connection, as shown in Figure 4-12. However, some connections, such
as those used for Unified Modeling Language (UML) diagrams, include special
features. Double-click a connection for a UML diagram, and you see the UML
Association Properties dialog box shown in Figure 4-13. The special properties
always modify the connection in a special drawing type in some way.

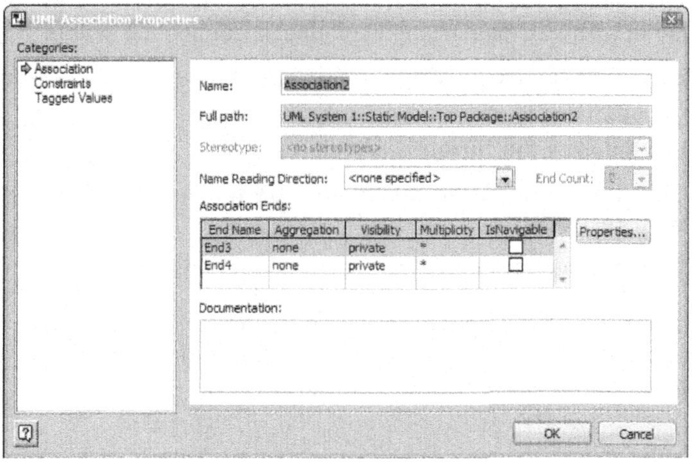

Figure 4-13:
Some
connectors
have special
properties
that help
you define
the
connection.

Using automatic connection points

One of the most interesting features of Visio 2007 is the ability to add connections between shapes automatically. Visio creates the connection using the default right-angle connection type, and the effect is the same as when you create the connection manually. All that this new feature does is make creating connections faster.

You can use one of three techniques to create connections automatically in Visio. The first technique helps you create the connection as you add shapes to a diagram using the following steps:

1. **Drag the shape from the Shapes window to the shape you want to use to make the connection.**

   You see four blue triangles around the shape. If you hover the mouse over a triangle, Visio displays "Auto Connect Shape" as the ToolTip.

2. **Choose one of the four triangles as a connection point.**

   Visio highlights the triangle.

3. **Drop the new shape.**

   Visio automatically places the new shape next to the existing shape in the direction that you selected and creates the connection for you.

The second technique is helpful when you already have the shapes on a diagram. Visio retains the current shape position, but creates the connection for you. Use the following steps for this technique:

1. **Select the shape you want to create a connection from using the Pointer Tool.**

   Visio selects the shape and displays all of the usual control handles, along with four blue triangle automatic connection points.

2. **Hover the mouse over one of the automatic connection triangles.**

   You see a red box around the shape that will receive the automatic connection from the currently selected shape.

3. **Click the triangle after you make sure the connection will go to the right recipient.**

   Visio automatically creates the connection for you.

The third technique automatically grabs a shape from the Shapes window and places it in the diagram for you, complete with a connection. The following steps tell you how to use this technique:

1. **Highlight the shape you want to use in the Shapes window.**

2. **Click one of the automatic connection triangles on the shape you want to use to create the connection without waiting for the red box to appear on other shapes in the diagram.**

   Visio places the highlighted shape on the diagram next to the selected shape and creates a connection from the existing shape to the new shape.

Finding the Shapes You Want

Visio offers so many different shapes on so many different stencils that keeping them all straight is difficult. For example, you might recall seeing a shape earlier, but not remember where you found it. On the other hand, you might not even know whether Visio supports a particular shape.

Visio makes it easy to find shapes by using the Search box right in the Shapes pane. Just type a word, such as *flag,* or a combination of words, such as *circuit breaker,* and Visio searches for shapes matching your description. The following steps help you search for a particular shape:

1. **Type a single word or a combination of words in the Search for Shapes field of the Shapes window.**

2. **Click the green arrow next to the Search box.**

   Visio searches for shapes that match your description. When Visio finds one or more shapes, it displays them in a new stencil that includes the search word or phrase you used as the title bar. Otherwise, Visio displays "Could not find a match. Please search again."

3. **Use any found shapes the same way you use other shapes; just drag them into your drawing.**

If your search word or phrase is too broad, Visio finds too many shapes. If the results found total more than 100 shapes, Visio displays a message asking whether you want to review the results. Click Yes to view them all, or click No to end the search and then type a more specific search word or phrase.

When you use Search for Shapes, Visio searches for shapes stored on your computer as well as on the Internet. This is the default setting for searching. You can change this search setting, among others, using the following steps:

1. **Choose Tools⇨Options.**

   The Options dialog box appears.

2. Click the Shape Search tab (see Figure 4-14).

In the Search Locations area, note that the Everywhere box is selected, as well as the My Computer and the Internet boxes. You can deselect any of these boxes to limit your search.

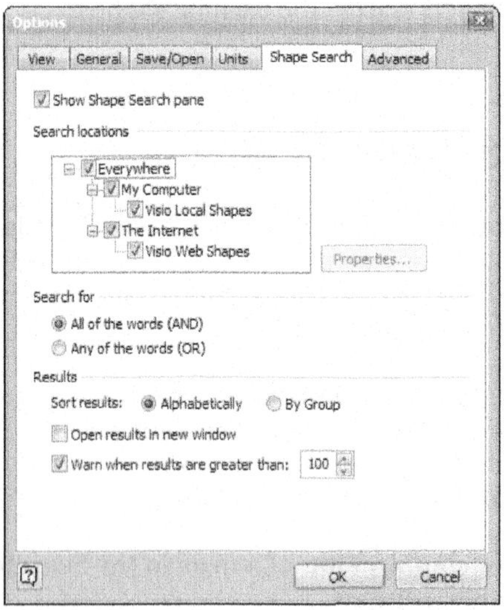

Figure 4-14:
You can customize the way Visio searches for shapes.

3. In the Search For area, choose All of the Words (AND) or Any of the Words (OR).

4. In the Results area, choose to sort results Alphabetically or By Group.

5. If you want results for each search to appear in a new window, select the Open Results in New Window check box.

This is a good option to choose if you want to save the shapes in a custom stencil. When this option is not selected, results from a new search replace old search results.

6. To change the Warn When Results Are Greater Than setting, use the up or down arrow or type a new number.

7. Click OK.

Another way to find a shape is to search for a shape that's similar to one already in your drawing. For example, suppose your drawing contains a personal computer shape and you want to find a similar shape. Use the following steps to search for similar shapes:

1. **Right-click a shape in your drawing and choose Shape.**

   The menu shown in Figure 4-15 appears.

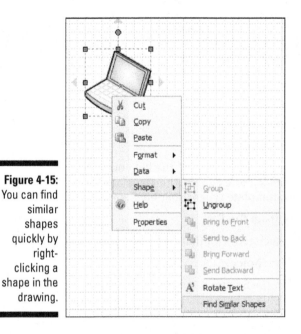

Figure 4-15:
You can find
similar
shapes
quickly by
right-
clicking a
shape in the
drawing.

2. **Choose Find Similar Shapes.**

   Visio searches for similar shapes and displays the results in a stencil in
   the Shapes pane.

3. **Drag the shape into your drawing just as you would from any other
   stencil.**

To find out more about creating custom shapes and stencils and saving them,
see Chapter 11.

Jazzing Up Your Drawings

Some drawings and charts are appropriate without any frills or fluff. But
sometimes, black shapes and text on a white background can be *really*
boring. This is especially true if you plan to use your drawings as part of a
presentation or add them to a publication. If you have the flexibility to add
interesting graphic elements and color, by all means, do so! Visio has some
slick features for jazzing up your drawings.

Loading stencils from other templates

Just because you're working with the Basic Diagram template found in the General category doesn't mean you can't use stencils from other templates. For example, you can easily use the Appliances stencil associated with the Building Plan template found in the Maps and Floor Plans category when you need it. The following steps tell you how to add an existing stencil to your current diagram:

1. **Choose File⇨Shapes.**

   You see a list of diagram categories.

2. **Select a diagram category from the list.**

   You see a list of template types. However, the list consolidates the templates into major divisions. For example, the Maps and Floor Plans category only contains two template types: Building Plan and Map.

3. **Select a template type from the list.**

   You see the stencils associated with that template type.

4. **Click the stencil of your choice.**

   Visio adds the stencil to the Shapes window.

Using the Visio Extras stencil shapes

There are times when you want to include in a drawing some graphical elements that don't qualify as clip art. They're more functional than clip art. Examples of this type of graphical element are borders, title blocks, legend blocks, and measurement scales. Visio includes a huge collection of stencils that contain these types of shapes.

To see a sample of these shapes, choose File⇨Shapes⇨Visio Extras. On the submenu, you find the following stencils:

✔ **Annotations:** A collection of shapes (callouts, text blocks, arrows, symbols) you can use to describe or call attention to parts of your drawing

✔ **Backgrounds:** Designs you can add as a backdrop to your drawing

✔ **Borders and Titles:** Predefined page border styles and title boxes from elegant to technical

✔ **Callouts:** A varied set of callout shapes used to grab attention and describe areas of a drawing (more choices than those found in the Annotations stencil)

- **Connectors:** A huge collection of every type of connector imaginable

- **Custom Line Patterns:** Options for custom line patterns for one-dimensional shapes

- **Custom Patterns (scaled and unscaled):** Options for custom fill patterns for two-dimensional shapes

- **Dimensioning (architectural and engineering):** Measurement specifications for scale drawings

- **Drawing Tool Shapes:** A collection of circles, arcs, lines, measuring tools, and polygon shapes

- **Embellishments:** Cool and weird stuff like Egyptian corners, Greek borders, art deco frames, and wave sections

- **Icon Sets:** A wealth of common icons such as emoticons, traffic signals, directional arrows, and ratings

- **Symbols:** Internationally recognized signs and symbols

- **Title Blocks:** A vast array of every conceivable title block, used in architectural drawings, maps, revisions, file names, drafts, and more

Using themes

In previous versions of Visio, you had to change colors manually, a potentially time-consuming process that didn't always guarantee acceptable results and virtually guaranteed inconsistencies between diagrams. Visual 2007 comes with a new theme feature that helps you create diagrams with a consistent appearance.

Themes consist of two formatting options. The first, *Theme Colors,* controls the colors of the shapes in your diagram. Each shape element receives a different, but coordinated, color treatment. The second, *Theme Effects,* changes the appearance of the color within the shape. A shape might use a graduated color scheme or a starburst pattern. Figure 4-16 shows an example of a diagram with both Theme Colors and Theme Effects applied (of course, you can't see color in a black-and-white book, but try the themes yourself and you'll see how they work).

You apply themes by using the Themes task pane shown in Figure 4-16. Display this task pane by clicking Themes on the Formatting toolbar or by choosing Format⇨Theme. You can also display the task pane by right-clicking the toolbar area and choosing Task Pane from the context menu. Select Theme - Colors or Theme - Effects from the drop-down list.

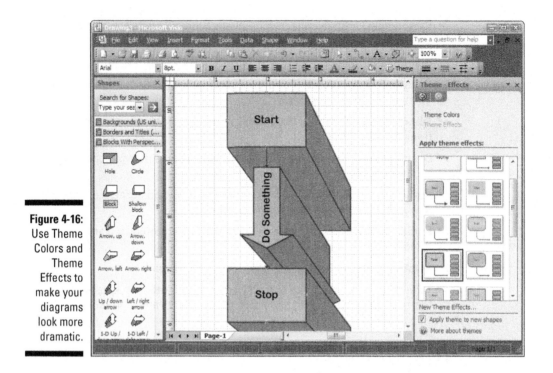

Add a theme to your diagram by clicking its entry in the task pane. Hovering the mouse over a color or effect choice tells you the name of that choice. You'll see the changes to your diagram instantly.

Sometimes a shape won't let you apply a theme. You can change this behavior by right-clicking the shape and choosing Format⇨Allow Themes from the context menu. You can also use this feature to format the shapes on a diagram using two different themes. Set the first theme, right-click any shapes that use that theme, and choose Format⇨Allow Themes from the context menu; now set the second theme. The shapes that you changed will still have the first theme set. Likewise, you might find that you don't want a particular shape to use a theme even though the rest of the diagram does. In this case, right-click the shape and choose Format⇨Remove Theme from the context menu.

The theme pictures in the Themes task pane are small. You can make the pictures larger by using the following steps.

1. **Hover the mouse over the picture.**

   You'll see a button with a down arrow, as shown in Figure 4-17.

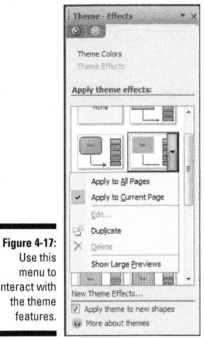

Figure 4-17:
Use this
menu to
interact with
the theme
features.

2. **Click the button and you'll see a menu of tasks you can perform.**

3. **Select Show Large Previews.**

   Visio changes the size of the theme previews.

Notice that the menu shown in Figure 4-17 also contains an Apply to All Pages option. Choose this option when you want to apply the same theme to all of the pages of a particular diagram. This option doesn't affect pages in other diagram files.

Chapter 5

Adding Text to Your Drawings

In This Chapter

▶ Understanding the role of text blocks

▶ Adding text to a drawing

▶ Manipulating text by editing, moving, resizing, and more

▶ Formatting margins and inserting tabs, bulleted lists, and numbered lists

▶ Altering the text style: color, font, and size

▶ Rotating text

*E*ven though they say one picture is worth a thousand words, a little bit of explanation can often help! It's highly unlikely that you'll create all your drawings without any text, so read on to find out how to add freestanding text as well as text to shapes, and then format it the way you want.

Understanding Text Blocks

All text in a Visio drawing is contained in a text block. A *text block* is a special frame for holding text. Most Visio shapes have a text block attached to them. For example, every shape in a flowchart has an attached text box, where you enter data to describe the process or decision represented by the flowchart symbol.

A shape's attached text block goes wherever the shape goes. However, you normally won't see a text block unless you enter text in it — and even then, you see only the text itself. Visio doesn't outline text blocks with a visible frame until you start typing text in the text block.

You'll see text in certain cases when a shape or connection has default text associated with it, but they're an exception. For example, when creating a connection between two shapes in a UML diagram, Visio labels the endpoints. You also see text in some shapes, such as a class, which has a default entry of Class1. In these two cases, you want to change the default text to something more appropriate. Other shapes have default text that you don't want to change. For example, when you add a Space shape to a floor plan, you want to maintain the existing text because it reflects the actual square footage of that room.

In some cases, you may want to add text to a drawing that's *not* attached to a shape. This is a *text shape* or *freestanding text.* A title for a drawing is a good example of freestanding text. It's obviously text, but you haven't attached it to any of the shapes in the drawing; the text block itself is the shape.

Generally, you'll find that Visio provides alternatives to freestanding text. Using a shape makes your text easier to see and maintain because Visio focuses many of its resources on shapes. For example, you can use any of the shapes in the Borders and Titles stencil to give your diagram a title. If you want a formal appearance, you can use any of the shapes in the Title Blocks stencil. Likewise, notes and annotations are easier to see when you use one of the shapes from the Annotations, Borders and Titles, or Callouts stencils.

Adding Text to a Drawing

In this section, you add text to a shape in a drawing and then add freestanding text. As you work with raw text (that is, the text itself before you format, color, or otherwise jazz it up), you use the buttons on the Standard toolbar shown in Table 5-1.

Table 5-1	Standard Toolbar Buttons for Working with Text	
Button	*Name*	*What It Does*
	Cut	Removes the selected text from the diagram and places it on the Windows Clipboard
	Copy	Places a copy of the selected shape on the Windows Clipboard
	Paste	Places the contents of the paste buffer in the drawing
	Pointer Tool	Lets you select a shape or shapes
	Text Tool	Lets you create a stand-alone text block (unattached to a shape)

Button	Name	What It Does
	Text Block Tool (drops down below the Text Tool button)	Lets you move, rotate, or resize a stand-alone text block or one attached to a shape
	Format Painter	"Picks up" the characteristics of the selected text so that you can apply it to other text

Most of the shapes you create require some type of identifying text. For example, when you create an electronic component, you'll want to assign it a name and value. Rooms in a floor plan have at least a name. The following steps tell you how to add text to a shape:

1. **Double-click a shape to select it and display its text box. (As an alternative, you can select the shape and press F2.)**

    You see the shape's text box, as shown in Figure 5-1. The shape's text box is a green dotted outline on a white background. It isn't always inside the shape; sometimes it's outside but near the shape.

    If your screen zoom is set to anything less than 100%, Visio immediately zooms in on the shape's text block so you can see where to type.

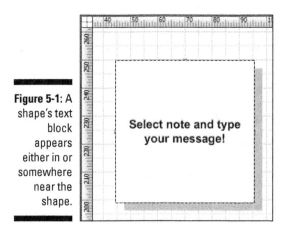

Figure 5-1: A shape's text block appears either in or somewhere near the shape.

Select note and type your message!

2. **Type text in the shape's text block.**

    You see the text you type appear within the text block. When you type more than one line of text, Visio automatically wraps the text to the next line. You can press Enter any time to begin a new line of text. If you enter more text than the text block can hold, Visio enlarges the text block as you continue to type.

 3. **Click anywhere outside the text block when you've finished typing.**

 You see the original shape again, along with your text.

If you enter a lot of text, the text block may become larger than the shape itself. You have a few options to make the text fit inside the shape:

 ✔ **Enlarge the shape and the text block (including the text in it).** Visio reformats the text automatically as you resize the shape. Refer to Chapter 4 for more about resizing shapes.

 ✔ **Change the size of the text block.** See the "Resizing a text block" section, later in this chapter, for details on changing the size of a text block.

 ✔ **Change the text's font size.** See the "Changing the font, size, color, and style of text" section, later in this chapter, for details on changing the font size.

 ✔ **Use more concise wording, remove extra words when possible, or find shorter words that mean the same thing as your original text using a thesaurus.** Highlight the word you want to change, right-click it, and choose Look Up from the context menu. Visio displays the Research task pane that includes a Thesaurus entry containing alternatives for the current word. Locate the word you want to use and choose Insert from the drop-down list box that appears when you click the down arrow next to the new word.

 ✔ **Select a different theme for your diagram.** Chapter 4 tells you more about using themes.

The formatting of text in a text block is different depending on the shape you work with. Some shapes left-align text, others right-align text, and still others orient the text vertically. Templates and themes control the way Visio aligns and formats text. For more information on changing text characteristics, see the "Changing the Way Your Text Looks" section, later in this chapter.

In some circumstances, you'll want to include text that's not part of a shape. Make sure you use a shape to add items, such as titles, to your diagram. However, fine print, such as copyright notices, is an example of freestanding text that you might not want to associate with a shape. You can include *freestanding text* in a drawing easily by following these steps:

 1. **Click the Text Tool button on the Standard toolbar.**

 Your mouse pointer changes to look like a sheet of paper with text.

 2. **Drag the pointer to draw a text box as large (or as small) as you want or click on an empty area of the diagram to have Visio draw a text block for you.**

 You see a text block outlined by a green dotted line. An insertion point appears in the center.

3. **Type your text.**

4. **Click anywhere outside the text block or press Esc.**

Note that in Step 2, the insertion point appears in the center of the text block because the text is set to be center-aligned. For more information on changing this setting, see the "Changing alignment" section, later in this chapter.

You can also type in a text block using the Pencil, Line, Freeform, Rectangle, or Ellipse Tool buttons to create your own shapes. Just double-click the shape and add text in the way just described. For more information about creating shapes, see Chapter 8.

Technically, freestanding text isn't actually freestanding. It's a shape named a *text shape*. However, you really don't need to know about text shapes to use them. The important issue is to remember that Visio always encloses text in a block; the text never just floats around aimlessly!

Working with Text and Text Blocks

In any drawing, you invariably manipulate text in *some* way, whether you edit, copy, paste, move, resize, change the alignment, alter the margins, shift the tabs, and so on. This section helps you make these changes after you enter text.

If you're familiar with word-processing programs such as Microsoft Word, you find that Visio handles text in nearly the same way. If you're already a pro at performing editing tasks, you can whiz right past these sections that discuss copying, pasting, moving, and deleting.

Editing text

It's inevitable. The moment you click outside a shape to save your text that you thought was perfect, you realize you need to change it. Maybe you want to add text, delete text, reword what you wrote, or just start all over again. Changing text in Visio is easy. Follow these steps:

1. **Select the Text Tool button, and then click a shape to display its text (refer to Figure 5-1).**

2. **Click the mouse where you want to change the text.**

   You see the insertion point after you click.

3. **Begin typing, selecting, deleting, or backspacing to make your changes.**

   - **To delete characters to the right of the insertion point:** Press the Delete key.

   - **To delete characters to the left of the insertion point**: Press the Backspace key.

   - **To select the text and type over it:** Highlight the text you want to delete (use the mouse or hold down the Shift key and use the arrow keys). Then begin typing new text. Whatever you type replaces the text you selected.

4. **After you make changes to your text, click anywhere outside the text block.**

   You see the modified text.

You can also open a text block by double-clicking the shape using the Pointer Tool (on the Standard toolbar), but watch out! If you use this method, Visio automatically selects all the text in the shape. If you don't want to replace all the text, be sure to click somewhere in the text block to position the insertion point before you begin typing. If you begin typing without positioning the insertion point, Visio replaces your text with whatever you type. If you replace text accidentally, choose Edit⇨Undo or press Ctrl+Z to bring back your old text.

Copying and pasting text

Sometimes you may want to copy text from one place to another — anything to avoid retyping! Actually, copying text is a good idea for another reason: consistency. If you want a chunk of text to be exactly the same somewhere else in your drawing, the best way to ensure this is to copy the text.

It doesn't matter whether the text you're pasting is attached to a shape or is freestanding text. You follow the same basic steps for copying and pasting. First, select the text to copy. If you don't select a text block to paste to, but instead paste the text by clicking a blank area of the drawing, Visio pastes the text into a new text block somewhere near the middle of the drawing page. You can then move the text block where you want it. Use the following steps to copy and paste text:

1. **Select the Text Tool on the Standard toolbar, and then click a shape.**

   The shape's text block appears.

2. **Highlight the portion of text that you want to copy.**

3. **Click Copy on the Standard toolbar, press Ctrl+C, or choose Edit⇨Copy.**

    Visio places the text on the Windows Clipboard.

4. **Choose where you want to paste the text:**

    • To paste into a shape's text block, double-click the shape.

    • To paste a text-only shape, click any blank area of the drawing.

5. **Click Paste on the Standard toolbar, choose Edit⇨Paste, or press Ctrl+V.**

    Visio copies the text to the new location.

The text that you copy remains on the Windows Clipboard until you copy something else. If you need to paste again and again, feel free!

After you select text, the quickest way to choose the Copy and Paste commands is from the pop-up shortcut menu. Just right-click after selecting text to display the shortcut menu.

Moving a text block

It isn't always obvious where Visio places a shape's text block until you enter some text in it or select the shape and press F2. In either case, you might find that you don't like the position of a text block and want to move it. In Figure 5-2, the text block for the star on the left covers up part of the shape. You could reduce the font size, but then your text might not be readable. Resizing the star will also work, but you may not always have that option. In this particular case, a better solution is to move the text out of the star, as shown in Figure 5-2.

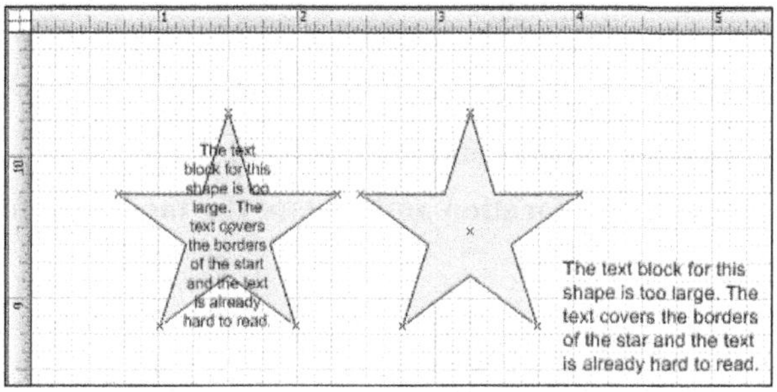

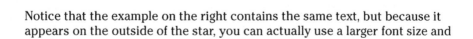

Figure 5-2:
Sometimes you need to move a text block to make the shape more visible.

The text block for this shape is too large. The text covers the borders of the start and the text is already hard to read.

The text block for this shape is too large. The text covers the borders of the star and the text is already hard to read.

Notice that the example on the right contains the same text, but because it appears on the outside of the star, you can actually use a larger font size and left-justify it, making the text easier to read. However, the text remains attached to the star. Try moving the star and the text moves with it. Use the following steps to move a text block independently of its shape:

1. **Click the Text Block button on the Standard toolbar.**

   Your mouse pointer changes to look like a sheet of paper with lines of text.

   To access the Text Block button, click the down arrow next to the Text Tool button on the Standard toolbar. Refer to Table 5-1 to see what both buttons look like.

2. **Click the shape that has the text you want to move.**

   The green text-block frame and handles become visible.

3. **Move the mouse over the text-block frame until the pointer changes to a double rectangle.**

   Notice when you hover the mouse pointer over the frame, the ToolTip says "Move Text Block."

4. **Drag the text block to reposition it.**

   Visio repositions the shape's text block to the position you choose.

5. **Click the Pointer Tool to bring back your normal mouse pointer.**

6. **Change the text font size and resize the text block as needed (see the next section in this chapter for details).**

Because freestanding text is its own shape, you can move it just like you move any other shape in a drawing. You don't need to use the Text Block button. Instead, just use the Pointer Tool button. Follow these steps:

1. **Click the Pointer Tool button (refer to Table 5-1) on the Standard toolbar.**

2. **Click the text-only shape that you want to move.**

   The green selection handles and frame appear.

3. **Drag the text to a new location and release the mouse button.**

Resizing a text block

Most shapes come with a text block of a reasonable size; that is, the text block usually fits the shape. If you don't like the size of a text block, it's possible to resize it. But it's questionable whether you should spend your time doing that, because text blocks automatically resize themselves when you enter too much text.

Even though Visio resizes text blocks for you as you type, you'll still want to resize text blocks in some situations. For example, when you move a text block outside of a shape, Visio doesn't optimize the text block size for the new location. You can also set the size of a text block as a *guideline* for when you enter text. As soon as you begin overfilling the text block, Visio resizes it. That's your cue to stop typing or change to a smaller font size when you need to enter more text. The following steps show you how to resize a text block:

1. **Click the Text Block button on the Standard toolbar.**

   When you move the mouse pointer over the text in the text block, the pointer changes to a double rectangle.

2. **Click the shape.**

   The green text-block frame and handles appear.

3. **Move the mouse pointer over a side handle to resize the shape's width, over a top or bottom handle to resize the shape's height, or over a corner handle to resize in both directions at once.**

   The mouse pointer changes to a double-headed arrow.

4. **Drag the handle to resize the text block, and then release the mouse button.**

5. **Click the Pointer Tool button to bring back the standard mouse pointer.**

Changing alignment

Whenever you create text in a drawing, you need to pay attention to how the text is aligned. *Horizontal alignment* refers to the way characters line up left to right in the text block. *Vertical alignment* refers to the way text lines up top to bottom in the text block. Many people also call the text alignment *justification*. For example, text that aligns on the right side of the text block is right-justified.

In many shapes, the default horizontal alignment is left alignment. However, center, right, distribute, and justified alignments have their place and are sometimes more appropriate. Figure 5-3 shows an example of each style.

When you work with a text document, you don't usually think about vertical alignment because your text typically starts at the top and fills the page to the bottom. However, when your text is contained in a text block (which is really nothing more than a box), you can choose to align the text with the top or bottom of the box, or you can center the text in the box, as shown in Figure 5-4.

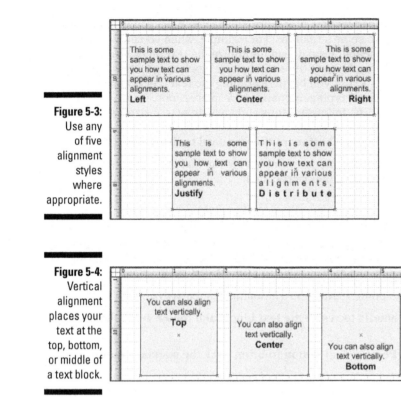

Figure 5-3:
Use any
of five
alignment
styles
where
appropriate.

Figure 5-4:
Vertical
alignment
places your
text at the
top, bottom,
or middle of
a text block.

You could use menu commands to change the text alignment, but it's much faster to use the toolbar. Toolbar buttons for text alignment appear on the Formatting and Format Text toolbars. Table 5-2 describes each of these buttons.

Table 5-2		Toolbar Buttons for Formatting Text	
Button	*Name*	*Toolbar*	*What It Does*
	Align Left	Formatting	Lines up text on the left side of the text block
	Align Center	Formatting	Lines up text around the center point of the text block
	Align Right	Formatting	Lines up text on the right side of the text block

Button	Name	Toolbar	What It Does
	Justify	Formatting	Lines up text on both the left and right sides of the text block by adding spaces between words
	Distribute	Formatting	Lines up text on the left and right sides of the text block by adding spaces between characters and words
	Align Top	Format Text	Aligns the first line of text with the top of the text block
	Align Middle	Format Text	Aligns the first line of text with the middle of the text block
	Align Bottom	Format Text	Aligns the last line of text with the bottom of the text block
	Decrease Indent	Formatting and Format Text	Moves text left to the previous indent point
	Increase Indent	Formatting and Format Text	Moves text right to the next indent point
	Decrease Paragraph Spacing	Formatting and Format Text	Brings lines of text in a paragraph closer together
	Increase Paragraph Spacing	Formatting and Format Text	Spreads lines of text in a paragraph farther apart

Unfortunately, only the Align Left, Align Center, and Align Right buttons normally appear on the Formatting toolbar in Visio 2007. You need to customize the toolbar to add the Justify and Distribute buttons. Right-click in the toolbar area and choose Customize from the context menu to display a list of commands you can add to the Formatting toolbar. Locate the Format Text category on the Commands tab of the Customize dialog box shown in Figure 5-5. Drag the Justify and Distribute commands from the Customize dialog box to the Formatting toolbar.

The text alignment (justification), vertical alignment, and paragraph spacing all modify the appearance of the text with a text block. The following steps tell you how to modify the appearance of the text using the tools in Table 5-2:

1. **Click the Text Tool button (refer to Table 5-1) on the Standard toolbar.**

2. **Click the shape that contains the text you want to change.**

   Visio displays the text block.

3. **Select the paragraph that you want to align.**

   If you want to align all the text in the text block, you don't need to select anything.

4. **Click the Align Left, Align Center, Align Right, Justify, or Distribute button (refer to Table 5-2) on the Formatting toolbar.**

   Visio reformats the selected text.

Note in Step 3 that because horizontal alignment applies to each paragraph individually, you can align separate paragraphs differently in the same text block. If you want to align all text the same way in the text block, you don't need to select anything; Visio formats all paragraphs the same way.

To justify or distribute — that is the question!

Most people are familiar with left, center, and right alignment but are stumped by justify and distribute. Justify fills the space between the left and right borders of a text block (except for "incomplete" lines, which often occur at the end of a paragraph) by adding spaces between words. Distribute fills the space between left and right borders (including short lines at the end of a paragraph) by adding spaces between words and characters.

Adjusting margins

Text-block margins define the white space that surrounds text in a text block. Visio sets very narrow text-block margins of 4 points. A point is approximately ¹⁄₇₂ inch. In most cases, these narrow margins are fine, because the outline of the text block isn't visible. However, if you decide to outline a text block with a frame, these margins can be so narrow that the text doesn't look right. For example, Figure 5-6 shows two text blocks. The text block on the left uses standard margins. The text block on the right uses 16-point margins. Not only does the text block on the right look better, but the words are also more readable. In addition, you don't get that claustrophobic feeling looking at it!

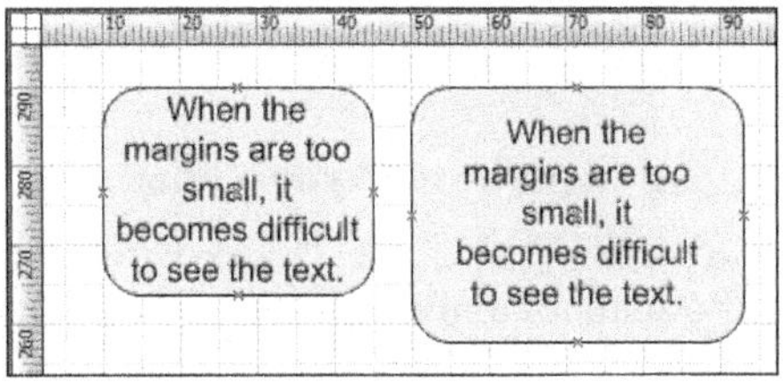

Figure 5-6:
Adjust a text block's margins to make text more pleasing to the eye and more readable.

If you prefer to have Visio measure text and margins in inches, you can change the default setting. Just choose Tools⇨Options, click the Units tab, and then change the Text setting. The drop-down box lists all the choices for units. The following steps describe how to change the margins for a text block:

1. **Click the Text Block button (refer to Table 5-1) on the Standard toolbar.**

   When you move the mouse pointer over the text in the text block, the pointer changes to a double rectangle.

2. **Click the shape that has the text block you want to change.**

   The green text-block frame and handles appear.

3. **Choose Format⇨Text or right-click and choose Format Text.**

   The Text dialog box appears.

4. **Click the Text Block tab, as shown in Figure 5-7.**

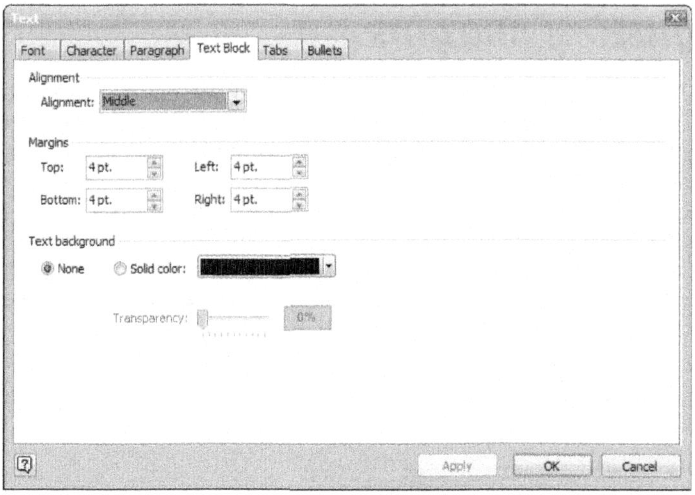

Figure 5-7:
You can
reset text-
block
margins.

5. **In the Top, Bottom, Left, and Right boxes, type a number.**

   Visio measures margins in points (72 points = 1 inch). If you prefer to use inches, enter them as decimal numbers and type **in** after the number (such as **.5 in**).

6. **Click Apply if you want to make more changes in the Text dialog box.**

   Visio applies the changes you've made. It's important to apply changes as you make them so you can track the appearance of your diagram by moving the Text dialog box and viewing the result of changes.

7. **Click OK.**

Using tabs in a text block

Some types of text call for a tabular format, even in a drawing. You may want to include a simple table in a drawing, with items aligned in rows and columns. To create this type of layout, you need to set *tab stops* (or just *tabs*) — the points where you want your cursor to jump when you press the Tab key.

You can set tabs as left aligned, right aligned, centered, or decimal aligned. You can see examples of each in Figure 5-8. When you use a decimal-aligned tab, be sure to type the decimal point in your entry. If you don't enter a decimal point, Visio left-aligns the entry.

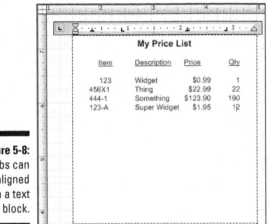

Figure 5-8:
Tabs can
be aligned
within a text
block.

The quickest and easiest way to set tabs is by clicking them onto the Text Block ruler. The following steps tell you how to perform this task:

1. **Click the Text Tool button on the Standard toolbar.**

2. **Click the shape with the text that you want to alter.**

   Visio displays the shape's text block.

3. **Right-click the text block and choose Text Ruler.**

   Visio displays a special ruler just for the text block. At the far left end of the ruler is a sample tab for a left-aligned tab.

4. **Choose the tab type (left, centered, right, or decimal aligned) by clicking the sample tab on the left side of the ruler until Visio displays the type you want.**

   A left tab looks like an *L,* a center tab looks like an upside-down *T,* a right tab looks like a backward *L,* and a decimal tab looks like an upside-down *T* with a decimal point (.) in it.

5. **Click directly on the ruler at the point where you want to set a tab.**

6. **Repeat Steps 4 and 5 to choose additional tabs.**

Now you can type text in the text block. Press the Tab key when you want the cursor to jump to a tab position.

To remove tabs, just drag them right off the ruler.

Using the ruler is fine when you can rely on approximate tab measurements. When you want to obtain a little more accuracy in setting the tab stops, you can use the Text dialog box to perform the task. The following steps tell you how to use this technique:

1. **Click the Text Block button on the Standard toolbar.**

   When you move the mouse pointer over the text in the text block, the pointer changes to a double rectangle.

2. **Click the shape that has the text that you want to alter.**

   The green text-block frame and handles appear.

3. **Choose Format⇨Text, or right-click and choose Format Text.**

   The Text dialog box appears.

4. **Click the Tabs tab.**

   Visio displays the dialog box shown in Figure 5-9.

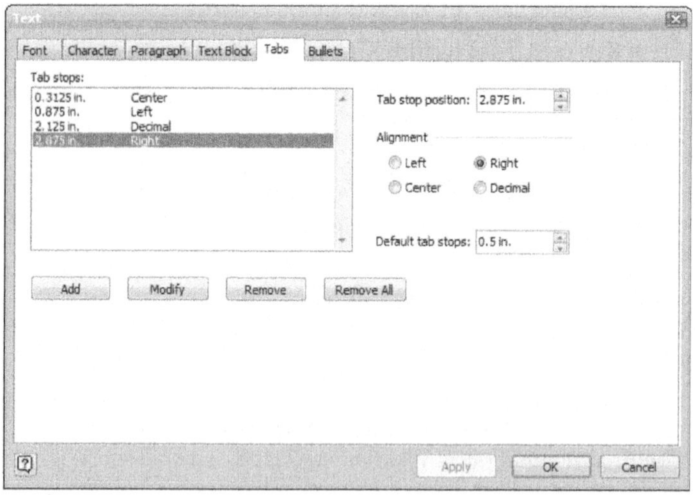

Figure 5-9:
Set tab
positions
here.

5. **Type a number (or click the up or down arrow) in the Tab Stops field and then click Add.**

6. **Choose an alignment style (Left, Center, Right, or Decimal) from the Alignment options.**

7. **Repeat Steps 5 and 6 to add more tabs.**

8. **Click OK when you're finished adding tabs.**

   The Text dialog box closes and you see the changes in the shape that you're editing.

To remove tabs using the Text dialog box, highlight the tab to remove in the Tab Stops field and then click Remove.

Creating bulleted lists

Bulleted lists are common in drawings and diagrams — probably because they help summarize and separate material. Fortunately, creating bulleted lists in Visio is easy because Visio does it for you automatically.

You can set up a bulleted format for text that you already typed or for a blank text block. If you set up a bulleted list in a blank text block, Visio inserts and formats the bullets as you type the text. The following steps describe how to create a bulleted list:

1. **Select the text that you want to format with bullets. If the text block is empty, select the text block itself.**

2. **Choose Format⇨Text or right-click and choose Format Text.**

   The Text dialog box appears.

3. **Click the Bullets tab to display the bullet options.**

   You see the dialog box shown in Figure 5-10.

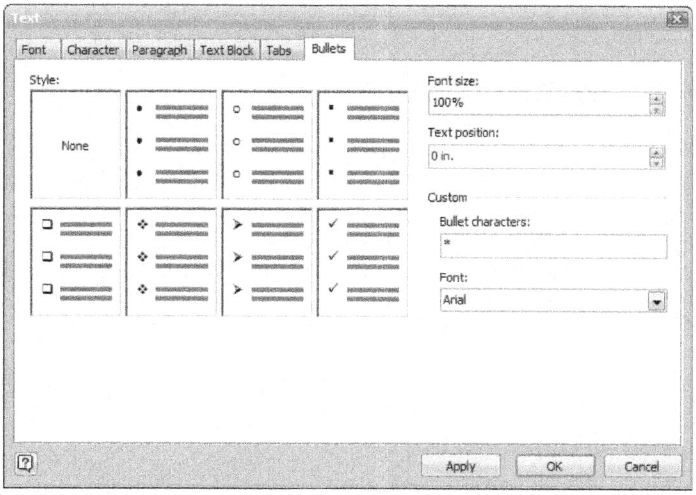

Figure 5-10:
Choose from several bullet styles and formats.

4. **Click a bullet style.**

5. **Type a percentage in the Font Size field if you want to change the bullet character size.**

   - To make the bullet character larger than the font text, enter a percentage greater than 100.

   - To make the bullet character smaller, enter a number smaller than 100.

6. **Enter the amount of space you want separating the bullet from the text (such as .25 in) in the Text Position field.**

7. **Use special characters for the bullet, if you want, by following these steps:**

   a. **In the Bullet Characters box, type the character or characters you want to use for the bullet.**

   b. **In the Font box, choose a font.**

   This is especially important when using a special font such as Wingdings or another special character font.

8. **Click OK when you have made all your choices.**

   Visio returns to your drawing. If you selected text in Step 1, it formats the text instantly.

If the text block is empty, the bullets will appear automatically when you begin typing. Press Enter at the end of a line to begin a new bullet point.

Creating numbered lists

The process for creating numbered lists is a bit more complicated than the process for creating bulleted lists. Visio doesn't add numbers automatically the way it does with bullets, so you need to type numbers and your text. Most people find it easier to format the text block for a numbered list *before* they enter the text and numbers. (It isn't required, however.) The following steps show you how to set up the indentation for a numbered list; keep in mind that you may want to alter the steps slightly for your particular text.

Follow these steps to set up an empty text block for a numbered list:

1. **Select an empty text block.**

2. **Choose Format⇨Text or right-click and choose Text.**

   The Text dialog box appears.

3. **Click the Paragraph tab.**

   You see the dialog box shown in Figure 5-11.

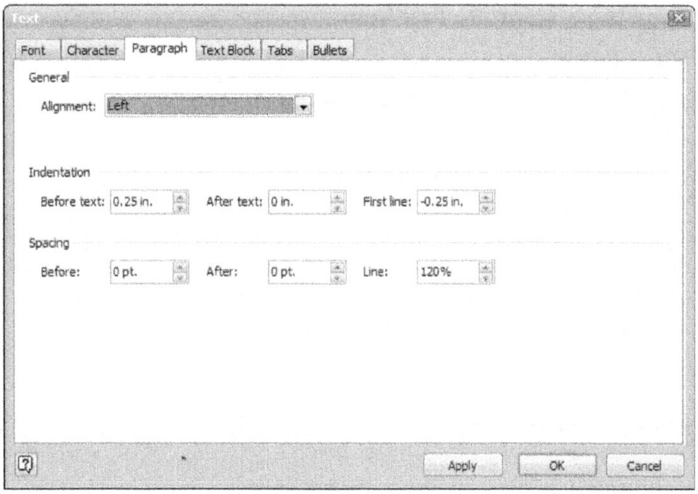

Figure 5-11:
Set up the
format for a
numbered
list.

4. **Choose Left in the Alignment field.**

5. **Type a measurement such as .5 in the Indentation Before Text field.**

   This sets the indentation from the left margin.

6. **Type a measurement such as –.5 in the Indentation First Line field.**

   This sets the position where you type the number for the numbered list.

   Many people use .5 inches for the indented text because it's convenient and standard, but you aren't required to use that measurement. You can just as easily use .2 or 1.2. Just make sure you use the same number for the Before Text and First Line options, with the Before Text number positive and the First Line number negative.

7. **Enter a measurement in the Indentation After Text field if you want to indent the right side of the paragraph.**

8. **Click OK.**

   Visio returns to your drawing.

In case you're wondering what you just did in these steps, you created a *hanging indent.* (The first line where the numbers begin *hangs* out to the left of the rest of the paragraph.) You set the *wrap* point (the point where text wraps on the second, third, and following lines) to .5 inches.

Now you can enter your information, as follows:

1. **Type the number for the first item (such as 1).**

2. **Press the Tab key.**

   This tab becomes the text wrap point if your text is longer than one line.

3. **Type the text for the first item.**

4. **Press Enter.**

5. **Repeat Steps 1–4 for all the items in the list.**

   You must follow this process for each numbered item to format the text correctly.

If you want to reformat existing text to a numbered list, use the same steps outlined previously to set up numbered list formatting for the text block. The difference is that you need to *insert* the item numbers in the existing text and then be sure to press Tab between the number and the text.

Setting the indentation and spacing of text

You use the Paragraph tab in the Text dialog box to set the indentation for a paragraph. Many people indent the first line of a paragraph to set off the beginning text. You also use indentation to create special effects such as numbered lists. In fact, you use indentation in many ways to make your text more readable.

The Paragraph tab in the Text dialog box also lets you adjust line spacing. For example, you can automatically add space before or after paragraphs or you can increase (or decrease) the spacing between lines within a paragraph. In many cases, you adjust line spacing in diagrams so that the text precisely fills a shape without going over the shape size. Adjusting the line spacing gives your diagram a finished appearance.

Visio measures line spacing in points unless you change the unit of measurement by using the Tools⇨Options command. (See the "Adjusting margins" section, earlier in this chapter, for more about margins.) For extra space before or after a paragraph, type a number in the Before or After box (refer to Figure 5-11). Use the following steps to set the indentation and line spacing for a paragraph:

1. **Click the Text Tool on the Standard toolbar.**

   The mouse pointer changes to look like a sheet of paper with text.

2. **In the text block or text-only shape, select all or part of the paragraph that you want to indent.**

3. **Choose Format⇨Text or right-click and choose Format Text.**

   The Text dialog box appears.

4. **Click the Paragraph tab.**

   You see the dialog box shown in Figure 5-11.

5. **Type a number (measured in inches or decimal inches) in the Before Text, After Text, and First Line fields to set the indentation for the paragraph you selected.**

6. **Type a number (measured in points) in the Before, After, and Line fields to set line spacing for the selected paragraph.**

   The Before and After boxes set the number of spaces preceding and following the paragraph; the Line box sets the spacing between lines in the paragraph.

7. **Click OK to return to your drawing.**

A quick way to indent a paragraph on the left side is to click Increase Indent on the Formatting toolbar (refer to Table 5-2). Highlight your paragraph, and then click this button. Visio automatically indents the entire paragraph ¼ inch for each click. Click Decrease Indent (also shown in Table 5-2) to reduce the amount of indentation.

Changing the Way Your Text Looks

When you draw a text block and enter text, Visio automatically displays the text as 8-point Arial black characters on a transparent background. Fortunately, you can use other fonts and special effects to improve the appearance of your diagrams and make them stand out. You have the option of changing the font, size, color, and style of text. You can also designate a case, position, and language. (No, Visio won't translate English into Portuguese for you!)

Changing the font, size, color, and style of text

The quickest way to change the appearance of text is by using toolbar buttons. Select the text that you want to change and click one of the toolbar buttons on the Format or Format Text toolbars (see Table 5-3). Some tools change the selected text immediately; others display a drop-down box where you can choose an option for changing the attributes.

Table 5-3	**Toolbar Buttons for Changing the Look of Text**		
Button	*Name*	*Toolbar*	*What It Does*
Arial	Font	Formatting	Lets you choose a font style
8pt.	Font Size	Formatting	Lets you choose a font size
B	Bold	Formatting	Changes the selected text to bold
I	Italic	Formatting	Changes the selected text to italic
U	Underline	Formatting	Underlines the selected text
A	Text Color	Formatting	Changes the color of the selected text
	Fill Color	Formatting	Changes the fill color of a shape
A	Increase Font Size	Format Text	Increases the font size incrementally (rather than selecting a specific size)
A	Decrease Font Size	Format Text	Decreases the font size incrementally (rather than selecting a specific size)
abe	Strikethrough	Format Text	Adds a strikethrough character to the selected text
ABC	Small Cap	Format Text	Converts the selected text to small caps
x^2	Superscript	Format Text	Raises the selected text to superscript level
x_2	Subscript	Format Text	Lowers the selected text to subscript level

Using the toolbar buttons works well when you change individual items. In some cases, you may want to use the Text dialog box instead so that you can change all of the features of a text block in one location. The following steps describe how to use the Text dialog box to change features of your text:

1. **Select the text that you want to change.**

2. **Choose Format⇨Text or right-click and choose Format Text.**

   The Text dialog box appears, as shown in Figure 5-12.

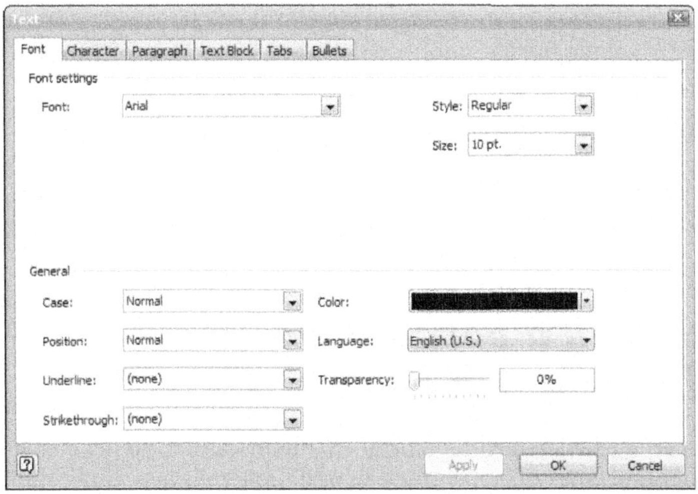

Figure 5-12:
You can change the look of text.

3. **Click the drop-down box of the attribute that you want to change:**

   - **To change the font:** Click the Font drop-down list and choose a font style. Unfortunately, the Font tab of the Text dialog box doesn't show you a preview of the font, so you can't see how a font looks before you choose it. The next best thing is to move the dialog box out of the way so that you can see your selected text. This way, when you click the Apply button, you can see how the text looks without closing the dialog box and starting all over again.

   - **To change the text style:** Click the Style drop-down list and choose Regular, Italic, Bold, or Bold Italic.

   - **To change the text size:** Click the Size drop-down list and choose a point size for the selected text.

   - **To change the case:** Click the Case drop-down list and choose Normal (the default setting), All Caps, Initial Caps, or Small Caps.

   - **To change the position of the text:** Click the Position drop-down list and choose Subscript or Superscript.

- **To underline:** Click the Underline drop-down list and choose Single or Double.

- **To add strikethrough:** Click the Strikethrough drop-down list and choose Single or Double.

- **To change the text color:** Click the Color drop-down list and choose a color for the selected text.

- **To change the language used by the Spell Checker:** Click the Language drop-down list and choose a language other than English.

- **To change the transparency of the text:** Drag the slider arrow along the bar until you find the transparency you want.

4. **Click Apply.**

5. **Repeat Steps 3 and 4 if you want to try other settings.**

6. **Click OK.**

   Visio returns to your drawing and reformats the selected text.

Choosing a background color for a text block

If you aren't satisfied with colorful characters alone, you can change the background color of a text block as well. Generally, you don't want to change the background color unless you have a specific reason to do so because changing the background color can reduce readability. The more contrast between the text and background colors, the better. (Text blocks are transparent by default.) For example, you might use a light yellow to highlight text that shows changes in the current document. A light yellow background with black text can make the information stand out and increase the chance that others will see the changes you make. The following steps describe how to change the background color of a text block:

1. **Click Text Tool on the Standard toolbar.**

2. **Select the text block that you want to change.**

3. **Choose Format⇨Text, or right-click the text block and choose Format Text.**

   The Text dialog box appears.

4. **Select the Text Block tab.**

5. **Choose a color from the Solid Color drop-down list, as shown in Figure 5-7 in the Text Background field. Choose white to make an opaque background on an unfilled shape.**

6. **Move the Transparency slider if desired to make the background less opaque.**

7. **Click Apply.**

   Visio changes the appearance of the text to match the setting you made.

8. **Click OK.**

The preceding steps change the background color of a text block. This is not the same thing as filling a shape with a color. The text block and the shape can fill independently of one another. See Chapter 8 for more information about filling shapes.

Painting the formatting to other text

When you use your precious time and energy to set up text with a magenta background, chartreuse text, Elephant font, 38-point font size, underline, bold, italic, and small caps, you don't want to have to do it all over again manually to make a matching text block. You can accomplish this task faster and easier by *painting* the format to another shape. Painting the formatting not only saves you time — it also ensures consistency. The following steps describe how to paint a format from one text block to another:

1. **Click the Pointer Tool button on the Standard toolbar.**

2. **Click the text block that has the formatting you want to copy.**

3. **Click the Format Painter button on the Standard toolbar.**

   Your mouse pointer now includes a paintbrush.

4. **Click the text block that receives the formatting information.**

   Visio applies the format instantly.

These steps copy all aspects of the text formatting (font, size, color, bold, italic, underline, and so on). The Format Painter also copies the vertical and horizontal alignment, margin settings, indentation, and tabs characteristics that belong to the original *text block*.

Rotating text

One of Visio's most versatile features is its capability to rotate text. For most Visio shapes, the text is oriented horizontally, but sometimes you may need to rotate the text at an angle. Figure 5-13 shows a triangle on the left with a horizontal text block. In the triangle on the right, the text block is rotated and moved so that the text runs parallel to the triangle's side.

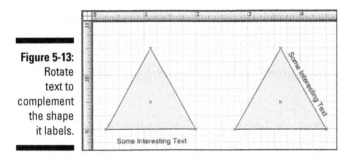

Figure 5-13:
Rotate
text to
complement
the shape
it labels.

You might think that you'll never need to use this feature and you could be right. An organizational chart doesn't usually require rotated text — at least not rotated to odd angles. However, when you create floor plans, engineering diagrams, and even software diagrams, you often need to use rotated text. The following steps describe how to perform this task:

1. **Click the Text Block button on the Standard toolbar.**

   When you move the mouse pointer over the text in the text block, the pointer changes to a double rectangle.

2. **Click the text block.**

   Green selection handles appear, along with round rotation handles at each corner of the frame.

3. **Move the mouse pointer over one of the rotation handles.**

   The mouse pointer changes to two curved arrows in the shape of a circle.

4. **Drag the text in the direction that you want to rotate the text.**

If you want to rotate the text to a specific angle, such as 45 degrees, watch the status bar as you rotate the text. Moving in a counterclockwise direction produces a positive angle up to 180 degrees; moving clockwise displays negative angles up to –180 degrees.

Rotating a text block usually moves it away from the object associated with it. After you finish rotating the text, make sure you move it back into position. For example, you might need to move it next to a border or other shape.

Chapter 6

Connecting Shapes

. . . .

In This Chapter

▶ Discovering connectors and their functions

▶ Adding connection points to shapes

▶ Unraveling a sticky glue mystery

▶ Gluing connectors to a shape

▶ Working with connectors that cross paths

▶ Gluing shapes to shapes

. . . .

*T*his chapter helps you discover two important Visio features: connectors and glue. *Connectors* are lines that show the relationships between individual shapes. In some cases, such as a flowchart, you can't create a diagram without using connectors because the shapes alone can't convey your meaning. *Glue* ensures that connectors remain attached to a shape. Imagine trying to move shapes around and then having to redraw the connectors with every move. The relationship among glue, connectors, and shapes is a close one. After you understand how each one works, you're on your way to becoming a powerful Visio user.

Discovering Connectors

Connector is a term that's unique to Visio. The simple explanation is that connectors are lines between boxes. A *connector* is a special, one-dimensional shape that you use to connect two-dimensional shapes to one another. This technical definition allows for the fact that connectors are not always lines; they can also be one-dimensional (1-D) shapes such as arrows, arcs, hubs, and other specialized shapes (for example, an Ethernet cable) that connect two-dimensional (2-D) shapes to each other. Given that connectors are a type of shape, they also have properties that let you define the relationship between the connector and the individual shapes and the two shapes. Connectors help you perform the following tasks:

✔ Show the connection between two shapes

✔ Define the relationship between two shapes

✔ Specify the hierarchy between shapes

✔ Create a path between shapes in a process

✔ Explain the criteria for moving from one shape to another

✔ Explore events, show motion, or consider other forms of dynamic data flow

Some drawings don't make any sense without connectors. Imagine an organization chart without connectors — you might have the president reporting to the copy-room clerk. Connectors show how components relate to each other and define the flow of power in an electrical diagram. A software diagram can't demonstrate the dynamic nature of an application without connectors. You find connectors in all sorts of drawings, from network diagrams, to process flowcharts, to Web-page diagrams.

In Figure 6-1, the 2-D Executive shape in the organization chart connects to the 2-D Manager shapes. Manager shapes connect to 2-D Position shapes. All the connectors are 1-D shapes. Notice how a single combined connector creates a connection between the positions and the associated manager. Visio performs this task automatically for you; all you need to worry about is creating the actual connections.

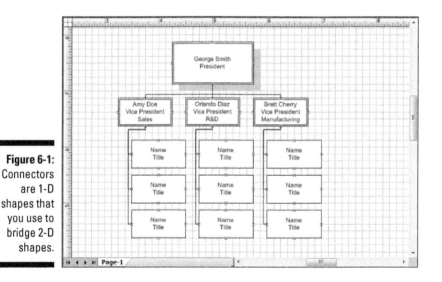

Figure 6-1:
Connectors are 1-D shapes that you use to bridge 2-D shapes.

REMEMBER

You can always distinguish a 1-D shape from a 2-D shape by the handles the shape displays when you select it. One-dimensional shapes always have two endpoints — small green squares with an x in the beginning point and a + in the ending point. Two-dimensional shapes always display a dotted green rectangle (the selection *frame*) with green selection handles at the corners and sides. (To review shape characteristics, refer to Chapter 4.)

Visio provides the following three methods for manually drawing connectors. (You can also use automatic drawing techniques; see the "Using the automatic connection feature" section, later in this chapter, for details.)

- ✔ Select the Connector Tool on the Standard toolbar
- ✔ Drag a connector shape from a stencil onto a drawing
- ✔ Click Connect Shapes on the Action toolbar

Visio connectors are more sophisticated than just simple lines or shapes. Some connectors are *dynamic,* meaning they can reconnect to a different point on a shape (if necessary) when you move the shape. Other connectors are *smart,* meaning they can change their form or path around shapes depending on the shapes you connect with them. These features may seem vague and meaningless now, but you'll soon discover how powerful they are.

In this chapter, you work with various tools on the Standard, Action, and View toolbars. Table 6-1 lists these tools. You might want to display the Action and View toolbars on your screen while working with connectors in a drawing. Just right-click in the toolbar area and select the toolbars you want to display.

Table 6-1	**Toolbar Buttons for Working with Connectors**		
Button	**Name**	**Toolbar**	**What It Does**
	Pointer Tool	Standard	The standard selection tool that lets you select any shape
	Connector Tool	Standard	Lets you draw connectors between shapes
	Connection Point Tool (below the Connector Tool button)	Standard	Lets you add connection points to a shape
	Connection Points	View	Displays or hides connection points in a drawing
	Connect Shapes	Action	Connects shapes automatically as you drag them into a drawing

You can access the Connection Point Tool by clicking the down arrow to the right of the Connector Tool. Consider adding the Connection Point Tool to your Standard toolbar (so it's visible all the time) by clicking Toolbar Options (the arrow at the right end of the toolbar) and choosing Add or Remove Buttons⇨Customize.

Working with Connection Points

The blue *X*s that appear on the sides of each shape are called *connection points* (refer to Figure 6-1). Connection points are the locations on a shape where you can attach a connector. Connection points appear only on your screen; they don't appear on a printout of your drawing.

Adding connection points to a shape

Visio usually provides ample connection points on its shapes. Sometimes, however, you might run across a shape that doesn't have a connection point where you want it. In that case, add one. Use these steps:

1. **Select a shape.**

2. **Click the drop-down arrow next to the Connector Tool on the Standard toolbar and choose Connection Point.**

   (Table 6-1 lists these tools.) The mouse pointer changes to an arrow with an *X*.

3. **Hold down the Ctrl key and click the location on the shape where you want to add a connection point. Then release the Ctrl key.**

You can add as many connection points as you like. You can place them on, inside, or outside a shape. Figure 6-2 shows an example of a triangle with connection points added. The connection points appear inside, outside, and on the triangle.

Having the ability to create connections wherever you want is important because some diagram types infer different meanings from a connection based on where the connection appears. For example, a block diagram can infer a connection from a subcomponent to another subcomponent, rather than between two major components, based on the positioning of the connection.

If you have trouble with Visio tugging your connection points away from where you want to place them, try turning off the Snap function. (Visio turns it on by default.) Snap "pulls" shapes and connectors to the nearest gridline, ruler subdivision, line on a shape, vertex, and so on. Choose Tools⇨Snap & Glue. On the General tab, deselect the Snap option and then click OK. (To find out more about the Snap function, see Chapter 7.)

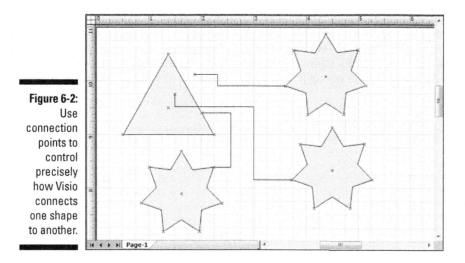

Figure 6-2:
Use
connection
points to
control
precisely
how Visio
connects
one shape
to another.

Deleting a connection point

Some shapes may have connection points that you don't want to use. Perhaps you added connection points that you no longer need. You can leave them there and just ignore them, or you can delete them.

Removing unneeded connection points has several advantages. Visio won't try to make a connection that you don't want when you eliminate an errant connection point. You can also control how the connections appear in the printed output with less effort and greater accuracy. The following steps describe how to perform this task:

1. **Click the drop-down arrow next to the Connector Tool on the Standard toolbar.**

2. **Click the Connection Point Tool, which looks like a blue *X*.**

3. **Click the connection point that you want to remove.**

   The connection point changes color to magenta.

4. **Press the Delete key.**

   Visio removes the connection point.

Using the automatic connection feature

The automatic connection feature can save you considerable time or it can prove extremely frustrating. The "Using automatic connection points" section of Chapter 4 demonstrates this Visio 2007 feature. However, it assumes that the connection is in the correct position. Unfortunately, many Visio shapes don't include the connection in the correct position. As a simple example, try using the automatic connection method to create a connection between a square and a hexagon. Very likely, you'll end up with the results shown at the top of Figure 6-3. The figure emphasizes the problem, but notice how the arrowhead is in the wrong place and the line doesn't take a straight path between the shapes.

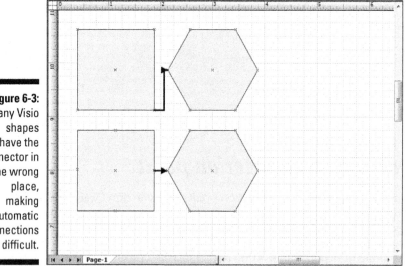

Figure 6-3:
Many Visio shapes have the connector in the wrong place, making automatic connections difficult.

The square shape comes with connectors in the corner, which is a good place, in some cases, but the incorrect place when you need to create a straightforward connection such as the one shown in the lower part of Figure 6-3. By combining the techniques described in the two previous sections, you can create a new square: one that has the connection points in the middle of each line segment, rather than in the vertices.

After you create the connection points on the shapes, save these shapes in a new stencil using the techniques shown in Chapter 11. You can create special stencils that let you use the automatic connection features of Visio effectively. The time you spend creating the new stencil is minimal compared with the time you'll save. Of course, you'll want to create a stencil only if you plan to use the automatic connection technique with the shape regularly. Don't take the time to create a stencil for a shape that you'll only use once.

Applying Glue (without the Mess)

Put your sticky white glue away — you don't need it when you use Visio. *Glue,* a feature built into Visio connectors, lets you stick connectors to shapes and keep them there. This may not seem like an important function now, but it's important when you start moving connected shapes all over the place.

Imagine for a minute creating a glueless drawing. Without glue, you have to move a connector each time you move a shape. If the distance between shapes changes, you have to adjust the length of the connector. Then you have to reattach the connector to the shape after you move it. If the path between two shapes changes, you have to reroute the connector. Now multiply those changes about 15 times, because you'll probably move shapes *at least* that many times in a drawing before it's finished. Without glue, creating and editing a drawing is more work than you ever imagined.

Choosing static or dynamic glue

Glue is such a great idea that Visio has two kinds: point-to-point (also known as *static* glue) and shape-to-shape (also called *dynamic* glue). As you see in this section, each one has a different purpose.

Point-to-point glue

Point-to-point glue forms a *static* connection between shapes. This means that if you connect two boxes from points on the top of each box, those connectors don't budge, no matter where you move the boxes. The connectors remain stuck to the top of each box, even if the drawing makes no sense. Point-to-point glue is *static, permanent, unchanging.*

Figure 6-4 shows what happens when you rearrange items that rely on point-to-point glue for a connection. As you rearrange the hexagons, the connectors maintain their original connection. Think of point-to-point glue as stubborn and unyielding. This form of glue is essential when you must maintain a specific connection. For example, you don't want the inputs and outputs to move in an electrical or software diagram, so you use point-to-point glue to ensure the connections remain stable.

When the way in which shapes are connected is important, or when you want connectors that stay exactly where you put them, use point-to-point glue. Point-to-point glue is also good for drawings you create quickly and for drawings that you aren't likely to change a great deal.

Shape-to-shape glue

Unlike point-to-point glue, shape-to-shape glue changes connections to provide the simplest display. When you move a shape that has a connector attached with shape-to-shape glue, the connector attaches itself to a different connection point if necessary — one that makes sense in the drawing. (You can always change the connection point if you don't like it.)

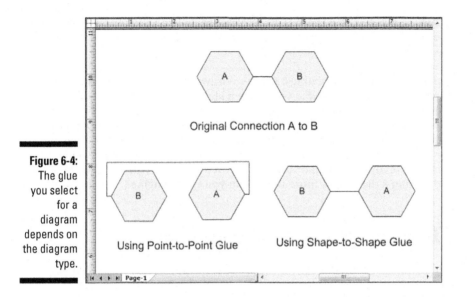

Figure 6-4:
The glue
you select
for a
diagram
depends on
the diagram
type.

Because shape-to-shape glue can attach to any connection point on a shape, it forms *dynamic* connections. The right-side hexagons at the bottom of Figure 6-4 show what happens when you use shape-to-shape glue. When you move shapes connected with shape-to-shape glue, the connectors move to more logical connection points (usually the nearest point) on each box instead of sticking to the original connection point. You commonly use this glue type for organizational charts and other diagrams where the point of connection isn't important, but maintaining a neat appearance is critical to ensure someone seeing your diagram will understand it.

Identifying glue types

With two types of glue, you need to be able to see in your drawing whether a connector uses shape-to-shape glue or point-to-point glue. After you select a connector (one that's connected at both ends to a shape), look at its endpoints. You see one of two things:

- ✔ **When a connector uses point-to-point glue,** the connector's endpoints are dark red squares and are the size of other endpoints and selection handles. The beginning point has an X in it; the ending point has a + in it.

- ✔ **When a connector uses shape-to-shape glue,** the endpoints are bright red squares and are larger than other endpoints and selection handles. The endpoint contains no + or X symbols.

Switching from one glue to the other

You can easily change a connection from one type of glue to the other. Knowing how to change glue types can be important depending on the type of drawing you create, how much you want to control connections, and how much you may want to change the drawing as you work on it. You might create a connection with shape-to-shape glue and then decide that you want the connector to *always* stay attached to a shape's lower-left corner no matter where you move the shape.

The trick to switching glue types lies in where you point your mouse as you move the connector's endpoint. When you point somewhere inside a shape, you get shape-to-shape glue; when you point directly to a connection point, you get point-to-point glue. The following steps describe how to create a shape-to-shape (dynamic) connection:

1. **Click the Pointer Tool (refer to Table 6-1) on the Standard toolbar.**

2. **Select the connector that you want to change.**

3. **Drag either endpoint away from the shape, and then drag the endpoint back toward the shape until a red border appears around the entire shape.**

   You must point somewhere inside the shape, not to a connection point. Move the mouse near, but not on, the connection point in the center of the shape.

4. **Release the mouse button when the red border appears around the entire shape.**

   When you release the mouse button, the endpoint attaches. The endpoint is bright red and slightly larger than other endpoints. This tells you that the connection is now shape-to-shape.

5. **Repeat Steps 2–4 for the other endpoint of the connector so that both endpoints now use shape-to-shape glue.**

When you use shape-to-shape glue, you don't get to choose the connection point; Visio chooses the *nearest* logical point to connect to. If you move the shape that the connector is attached to, the connector might attach to a different point.

Shape-to-shape glue is available only to dynamic connectors because dynamic connectors have *elbow joints:* points on the connector at which it can bend. Without them, the connector wouldn't be able to change its path when you move the shape that's attached to it. If you don't see elbow joints, the connector is a *straight* connector, and you can use only point-to-point glue. See the "Drawing connectors using the Connector Tool" section, later in this chapter, for more information about dynamic connectors and elbow joints. The following steps describe how to create a point-to-point (static) connection:

1. **Click the Pointer Tool on the Standard toolbar.**

2. **Select the connector that you want to change.**

3. **Drag either endpoint away from the shape, and then drag the endpoint toward the connection point where you want to attach the connector.**

   A bright red border appears around the connection point only.

4. **Release the mouse button.**

   The endpoint is attached to the connection point. The connection point is a small dark red square, which tells you that the connector is now using point-to-point (static) glue.

5. **Repeat Steps 2–4 with the other endpoint of the connector so that both ends now use point-to-point glue.**

Setting glue options

You might think that connection points are the only areas on a shape where you can attach connectors. In fact, you can attach connectors to guides, shape handles, and shape vertices as well. You also can glue to a shape's *geometry* (anywhere along the lines or curves that define the shape) even without a connection point. You can choose from five options in the Glue To group located in the Snap & Glue dialog box (see Figure 6-5).

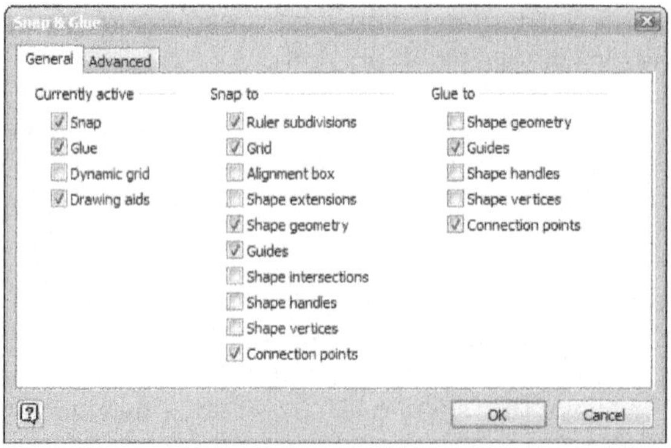

Figure 6-5:
Choose the items you want to glue to from the Snap & Glue dialog box.

Follow these steps to select glue options:

1. **Choose Tools⇨Snap & Glue.**

   The Snap and Glue dialog box appears, as shown in Figure 6-5.

2. **Select the check boxes of the points to which you want to glue connectors in the Glue To group.**

   The Guides and Connection Points options are selected for you automatically. (Guides are lines that you can add to a drawing to help you position shapes accurately. See Chapter 7 for more on guides.)

   If you want to glue connectors to shape geometry, shape handles, or shape vertices, select these check boxes as well, or you can deselect any of the five options.

3. **Click OK.**

When you choose the Shape Geometry option, you can glue a connector to any point that defines the shape. A circle is a perfect example. A circle typically has five connection points: top, bottom, right, left, and center. When Shape Geometry is *not* selected as a glue option, you can glue a connector to only one of these five points. When Shape Geometry *is* selected, you can attach a connector to any point along the circumference of the circle. The best part is that you can drag the connector clockwise or counterclockwise, and it stays attached to any point you choose along the circumference of the circle.

Gluing Connectors to Shapes

Visio offers several methods for connecting shapes in a drawing. Some let you connect shapes as you drag them into your drawing, and others let you add connectors later. This section discusses each of the methods for connecting shapes. The method you use pretty much comes down to the type of glue you want to use and personal preference.

Connecting shapes as you drag them

Connecting shapes as you drag them into your drawing is by far the quickest, easiest way to connect shapes. This method is fast because it combines two steps: adding the shape and creating the connection. The resulting connection uses shape-to-shape glue and dynamic connectors, so if you move shapes later, the connectors reconnect to the closest logical points. The following steps describe how to connect shapes when you drag a shape from the Shapes window:

1. **Select the Connector Tool (refer to Table 6-1) on the Standard toolbar.**

   The mouse pointer changes to the connector tool, which looks like an elbow-shaped arrow.

2. **Select the shape you want to use to create a connection.**

   You see the green resizing handles surrounding the selected shape. Visio won't create a connection when you haven't selected any of the shapes in the diagram.

3. **Drag a shape from the Shapes window to the diagram.**

   Visio uses shape-to-shape glue to connect the two shapes automatically with a dynamic (elbow-jointed) connector.

4. **Repeat Step 3 until all the shapes that you want are in the drawing.**

   Visio continues to connect each additional shape to the selected shape one using shape-to-shape glue.

5. **Click the Pointer Tool to display the regular mouse pointer.**

As you work through these steps, you may notice that Visio automatically selects the most recent shape you dragged into the diagram. After you drag another shape into the drawing, Visio selects that shape. You can always manually select a different shape or click on the currently selected shape to deselect it.

If the automatic connection feature isn't working for you, you may be trying to connect 1-D shapes. This feature automatically connects only 2-D shapes. (If you need to connect 1-D shapes — which is a rarity — you can draw connectors. See the next section to find out more about drawing connectors.)

Drawing connectors using the Connector Tool

You can use the Connector Tool to add connections to 2-D shapes. Depending on how you create the connection, you end up with either a shape-to-shape or a point-to-point connection. The following steps describe how to create a point-to-point connection:

1. **Select the Connector Tool on the Standard toolbar.**

   The mouse pointer changes to an elbow-shaped arrow.

2. **Move the mouse pointer over a connection point on a shape.**

   You see a bold red border around the connection point.

3. **Click the connection point and then drag the mouse pointer to a connection point on another shape.**

   You see a bold red border around the connection point on the second shape.

4. **Release the mouse button.**

   The connector is selected and you can see that the endpoints are small dark red squares, indicating a static (point-to-point) glue.

If you want to use shape-to-shape glue instead with a dynamic connector, the method is similar but not quite the same as in the preceding steps. The following steps describe how to perform this task:

1. **Click the Connector Tool on the Standard toolbar.**

   The mouse pointer changes to an elbow-shaped arrow.

2. **Move the mouse pointer over the first *shape* you want to connect. (Be sure to point inside the shape, not at a connector.)**

   You see a bold red border around the entire shape.

3. **Click and then drag the mouse pointer to point to another *shape*. (Be sure to point inside the shape, not at a connector.)**

   When you point to a second shape, you see a bold red border around it. The connector attaches to the most logical point on the second shape, automatically using dynamic glue.

You can also create combinations of connections. For example, by starting at a specific connection on the first shape and ending inside the second shape, you create a point-to-point connection on the first shape and a shape-to-shape connection on the second shape. Likewise, when you start within the first shape and end at a specific connection on the second shape, the second shape has the point-to-point connection. These combination connections make it possible to anchor the connection at one end while letting it float at the other. Sometimes you need a connection of this kind when working with specific diagrams. For example, you might want to create a connection where the viewer sees output at a specific connection, but input at any convenient connection. Figure 6-6 shows the effects of using a combination of glue types. Compare these effects with those in Figure 6-4 and you'll see how you can obtain any connection setup you might require.

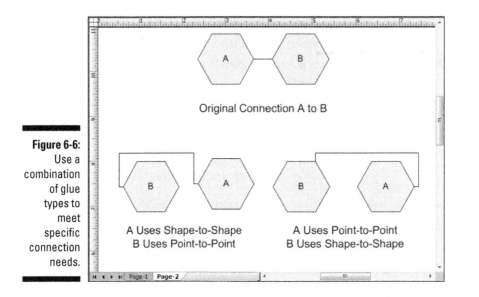

Figure 6-6:
Use a
combination
of glue
types to
meet
specific
connection
needs.

Saving time with the Connect Shapes feature

The Connect Shapes feature is a powerful timesaver. It connects two or more 2-D shapes automatically in the order that you select. You can use this method as an alternative to connecting shapes one at a time using the Connector Tool. The following steps describe how to perform this task:

1. **Select the Pointer Tool on the Standard toolbar.**

2. **Hold down the Shift key and click all the shapes (one by one) in the order that you want to connect them.**

3. **Click Connect Shapes (refer to Table 6-1) on the Action toolbar, or choose Tools⇨Connect Shapes.**

   Visio connects all of the shapes automatically using shape-to-shape glue and dynamic connectors.

Choosing a custom connector to connect shapes

A variation of the Connect Shapes feature lets you connect shapes with the type of connector you choose (something other than a plain line). Suppose, for example, that you want to connect four boxes with block-style arrows or arrow-tipped lines. These are just two examples of 1-D shapes that you can choose from the File➪Shapes➪Visio Extras➪Connectors stencil shown in Figure 6-7.

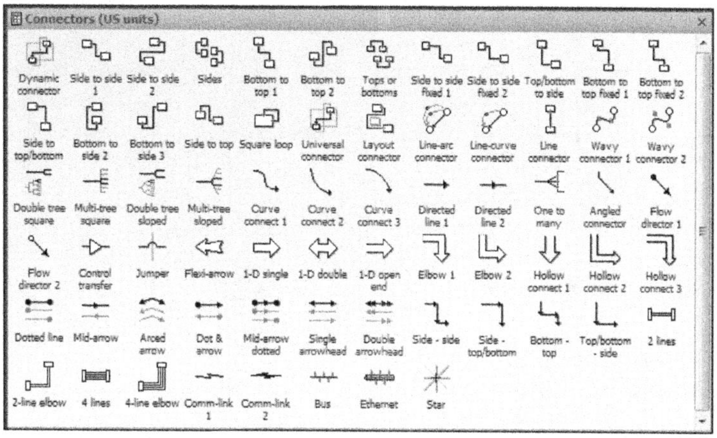

Figure 6-7:
Use any of the special connector stencils to connect two shapes.

As shown in Figure 6-7, Visio includes a number of special connection types. For example, when working on an electronics project, you can choose the Comm-link shape to create a radio connection. When you choose one of these connectors and follow the next set of steps, Visio automatically uses that shape as a connector.

1. **Select the Pointer Tool on the Standard toolbar.**

2. **Choose File➪Shapes➪Visio Extras➪Connectors.**

   The Connectors stencil appears.

3. **Click the connector that you want to use.**

4. **Hold down the Shift key and click all the shapes in the order that you want to connect them.**

5. **Click Connect Shapes on the Action toolbar.**

   Visio automatically creates connections between all the shapes that you selected using the connector you chose.

All connectors are 1-D shapes. Some stencils contain 1-D shapes that Visio calls *connectors*.

Figure 6-8 shows a number of the special connectors in use. Each of these connectors appears in the Connectors stencil, so you can access them easily any time you need them.

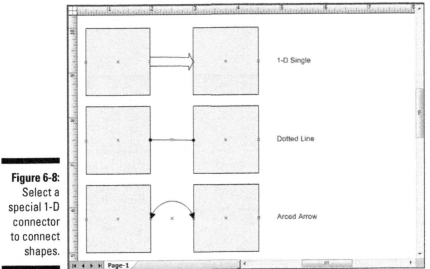

Figure 6-8:
Select a
special 1-D
connector
to connect
shapes.

 If you try these steps and the "connector" you chose doesn't work, it's probably because it's not a 1-D shape. To act as a connector, a shape must be one-dimensional. A 1-D shape has two endpoints (visible when selected); a 2-D shape has a selection frame and handles. (To review shapes, refer to Chapter 4.)

Dragging connector shapes into your drawing

You can also connect shapes by dragging 1-D connector shapes from stencils into your drawing. The shape you use *must* be one-dimensional, and you can connect only at connection points.

 Most of the connectors appear in the Connectors stencil. Choose File⇨ Shapes⇨Visio Extras⇨Connectors to display this stencil. Other stencils (for instance, the File⇨Shapes⇨Block Diagram⇨Blocks stencil) contain a connector or two as well. The easiest way to find connectors is to type **connector** in the Search field of the Shapes window and press Enter. Visio will display what appears to be an overwhelming number of connections. Unfortunately, some of these items are shapes. For example, a Small D Connector actually finds use in electronics diagrams. However, you'll still end up with a number of additional connectors for your diagram.

After you locate a connector you want to use, you can start placing it on your diagram. The following steps describe how to place the connector and connect it to the shapes:

1. **Click the Pointer Tool on the Standard toolbar.**

2. **Select the connector you want to use and drag it onto the diagram.**

3. **Do one of the following:**

   • **To make a connection using point-to-point (static) glue,** drag one endpoint of the connector, point to a connection point on the shape, and then release the mouse button.

   You see a bold red border around the connection point. When you release the mouse button, you see the small dark red endpoint (indicating a point-to-point connection).

   • **To make a connection using shape-to-shape (dynamic) glue,** drag one endpoint of the connector, point to an empty area inside the shape (usually near the center connection), and then release the mouse button.

   You see a bold red border around the entire shape. When you release the mouse button, you see a large red square endpoint (indicating a shape-to-shape connection).

4. **Repeat Steps 2 and 3 to connect more shapes.**

Moving connectors

When you want absolute control over where your connectors attach to a shape, you choose point-to-point (static) glue. However, if you change your mind about where you attached a connector, you can always move it. Suppose you originally attached a connector to the bottom of a shape and now you want to attach it to the top. The following steps describe how to move a connector:

1. **Click the Pointer Tool on the Standard toolbar (refer to Table 6-1).**

2. **In the drawing, click the connector you want to move.**

   Visio highlights the connector.

3. **Drag the endpoint away from the shape, and then drag it to the connection point (point-to-point glue) or to an area within the shape (shape-to-shape glue) you want to use for the new connection.**

   Visio breaks the original connection and then outlines the new connection point in red (point-to-point glue) or the entire shape in red (shape-to-shape glue) when you point to it.

4. **Release the mouse button.**

   Visio displays the new connection point.

Managing Connectors

Some drawings can become quite complex, with connectors running everywhere! You need to have a strategy for making your drawings clearly understood. This section discusses what to do when connectors cross paths and how to route connectors in the direction you want them to go.

Handling connectors that cross paths

In some drawings, such as flowcharts, network diagrams, and electronics diagrams, you might run into problems when connectors cross each other. In a simple drawing, this might not be an issue. However, when a drawing is complex, it can be difficult to follow connectors that cross paths.

To solve this problem, Visio adds a *jump* — sort of a wrinkle in a line — to all horizontal connectors in a drawing that cross vertical connectors. The jump makes it easier to see which shapes you have connected. A special shape, the Junction, shows which shapes have multiple connections. Generally, you only need to use junctions with special diagrams, such as an electrical layout, but it's good to know that both connection options exist. Figure 6-9 shows an electrical layout that includes a jump at the top and a junction at the bottom.

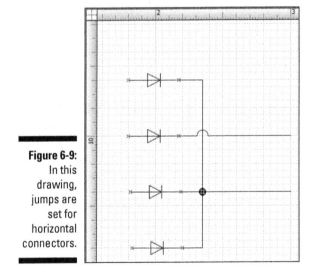

Figure 6-9:
In this drawing, jumps are set for horizontal connectors.

You control line jumps using the settings on the Layout and Routing tab of the Page Setup dialog box (see Figure 6-10). By default, Visio adds an arc-shaped jump to horizontal lines, but you can change the default settings. If you do, the changes apply to all new lines you draw in the current drawing. To make these choices, use the following steps:

1. **Choose File⇨Page Setup.**

2. **Click the Layout and Routing tab (see Figure 6-10).**

3. **Choose the type of lines for which you want to display line jumps in the Add Line Jumps To field.**

4. **Choose a style in the Line Jump Style field.**

   Visio provides a number of standard styles including the arc, a gap, a square, and everything from a 2-sided to a 7-sided polygon. The arc is the standard for electrical and electronics diagrams. Using other jumps with other diagram types provides a means of adding pizzazz to your diagram.

5. **Alter the width of the jump as necessary by dragging the Horizontal Size bar.**

6. **Alter the height of the jumps as necessary by dragging the Vertical Size bar.**

7. **Click Apply to preview the settings in your drawing.**

8. **When all settings are correct, click OK.**

Performing changes on single connections quickly

If you just want to alter jumps on a case-by-case basis rather than changing the default settings, use the buttons on the Layout & Routing toolbar. Display this toolbar by right-clicking in the toolbar area and choosing Layout & Routing, or choose View⇨Toolbars⇨Layout & Routing. Table 6-2 describes the two essential buttons on this toolbar for changing connector routing.

Table 6-2		Toolbar Buttons for Adding Line Jumps	
Button	*Name*	*Toolbar*	*What It Does*
	Add Line Jumps To	Layout and Routing	Adds jumps to the selected line. The ToolTip for this button always shows the currently selected option. The default setting is No Lines.
	Line Jump Style	Layout and Routing	Lets you choose a style for the line jump. The ToolTip for this button always shows the currently selected option. The default setting is Page Default.

Laying Out Shapes Automatically

Visio provides an automatic layout feature called Lay Out Shapes for drawings that typically include connected shapes, such as organization charts, network diagrams, flowcharts, and tree diagrams. This feature saves you the trouble of rearranging shapes manually when you need to make a change in a large drawing. For instance, suppose your company is reorganizing and adding two departments. You need to update the organization chart by inserting new boxes for managers and workers. Inserting is the easy part, but rearranging and realigning the shapes can prove time consuming.

You can also use Lay Out Shapes when you're in a hurry to create a connected drawing. You can quickly drag new shapes into a drawing without paying too much attention to position or alignment and then let Visio do that part for you.

To use the Lay Out Shapes feature, you must establish connections between the shapes in the drawing. If you're creating a drawing, the easiest way to do this is by clicking the Connector Tool before you start dragging shapes into your drawing. After all the shapes are in the drawing and connected, you're ready to use Lay Out Shapes. The following steps describe how to use this feature:

1. **Drag all the shapes and connectors into the drawing.**

2. **Choose one of the following:**

   • **To arrange all shapes,** click a blank area of the drawing.

   • **To arrange only certain shapes,** select the shapes you want Visio to arrange.

3. **Choose Shape⇨Configure Layout.**

   The Configure Layout dialog box appears, as shown in Figure 6-11.

Figure 6-11: Choose automatic layout settings here.

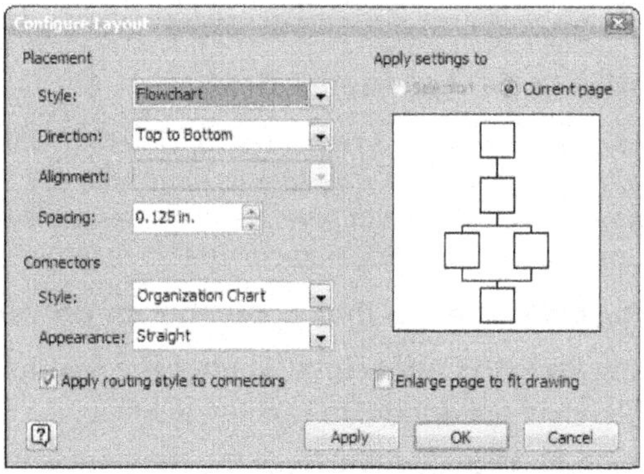

4. **Perform the following tasks in the Placement area:**

   a. **Click the drop-down arrow next to the Style field and highlight your choice.**

      Visio displays a preview of each style on the right side of the dialog box.

      Note: As you work your way through this dialog box, some of the drop-down boxes listed in these steps may become unavailable based on previous choices you made.

   b. **Select an option in the Direction field.**

      Visio changes the preview to match the direction you choose. Top to Bottom is the most common choice for organizational charts, while Left to Right is the most common choice for block diagrams. Use a direction that best suits the diagram you have created.

   c. **Select an option in the Alignment field.**

      Visio changes the preview to match the alignment you choose. Left is the most common choice for flowcharts. Center is the most common choice for organizational charts. You'll seldom have a reason to choose Right, but the option is available when you need it.

d. Select an option in the Spacing field.

This selection doesn't provide a change in the preview area, so you might need to adjust it several times to obtain the best results. This field controls the distance between shapes. You should select a spacing that provides the best viewing and aesthetic appeal.

5. **Perform the following tasks in the Connectors area:**

a. Select an option in the Style field.

Visio displays a preview to the right. This field has selections for organizational charts, trees, and flowcharts. If you're creating another diagram type, choose an option that best meets the diagram requirements.

b. Select an option in the Appearance field.

Visio displays a preview to the right. The options for this field are Curved and Straight. Most charts and diagrams use Straight. However, using curved lines can give some charts a pleasing appearance and you might try using curved lines when appropriate.

6. **Select the following options when they apply to your drawing:**

- **Apply Routing Style to Connectors:** Applies the routing style you choose in Step 5a to *all* connectors on the page.

- **Enlarge Page to Fit Drawing:** Enlarges the drawing, if necessary, to adjust the spacing for all shapes during auto-layout.

7. **Choose the Selection or Current Page option in the Apply Settings To area.**

Visio only enables this option when you have selected shapes on the diagram. The preview doesn't change for this option. Choose the Selection option when you want changes to apply only to the shapes you selected.

8. **Click Apply to preview your changes.**

If you don't like the way Lay Out Shapes arranges your drawing, choose Edit➪Undo or press Ctrl+Z. You can always follow the preceding steps again to make different layout choices.

9. **Click OK.**

Visio arranges the shapes in the drawing using the settings you select.

Part II
Creating Visio Drawings

The 5th Wave   By Rich Tennant

"You might want to adjust the value on your 'Nudge' function."

In this part . . .

*T*his part contains all of the information you need to know to create a drawing. You find out how to add shapes to a drawing and work with them, how to connect shapes, and how to add text so you can describe your drawings. This part also demonstrates a new Visio feature called themes that make you more productive. You won't perform any fancy drawing here, but you will understand enough features of Visio to be productive.

Chapter 7

Perfecting Your Drawings

. . . .

. . . .

*Y*ou may or may not feel the need to have everything neat and clean when
it comes to your diagrams, but when you need to straighten things up,
Visio provides everything you need to do it. This chapter shows you how to
use Visio's tools to measure, place, and line up elements in a drawing. These
tools make "perfecting" tasks easy and save you time. Don't feel that you
must use all these ideas. Choose the ideas that make the most sense for your
particular drawing.

Visio has a lot of functionality packed into a very small package. With all the
functionality, some people become overwhelmed by this chapter in the book
because they think they have to do everything the book has discussed.
Nothing is farther from the truth. Think of this book as the menu and you can
choose the items you want. If all you need is a sketch that no one else will
ever see, you really don't need to place shapes precisely. That's the point of
Visio: You can make diagrams as simple or as complex as you need them. In
short, you can use Visio today; don't let the features you really don't need
overwhelm you.

All about Measurements and Placement Tools

This section gives you a preview of the terms used in this chapter. You can use this list to understand the concepts in this chapter with greater ease.

- ✔ **Alignment and distribution:** *Alignment* refers to shapes lining up evenly. For example, you can align the tops of all of the shapes so they look even from the top even though they might be different sizes. *Distribution* refers to objects being spaced evenly across a given area so the space between each shape is the same. When shapes aren't aligned and distributed evenly in a drawing, your eyes sense that something is wrong. Visio helps you automatically align and distribute shapes.

- ✔ **Gridlines:** These prominent vertical and horizontal lines make the drawing area look like graph paper. The *grid* is a useful tool for measuring and placing shapes. (Many of the figures in this book don't show the grid so that you can focus on the topic at hand.)

- ✔ **Guides:** You can add guidelines and guide points to a drawing to help position and place shapes accurately. If you were to draw a furniture layout on paper, you might lightly sketch lines that represent the boundaries of the room so you could place the furniture precisely. Guides serve the same purpose in Visio.

- ✔ **Rulers:** These are the objects on the top and left side of the drawing area that look curiously like — well, rulers. Rulers, as you may expect, act as measuring devices.

- ✔ **Scale:** *Scale* is the ratio of the size of real-life objects to the shapes in your drawing. Because you can't represent something as large as a building using true measurements, which would make the diagram as large as the building itself, you use a standard reduction in the diagram. A measurement of ½ inch in the diagram might represent 1 foot in the building. In a few cases, such as electronics diagrams, you might actually end up making the diagram larger than the actual object so that someone viewing your diagram can see the details of your design. In this case, ½ inch might represent ⅟₁₀₀ inch in the diagram. Using an accurate scale is important for floor plans and engineering diagrams where you model a physical entity. You won't ever use scale for an abstract entity such as a flowchart.

- ✔ **Snap:** This feature pulls, or attracts, shapes to any object that you specify such as another shape, a gridline, a guide, or a connection point. This is a terrific feature that helps you place shapes accurately.

As you work through this chapter, it's helpful to have Rulers, Grid, Guides, and Connection Points selected on your View menu. Just click the item to place a check mark next to its entry on the View menu.

You might also find it useful to display the View toolbar (choose View⇨Toolbars⇨View). The View toolbar buttons are listed in Table 7-1. Each button is a toggle that turns the named feature on or off.

Table 7-1		Toolbar Buttons That Help You Place Shapes	
Button	*Name*	*Toolbar*	*What It Does*
	Rulers	View	Displays or hides rulers at the top and left of the drawing window
	Grid	View	Displays or hides a grid in the drawing area
	Guides	View	Displays or hides guides in a drawing
	Connection Points	View	Displays or hides connection points in a drawing

Another toolbar you might want to display is the Snap & Glue toolbar because it provides features that help you create diagrams faster and with less effort. For example, you can snap new shapes to the grid to make it easier to create great-looking diagrams without having to align the shapes first. Table 7-2 describes the Snap & Glue tools. All the buttons in Table 7-2 toggle features on or off each time you click the button, so you can turn these features on or off whenever you choose.

Table 7-2		Toolbar Buttons That Help You Snap & Glue Shapes	
Button	*Name*	*Toolbar*	*What It Does*
	Toggle Snap	Snap & Glue	Pulls shapes to items you specify in the Snap & Glue dialog box
	Toggle Glue	Snap & Glue	Attaches shapes to items you select in the Snap & Glue dialog box
	Snap to Dynamic Grid	Snap & Glue	Displays dotted lines as you drag shapes into a drawing to help you place the shapes accurately

(continued)

Table 7-2 *(continued)*

Button	Name	Toolbar	What It Does
	Snap to Drawing Aids	Snap & Glue	Helps you draw shapes such as circles, squares, or lines at a particular angle
	Snap to Ruler Subdivisions	Snap & Glue	Pulls shapes to the nearest ruler subdivision
	Snap to Grid	Snap & Glue	Pulls shapes to the nearest gridline
	Snap to Alignment Box	Snap & Glue	Pulls shapes to another shape's alignment box
	Snap to Shape Intersections	Snap & Glue	Pulls shapes to specific points on other shapes (such as the center point or apex of an arc, or the endpoint or midpoint of a line)
	Glue to Shape Geometry	Snap & Glue	Attaches shapes to the visible edges of another shape
	Glue to Guides	Snap & Glue	Attaches shapes to guide lines and guide points
	Glue to Shape Handles	Snap & Glue	Attaches shapes to other shapes' handles
	Glue to Shape Vertices	Snap & Glue	Attaches shapes to other shapes' vertices
	Glue to Connection Points	Snap & Glue	Attaches shapes to other shapes' connection points

Using the Drawing Grid

Whenever you create a new drawing, Visio automatically displays a *drawing grid* — horizontal and vertical lines that make the drawing area look like graph paper. The grid helps you place shapes where you want them in a drawing.

Just as you can buy graph paper in different grid sizes, you can set the grid *density* (fine, normal, or coarse) for your drawing. Why would you care about density? If you create a drawing with very small shapes that you want to place precisely, you probably want a finer density — say, lines every ⅛ inch or so. On the other hand, if you use very large shapes in your drawing, a ½-inch grid is more than adequate. You don't want to use a small grid with large shapes because the grid ends up cluttering the drawing area.

Keep in mind that what you see on your screen depends on your monitor and the resolution you use. To figure out what fine, normal, and coarse mean on your monitor, experiment with them by changing the grid density. (The steps to do so appear later in this section.)

The grid in Visio is *variable*. When you zoom in on a drawing, gridlines become more dense; when you zoom out, the gridlines are less dense. This feature keeps the gridlines from looking like one black square. The number of gridlines you see is the amount that Visio can display without making the grid too dense.

If your mouse is equipped with a wheel, the quickest way to zoom in and out is by holding the Ctrl key as you roll the mouse wheel forward or backward. To make the increments a little more predictable, start at 100%. Zooming out produces values of 50%, 25%, 13%, and so on, until the zoom factor reaches 1%. Zooming in produces values of 200%, 400%, and so on, until the zoom factor reaches 3,098%.

Like most settings in Visio, you can turn off the variable grid and instead use a fixed grid (see the steps that follow). When you use a fixed grid, the density stays the same, regardless of the zoom percentage you use. Typically, Visio spaces the grid evenly both horizontally and vertically; when horizontal lines occur every ½ inch, vertical lines do, too. However, you can set an uneven grid if you like, with ½-inch horizontal gridlines and ¼-inch vertical gridlines, for example. Fixed grids work best when you need to provide a grid for physical measurement, such as creating a floor plan.

You can also choose something other than the lower-left corner of the drawing area as a starting point for the grid. For example, you could create a 1-inch grid for general shape positioning and then offset the grid by ½ inch to adjust for the margins on your page. Figure 7-1 shows how such an arrangement would look.

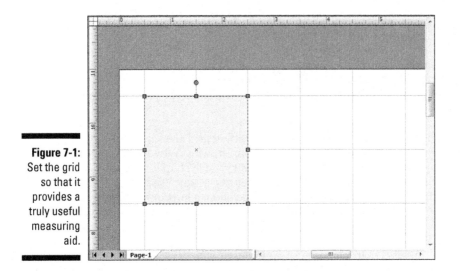

Figure 7-1:
Set the grid
so that it
provides a
truly useful
measuring
aid.

Because the shapes in this diagram are multiples of 1 inch in size, every shape fits neatly within a grid area. The half-inch offset ensures that none of the shapes prints off the side of the page. Using this approach saves considerable time when you know how you want the page to appear. The following steps describe how to set a grid:

1. **Choose Tools➪Ruler & Grid.**

   The Ruler & Grid dialog box appears, as shown in Figure 7-2. Notice that the dialog box includes separate areas for horizontal and vertical gridlines so that you can set the grid scales independently.

Figure 7-2:
Use the
Ruler & Grid
dialog box
to set grid
variables.

2. **Click the drop-down lists for Grid Spacing Horizontal and Grid Spacing Vertical and then choose Fine, Normal, Coarse, or Fixed.**

3. **Type a number (in inches) in the Minimum Spacing fields when you want to control the minimum grid spacing.**

4. **Choose a grid origin when you need to use something other than the upper-left corner of the display as the starting point for your measurement.**

5. **Click OK.**

Note: The grid doesn't appear when you print the drawing. It's an on-screen visual aid only.

If you ever want to turn off the drawing grid, click the Grid button on the View toolbar or choose View➪Grid. Turning off the grid helps you see how the drawing will look when you print it.

Using Dynamic Grid

Even though many people associate dynamic grids with flowcharts or block diagrams, any diagram can benefit from the dynamic grid feature. The *dynamic grid* helps you position new shapes vertically and horizontally relative to the shapes you've already placed in the drawing. Whenever you drag a flowchart or block diagram shape into your drawing, horizontal and vertical reference lines appear along with the shape. These reference lines appear when the two shapes are aligned on a side or in the middle. You'll also see a ToolTip that says "Snap to Dynamic Grid."

Using the dynamic grid simplifies drawing by helping you align shapes quickly. As you move the shape around the drawing, the reference lines "jump" to show you when the shape is in alignment with another shape. When the two shapes align, release the mouse button; the reference lines disappear.

Dynamic grid is automatically active when you create a flowchart. To activate dynamic grid for block diagrams or other drawings, click Snap to Dynamic Grid on the Snap & Glue toolbar (refer to Table 7-2) or choose Tools➪Snap & Glue, select the Dynamic Grid option in the Currently Active list of the Snap & Grid dialog box, and click OK. Each time you click Snap to Dynamic Grid on the Snap & Glue toolbar, the dynamic grid feature toggles on or off.

Setting Drawing Scale

When you create a drawing that doesn't represent a real-life object, such as a flowchart, you don't need to worry about scale. Who cares whether your decision shape is 1⅛ inches wide and your process shape is 1¾ inches wide?

When you use a template to create a flowchart (or any other type of drawing with abstract shapes), Visio automatically sets the drawing scale to 1:1 (making the drawing actual size).

However, when you create a drawing with shapes that represent any real-life objects larger or smaller than a page, the drawing must be *scaled* so that all the objects fit on the page in proper relation to one another. For example, suppose you want to create an office layout. If you choose the Building Plan category and the Office Layout template, Visio automatically sets the drawing scale to ½ inch:1 foot. That is, every ½ inch shown on the printed page represents 1 foot of office space. Figure 7-3 shows an example of a diagram that uses a scale of ½ inch:1 foot.

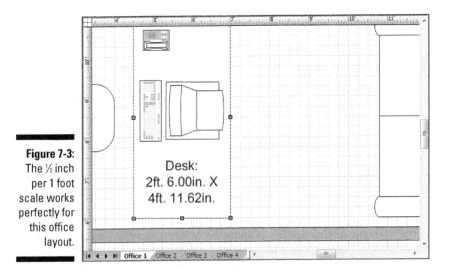

Figure 7-3:
The ½ inch
per 1 foot
scale works
perfectly for
this office
layout.

Notice that the rulers in this diagram reflect the scale. The desk is 2' 6" (2 feet, 6 inches) in depth. The text at the bottom of the desk is part of a Room Measure shape that you can find in the Dimensioning - Architectural stencil. The Room Measure shape is misnamed; you can use it to measure anything. Look at the ruler and you can see that it also shows the desk is precisely 2' 6". By moving the shape so that its lines intersect the ruler, as shown in Figure 7-3, you can make precise measurements.

If you're not using a template or if you want to adjust the scale set by a template, you can set a drawing scale yourself. Here's the terminology you need to understand first:

✔ **Page units** represent the measurements on the printed page. For example, in a room layout drawing that uses ¼ inch to represent 1 foot of real-life objects, *inches* are the page units. An 8-foot couch measures 2 inches in page units.

✔ **Measurement units** represent the real-life measurement of objects in a drawing. For example, in the same room layout drawing that uses ¼ inch to represent 1 foot, *feet* are the measurement units. Therefore, 2 inches on the drawing represents 8 feet of a real-life object.

✔ **Drawing scale** is the ratio between page units and measurement units.

The larger the spread between page units and measurements units, the larger the area you can illustrate in a drawing. For example, you can represent a much larger area with a drawing scale of ⅛ inch:1 yard than you can with a drawing scale of ¼ inch:1 foot. However, as you decrease the scale, you also lose detail. It may be possible to see the details of a cabinet when you use a scale of ½ inch:1 foot, but these details are all but invisible when you set the scale to ⅛ inch:1 yard.

You can set a different drawing scale for individual pages in a drawing. For example, you might use a small scale to show the outside of an office building, a medium scale to show the office layout, and a large scale to show the details of an individual office. Likewise, you might draw a circuit board layout using a 1:1 scale, but you might show details of the Plated Through Hole (PTH) layout of an individual circuit element at a scale of 1 inch:¼ inch. The diagram is now actually larger than the physical device. The following steps describe how to set the scale for a diagram:

1. **Choose File⇨Page Setup.**

2. **Click the Drawing Scale tab.**

   You see the Page Setup dialog box shown in Figure 7-4.

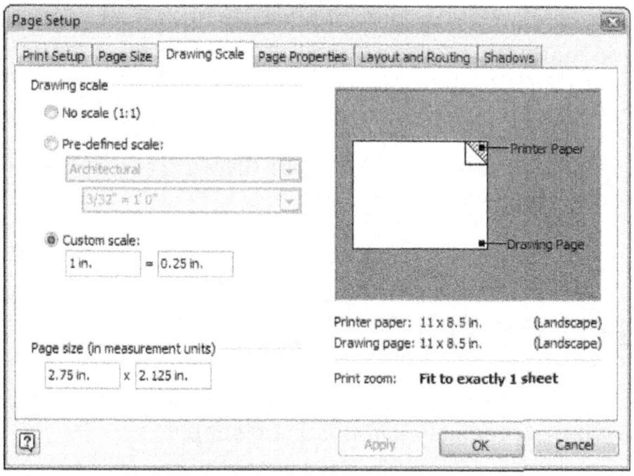

Figure 7-4:
Choose a predefined drawing scale or enter measurements for a custom scale.

Page Setup	
Print Setup | Page Size | **Drawing Scale** | Page Properties | Layout and Routing | Shadows	
Drawing scale	
○ No scale (1:1)	
○ Pre-defined scale:	Printer Paper
Architectural	
3/32" = 1' 0"	
● Custom scale:	Drawing Page
1 in. = 0.25 in.	
	Printer paper: 11 x 8.5 in. (Landscape)
Page size (in measurement units)	Drawing page: 11 x 8.5 in. (Landscape)
2.75 in. x 2.125 in.	Print zoom: **Fit to exactly 1 sheet**
?	Apply OK Cancel

3. Select the No Scale, Pre-defined Scale, or Custom Scale option.

- Select the No Scale option for diagrams that don't require a scale, such as a flowchart or block diagram.

- Choose Pre-defined Scale for an architectural, civil engineering, metric, or mechanical engineering scale. The options in the first drop-down list box contain the scale type: Architectural, Civil Engineering, Metric, and Mechanical Engineering. Visio automatically selects the most common scale for the scale type in the second drop-down list box. However, you can choose other common scales from this second drop-down list box.

- Choose Custom Scale when none of the predefined scales fit your particular need. Type a number and units in the first box for page units and a number and units in the second box for measurement units. For fractional units, enter the decimal equivalent, such as .125 in. for ⅛ inch.

4. Type the length and width of your diagram in the Page Size field when necessary.

These numbers tell you how large an area you can represent in your drawing. The default page size shows how much area you can represent on a single sheet of paper. For example, when you use an 8½-inch-x-11-inch piece of paper, a diagram drawn to a scale of ½ inch:1 foot provides 17 feet x 22 feet of drawing space. If the area isn't large enough, either increase your page units or change the page size. Changing the page size means that you'll need more than one sheet of paper to print the diagram or that you'll need to use a larger sheet of paper.

5. Before leaving this dialog box, click the Page Properties tab.

Notice that Visio automatically sets the measurement units for the current page to match the setting you chose in Step 4.

6. Click OK.

Visio automatically adjusts the scale in your drawing (as well as the ruler scale) to the new settings you chose.

Snapping Shapes into Place

Snap is a terrific Visio feature. You can't imagine how much time you waste trying to place shapes precisely *without* using snap.

The Snap feature in Visio works like a magnet. When snap is turned on, a shape jumps to certain points as you drag it around the drawing area. You can attach a shape to any of the following elements:

- **Ruler subdivisions:** Tick marks that appear on the ruler (1 inch, ½ inch, ¼ inch, and so on)

- **Grid:** Horizontal and vertical graph lines in the drawing area

- **Alignment box:** A shape's frame (displayed only when a shape is selected)

- **Shape extensions:** Dotted lines that extend out from a shape (such as the horizontal or vertical line of the edges of a rectangle)

- **Shape geometry:** The visible edges of a shape

- **Guides:** Special lines or points that you add to a drawing to help you align shapes

- **Shape intersections:** The points at which shapes intersect

- **Shape handles:** The square green handles on a selected shape that you use to resize the shape

- **Shape vertices:** The green diamond-shaped points on a shape where lines come together

- **Connection points:** Blue *X*s that appear on shapes when View➪ Connection Points is selected

When using snap features, it's helpful to display the Snap & Glue toolbar, which includes the buttons shown in Table 7-2. Note that many of these buttons mirror the Snap & Glue dialog box settings in the preceding list.

Visio turns on snap automatically for rulers, gridlines, connection points, and guides. This means that whenever you drag a shape around the drawing area, the shape jumps (whether you notice it or not) to align itself to ruler subdivisions, gridlines, guides, or connection points on other shapes. For example, suppose you want to space three rectangles ½ inch apart. As you drag the shapes, they jump to the nearest gridline or ruler subdivision, placing the rectangles exactly ½ inch apart. You could line up these shapes using the rulers and the grid as a visual guide, but why spend more time than you need to when Visio's snap feature helps you do it automatically?

Of course, it's easy to introduce too much snap into your diagram as well. The type of snap you use depends on the diagram you're creating. In many cases, such as a flowchart, all you really need to do is snap to a fixed grid. Floor plans may require that you snap only to the ruler. Organizational charts or UML diagrams may require that you snap only to the connection points because the connection point is the focus of the diagram's connectivity. Some diagrams, such as electrical layouts or engineering diagrams, work out best when you don't use any snap because using snap makes it difficult to place shapes precisely. The problem with introducing too much snap is that you can actually make it more difficult to align shapes. Maintain the simplest work environment that you can by keeping snap under control.

Along with choosing snap elements, you get to set the *strength* of snap. It's like choosing between a tiny refrigerator magnet and a 10-pound horseshoe magnet. The bigger the magnet, the harder snap pulls. Generally, you must set the strength of the snap when you combine multiple forms of snap. Setting the snap strength lets you bias the snap from a ruler over the snap from the grid when you want to favor ruler positions. The following steps describe how to set the snap strength:

1. **Choose Tools⇨Snap & Glue.**

   The Snap & Glue dialog box appears, as shown in Figure 7-5.

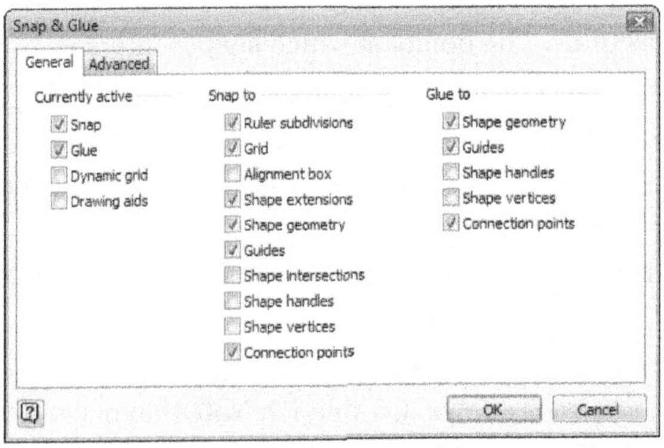

Figure 7-5:
Choose the elements you want shapes to snap to.

2. **Select the snap types that you want to activate in the Snap To area.**

3. **Click the Advanced tab.**

   You see the advanced options shown in Figure 7-6. Notice the Snap Strength options. The number of pixels is the important factor. In this case, the object you want to snap must appear within 4 pixels of a ruler increment in order to snap to the increment. If the shape is 5 pixels away, the shape won't snap. Items with higher numbers have a stronger snap.

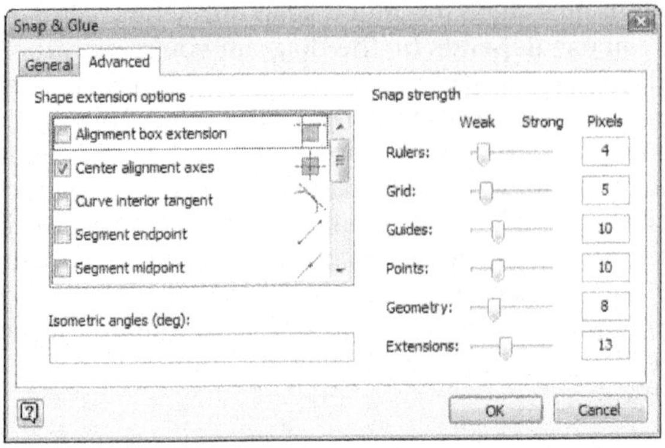

Figure 7-6:
Define the strength of snap for each of the snap types you selected.

4. **Set the snap strength for each of the snap types you selected in Step 3.**

5. **Click OK.**

 If you want to turn snap off altogether, click the Toggle Snap button on the Snap & Glue toolbar, or choose Tools➪Snap & Glue and deselect the Snap box in the Currently Active area of the dialog box. Shapes move freely as you drag them around the drawing area when you turn snap off.

Measuring Up with Rulers

Some drawings don't require rulers. For instance, if your drawing is completely abstract (that is, completely unrelated to real-world shapes), such as a flowchart or an audit diagram, rulers are meaningless. You don't care whether your shapes are 1 inch wide or 1¼ inches wide; it doesn't change the meaning of the information your drawing conveys. The only thing you really care about is whether your drawing fits on the page. When you work with a scaled drawing, however, accurate measurements are essential. By displaying vertical and horizontal rulers in a drawing, you can instantly see the size of a shape and how much space you have on the drawing page.

In unscaled Visio drawings, rulers typically display either inches or centimeters, depending on the template of the drawing type you chose. (Recall that almost all drawing types are available in English or metric units.) Scaled drawings typically display either feet or meters, but you have many other choices. For example, you might want to use yards for drawings that represent real-life objects, such as landscape plans. If you use the metric system, you might want to switch ruler units to centimeters or millimeters.

Don't always associate the ruler with physical elements. For example, you can set the ruler to points (½ inch) or picas (⅙ inch) when you're working with text. Speaking of text, Visio also supports esoteric units of measure such as the *didot* (1 didot ≈ 1.07 points; 67.567 didots ≈ 1 inch) and the *cicero* (12 didots, 5.63 ciceros ≈ 1 inch).

 Using a larger scale on the ruler makes the ruler easier to read, but reduces the accuracy of the measurements you can take. Using a smaller increment has the opposite effect. Zooming in adds increments to the rule, while zooming out removes them. You can choose to measure inches in fractions or as a decimal value; the same holds true for feet. Using a decimal scale changes the increments on the ruler. The point is that the rule is extremely flexible so you should try various settings to see which one works best for your particular diagram.

Changing the units that the ruler displays does nothing to change the drawing scale. Scale is a *ratio* of units displayed on the page (or screen) to real-life measurements. The ruler changes only the units displayed in a drawing, not their scale. The following steps describe how to change the ruler settings:

1. **Choose File➪Page Setup.**

   The Page Setup dialog box appears.

2. **Click the Page Properties tab.**

3. **Click the drop-down arrow for Measurement Units (see Figure 7-7) and select the units you want to use for the current page.**

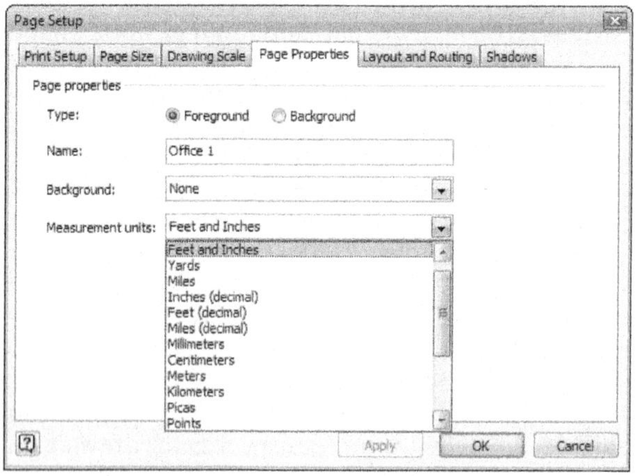

Figure 7-7:
Select the measurement units for the current page.

4. **Click OK.**

Visio changes the ruler's measurement units for only the current page. If your drawing contains multiple pages, you can display different ruler units on other pages. Just display the correct drawing page before using the preceding steps, or choose the correct page in the Name drop-down list in the Page Setup dialog box.

The *zero point* for the rulers (the point where 0 appears on a ruler) is generally in the lower-left corner of the drawing page, but you can change this position. If you want a symmetrical drawing, you might move the ruler's zero points to the middle of the page, draw half of a drawing, and then mirror it. Or suppose you're drawing an office layout. You might find the drawing easier to work with if you move the zero points to align with the left and upper walls so you can measure distances from that point (see Figure 7-8).

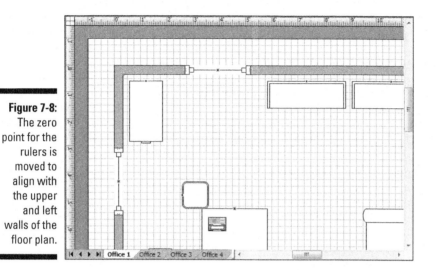

Figure 7-8:
The zero point for the rulers is moved to align with the upper and left walls of the floor plan.

You can set the ruler using the Ruler & Grid dialog box shown in Figure 7-1 (see the "Using the Drawing Grid" section, earlier in this chapter, for details). However, the faster method is to make changes directly to the ruler on-screen. The following steps describe how to perform this task:

1. **Move the mouse pointer to the gray square where the vertical ruler and horizontal ruler intersect (in the upper-left corner of the drawing area).**

    The mouse pointer changes to a four-headed arrow.

2. **Hold down the Ctrl key and drag the mouse to the new location for the zero point of both rulers.**

    As you move your mouse, watch the faint dotted line that appears on each ruler, marking the position of the mouse.

3. **Release the mouse button when the zero point is positioned where you want it.**

If you want to change the zero point of just one ruler, use the same basic procedure, but drag from one ruler only. For example, if you want to place the zero point on the horizontal ruler 2 inches in from the left edge of the paper, follow these steps:

1. **Point to the vertical ruler until you see the double-headed arrow mouse pointer.**

    That's right. To change the zero point on the horizontal ruler, you point to the vertical ruler.

2. **Hold down the Ctrl key and drag the mouse until the vertical line is positioned where you want the zero point on the horizontal ruler.**

To reset the zero points of both rulers to their default position, double-click the intersection of the rulers (in the upper-left corner of the drawing area).

Using Guide Lines and Guide Points

Any diagram that requires you to create complex combinations of shapes and text can benefit from guide lines and guide points. *Guide lines* and *guide points* work in combination with the Snap feature. Use guide lines when you want a number of shapes to line up with each other. Use guide points when you want to pinpoint a shape in an exact location. Many people call guides by other names, the most popular of which is construction lines.

You have two options for aligning shapes with guide lines and guide points. Visio lets you glue or snap the shapes to the guide. Gluing the shapes is preferable when you want to use connection points as a source of alignment. Snapping the shapes is preferable when you want to use the sides as a source of alignment. Before your guides will perform any work, you must enable this feature. The following steps tell you how to perform this task:

1. **Choose Tools⇨Snap & Glue.**

   You see the Snap & Glue dialog box.

2. **Select Guides in either the Snap To or Glue To list.**

3. **Click the Advanced tab.**

4. **Set the Guides Snap Strength value high enough to ensure the guides work as anticipated.**

   Use your personal preference when setting this value. Generally, higher is better. A value of between 20 and 30 normally provides the best performance.

5. **Click OK.**

After you finish enabling the guides, you can create diagrams that have horizontal or vertical guides. Figure 7-9 shows a simple use for both guide orientations. Notice that the lines help you align the shapes faster and with less effort. As with most objects, guides change color when you select them to move them or perform other tasks. The default colors for guides are green when selected and blue when not selected.

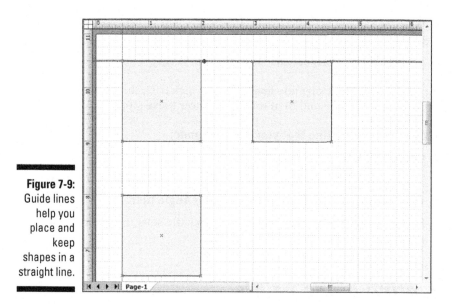

Figure 7-9:
Guide lines
help you
place and
keep
shapes in a
straight line.

The useful thing about guide lines and guide points is that you can move them. When you glue the shapes to the guide line or guide point, the shape moves with it. This feature is helpful when you want to move a number of shapes at once and ensure they remain aligned. Otherwise, when you simply snap the shape to the guide line or guide point, only the guide line or guide point moves; the shape remains in place. This feature lets you change the guide to meet new alignment needs without changing existing shapes. In fact, you can use the existing shapes as a means of ensuring correct placement of the guide line or guide point.

Creating guide lines

Guide lines appear as single lines across the display. You can orient them horizontally or vertically as needed. A guide line includes a center of rotation handle that you can move. Choose one of the options from the Shape⇨Rotate or Flip menu to rotate the guide line as needed around the center of rotation. The following steps describe how to create a guide line:

1. **Move your mouse pointer over the vertical ruler (to create a vertical guide) or over the horizontal ruler (to create a horizontal guide) until the mouse pointer changes to a double-headed arrow.**

2. **Drag the mouse pointer.**

   As you drag, the guide appears as a blue line that runs up and down (or across) the drawing page.

3. **When the guide is positioned where you want it, release the mouse button.**

   The line turns green because it's selected.

Want to create a diagonal guide line? Here's a slick trick. Just create a horizontal or vertical guide and then rotate it. Follow these steps:

1. **Select the guide line that you want to rotate.**

2. **Choose View➪Size & Position Window.**

   The Size & Position window appears near the bottom of your screen.

3. **Type the degree angle of rotation in the Angle field.**

   For a diagonal guide, type **45**. Visio rotates the selected guide to the angle that you specify.

Creating guide points

When you want to pinpoint a shape in an exact location, create a *guide point*. Guide points are an excellent method for creating a shape-within-a-shape and align the shapes automatically. A guide point looks like a circle with a cross through it on-screen. The following steps describe how to create a guide point:

1. **Move your mouse pointer over the intersection of the vertical and horizontal rulers.**

   The mouse pointer changes to a four-headed arrow.

2. **Drag the mouse.**

   Two blue lines — one vertical and one horizontal — follow the movement of the mouse pointer on the drawing page.

3. **When the intersection of the guides is positioned where you want it, release the mouse button.**

   The blue lines disappear, and the guide point (a circle with a cross through it) is displayed on the screen.

As with guide lines, guide points rely on snap or glue. When you glue the shapes to the guide point, you can move all of the shapes by moving the guide point. The biggest difference is that all of the shapes align to the same center, as shown in Figure 7-10.

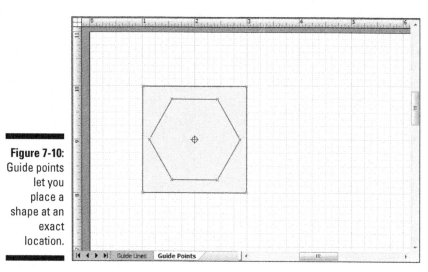

Figure 7-10:
Guide points
let you
place a
shape at an
exact
location.

If you want to use multiple guides spaced evenly across your drawing, here is a great way to create them:

1. **Create the first guide.**

2. **Hold down the Ctrl key as you drag a copy of the guide to the next increment you want — say, 1 inch.**

3. **Press the F4 key.**

   Visio automatically creates another guide 1 inch from the last guide.

4. **Press F4 as many times as you want to keep creating guides spaced at the same increment.**

Aligning and Distributing Shapes

Besides using guides, Visio gives you another way to align shapes automatically using the alignment tools. With the click of a toolbar button (or through a menu command), you can horizontally align the top, bottom, or middle of selected shapes, or you can vertically align the left edge, right edge, or middle of selected shapes. You first select the shape you want other shapes to align to and then select all the other shapes using the Ctrl+Click method. The first shape you select becomes the reference point for the alignment of other shapes.

To use the alignment tools, display the Action toolbar. The Align Shapes button has a drop-down box, which displays a miniversion of the alignment options available. These options are also available in the Align Shapes dialog box when you choose Shape⇨Align Shapes, as shown in Figure 7-11. (To make this menu command active, you must first select at least two shapes in the drawing.)

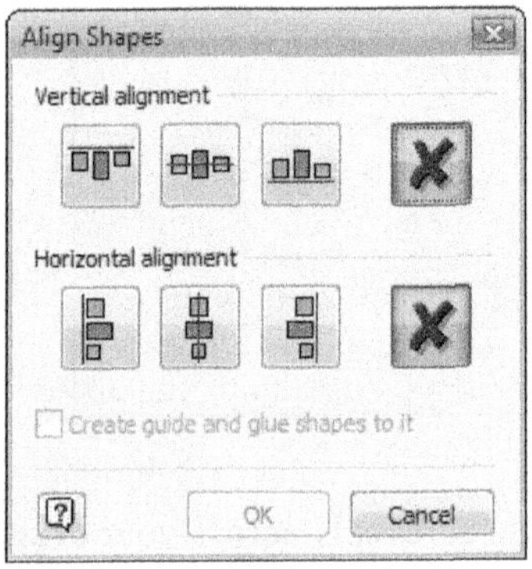

Figure 7-11:
Choose a
vertical or
horizontal
alignment.

To align several shapes horizontally, vertically, or both, use these steps:

1. **Select the shape to which you want the other shapes to align.**

2. **Hold down the Ctrl key and at the same time select all the other shapes that you want to be aligned to the first shape.**

3. **Choose Shape⇨Align Shapes or click the drop-down arrow next to the Align Shapes button on the Shapes toolbar.**

   The Align Shapes dialog box appears (refer to Figure 7-11).

4. **Click the alignment style that you want.**

   If you think you'll be adding more shapes that you'll want to have aligned with these, consider selecting the Create Guide and Glue Shapes to It check box, which is at the bottom of the dialog box.

5. **Click OK.**

   Visio aligns all shapes to the first shape that you selected.

Have you ever tried to space several shapes evenly — say, ½ inch apart — across an area? Doing it manually can be frustrating. Visio refers to the process of spacing shapes evenly as *distributing* shapes. You can distribute shapes by clicking the Distribute Shapes toolbar button (or by using a menu command, if you prefer). Like the Align Shapes toolbar button, the Distribute Shapes button also has a drop-down box, which displays a miniversion of the Distribute Shapes dialog box shown in Figure 7-12.

Use these steps to distribute shapes across an area:

1. **Select all the shapes that you want to distribute.**

2. **Choose Shape⇨Distribute Shapes or click the drop-down arrow on the Distribute Shapes button on the Action toolbar.**

   The Distribute Shapes dialog box appears, as shown in Figure 7-12.

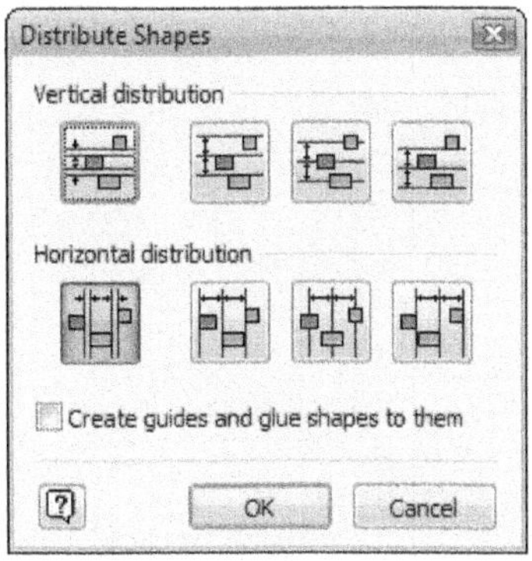

Figure 7-12:
Choose a
distribution
style.

3. **Click the distribution style that you want to use.**

   If you think that you may add more shapes that you'll want to distribute, consider selecting the Create Guides and Glue Shapes to Them check box at the bottom of the dialog box.

4. **Click OK.**

   Visio automatically distributes the shapes.

Visio has many timesaving features. Take advantage of the flexibility you have to focus on the content of a drawing, and then use Visio's features to help you perfect your drawing.

Chapter 8

Creating and Customizing Shapes

. . . .

In This Chapter

▶ Customizing shapes by using fun Visio tools

▶ Creating your own shapes

▶ Manipulating shapes

▶ Adding character to your shapes

▶ Grouping and stacking shapes

. . . .

Because Visio provides so many shapes in its stencils, you can use the program successfully without ever needing to customize shapes. However, sometimes you need to create your own shapes. For example, you might need a new shape for a floor plan that isn't included in the standard stencil. Developers might need to add new shapes when describing an application's structure. Because Visio is so flexible, you might decide to create specialized stencils for your own diagram types. For example, imagine you work in a store and want to organize products on shelves to see how they fit best. A special stencil that has all of the standard product sizes would help you perform this task.

In this chapter, you discover how to get creative with Visio by changing existing shapes and drawing your own shapes. Although this chapter uses a diagram to hold the new shapes, you'll eventually discover how to add these shapes to a stencil in Chapter 11. It's also important to realize that you don't have to be a draftsperson or budding artist to create new shapes. Many shapes are combinations of existing shapes and perhaps a few well-placed lines. Generally, you can let the professionals do all of the heavy lifting for you and concentrate on a few tweaks.

Creating Unique Shapes the Fun Way

In many cases, you can create all of the new shapes you need by combining existing shapes. Near the middle of the Visio Shape menu is a submenu named Operations that contains a number of tools you use to combine shapes in various ways. The following list explains each tool:

- **Union:** Creates a shape from overlapping shapes by using the perimeter of all the shapes as the new outline

- **Combine:** Creates a shape from overlapping shapes by cutting out the areas that overlap

- **Fragment:** Breaks shapes into separate shapes along the lines where they overlap

- **Intersect:** Creates a shape from *only* the area where two or more shapes overlap (all other areas are deleted)

- **Subtract:** Cuts away the areas that overlap the first shape you select

It might take you a while to remember exactly what each command does. That's okay; just experiment with them. If you don't like the result, choose Edit⇨Undo and try another one. The following sections illustrate how each of these commands work — they're easier to see than read about.

The first shape you select determines the attributes of the resulting shape after an operation. For example, when the first shape you select is yellow, the resulting shape is also yellow. Consequently, the order in which you select the shapes is important. However, the order doesn't affect the result. No matter which order you use to select the shapes, a combination always produces the same result.

You can always undo an operation by clicking Undo on the Standard toolbar. However, after you perform an operation and close Visio, the change is permanent; you can't undo it by performing one of the other operations. In many cases, you can still use the resulting shape as a template for re-creating the individual shapes used to create it. Simply drag and drop the original shapes onto the resulting shape and align the various shape lines.

You'll discover how to use a lot of Visio's drawing, formatting, and manipulation tools throughout this chapter, so you might want to open some of the toolbars listed in Table 8-1 now. Unless stated otherwise, use the Pointer Tool in the instructional steps for selecting shapes.

Table 8-1   Toolbar Buttons for Drawing and Manipulating Shapes

Button	Name	Toolbar	What It Does
	Arc Tool	Drawing	Lets you draw an arc shape
	Bring to Front	Action	Brings a shape to the top of the stack in the stacking order
	Ellipse Tool	Drawing	Lets you draw circles and ovals (ellipses)
	Flip Horizontal	Action	Flips a shape from the left to the right
	Flip Vertical	Action	Flips a shape from the top to the bottom
	Format Painter	Standard	Lets you apply formatting from one shape to another
	Freeform Tool	Drawing	Lets you draw freehand using curves and lines
	Lasso Select	Standard	Allows you to draw a lasso (an irregular shape) around the shapes you want to select
	Line Tool	Drawing	Lets you draw a straight line
	Pencil Tool	Drawing	Lets you draw lines, arcs, or circles depending on how you move the mouse
	Pointer Tool	Standard	The standard pointer tool for selecting shapes
	Rectangle Tool	Drawing	Draws rectangles and squares

(continued)

Table 8-1 *(continued)*

Button	Name	Toolbar	What It Does
	Rotate Right	Action	Turns a shape 90 degrees to the right
	Rotate Left	Action	Turns a shape 90 degrees to the left
	Send to Back	Action	Sends a shape to the bottom of the stack in the stacking order

Uniting shapes

The Union command does as its name suggests — it *unites* two or more over-lapping shapes. The Union command combines these shapes by maintaining the perimeters of all the shapes and erasing their inside boundaries to form one new shape.

The following steps describe how to unite several shapes.

1. **Drag the shapes that you want to unite into the drawing area.**

   If you want to draw shapes, draw them now.

2. **Move the shapes where you want them, making sure each one over-laps at least one other shape.**

3. **Select all the shapes that you want to unite using the Pointer Tool.**

4. **Choose Shape⇨Operations⇨Union.**

   Visio unites all the shapes, as shown in Figure 8-1.

If some of the shapes you select don't overlap, the Union command still unites them, even though they don't appear to be any different. Try selecting one by itself and you'll see that Visio now treats them as one shape.

Union is different from Group in that the borders where shapes overlap are eliminated when you unite them. Grouping simply treats selected shapes as a single shape.

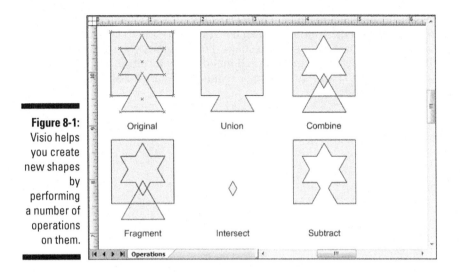

Figure 8-1:
Visio helps
you create
new shapes
by
performing
a number of
operations
on them.

Combining shapes

The Combine command does as its name says; it combines several shapes into a single shape. Combining shapes creates a cutout where two shapes overlap. If a third shape overlaps the previous two shapes in an area, you see the part of the shape that overlaps both. The cutout and inclusion of shape elements continue to alternate until Visio runs out of shapes to combine. Figure 8-1 shows how three shapes will look when combined. The diamond shape in the center is the result of an overlap of three shapes. The following steps describe how to combine several shapes:

1. **Draw all the shapes that you want to combine.**

2. **Arrange the shapes so that they overlap.**

3. **Select all the shapes that you want to combine using the Pointer Tool.**

4. **Choose Shape➪Operations➪Combine.**

    Visio combines the shapes as shown in Figure 8-1.

When you combine shapes that don't overlap, there isn't anything for Visio to do. However, Visio still combines the shapes and treats them as a single shape, just as the Union command does.

Fragmenting shapes

Fragmenting cuts overlapped shapes apart wherever they overlap, as shown in Figure 8-1. Many people miss the opportunity to use fragmentation because it doesn't appear to do anything worthwhile, so this section spends a little more time with this operation. You can use fragmentation to create a new shape that is only part of an original shape. For example, you might take the middle out of a couch and create a sectional piece of furniture by fragmenting the standard couch shape with a line or rectangle. Figure 8-2 shows an example of this technique.

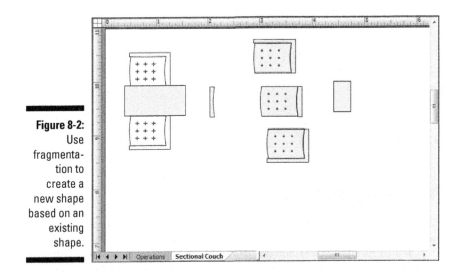

Figure 8-2:
Use fragmenta-
tion to
create a
new shape
based on an
existing
shape.

To create this shape, you begin by dragging and dropping the Sofa shape from the Furniture stencil. Draw a rectangle over the top of the sofa as shown on the left side of Figure 8-2; make sure that the top and bottom of the rectangle align with the center section. The right and left of the rectangle must appear outside of the sofa. The following steps describe how to fragment several shapes:

1. **Drag all the shapes that you want into the drawing area or draw new ones.**

2. **Arrange the shapes so that they overlap.**

3. **Select all the overlapping shapes using the Pointer Tool.**

4. **Choose Shape⇨Operations⇨Fragment.**

   Visio breaks all the shapes into separate shapes along their overlapping lines.

At this point, you can finish the sectional sofa. Draw a box around the right remainder of the rectangle and click Group on the Action toolbar. Drag this piece of the rectangle away from the remainder of the sofa just to be sure that you didn't group part of the sofa that you need. Now, you can delete that unnecessary portion. Group each remaining piece of the sofa in turn. You'll end up with five pieces, as shown on the right side of Figure 8-2, two of which you'll delete.

Intersecting shapes

The Intersect command makes a radical change in your shapes. Visio keeps only the parts where *all* the shapes overlap and cuts away the rest. As with fragmenting, you can use this technique to use parts of existing shapes. Unlike fragmentation, you don't get to keep the whole shape, just the part that all of the selected shapes overlap. The following steps describe how to intersect several shapes:

1. **Drag all the shapes that you want into the drawing area or draw them.**

2. **Arrange the shapes so that they *all* overlap every other shape at some point.**

3. **Select all the shapes that you want to intersect using the Pointer Tool.**

4. **Choose Shape⇨Operations⇨Intersect.**

   Visio leaves only the portion where *all* shapes overlap, removing the extraneous parts, as shown in Figure 8-1.

Subtracting shapes

Subtract is a feature that works just like it sounds: When two shapes overlap, the overlapping part is subtracted, or removed, from the first shape that you select. This command subtracts the *second* shape you select from the *first* shape you select. The first shape you select, then, is the shape that remains — in part — after using the Subtract command. The following steps describe how to subtract several shapes:

1. **Drag the shapes that you want to work with into the drawing area or draw new shapes.**

2. **Position the shapes so that they overlap.**

3. **Select the shape that you want to keep using the Pointer Tool.**

4. **Select the shape that you want to subtract.**

5. **Choose Shape⇨Operations⇨Subtract.**

   Visio removes the shape that you selected in Step 4 and leaves what remains of the shape that you selected in Step 3, as shown in Figure 8-1.

Subtraction is the one operation where selection order does matter. The first shape is the one that provides the base material. All subsequent selections subtract from the first. Figure 8-3 shows an example of three different results using the same starting point. Notice that selecting the star first subtracts everything because the rectangle completely encloses the star. Visio places a heavier magenta selection rectangle around the first shape you select so you can see how other selections will affect it.

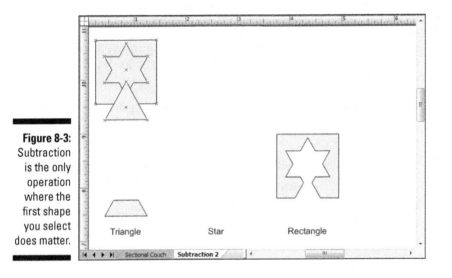

Figure 8-3:
Subtraction is the only operation where the first shape you select does matter.

Restacking shapes

Each time you draw or drag a new shape into the drawing area, Visio places it on top of other, existing shapes. (If you don't overlap the shapes, you never notice this.) To understand how Visio keeps track of the order of shapes, pretend that you are drawing each shape on a separate piece of paper. Each time you draw a shape, you drop the paper on your desk. The first one to fall is at the bottom of the stack. Those that fall on top of others clearly overlap one another. Those that don't overlap *still fall in a stacking order,* whether you pay attention to it or not. The last one you drop is at the top of the stack.

Visio has two commands — Bring to Front and Send to Back — to help you rearrange the stacking order of shapes. You can find both buttons on the Action toolbar. You also can go to the Shape menu and find two other commands for restacking: Bring Forward and Send Backward. (You can display the Action toolbar by right-clicking the toolbar area and choosing Action.) What's the difference between all these? Here's the lowdown:

✔ **Bring to Front:** Brings a shape to the top of the stack

✔ **Bring Forward:** Brings a shape up one level in the stack

✔ **Send to Back:** Sends a shape to the bottom of the stack

✔ **Send Backward:** Sends a shape down one level in the stack

Bring Forward and Send Backward are found only on the Shape menu, but you can add buttons for these commands to the Action toolbar by customizing your toolbar. To find out more about customizing toolbars, refer to Chapter 1.

Figure 8-4 shows the results of using several of these commands on the star. The star is in the middle of the shapes at the beginning. Using each of the commands moves the star to a new position within the stack.

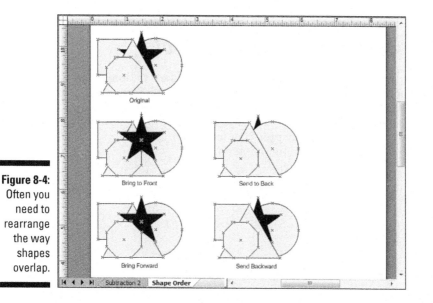

Figure 8-4:
Often you need to rearrange the way shapes overlap.

You can see a little more of the star when you use the Bring Forward command, but the Bring to Front command shows everything. The following steps describe how to rearrange several shapes:

1. **Select the shape that you want to move.**

2. **Determine which command or button you need to use: Bring Forward, Bring to Front, Send Backward, or Send to Back.**

3. **Click the Bring to Front button or the Send to Back button on the Shape toolbar, or choose Shape⇨Order⇨Bring Forward or Shape⇨Order ⇨Send Backward.**

   Visio moves the shape as you specify within the stack order.

4. **Repeat Step 3 if necessary.**

If you prefer using shortcut keys, press Ctrl+Shift+F for Bring to Front or Ctrl+Shift+B for Send to Back.

Drawing Your Own Shapes

As if there weren't enough shapes for you to choose from in Visio, you can make your own, too. You might find that you often make your own shapes, particularly if you work in a specialized field. Visio gives you many buttons on the Drawing toolbar for drawing shapes (refer to Table 8-1).

Drawing with the Line Tool

You can use the Line Tool button on the Standard toolbar to draw lines or shapes that are made up of straight lines. The points at which you start and stop drawing a line are called *endpoints* (see Figure 8-5). Between the two endpoints is a *control point,* which you use to control the shape of a shape, as discussed later in this chapter. (For more information about working with control points, refer also to Chapter 4.)

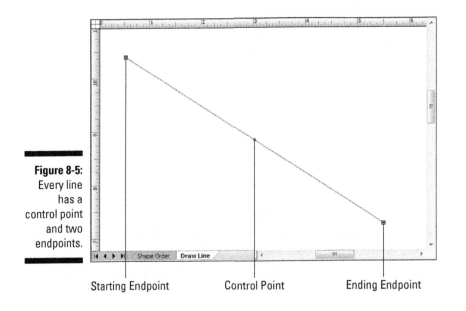

Figure 8-5:
Every line
has a
control point
and two
endpoints.

Starting Endpoint   Control Point   Ending Endpoint

As shown in Figure 8-5, Visio marks the ends of the lines using two boxes. The first, the beginning endpoint, includes an *X*. The second, the ending endpoint, includes a plus symbol (+). The following steps describe how to draw a line:

1. Click the Line Tool (refer to Table 8-1) on the Drawing toolbar.

The mouse pointer changes to a line and a plus symbol.

2. Place the mouse pointer where you want to begin the line; then drag the mouse to the point where you want the line to end.

As you drag the mouse, you see a guide line that extends from the starting point to the location of your pointer. The guide line shows you where Visio will draw the line when you release the mouse button. Move the mouse around in a circle and you see that the guide line follows your movement. At every 45-degree interval, the guide line shoots out into a ray. This feature helps you draw lines at perfect 45-, 90-, 135-, and 180-degree angles from your starting point.

3. Release the mouse button.

Visio draws the line, selects it, and displays the endpoints. (Switch to the Pencil Tool on the Drawing toolbar if you want to display the control point.)

4. Click any blank area of the drawing to deselect the line.

It's not often that you draw a single line by itself. More than likely, you'll want to draw a shape by connecting a series of line segments. The trick, here, is that you must draw all segments consecutively if you want to create a closed shape. If you don't draw them consecutively, Visio won't close the shape, even if the segments appear to be connected. The following steps describe how to draw a line that connects to a line that you drew previously:

1. Select the line you want to connect to using the Pointer Tool if you have already drawn a line.

Visio highlights the line.

2. Click the Line Tool on the Drawing toolbar.

The mouse pointer changes to a line and a plus symbol.

3. Draw your first segment by dragging the mouse and releasing if you haven't already created a line.

Visio draws the line, selects it, and displays the endpoints.

4. Point to the endpoint of the selected segment; then drag the mouse to draw the next segment of your shape.

Visio draws the next line in the sequence and selects it. You see an Extend Shape pointer, rather than the standard endpoint, as shown in Figure 8-6.

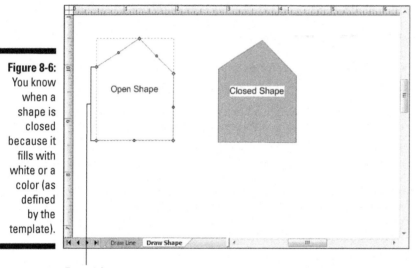

Figure 8-6:
You know
when a
shape is
closed
because it
fills with
white or a
color (as
defined
by the
template).

Extend Shape

5. **Repeat Step 4 as many times as you want.**

6. **To close the shape, draw another segment from the endpoint of the last segment that you drew, to the beginning point of the first segment that you drew, and then release the mouse button.**

The shape becomes a *closed* shape. You see the shape fill with white (or another color, depending on the template or theme you choose). The ability to use a theme is new in Visio 2007 and makes setting the shape attributes significantly easier. The "Using Themes" section of Chapter 4 contains details about using themes. See Figure 8-6 to see the effect of closing a shape.

If your background color is white and your grid is turned off, you can't see the white fill.

Whenever you draw shapes by connecting segments, turn on Snap (choose Tools➪Snap & Glue), the feature that pulls shapes into place. Snap helps you connect segments automatically. To find out more about how Snap works, refer to Chapter 7.

Drawing with the Pencil Tool

The Pencil Tool works almost exactly like the Line Tool. If you select the Pencil Tool and move the mouse in a straight line, you draw a straight line. If you move the mouse in a curved direction, you draw a portion of a circle. The size and circumference of the circle depend on how far you move the mouse. Use the Pencil Tool when you want to draw a shape that includes both curves and lines.

To create a closed shape, you must draw all segments (lines and arcs) consecutively as you would when using the Line Tool. The following steps describe how to draw using the Pencil Tool:

1. **Click the Pencil Tool (refer to Table 8-1) on the Standard toolbar.**

2. **Draw the first segment by dragging the mouse and then releasing the mouse button.**

   Drag in a straight line to create a line; drag in a circular direction to create a curve.

3. **Draw the next segment by pointing to the endpoint of the previous segment, dragging the mouse and then releasing the mouse button.**

4. **Repeat the motion in Step 3 as many times as you like.**

5. **Finish the shape by connecting the endpoint of the last segment to the beginning point of the first segment.**

Drawing with the Arc Tool

It might seem obvious that you draw an arc by using the Arc Tool, but you might be wondering how the Arc Tool differs from the Pencil Tool, which also lets you draw arcs. The Arc Tool lets you draw one quarter of an ellipse, whereas the Pencil Tool enables you to draw a portion of a circle (not an ellipse and not limited to one quarter). Use the Arc Tool when you want a less-than-circular curve (such as an oval). Use the Pencil Tool when you want to draw true circular curves. (See the "Creating shapes with the Ellipse and Rectangle Tool" section, later in this chapter, to find out how to use the Ellipse Tool button to draw complete circles and ellipses.) The following steps describe how to draw an arc:

1. **Click the Arc Tool (refer to Table 8-1) on the Standard toolbar.**

2. **Place the mouse where you want the arc to begin.**

3. **Drag the mouse in the direction that you want the arc to go.**

4. **Release the mouse button where you want the arc to end.**

Creating irregular shapes
with the Freeform Tool

The Freeform Tool helps you create lines that aren't straight or circular. You use it the same way you use a pencil when you're doodling. The Freeform Tool obediently displays every curve and scribble you make. Just click the Freeform Tool to create freeform shapes. To create a closed shape like the one shown in Figure 8-7, end your drawing at the point where you began.

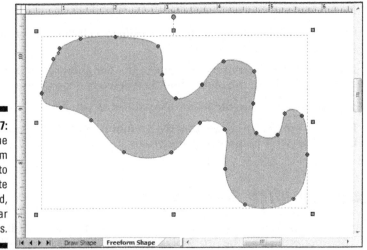

Figure 8-7:
Use the
Freeform
Tool to
create
curved,
irregular
shapes.

If you have a tablet PC or a tablet attached to your computer, the Freeform Tool is great because it's easier to draw with a pen than with a mouse.

Creating shapes with the Ellipse
Tool and Rectangle Tool

You can use the Arc Tool and Pencil Tool to draw curves (elliptical or circular), and you can use either of these buttons to draw four connected segments that form a complete circle or ellipse. Fortunately, Visio provides an easier way to draw both ellipses and circles. Just use the Ellipse Tool to draw perfect circles or ellipses. The following steps describe how to draw an ellipse or circle:

1. **Click the Ellipse Tool (refer to Table 8-1) on the Standard toolbar.**

2. **Put the mouse pointer where you want to place the ellipse.**

3. **Drag the mouse in any direction.**

   To draw a perfect circle, hold down the Shift key as you drag the mouse.

4. **Release the mouse button when the ellipse is the size and shape that you want.**

If you want the ellipse to be a particular size, watch the status bar as you drag the mouse. The status bar tells you the exact width and height of your ellipse as you draw. You can also choose Shape⇨Size and Position after you draw the shape and then enter exact dimensions in the Height and Width boxes.

The Rectangle Tool works in the same way as the Ellipse Tool. You could use the Line Tool to create a rectangle by drawing and connecting four segments, but it's easier to draw a rectangle by using the Rectangle Tool. The following steps describe how to draw a rectangle or square:

1. **Click the Rectangle Tool (refer to Table 8-1) on the Standard toolbar.**

2. **Put the mouse pointer where you want to place the rectangle.**

3. **Drag the mouse in any direction.**

   To draw a perfect square, hold down the Shift key as you drag the mouse. To create a rectangle of a specific size, watch the status bar for height and width measurements as you draw.

4. **Release the mouse button when the rectangle is the size and shape that you want.**

Manipulating Shapes

Visio provides a wealth of shapes, but they might not always appear precisely as you need them. For example, an electronic component might not have the leads oriented in the correct direction or a piece of furniture might point toward the wall when you drag it out of the stencil. A shape might also require a small correction to provide the correct appearance. For example, you might have to add a feature to a flowchart shape to account for a new instruction or flow control type. The following sections describe the methods you can use to manipulate shapes in Visio.

You can make your changes more precise by zooming in on your shape and using the rulers to track the movement of a control point. Avoid using Snap on irregular shapes because using Snap will cause the control points to move unevenly. Turn off Snap by choosing Tools⇨Snap & Glue. Deselect the Snap option on the General tab of the Snap & Glue dialog box and click OK.

Moving and adding vertices

With Visio, it's easy to change the form of a shape by dragging part of the shape to a new position. Figure 8-8 shows how you can change a standard triangle to another form by dragging one of the vertices to a new location. Remember that a *vertex* appears at the end of every line and at points where lines intersect, which means that you see a vertex at each point of the triangle. Green diamond shapes mark the vertices, but you can see them only when you select the shape by using one of the following buttons on the Standard toolbar (just click the button and then select the shape):

✔ Arc Tool

✔ Freeform Tool

✔ Line Tool

✔ Pencil Tool

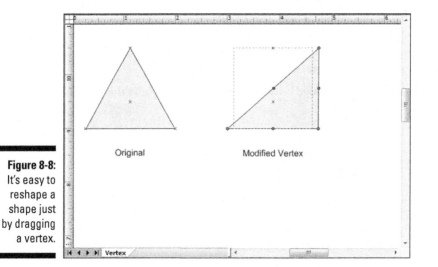

Original   Modified Vertex

Figure 8-8:
It's easy to
reshape a
shape just
by dragging
a vertex.

The following steps describe how to move a vertex:

1. **Select the Pencil, Freeform, Line, or Arc Tool (refer to Table 8-1).**

2. **Point to the vertex that you want to move.**

   When you're within *selection range* of the vertex, the mouse pointer changes to a four-headed arrow.

3. **Click the vertex.**

   The color changes from green to magenta.

4. **Drag the vertex where you want it, and then release the mouse button.**

You also can add a vertex to any shape by following these steps:

1. **Select the Pencil Tool.**

2. **Select the shape.**

   You see the vertices and control points of the shape.

3. **Hold down the Ctrl key, and click a point where you want to add a vertex.**

   Visio adds the vertex (diamond shape) and a control point (round shape) between the new vertex and the previous one.

4. **Repeat Step 3 for as many vertices as you want to add.**

When you add a vertex to a shape, you're actually adding a *segment*. That's because Visio automatically adds a control point between the new vertex and the previous one. You can use the control point to change the shape of the segment. See the next section of this chapter for details.

Why would you want to add a vertex to a shape? Check out the five-pointed star on the left side of Figure 8-9. It's not bad, but perhaps you want it to look a little snazzier — maybe with five smaller points between the five existing points. To accomplish this task, you need to add some vertices and move others. Currently, vertices appear at the tip of each point on the star and at each inverted angle of the star. (Even though the vertices are small and difficult to see in the figure, you'll see them clearly on your screen.)

To create the ten-pointed star (shown on the right side of Figure 8-9), add the vertices labeled B and C in the figure to each side of the star. After you add the vertices, pull the inverted angle vertex A out to a point. If you pull A without adding B and C, you just make a fatter star with shallower inverted angles. Adding the vertices B and C gives the new tip two new points from which to begin.

You always have alternatives in Visio. For example, perhaps you don't want to create the star shown in Figure 8-9 by adding vertices and moving out the corners. An alternative is to use two stars, one that is bigger (say 2 inches) and one that is smaller (say 1.5 inches). Use the Size & Position window to set the X and Y values for both stars the same. Now, set the Angle property of the smaller star to 36 for a five-pointed star (use 180 divided by the number of star points to determine the Angle property value). Select both stars and choose the Shape➪Operations➪Combine command to create a combined star. The result is the same as moving the vertices in most cases.

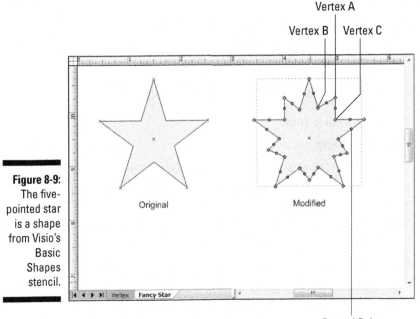

Vertex A

Vertex B   Vertex C

Original

Modified

Figure 8-9:
The five-
pointed star
is a shape
from Visio's
Basic
Shapes
stencil.

Control Point

Moving control points

Suppose that instead of adding five new points to the star in Figure 8-9, you just want to round out the lines of the star and make it look like one of the stars in Figure 8-10. You use the *control points,* the round shapes that appear between two vertices, to perform this task.

The following steps describe how to move a control point:

1. **Select the shape by using the Pointer Tool on the Standard toolbar.**

   You see the selection handles of the shape.

2. **Select the Pencil Tool.**

   You see the shape's vertices and control points.

3. **Point to the control point that you want to move.**

   The mouse pointer changes to a four-headed arrow.

4. **Click the control point.**

   The selected control point switches from green to magenta.

5. **Drag the control point, and then release the mouse button.**

   Visio rounds the line segment and moves it in or out with the mouse.

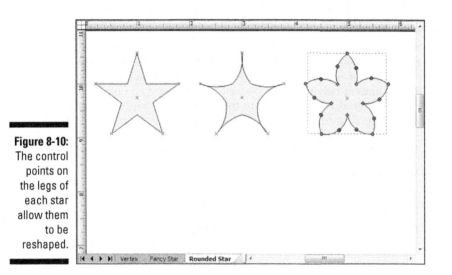

Figure 8-10:
The control points on the legs of each star allow them to be reshaped.

Rotating shapes

Rotating shapes helps you change the orientation of the shape to other shapes in the diagram. A shape might not be facing the correct angle when you drag it into the drawing or it might be easier to draw a shape at one angle and rotate it later.

You can rotate nearly all Visio shapes. If the shape has large, round handles that appear at the corners of its frame, you can rotate the shape. You also see a *rotation pin* (a round handle with a plus symbol) at the center of the shape. This is the point around which the shape rotates. (If a Visio shape can't rotate, it's for good reason — probably because it doesn't make sense to rotate it.) You can use any of the following methods to rotate a shape:

- ✔ **Rotation handles** on a shape let you drag the shape to rotate it. Use this method when you want to change a shape's angle quickly but not necessarily precisely.

- ✔ **Rotate Right and Rotate Left buttons** on the Action toolbar let you rotate a shape 90 degrees at a time (clockwise or counterclockwise). Use this method when you know you want to rotate a shape in 90-degree increments.

- ✔ **The menu command** (View➪Windows➪Size & Position) opens the Size & Position window, which lets you specify a rotation angle using the Angle property. This is the best method to use when the precise angle of rotation is a priority.

Rotation handles

A *rotation handle* is attached to a single shape or shapes that you group together. If you want to move a number of shapes to the same angle, select them and click Group on the Action toolbar. Even if you want to manipulate the shapes individually later, temporarily group them so you can change the angle. Click Ungroup when you want to manage the shapes individually. The following steps describe how to rotate a shape using the rotation handles:

1. **Click the Pointer Tool on the Standard toolbar.**

2. **Click the shape that you want to rotate.**

   The rotation handle, a large green circle, is visible usually somewhere near the top of the shape.

3. **Move the mouse pointer over the rotation handle.**

   The pointer changes to the rotation pointer, which looks like a circular, single-pointed arrow.

4. **Drag the mouse pointer clockwise or counterclockwise, depending on the direction that you want to rotate the shape.**

   As you drag the mouse, the mouse pointer changes to four arrows in a circular shape. Watch the status bar to see how far (in degrees) the shape is rotating.

5. **Release the mouse button when the shape is in the position that you want it.**

The closer you place the mouse to the rotation pin as you're rotating a shape, the more the rotation angle jumps, sometimes skipping degrees. The farther away you place the mouse pointer from the rotation pin, the more precise the angle of rotation.

Rotation buttons

Many diagrams require that you rotate a shape by 90 degrees. For example, you can create most floor plans by rotating shapes in 90-degree increments because many floor plans place walls in 90-degree angles. Electrical and electronic diagrams normally require only 90-degree angle changes as well. Consequently, the fastest way to rotate your shape in many cases is to use the rotation buttons. The following steps describe how to rotate a shape using the rotation buttons.

1. **Click the shape that you want to rotate.**

2. **Click the Rotate Right or Rotate Left button on the Action toolbar.**

   Visio rotates the shape in response to the command you select.

You can click the Rotate Right or Rotate Left button repeatedly to continue rotating the same shape in 90-degree increments. This method saves you the trouble of rotating a shape manually or using a menu command.

Size & Position window

When precision is important to you, use the Size & Position window to rotate shapes. You can rotate a shape at a precise angle, as little as .01 degrees. Use these steps to rotate a shape at a precise angle:

1. **Select the shape that you want to rotate.**

2. **Choose View⇨Size & Position or click Size & Position Window on the View toolbar.**

   The Size & Position window appears, as shown in Figure 8-11.

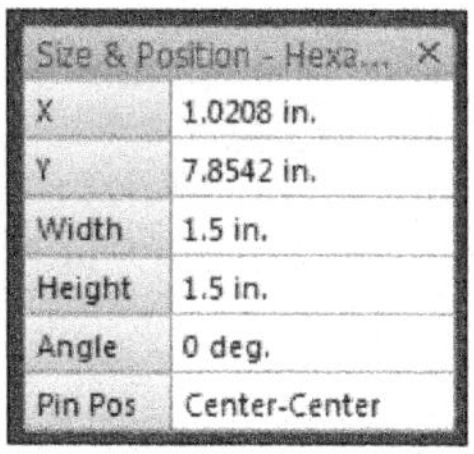

Figure 8-11:
Type a
positive
number for
countercloc
kwise
rotation,
negative for
clockwise.

Size & Position - Hexa... ✕	
X	1.0208 in.
Y	7.8542 in.
Width	1.5 in.
Height	1.5 in.
Angle	0 deg.
Pin Pos	Center-Center

3. **Type a number for the angle of rotation in the Angle field.**

   Type a positive number for a counterclockwise angle of rotation or a negative number for a clockwise angle of rotation.

4. **Click OK.**

   Visio rotates the shape to the angle you specify. Notice that the angle you entered is now reflected on the status bar.

Rotation pin

On most Visio shapes, the rotation pin is right in the center of the shape. If you want a shape to rotate around a different point, you can move the rotation pin. You might need to do this if you want to keep a particular point on the shape anchored. For example, Figure 8-12 shows a technique for rotating text around the right side to produce a particular effect. To produce this effect, you set the Pin Pos property to Center-Right, make as many copies of the text as needed, and then change the Angle property for each copy of the text. All of the text shapes have the same X and Y values.

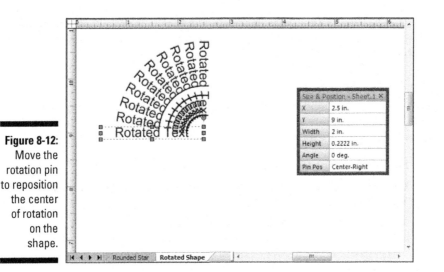

Figure 8-12:
Move the
rotation pin
to reposition
the center
of rotation
on the
shape.

You can use also use the Size & Position window to change the location of the rotation pin (see Figure 8-12). Choose Top-Left, Top-Center, Top-Right, Center-Left, Center-Center, Center-Right, Bottom-Left, Bottom-Center, or Bottom-Right in the Pin Pos field of the Size & Position Window. You can also move the pin position manually using these steps:

1. **Click the Pointer Tool (on the Standard toolbar).**

2. **Select the shape.**

3. **If you don't see the rotation pin, move the mouse pointer over the shape's rotation handle.**

   Visio displays the shape's rotation pin. Look for a line from the rotation handle to the rotation pin.

4. **Point to the rotation pin and drag it to a new position.**

5. **Release the mouse button.**

   The value in the Pin Pos field of the Size & Position Window changes as you drag the rotation pin to a new location. The change only appears after you release the mouse button.

To return a rotation pin to the center of a shape, choose View➪Windows➪ Size & Position or click Size & Position Window on the View toolbar. Change the Pin Pos property value to Center-Center.

Flipping shapes

Sometimes you find just the right shape, but it's facing the wrong direction. In that case, you can flip the shape so that it faces the opposite direction. Your choices are Flip Horizontal (which flips a shape right to left) or Flip Vertical (which flips the shape top to bottom). To flip a shape, use the Flip Horizontal or Flip Vertical buttons shown in Table 8-1. Select the shape first and then click one of the flip buttons.

Adding Style to Your Shapes

Most Visio shapes are functional, but also very generic in appearance. A sofa has all of the basic lines for a sofa, but none of the color and certainly none of the cloth patterns of the real thing. The shapes used for flowcharts, graphs, charts, and other business data are generic as well. Visio helps you jazz up these basic shapes by adding features such as line color and weight, fill color and pattern, and shadowing. Many people refer to such features as *formatting*.

In the past, Visio forced you to change the formatting for shapes individually or as a group. However, you had no way to save the settings, so repeating the formatting from diagram to diagram was difficult. In addition, when you added new shapes to a diagram, you still had to format them manually. Fortunately, Visio 2007 includes *themes*. You use themes in the same way as you use manual formatting; you have the same options available. However, now you can store the settings for future use so you can repeat formatting quite easily. In addition, you can tell Visio to use a particular theme for all new shapes, so you can apply the theme automatically.

The following sections describe how to make individual changes first. You can then apply what you know to create new theme colors and theme effects. A *theme color* is a list of the colors used for particular diagram elements. A *theme effect* determines how the shape appears: the line style, corner types, and so on.

Changing line style

Every shape has an outline, usually a thin black line. Not only can you change the color of the line, but you can also change the *weight* (thickness) of it as well as the pattern and transparency. You can make it fat and green and dash-dot-dashed, or dainty and pink and dot-dash-dotted. If you decide you don't like square corners, you can round them.

When you work with a 1-D shape like a simple line, you can also add line ends (such as arrowheads) to the beginning or end of the shape, and determine the size of the line ends. The Line dialog box (shown in Figure 8-13) has a preview window so you can see the changes you make.

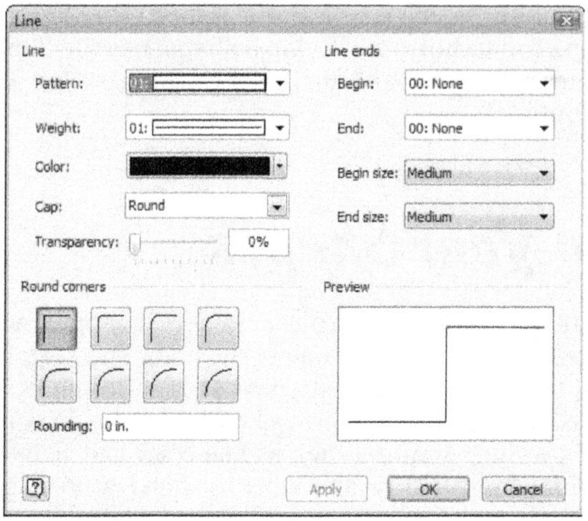

Figure 8-13:
Use the Line
dialog box
to change
many
character-
istics of a
shape's
outline or a
line itself.

Although Figure 8-13 shows all of the line options at your disposal, you can also make many changes using the features of the Format Shape toolbar. Generally, using the toolbar whenever you can is faster. The following steps describe how to change the line format:

1. **Select the shape or shapes that you want to change.**

2. **Choose Format⇨Line, or right-click and choose Format⇨Line.**

   Visio displays the Line dialog box, as shown in Figure 8-13.

3. **Choose a line pattern in the Pattern field.**

   Visio shows any changes as you make them in the Preview area.

4. **Choose a line thickness in the Weight field.**

5. **Choose a line color in the Color field.**

6. **Choose blunt lines (Square) or soft lines (Round) in the Cap field.**

7. **Change the transparency of the line by sliding the Transparency bar.**

8. **Round the corners of your shape by clicking one of the rounding styles in the Round Corners area.**

   If you want the rounding to be a specific size (such as beginning ⅛ inch from the corner), type a decimal number in the Rounding box.

9. **If your shape is 1-D, choose line ends and their size in the Begin, End, Begin Size, and End Size fields.**

10. **View your choices in the Preview area.**

11. **When the shape appears as you want it, click OK.**

In the next section, you learn that you can also set the transparency of the fill in a 2-D shape. When you change the shape's fill transparency, it also affects the transparency of the shape's line (whether you change it using the previous steps or not).

Visio provides the buttons shown in Table 8-2 to apply line style changes without opening a menu. Note that the Transparency setting affects both the line and the fill of a 2-D shape, but that you can also use it to change the transparency of a line. These buttons appear on the Formatting and Format Shape toolbars, which you can display by choosing View➪Toolbars➪Format and View➪Toolbars➪Format Shape. To use any of these buttons, first select the shape or shapes you want to change, and then click the tiny down arrow next to the button to display a list of choices.

Table 8-2	Toolbar Buttons for Changing Line Styles		
Button	*Name*	*Toolbar*	*What It Does*
	Line Color	Formatting	Lets you choose the line color for the selected shape
	Line Weight	Formatting	Lets you choose the line thickness for the selected shape
	Line Pattern	Formatting	Lets you choose the line pattern for the selected shape
	Line Ends	Formatting	Lets you choose endpoints for a line
	Transparency	Format Shape	Lets you set a transparency level for the fill and the line
	Corner Rounding	Format Shape	Lets you choose a line corner style for 2-D shapes
Theme	Theme	Formatting	Lets you choose a theme to perform all formatting tasks, rather than perform them individually (refer to Chapter 4 for details)

Adding fill color, pattern, and shadow

White, white, white can become monotonous after a while. Why not add some excitement to your shapes by making them patterned and colorful with shadows? Color and shadows aren't just aesthetic qualities; they also attract attention, hold interest, and help the reader interpret data more easily.

Filling a shape with a solid color is straightforward. Just choose the color and that's that. If you fill a shape with a pattern, however, you have to choose two colors — one for the foreground and one for the background. The foreground color comprises the pattern, such as dots, hash marks, stripes, or crisscrosses. The background color is the one that shows through the pattern. Often, patterns show up in black and white, so you don't even think about the possibility of choosing colors for the foreground and background. You can use black and white in Visio as well, but it's good to know what foreground and background colors are so that you get the results you expect.

A shape's shadow doesn't have to be a solid color. You can choose a shadow style, pattern, foreground color, background color, and transparency for the shadow as well. The following steps describe how to change the shape format:

1. **Select the shape or shapes that you want to change.**

2. **Choose Format⇨Fill, or right-click and choose Format⇨Fill.**

   The Fill dialog box appears, as shown in Figure 8-14.

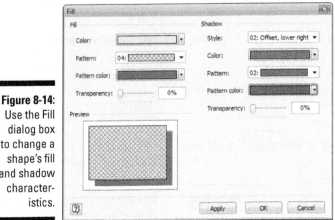

Figure 8-14: Use the Fill dialog box to change a shape's fill and shadow characteristics.

3. **Choose the color, pattern, pattern color, and transparency in the Fill area.**

4. **Choose the style, color, pattern, pattern color, and transparency in the Shadow area.**

   The Preview area shows a sample of the choices that you selected.

5. **Click OK.**

   Visio returns to your drawing and reformats the selected shape.

To make further refinements to the shadow (beyond what's available in the Fill dialog box), choose Format⇨Shadow, which displays the Shadow dialog box. Here you can also change the size, position, offset, direction, and magnification of a shadow. To change these settings, select the shape you want to change, and then choose Format⇨Shadow.

Visio also provides timesaving toolbar buttons for fill color, transparency, fill pattern, and shadow color, as shown in Table 8-3. Select a shape or shapes you want to change, and then click the down arrow next to the button to display a list of choices.

Table 8-3	Toolbar Buttons for Changing Fills and Shadows		
Button	*Name*	*Toolbar*	*What It Does*
	Fill Color	Formatting	Lets you choose a fill color for 2-D shapes
	Transparency	Format Shape	Lets you set a transparency level for the fill and the line
	Fill Pattern	Format Shape	Lets you choose a fill pattern for 2-D shapes
	Shadow Color	Format Shape	Lets you choose the shadow color, the style, and other settings for 2-D shapes
Theme	Theme	Formatting	Lets you choose a theme to perform all formatting tasks, rather than perform them individually (refer to Chapter 4 for details)

Copying formats

You might have used Visio to create diagrams before Visio 2007 appeared on the scene with themes. Many of your older diagrams will contain formatting that you still want to use with new shapes. Even though the best way now to format shapes is to use themes, you can still copy formatting from existing shapes to new shapes and save time. The Format Painter button lets you paint a format from one shape to another. This truly is a timesaving feature. Use it when you don't want to create a new theme based on an existing shape format. The following steps describe how to copy a shape format:

1. **Click the shape that has the format you want to copy.**
2. **Click the Format Painter (refer to Table 8-1) on the Standard toolbar.**

   Your mouse pointer changes to a paintbrush.
3. **Click the shape that you want to apply the format to.**

   Presto! All that beautiful color and style is instantly copied to your shape.

Reformatting a shape

So, you decide that you don't like violet polka dots on an orange background with a green frame and a green-and-purple crisscross shadow pattern. How do you get rid of it? Unfortunately, you can't click a button that magically removes all the formatting that you add to a shape. The fastest way to get rid of formatting you don't want and return the formatting to its default state is to drag and drop a new shape onto the diagram. Select the new shape first, and then all of the shapes that you want to change. Now, click the Format Painter to change all of the existing shapes to their default settings.

Setting the shapes to a default setting is essential when you want to use themes. Visio won't override any custom changes you make to a shape; the shape must use default formatting to use a theme. Consequently, when you change the fill color to blue, a change in theme won't change the fill color, but it will change the line color, pattern, and other formatting.

Creating new theme colors

The easiest way to change colors in a diagram is to use a theme. Chapter 4 shows you how to use themes to change diagram colors. However, you might not find a theme that you want to use. Perhaps your company has custom color requirements that you must consider when creating diagrams. Defining a new theme color is essentially the same as defining the color for an individual shape. The only difference is that you store the color information for future use and have the option to apply the color to any new shapes automatically. In addition, if you choose to change colors, all you do is select a new theme, rather than change the colors individually. The following steps describe how to create a new theme color:

1. **Click Theme on the Formatting toolbar (refer to Table 8-3).**

    You see the Theme - Colors or Theme - Effects task pane.

2. **Click the Theme Colors link when it's enabled.**

    You see the Theme - Colors task pane.

3. **Click the New Theme Colors link.**

    The New Theme Colors dialog box shown in Figure 8-15 appears.

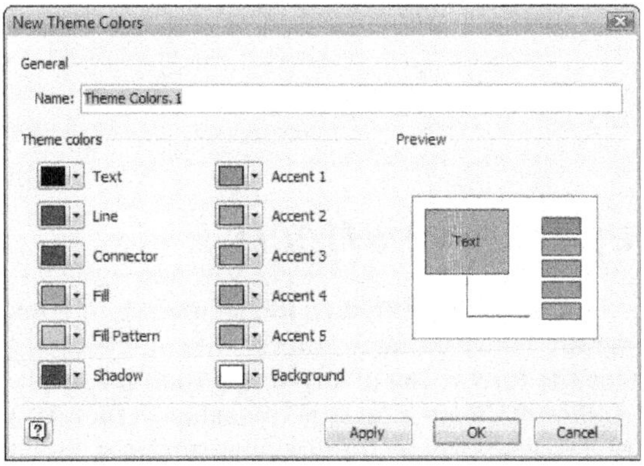

Figure 8-15: Themes help you control the individual colors of every diagram element.

4. **Type a name for your theme in the Name field.**

5. **Choose colors for each of the shape, line, text, and diagram elements.**

    Visio displays changes you make in the Preview area.

6. **Click OK.**

    Visio saves your changes and displays the new theme in the Custom category of the Theme - Colors task pane, as shown in Figure 8-16. You can now select this theme whenever you need to use your custom colors. Any shapes and lines that don't have special color settings will use your theme's color settings.

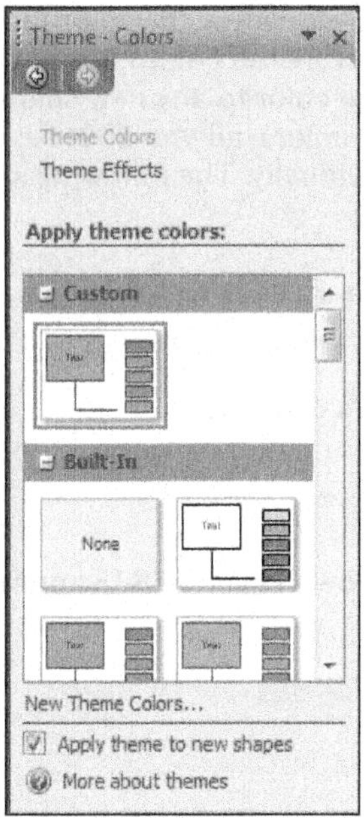

Figure 8-16:
Visio
displays any
custom
themes you
create in a
special
Custom
category.

Creating new theme effects

Theme effects help you define the text, line, fill, shadow, and connector formatting for your diagram. As with theme colors, choosing a theme effect automatically changes the formatting of any shape that doesn't have custom formatting applied. Defining theme effects is the same as manually changing the physical appearance of shapes by modifying formatting such as line thickness. The following steps describe how to create a new theme effect:

1. **Click Theme on the Formatting toolbar (refer to Table 8-3).**

   You see the Theme - Colors or Theme - Effects task pane.

2. **Click the Theme Effects link when it's enabled.**

   You see the Theme - Effects task pane.

3. **Click the New Theme Effects link.**

   The New Theme Effects dialog box shown in Figure 8-17 appears.

4. **Select the General tab. Type a name for your theme in the Name field.**

5. **Select the Text tab. Choose text formatting features such as the font.**

   Visio displays changes you make in the Preview area.

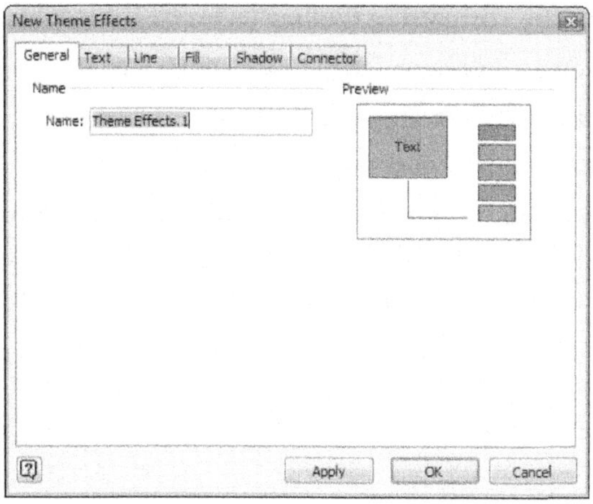

Figure 8-17:
Themes
help you
control the
effects used
to display
shapes.

6. **Select the Line tab. Choose line formatting features such as the line weight, line pattern, transparency, and round corners.**

   You won't see the line ends on this tab. The line-end settings appear on the Connector tab. In addition, you won't see any line color settings. Remember that you change color using a theme color, as described in the previous section of this chapter.

7. **Select the Fill tab. Choose fill formatting features such as pattern and transparency.**

8. **Select the Shadow tab. Choose shadow formatting features such as style, transparency, X offset, Y offset, magnification, and direction.**

9. **Select the Connector tab. Choose connector formatting features such as pattern, weight, transparency, and round corners. Set up any connector end features such as the beginning and ending end type (arrows) and size.**

10. **Click OK.**

    Visio saves your changes and displays the new theme in the Custom category of the Theme - Effects task pane. You can now select this theme whenever you need to use your custom effects. Any shapes and lines that don't have any special effect settings will use your theme's effects settings.

Copying new themes

Sometimes you won't want to take the time to create a theme from scratch. You can copy existing color or effects themes and use them as the starting point for your own custom theme. The following steps describe how to duplicate a theme color or effect:

1. **Click Theme on the Formatting toolbar (refer to Table 8-3).**

    You see the Theme - Colors or Theme - Effects task pane.

2. **Click the Theme Colors or Theme Effects link as needed.**

    You see the appropriate theme task pane.

3. **Select the theme you want to duplicate. Hover the mouse over the entry and click the down arrow.**

    The menu shown in Figure 8-18 appears.

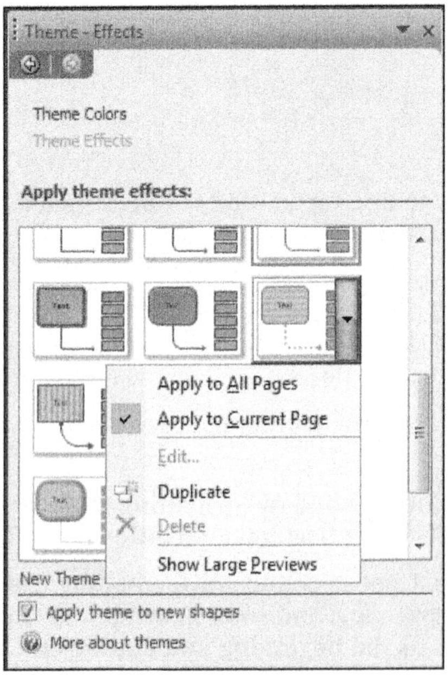

Figure 8-18:
Every theme
entry has a
menu of
tasks
associated
with it.

4. **Select Duplicate.**

    Visio copies the theme to the Custom category.

5. **Select the duplicated theme in the Custom category. Hover the mouse over the entry and click the down arrow.**

    The menu shown in Figure 8-18 appears.

6. **Select Edit.**

    You see the Edit Theme Colors or Edit Theme Effects dialog boxes, where you can change the theme colors or theme effects settings.

Managing Shapes by Grouping

Nothing is more frustrating than spending a good deal of time creating a shape out of many shapes, getting everything perfectly aligned, and then messing it all up when you try to move it or resize it. One way to avoid this problem is to group shapes so that they behave as a unit. Grouping also enables you to size, rotate, flip, and otherwise treat the whole shape as a unit.

Creating groups

You can group any set of shapes that you select; their proximity to one another makes no difference. In many cases, you'll create temporary groups to perform drawing tasks with greater ease. For example, you might want to change the angle of a group of shapes, so creating a temporary group makes sense. You can also create temporary groups to make manual formatting easier. Temporary groups make it easier to move elements in a flowchart, floor plan, or other diagram with greater ease. The steps that follow specify menu commands as well as toolbar buttons, which appear in Table 8-4.

Table 8-4	Action Toolbar Buttons for Grouping Shapes	
Button	*Name*	*What It Does*
	Group	Groups all selected shapes
	Ungroup	Ungroups the selected shape

To create a group, use these steps:

1. **Select all the shapes that you want to group.**

2. **Choose Shape⇨Grouping⇨Group or click the Group button on the Action toolbar.**

   Visio reframes the shapes with a single frame and handles.

To ungroup a shape, follow these steps:

1. **Select the grouped shape.**

2. **Choose Shape⊅Grouping⊅Ungroup or click the Ungroup button on the Shape toolbar.**

   Visio separates the grouped shape into its original shapes and selects each one individually.

If you prefer to use shortcut keys, you can press Ctrl+Shift+G for Group and Ctrl+Shift+U for Ungroup.

Editing a group

When you click a group, Visio selects the entire group. Clicking a component shape in that group lets you *subselect* just that component. When you click a group once, you see green selection handles around the entire group. Click again on a member of the group to subselect it. You see green selection handles for only that shape, and the handles that defined the boundaries of the entire group change to a faint line of gray dashes.

This feature of subselecting allows you to easily edit a shape in a group. (You don't have to ungroup shapes to edit an individual shape.) After you subselect a shape, you can move it, resize it, reshape it, change its line color, fill it, or make any other changes without affecting other shapes in the group. When you finish making changes, click anywhere outside the group or press Esc to deselect the shape.

If you prefer to have Visio select members of a group with the first mouse click and then select the entire group with a second mouse click, you can set Visio to behave this way. Another option is to have Visio select only the group and *never* subselect shapes. The following steps describe how to change the group selection behavior:

1. **Click a grouped shape.**

2. **Choose Format⊅Behavior.**

   The Behavior tab in the Behavior dialog box appears. Look in the Group Behavior area of the dialog box.

3. **Indicate your preference in the Selection drop-down list:**

   • To disable subselecting, choose Group Only.

   • To change back to Visio's default setting, in which you select a group with a single click and individual shapes with a second mouse click, choose Group First.

- To select members of a group with a single click and the entire group with a second mouse click, choose Members First.

4. **Click OK.**

Adding a shape to a group

Sometimes when you create a group, you'll want to add another shape to the group. Visio has a special command for adding shapes to an existing group. Use these steps:

1. **Select the shape to which you want to add a shape.**

   Visio displays the shape's selection frame and handles.

2. **Select the shape you want to add.**

   Visio adds the shape to the selection frame.

3. **Choose Shape➪Grouping➪Add to Group.**

   Visio adds the shape to the group selection frame.

Never create a group, add shapes to it, and then group it again. Adding shapes to an already-grouped group creates what Visio calls a *nested* group. Each time you group a group, the file size increases unnecessarily and performance (load time and save time) declines.

Removing a shape from a group

You can remove a shape from an existing group just as easily as you can add one. Just click the group to select it, and then click the component of the group that you want to remove. Visio displays the selection frame and handles for just that component shape. Choose Shape➪Grouping➪Remove from Group. Visio removes the component from the group. The shape remains in the drawing but is now ungrouped from the original group.

Adding text to grouped shapes

Normally, if you double-click a shape, Visio displays the shape's text block so you can add or edit text. However, you can't double-click a shape in a group to display its text box. To add text to a shape that's part of a group, you need to use a separate window. The following steps describe how to add text to a shape in a group:

1. **Select the group.**

2. **Choose Edit⇨Open Group.**

   Visio opens a separate window and zooms in on the group.

3. **In this window, double-click the shape that you want to add text to.**

   Visio zooms in on the shape's text block.

4. **Type the text you want to add to the shape, and then press Esc or click somewhere outside the text block.**

5. **Click the window's Close button.**

   Visio returns to your drawing window, and the text you added appears in the shape.

Chapter 9

Working with Pages

. . . .

. . . .

*J*ust about now you may be thinking, "A page is a page; what's to know? Pretty boring stuff." There's a lot to know about pages in Visio. Visio files aren't like documents, where text flows smoothly from one page to the next with a few interesting figures thrown in here and there. Some drawings have only one page; others may have multiple pages. And in Visio, pages are independent of each other. You can set a different page size, orientation, drawing scale, background, shadow, and even header and footer for each page in a single Visio file. You can also rotate a page to make drawing angled lines and shapes easier — and then rotate it back again when you've finished drawing. This makes Visio flexible, but it also makes it more complex than your average text editor.

The Role of the Template

A *template* is designed to make creating a drawing easier because it sets up a drawing scale (such as a typical architectural scale of ¼ inch:1 foot), and it automatically opens the stencils that you need to create a particular type of drawing (such as the Office Layout stencil for creating a space plan). Refer to Chapter 2 if you need a refresher on using templates to create a Visio file.

A template also sets up the size of the drawing page and the printer paper (both usually 8½ by 11 inches) and the orientation of the page (portrait or landscape). You need to be aware of these settings when you work with pages in a drawing. Using a template is a definite advantage because it automatically matches the size and orientation of the drawing page to the size and orientation of the printed page, which ensures that your drawing prints correctly.

Drawing page size refers to the drawing area that you see on the screen, *printer paper* refers to the paper you print on, and *printed drawing* refers to the drawing as printed on paper. (Refer to Chapter 3 for more details on these printing terms.)

Reorienting a Page

Suppose that you're creating a network diagram in portrait orientation, and you realize that the drawing is too wide to fit on 8½-inch-wide paper. You can change the paper orientation to landscape rather than adjust the layout of your drawing. Switching to landscape orientation turns your drawing page 90 degrees so that its width is greater than its length.

When you change the orientation of your drawing page, however, you need to make sure that the printer settings match. Follow these steps:

1. **Choose File⇨Page Setup.**

   The Page Setup dialog box appears.

2. **Select the Print Setup tab.**

   You see the Print Setup tab of the Page Setup dialog box, as shown in Figure 9-1.

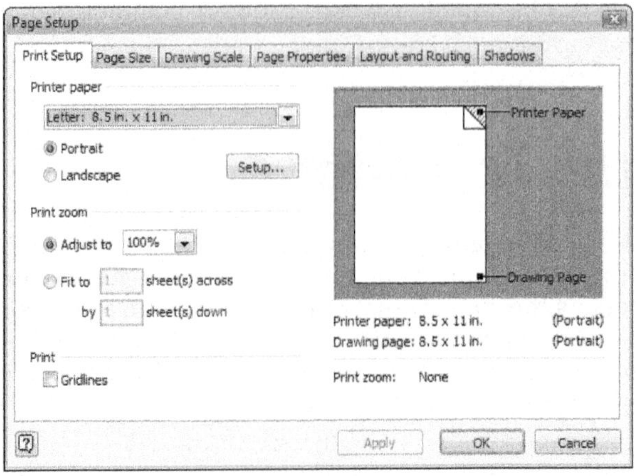

Figure 9-1: You can change the orientation for a page on the Print Setup tab of the Page Setup dialog box.

3. **Click either Portrait or Landscape in the Printer Paper area.**

4. **Click the Page Size tab.**

   You see the Page Size tab, as shown in Figure 9-2. Note that Visio changes the Page Size to the orientation you chose in Step 2. The preview looks identical to the one shown on the Print Setup tab. The printer paper and drawing page orientations match because the Same as Printer Paper Size option is selected by default.

Figure 9-2:
The preview on the Page Size tab shows that the drawing page size and printer paper size match.

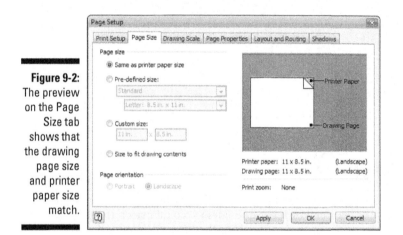

5. **Click OK.**

When you switch page orientation, the shapes in your drawing don't mysteriously disappear or get erased, but it's possible that some of them are either straddling the page borders or are completely off the page (see Figure 9-3). You just moved the boundaries of the page, but the shapes are placed where they always were (within the old page boundaries — sort of like the Incredible Hulk bursting out of his shirt). Now that you have new boundaries, you need to move your shapes to get them back onto the drawing page.

Choosing Shape➪Center Drawing helps you begin rearranging shapes by placing the drawing in the center of the new page boundaries. Some specialty diagrams include special commands for rearranging the elements. For example, when working with an organizational chart, you can use either the Organizational Chart➪Re-layout or Organizational Chart➪ Best Fit to Page command. You may still need to move some shapes around to fit them on the page, but these diagram reorganization options give you a head start.

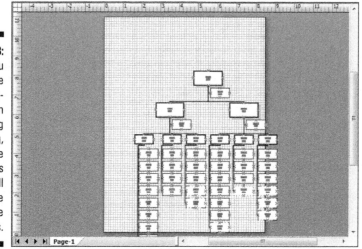

Figure 9-3:
When you change the page orientation in an existing drawing, some shapes might fall outside the new page boundaries.

Setting a Page Size

Page size refers to the size of your drawing; it has nothing to do with the paper size in your printer. For most documents, you'll match the page size (drawing size) to your paper size, whether the paper is standard size (8½ x 11 inches), legal size (8½ x 14 inches), or larger, such as 11 x 17 inches. Drawings, however, are often different from standard text documents because you must display the drawing in its entirety on one page (even if you print it out as multiple sheets), rather than spread words across multiple pages. Drawings can come in all shapes and sizes, especially in engineering and architectural fields. Some drawings won't fit on standard-size paper and must be printed across several sheets (unless you're fortunate enough to have a plotter). Visio lets you determine your drawing page size in the following ways:

✔ Using predefined sizes

✔ Entering custom measurements

✔ Using the drawing content as size boundaries

Letting Visio determine the size based on the drawing content is a good one to choose when you want your drawing to fill the entire page.

Some of the predefined sizes you can choose from include Metric, such as 148 x 210 millimeters defined by the International Organization for Standardization (ISO); American National Standards Institute (ANSI) Engineering (sizes A through E), such as 22 x 34 inches; and ANSI Architectural, such as 24 x 36 inches. You can find a comparison of ISO to American drawing sizes and a description of drawing sizes A through E at www.engineeringtoolbox.com/paper-drafting-sizes-d_41.html.

Drawing pages are independent, even when they belong to the same Visio file. This means you can make different pages in a file different sizes. The ability to use different-size pages comes in handy especially for floor plans and engineering drawings, where a user expects to see drawings in specific sizes depending on content and purpose.

You use the Page Size tab in the Page Setup dialog box for all three methods of sizing your drawing. In this example, the page size begins smaller than the paper size. The following steps describe how to modify the drawing page size:

1. **Choose File➪Page Setup.**

2. **Click the Page Size tab.**

   You see the Page Setup dialog box shown in Figure 9-4. Notice that the page size is less than the paper size so the page doesn't consume the entire piece of paper.

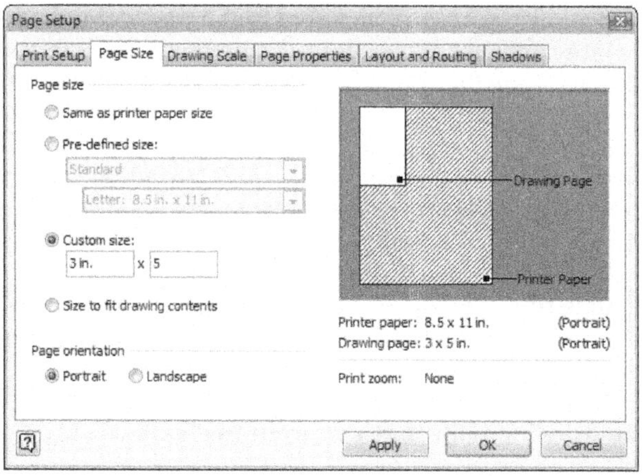

Figure 9-4:
Set the size of your drawing on the Page Size tab of the Page Setup dialog box.

3. **Select one of the following options for the page size:**

   • **Same as Printer Paper Size:** Sets your drawing size to the same size as your printer paper. This is the standard size for business and personal output when the diagram is for personal, rather than presentation, purposes.

   • **Pre-defined Size:** Uses a predefined size in one of the following categories: Standard, Metric (ISO), ANSI Engineering, or ANSI Architectural. For this option, you select a category in the top box and then select a size in the category you chose. Make sure that engineering and architectural drawings conform to company guidelines and local code.

- **Custom Size:** Enables you to set a custom size. Type the width in the first field, followed by the length in the second field. (You may optionally type **in** for inches or **mm** for millimeters following the number; Visio uses the default settings when you don't specify a unit of measure.) You use this feature for nonstandard output. For example, one teacher used this feature to create flash cards for school children using 3-x-5-inch recipe cards.

- **Size to Fit Drawing Contents:** Sizes the drawing based on its contents. This feature comes in handy for presentation materials such as organizational charts, flowcharts, business charts and diagrams, pivotdiagrams, and other data presentations. Using this setting ensures the content fills the page so there isn't too much or too little white space.

 4. Click OK.

Setting a custom size can be useful if you're printing on nonstandard-sized paper. You can also use this option to *position* or *isolate* a drawing on standard-sized paper. For example, suppose that you want to print a 3-x-5-inch Visio drawing in the upper-left corner of an 8½-x-11-inch piece of paper and leave the remaining white space for reviewers to write comments. When you set a unique page size that's smaller than your paper, the drawing prints in the upper-left corner of the page.

If you reduce the page size of an existing drawing, the shapes in that drawing don't move or change size. If some of the shapes are outside the new page dimensions, you need to move them inside.

You can also change the size of your drawing page dynamically by dragging the page edges with your mouse. (This method saves you the trouble of opening the Page Setup dialog box.) Here's how it works:

 1. Display the drawing page that you want to change.

 2. Select the Pointer Tool.

 3. Press and hold down the Ctrl key and move the mouse pointer over the edge of the drawing page that you want to drag.

 The mouse pointer changes to a double-headed arrow (horizontal or vertical, depending on the page edge you choose).

 4. Drag the mouse in the direction you want to expand (or contract) the borders.

 A dotted outline shows the location of the new page dimensions, as shown in Figure 9-5.

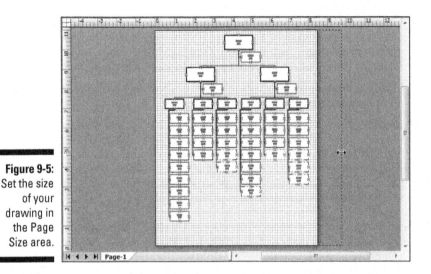

Figure 9-5:
Set the size
of your
drawing in
the Page
Size area.

To resize the page's height and width at the same time, move the mouse pointer near (but not directly on) one of the page's corners. The double-headed mouse pointer now points diagonally.

5. **Still holding down the Ctrl key, drag the mouse until the page is the size that you want, noting the page dimensions on the status bar.**

To see how your drawing page size differs from the current paper size settings, choose File⇨Page Setup. To change the paper size, click the Print Setup tab in the Page Setup dialog box. Refer to Chapter 3 for more information about printing.

Adding and Deleting Pages in a Drawing

When you create a new Visio drawing, it includes only one page. You can add pages to a drawing. Following are some good reasons for doing so:

- ✔ **Keep a set of related drawings,** such as a collection of maps with driving directions for your city, on separate pages in one Visio file.

- ✔ **Use pages to create overview drawings and detail drawings** of your corporate, regional, and branch organization charts, for example. You can even add *jumps,* similar to links between Web sites, from one page to another.

✔ **Use pages to keep track of the history and revisions of a drawing,** which can work something like this: Page 1 is the original draft, Page 2 is the second draft, Page 3 is the review drawing, Page 4 is the revised drawing, Page 5 is the second review drawing, and Page 6 is the final drawing.

✔ **Create a mini-slideshow** with a series of drawings on separate pages and present them in full-screen view.

✔ **Include your company name and logo on background pages** so that the logo shows through on every page without being part of your drawing. The icing on the cake is that each page in your drawing can have its own background page, so you can vary the background content from page to page. (Background pages are discussed in detail in the "What's in a Background?" section, later in this chapter.)

You can add as many pages to a drawing as you like. Pages are always added at the end of the drawing, so technically speaking, you can't *insert* pages between other pages (even though Visio uses that terminology). You can, however, reorder pages, as discussed later in the "Reordering pages" section. The new page that you add takes on all the attributes of the page that's currently displayed. If you want to change some of these attributes, you can do so when you create the page or later, using the File⇨Page Setup command. The following steps describe how to add a page to a drawing:

1. **Display the page with the attributes that you want the new page to have.**

   The new page always takes on the attributes of the selected page, even if you haven't defined any attributes for that page. Visio assigns default attributes to the page it provides for you. The default attributes depend on the template you choose and any changes you have made to that template.

2. **Right-click the page tab at the bottom of the drawing window and choose Insert Page, or Choose Insert⇨New Page.**

   The Page Properties tab of the Page Setup dialog box appears, as shown in Figure 9-6. Visio suggests a temporary name in the Name box.

3. **For the Type, select Foreground to create a "regular" Visio drawing page.**

   Background pages are discussed later in the "What's in a Background?" section.

4. **In the Name field, type a new name or use the suggested name.**

   At this point, you're free to click the Page Size or Drawing Scale tab to change settings for the new page. However, this isn't necessary if you want the new page to take on the attributes of the page that you displayed in Step 1.

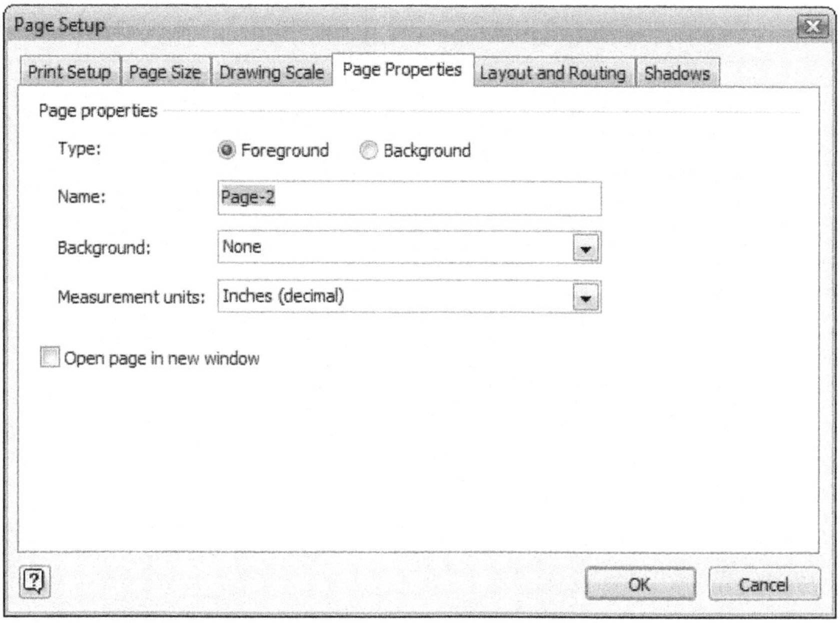

Page Setup

| Print Setup | Page Size | Drawing Scale | Page Properties | Layout and Routing | Shadows |

Page properties

Type: ⦿ Foreground   ○ Background

Name: Page-2

Background: None

Measurement units: Inches (decimal)

☐ Open page in new window

[?]   OK   Cancel

Figure 9-6:
Set attributes for a new page.

5. **Choose a background page if desired.**

   The "What's in a Background?" section describes this option in more detail.

6. **Choose the measurement units when different from the current page.**

7. **Select the Open Page in New Window check box when you want to create the page in a new window, rather than using an existing window.**

   Visio 2007 lets you create pages in multiple windows so that you can perform a side-by-side comparison of the new page with an existing page. You can also create a new window by choosing Window⇨New Window. Choose Window⇨Tile to display the windows side by side for comparison purposes, as shown in Figure 9-7. Notice that each new window has a : (colon) followed by a number. In this case, there are two windows. The first has a :1 attached to the file name, while the second has a :2 attached to the file name. Each window can have a separate set of templates. Closing a window doesn't close the file unless it's the last open window for that file. See the "Displaying multiple pages at once" section, later in this chapter, for additional information.

8. **Click OK.**

   The new page appears after all the other pages in the drawing, and Visio adds a tab to the bottom of the drawing window.

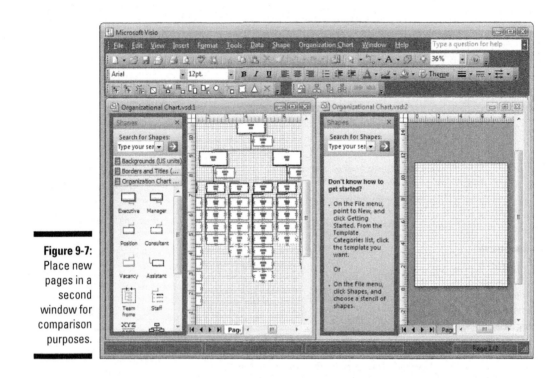

Figure 9-7:
Place new
pages in a
second
window for
comparison
purposes.

The precise term for a drawing page is *foreground page*. The foreground page gets its name because it appears in front of the background page. See the "What's in a Background?" section, later in this chapter, for more information about creating and using background pages.

Sometimes after you add a page to a drawing, you decide later that you want to delete it. You can delete one page at a time quickly by right-clicking the page tab and choosing Delete Page from the context menu. The following steps describe how you delete several pages:

1. **Choose Edit⇨Delete Pages.**

   The Delete Pages dialog box appears and lists all the pages in the drawing by name, as shown in Figure 9-8.

2. **Click the page or pages that you want to delete.**

   To select a contiguous range of pages, click the first page, hold down the Shift key, and select the last page. To select a noncontiguous range of pages, hold down the Ctrl key as you click each page name.

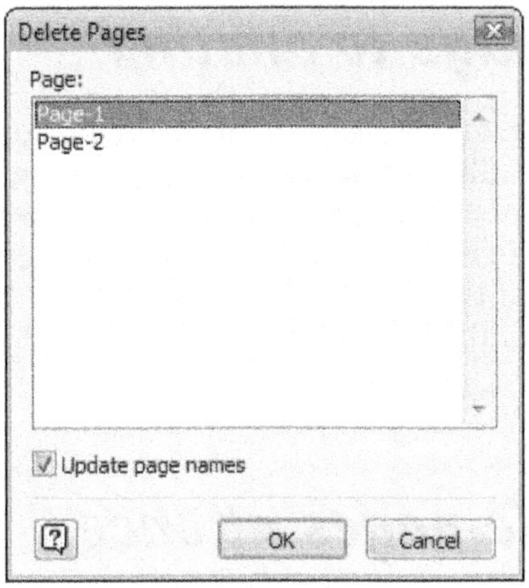

Figure 9-8:
Select the
page you
want to
delete.

[Delete Pages dialog box: Page list showing "Page-1" (highlighted) and "Page-2", with "Update page names" checkbox checked, and OK and Cancel buttons]

3. **Select the Update Page Names check box when you want Visio to renumber pages for you.**

   This option only works when a page number appears at the end of each page tab.

4. **Click OK.**

   Visio removes the selected pages from the drawing, renumbers the pages when you choose this option, and closes the dialog box.

Page deletion is permanent when you save the diagram file to disk. Clicking Undo won't retrieve the page for you. However, you can retrieve an accidentally deleted page before saving. Simply close the file without saving your changes. Reopen the file and you'll see the page that you deleted. Of course, using this technique also means you lose any changes you made after the last save, so it always pays to save your document immediately before you begin deleting pages.

Working with Multiple Pages

A drawing with multiple pages is more complex than a single-page drawing. You need to know how to get from one page to another and how to rearrange pages, if necessary. You also might find it useful to display more than one page at a time so you can compare pages. Read on to find out how to work with multiple pages in a drawing.

Getting from one page to another

When you add pages to a drawing, Visio creates a tab at the bottom of the drawing area identifying the page. Clicking a page tab is by far the fastest way to switch from one page to another. If your file contains just a few pages, all tabs are usually visible at one time. If your file contains many pages, Visio can't display all the tabs at once at the bottom of the window. In that case, use the scroll buttons to the left of the page tabs to go to the first page, previous page, next page, or last page.

Displaying multiple pages at once

When your drawing contains multiple pages, viewing more than one page at a time lets you compare one page to another quickly and easily. It also lets you edit each page without repeatedly closing one and opening another. Visio opens another page in a separate window. Use these steps to open additional page windows:

1. **Choose Edit⇨Go To⇨Page option.**

   (The Page option is at the bottom of the submenu.) The Page dialog box appears, and lists all the pages in the drawing. Notice that the currently selected page is grayed out.

2. **Highlight the page that you want to view.**

3. **Select the Open Page in New Window check box, as shown in Figure 9-9.**

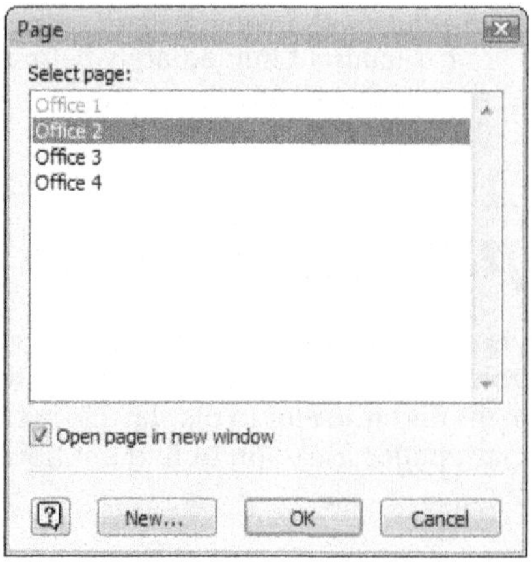

Figure 9-9:
Choose a page to display using the Page dialog box.

4. **Click OK.**

   Visio opens the page in a new window.

5. **Repeat Steps 1 through 4 to open additional pages in a new window.**

   Each time you open a new page, it becomes the current page on your screen, so you still aren't viewing multiple windows yet. You won't see them until you change the way they are displayed.

Choose Window⇨Tile or Window⇨Cascade to arrange the open windows on your screen. The Tile option displays all open page windows next to each other on the screen like tiles on the floor.

The Cascade option staggers the windows so that the title bar of each window is visible. The title bar looks similar to this: *MeetingRoom:1,* where *MeetingRoom* is the file name for the drawing and *1* is the number of the page window you opened. The second page window you opened would be called *MeetingRoom:2.* (Note that the number in the title bar does not correspond to the page number in the drawing; it refers only to the order in which you opened additional pages.)

If your only goal is to open a second window, choose Window⇨New Window. You can still choose any of the diagram pages in either window as you would normally. This technique opens a second window showing the current page, which comes in handy when you want to compare two areas of the same page.

Reordering pages

When you add pages to a drawing, Visio automatically adds them to the end of the drawing (although the menu name is Insert — go figure). Because Visio doesn't let you insert pages in a drawing (such as between Pages 3 and 4), the only way to put new pages in the order that you want them is to reorder them.

Reordering pages in Visio couldn't be easier. Just drag the page tab (at the bottom of the drawing window) and drop it in the spot you want. As you drag the page tab, the mouse pointer displays a small page, and a small arrowhead appears just above the tabs to indicate where Visio will insert the page when you release the mouse button.

Renaming Pages

Visio doesn't provide a very interesting name for the pages of your diagram, so you'll probably want to rename it at some point. You can change the title of a page at any time using one of two methods.

The first and easiest is to simply right-click the page tab at the bottom of the drawing window and choose Rename Page. Visio highlights the page name on the tab. Type the new page name right on the tab and press Enter. This method works for both foreground and background pages.

If the page has a background assigned to it, the name change doesn't affect the association between the background and foreground pages. For more information about background pages, see the "What's in a Background?" section, later in this chapter.

Sometimes, it's not convenient to use the right-click method. For example, you might use the keyboard for most tasks, rather than the mouse. The following steps describe the second method for renaming a page:

1. **Display the page you want to change in the drawing window.**

2. **Choose File⇨Page Setup to display the Page Setup dialog box.**

3. **Select the Page Properties tab.**

   You see the Page Properties for the current page, including the page name.

4. **Type the page's new title in the Name field.**

5. **Click OK.**

   Visio changes the displayed name on the page tab.

Viewing on the Big Screen

If you want to see how your drawing will look on the printed page, you can always click Print Preview on the Standard toolbar (refer to Chapter 3 for information about using Print Preview). However, Print Preview is more for checking final details before you print. What if you want to view your drawing pages like a miniature slide show? You can display your drawing using the *entire* screen, without title bars, menu bars, status bars, scroll bars, or any other windows. You can even control the drawing like a slide show, moving forward or backward through the pages.

Using the entire screen is a great way to create a mini-presentation for a small group of viewers. Because you don't need a slide projector, you avoid the hassle of setting up special equipment. The following steps describe how to display your diagram in full-screen mode:

1. **Select the first page of your drawing.**

2. **Choose View⇨Full Screen, or press F5.**

   Visio switches to full-screen mode and displays the first page of your drawing.

3. **To move to another page:**

   • To move to the next page, press N, the Page Down key, the right-arrow key, or the left mouse button.

   • To move to the previous page, press P, the Page Up key, or the left-arrow key.

4. **Press Esc or F5 to return to the Visio window.**

You can also navigate pages using the pop-up menu shown in Figure 9-10. To display this menu, click the right mouse button. Using the pop-up menu is important if you're on Page 3, say, and want to move quickly to Page 42.

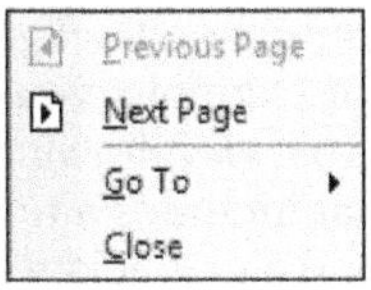

Figure 9-10:
In full-screen mode, all of Visio's menus, toolbars, task panes, and other window attributes are hidden.

◁	Previous Page
▷	Next Page
	Go To ▶
	Close

Hyperlinks — shapes that you click to go to another page — are a cool feature of Visio. If your drawing contains hyperlinks, you can click the hyperlink shape to leap to the link. For details about adding hyperlinks to a drawing, see Chapter 14.

What's in a Background?

As if foreground pages weren't enough, you can also add background pages to a drawing. Why would you want to do that? The best answer is that they offer consistency. If you want to show a file name, a date, a company name, a logo, a page number, or any other information about a drawing — but you don't want it on your drawing page — you can put all that information on a background page. Using a background page is sort of like printing your drawing on a transparency and slipping the background page underneath. The information on the background page shows through the transparency — visible and printable — but the drawing itself isn't mucked up with all sorts of extraneous information. However, you do see the contents of the background pages; otherwise, you wouldn't be able to place your diagram in such a way that it works with the background page features.

You can create as many background pages as you want in a drawing file. What can you do with a background? You *assign* it to a foreground page. Assigning makes the association between the two. You can assign the following:

✔ A single background page to one or more foreground pages

✔ A different background page to each foreground page

✔ A background page to another background page

The most important rule to remember is that you *can't* assign more than one background page to any foreground page. However, each background page can also have a background page assigned to it. You can piggyback background pages on a foreground page by assigning a background to a background and then assigning that background to a foreground. For example, your company might have a logo background that you must assign to every drawing. Your engineering diagrams require a background diagram that includes a title block. To make this setup work, assign the logo background as a background to the title block background; then assign the title block background to your diagram. Figure 9-11 shows this three-page setup.

In this case, the diagram begins with the Logo tab shown in the upper-left corner of the display. This page acts as a background for the Frame page that appears in the upper-right corner. Finally, the sole foreground page uses the Frame page as a background. You see the cumulative effect of using the two background and the foreground pages in this example.

It's also important to notice the three window setups in this case. The Logo page doesn't require any stencils, so it doesn't display the Shapes window. The Frame page requires the Frame shape from the Title Blocks stencil, so it displays only that stencil. Finally, because this is a Circuits and Logic diagram, you see the standard stencils displayed in the Shapes window for the Diagram page.

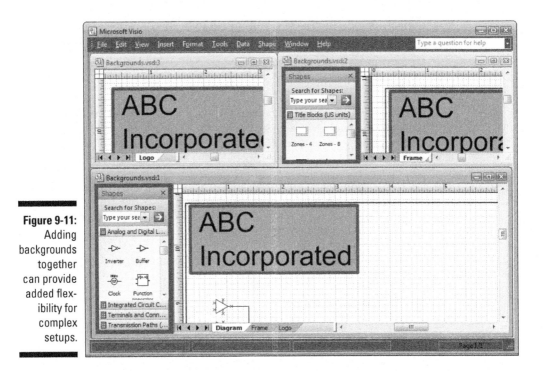

Figure 9-11:
Adding
backgrounds
together
can provide
added flex-
ibility for
complex
setups.

One of the most important concepts to understand about background pages is that the content is separate from the parent (foreground or other background) page. You can't select, edit, delete, or do anything else with the background page. This feature makes background pages an excellent way to add content that you don't want to change while working on your diagrams.

Creating and assigning a background page

Background pages aren't useful by themselves. To use a background page, you must create it and then *assign* it to another page. Unassigned, you can still print a background page, but it prints by itself, without any foreground information. The following steps describe how to create a background page:

1. **Display any page in your drawing.**

2. **Choose Insert⇨New Page.**

   Visio displays the Page Properties tab of the Page Setup dialog box. (Refer to Figure 9-6.)

3. **Click the Background option.**

4. **Type a new name in the Name field.**

5. **Choose an existing background or None in the Background field.**

6. **Choose the units you want to use for the background page in the Measurement Units field.**

7. **Click OK.**

That's all there is to creating a background page. Next, you add the information you want the background page to contain. For details on modifying a background page's content, see the "Editing a background page" section, later in this chapter.

The last step — and it's an important one — is to assign the background page to another page (foreground or background) in the drawing. Until you assign it, it just sits there in the drawing doing nothing. The following steps describe how to assign a background page to another page:

1. **Display the page that you want to assign the background page to.**

   Think of this as the parent page.

2. **Choose File⇨Page Setup.**

   You see the Page Setup dialog box.

3. **Click the Page Properties tab.**

   The Name field displays the name of the current page.

4. **Click the Background drop-down arrow.**

   You see a list of the background pages that you created.

5. **Choose the background page that you want to assign to the page you displayed in Step 1.**

6. **Click OK.**

   Visio creates the association between the two pages, closes the dialog box, and returns to your drawing.

Unassigning a background page

At some point, you may need to use a different background page or choose not to use a background page at all. You can always *unassign* a background page. Unassigning breaks the association between two pages. Unassigning doesn't delete the background page; it just leaves it sitting unassigned until you choose to assign it again.

To unassign a background page, display the parent (foreground or other background) page in the drawing area, and then click the Page Properties tab of the Page Setup dialog box. Choose None in the Background field, and then click OK. The background page still exists, but you can't see it when viewing the parent page.

Displaying a background page

When you assign a background page to another page, Visio displays the contents of the background page on the screen whenever you display its foreground page. This can become distracting while you work on the foreground page. If you don't want to see the background page content while you're working on the foreground page, you must unassign the background from the foreground. See the preceding section to unassign a background page. However, removing the background page means that you might create content on the foreground page that conflicts with it. For example, a diagram element might appear over the logo when you finish. In most cases, you'll want to retain the background elements to avoid conflicts.

Editing a background page

Because a background page is just a drawing page, you edit it just as you do a foreground page. Display the background page by clicking the page tab at the bottom of the drawing window. You can add, delete, move, or format shapes or text on the background page just like on any other page.

Are you driving yourself crazy trying to select a shape that refuses to be selected? That's probably because the shape is on the background page assigned to your foreground page. It just appears to be on the foreground page. It's hard to tell which is which because Visio makes no distinction between foreground and background pages on the screen.

Using a background shape

Visio provides some special shapes designed just for background pages. They're provided to add interest and style to your drawings. Most of the backgrounds are abstract designs, although some represent real-world objects or scenes such as world maps, city scenes, or mountains. Background shapes are usually set to high transparency so that the shapes in your drawing show through easily.

Background shapes reside on their own stencil called Backgrounds. To display them, choose File➪Shapes➪Visio Extras➪Backgrounds. To use a background shape, just open the Backgrounds stencil and drag a shape onto your drawing.

In previous versions of Visio, you couldn't assign a shape from the Backgrounds stencil to a foreground page. Visio automatically created a background page, placed the shape there, and assigned that background to the foreground page. In Visio 2007, you can assign a background shape directly to a foreground page, which saves you considerable time and effort.

Background shapes fill the entire page, regardless of the size of your drawing page. So if you start with a page size for your background page of 8½ x 11, and then change it to 3 x 5, the background shape automatically resizes to fill the page.

Rotating Pages

The best computer software programs work the way you worked before you had the program. Think about the following example. When using a pencil and paper to draw a floor plan, you'd probably draw all the straight lines on the paper and then *turn the paper at an angle* and draw any angles. You can work exactly the same way in Visio by rotating a drawing page. The program lets you work the way you work when you're drawing on paper.

When you rotate a page, the shapes stay in position, just as they do when you rotate a piece of paper. *Guide lines,* those vertical and horizontal lines you drag into your drawing from the rulers to help you place shapes, also stay in position when you rotate a page. (To review creating and using guide lines, refer to Chapter 7.) When you know that you're going to rotate a page, you can use guide lines as a custom grid.

Unlike on your drawing paper, rulers and the drawing page grid *do not* rotate when you turn a page. This is a good thing — you can always maintain a horizontal and vertical baseline from which to work, regardless of the angle of the paper.

Figure 9-12 shows a rotated view of an office layout. You could add guide lines and other features to make it easier to line items up using the new orientation.

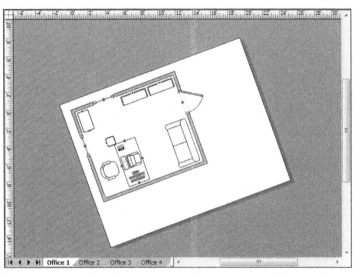

Figure 9-12:
It's easy
to draw
objects at
an angle
after you
rotate a
diagram.

Rotating a page doesn't affect the page orientation settings (that is, portrait or landscape) or the way the page prints. Page rotation is simply an on-screen tool to aid you in drawing. The following steps describe how to rotate a page:

1. **Select the Pointer Tool.**

2. **Display the drawing page you want to rotate by clicking its page tab.**

3. **Press and hold down the Ctrl key and then move the mouse pointer over any corner of the page.**

   The pointer changes to a circular rotation pointer.

4. **Drag the mouse either clockwise or counterclockwise, depending on the direction that you want to rotate the page.**

   To rotate to a specific angle, watch the status bar as you drag the page; it tells you the exact angle (in degrees) of the page as you rotate it.

   The farther you move the mouse pointer away from the page corner, the more precise the angle you can choose.

5. **Release the mouse button and the Ctrl key when the page is rotated to the angle that you want.**

After you try rotating a drawing page, you'll realize how useful this feature is, whether you're drawing floor plans or any other type of drawing requiring angled lines.

Chapter 10

Layering Your Drawings

. . . .

. . . .

*V*isio defines a *layer* as a named category of shapes. Think of the layer as a surface on which you can place shapes that's separate from other surfaces on a page of a diagram. When you were a child, did you ever have one of those anatomy books with the transparent sheets? The bottom sheet had the skeletal structure, the next sheet had internal organs, and then you added the nervous system, the muscular structure, and finally the skin. Well, the layer system in Visio works in much the same way. You can create layers in a Visio drawing for the same purpose as your anatomy book: to show groups or categories of shapes independently of others or as part of the whole. Many other graphics applications, such as Photoshop and Paint Shop Pro, include the concept of layers, so this isn't a Visio-specific convention.

How can you use layers? In a landscape drawing, you may want to include structural walls and pathways on one layer; grass, ground cover, and small shrubs on another; trees on a separate layer; and ornamental flowers on another layer. Another example is a layout for a building or home in which the walls, doors, and windows appear on one layer, and the wiring, electrical system, plumbing, and HVAC (heating, ventilation, and air conditioning) system appear on individual layers. You can display just one layer to view the shapes in a particular group or display all layers to view the complete plan.

Layers work well for most diagrams. A floor plan can show the building layout at the lowest layer, the furniture on another layer, electronics on another layer, and so on until you build the entire floor plan. Electronic diagrams can place the circuit board at the lowest layer and add components. Even flowcharts benefit from layers. You can lay out the shapes on one layer, general text on the next layer, specifics on the next layer, and your notes on another layer. The whole purpose of layering is to reduce complexity while improving the overall amount of available information.

Getting the Essential Facts on Layers and Layering

You need to know the essential facts about layers so that you can make decisions about how and when to use them. Don't let all of these facts scare you. As you read the following list, try to form a mental picture of what's going on:

- ✔ A Visio drawing can have more than one page.
- ✔ Each page can have its own set of layers.
- ✔ Visio automatically assigns some shapes to predefined layers (based on the template that you choose).
- ✔ A shape can be assigned to (and therefore, appear on) one or more layers.
- ✔ A Visio page (with or without layers) can have one background page. However, each background page can have a background page, which means that each Visio page can inherit multiple background pages. (Refer to Chapter 9 for details.)
- ✔ Although similar in behavior, a background page is not the same as a layer. You can always edit the shapes on a layer, but you can't edit the shapes on a background page unless you display the background page.
- ✔ A background page can have its own layers.

The concepts of layers, pages, and diagrams can be confusing. It becomes clearer if you visualize a *layer* as one transparent sheet, a stack of transparent sheets as a *page,* and multiple stacks as separate pages in a *drawing* (see Figure 10-1). Although a Visio background page is also transparent, its purpose is to display repetitive information (such as a company logo or the document's title and date) rather than a category of shapes, as a layer does. If the bottom transparent sheet of the anatomy book had only a title, such as "The Human Body," it would be analogous to a Visio background page.

When you want to group and display categories of shapes in a drawing, use layers. When you want repetitive information to appear on each page of a drawing, use a background page.

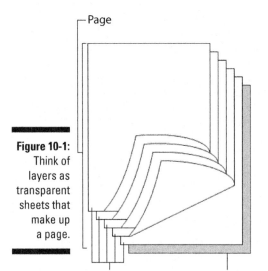

Figure 10-1:
Think of
layers as
transparent
sheets that
make up
a page.

Page

Transparent layers   Background page

In general, you *assign* shapes to a specific layer. However, some shapes naturally appear on more than one layer, even when you place them on a specific layer. Some Visio templates include predefined layers. In these cases, Visio assigns the shapes in the template's stencils to a particular layer. Visio automatically adds the layers to your drawing when you add the shapes. The number of automatic layers depends on which shapes you include in the diagram.

The Floor Plan template is a good example of a template with predefined layers. Some of the layers in this template include the following:

- ✔ **Building Envelope** (exterior walls, doors, windows)
- ✔ **Computer** (all computer-related equipment)
- ✔ **Dimensions** (any text used to show the size of a shape)
- ✔ **Door** (all doors within the floor plan)
- ✔ **Electrical Appliance** (room features such as lamps that aren't electronic devices)
- ✔ **Equipment** (fax and copy machines)
- ✔ **Furniture** (desks, chairs, tables)
- ✔ **Movable Furnishings** (plants, lamps, coat racks)
- ✔ **Power/Comm.** (electrical outlets and telephone jacks)
- ✔ **Nonmovable furnishings** (corner work surfaces, panels)
- ✔ **Wall** (shapes that delineate floor space)
- ✔ **Window** (all windows within the floor plan)

The Floor Plan template contains a reasonable number of layers. Other templates, such as the Space Plan template, contain several dozen layers. The number and type of shapes you include in a drawing determine the exact number of layers that the drawing has.

If you add a page to your drawing, it doesn't contain any layers until you drag a shape that's preassigned to a layer onto the diagram or you create a layer, as described in the "Adding a layer and removing one" section, later in this chapter.

Working with Layers

As you might suspect, there are many different operations for working with layers: adding, naming, deleting, renaming, hiding, activating, assigning shapes, and so on. In this section, you learn the significance and the steps for doing all these tasks. However, don't feel you need to do all these at once to work with layers. Just use whatever tasks seem appropriate for your particular drawing.

When you use a Visio template to create a drawing, Visio adds layers automatically as you drag shapes in. You're never *required* to create layers or do anything with existing layers. However, layers are important for a number of reasons, as described in the following list:

- **Hiding data:** Sometimes you don't want others to see sensitive information, so you can place it on a separate layer that only people with the proper permissions can see.

- **Reducing complexity:** Diagrams can quickly become so complex that even you can't understand them with ease. Using layers lets you hide data that is essential to the diagram, but unnecessary for the current task.

- **Explaining concepts:** You can reveal a plan, theory, strategy, or other concept one layer at a time when explaining it to other people.

- **Seeing details:** It's possible that one shape will reside on top of another shape. Removing the upper shape lets you see the shape below it.

- **Organizing shapes:** One of the best reasons to use layers is to organize the shapes on your diagram. You can view the layout of individual layers to determine how to use the shapes better, improving the overall appearance and usability of the diagram.

- **Teaching others:** A teacher might create Visio diagrams with a layer for the question and another for the answer. A third layer contains details about the question and a fourth includes personal notes. It's important to understand the layers to help you extend Visio's functionality by letting you perform tasks that Microsoft might not have envisioned.

Toolbars for working with layers

Two toolbars are helpful when working with layers. The first is the View toolbar. It has a lone button for working with layers, the Layer Properties button, which is shown in Table 10-1.

Table 10-1		Toolbar Buttons for Working with Layers	
Button	*Name*	*Toolbar*	*What It Does*
[Multiple Layers]	Layer Properties	View	Displays the Layer Properties dialog box shown in Figure 10-2
	Layers	Format Shape	Displays the Layer dialog box shown in Figure 10-4, which lists the layer(s) to which a selected shape is assigned

The second toolbar, Format Shape, contains a box called Layers. When you select a shape in a drawing, the layer to which that shape is assigned appears in this box. If the shape is assigned to multiple layers, this box tells you so. If the selected shape is unassigned, this box simply says "No Layer."

To display the View toolbar and the Format Shape toolbar, right-click the toolbar area and choose the toolbar name from the pop-up menu, or choose View➪Toolbars and select their names from the list.

Adding a layer and removing one

When the template you're using doesn't include the layers you want or if you're not using a template, you can create layers of your own. Suppose your drawing contains a layer called *Computer Equipment.* You might want to refine that further by creating a layer called *Rented Computer Equipment.* That way, you could easily distinguish rented equipment from owned equipment. The following steps describe how to add a layer:

1. **Choose View➪Layer Properties or click Layer Properties on the View toolbar.**

   Visio displays the Layer Properties dialog box, showing a list of layers for the current page, as shown in Figure 10-2.

   If your Layer Properties dialog box is empty, it doesn't necessarily mean that the template you're using doesn't include predefined layers. The layers appear in the dialog box only after you've dragged preassigned shapes onto your drawing page.

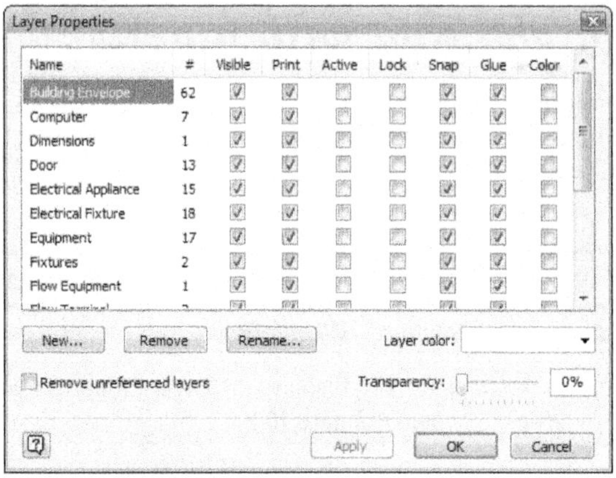

Figure 10-2:
Visio displays all layers on the current page of the drawing.

Name	#	Visible	Print	Active	Lock	Snap	Glue	Color
Building Envelope	62	✓	✓			✓	✓	
Computer	7	✓	✓			✓	✓	
Dimensions	1	✓	✓			✓	✓	
Door	13	✓	✓			✓	✓	
Electrical Appliance	15	✓	✓			✓	✓	
Electrical Fixture	18	✓	✓			✓	✓	
Equipment	17	✓	✓			✓	✓	
Fixtures	2	✓	✓			✓	✓	
Flow Equipment	1	✓	✓			✓	✓	

New... Remove Rename... Layer color: ▼

Remove unreferenced layers   Transparency: 0%

Apply OK Cancel

2. **Click New.**

The New Layer dialog box appears, as shown in Figure 10-3.

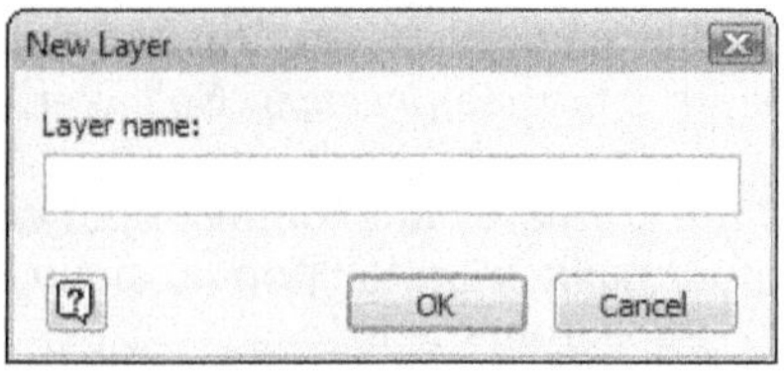

Figure 10-3:
Name your new layer.

New Layer

Layer name:

OK Cancel

3. **Type the name that you want for the new layer in the Layer Name field and then click OK.**

Your new layer is added to the list in the Layer Properties dialog box.

4. **Click Apply and then repeat Steps 2 and 3 if you want to add more layers.**

5. **Click OK to close the Layer Properties dialog box.**

When you add or remove layers, Visio adds or removes them from only the current page. If you want to add or remove layers from multiple pages, you need to do so for each page. The following steps describe how to remove a layer:

1. **Choose View➪Layer Properties or click Layer Properties on the View toolbar.**

Visio displays the Layer Properties dialog box, which shows a list of layers for the current page.

2. **Choose the layer name that you want to remove and then click Remove.**

Visio displays a message box warning that it will delete all shapes that belong to the current layer. The shapes are deleted even when they belong to other layers. You always see the warning dialog box, even when no shapes belong to the selected layer.

3. **Reply to the warning asking whether you really want to remove the layer.**

   If you're willing to sacrifice the shapes on the layer, go ahead and click Yes. If not, click No and then reassign the shapes to a different layer before you remove the layer. (See the "Assigning Shapes to Layers" section, later in this chapter.)

4. **Click OK.**

If you respond No to the warning message and then immediately try to remove another layer, beware: Visio will not display the warning message again! If you click Yes for the second layer, Visio deletes it, whether or not it contains shapes. You can restore the layer by clicking Cancel before the Layer Properties dialog box closes. If you close the dialog box, you can restore the layer by immediately clicking Undo or choosing Edit⇨Undo.

Renaming a layer

You may want to change the name of a layer that you create to something that better describes the shapes that it contains. Even though Visio lets you rename predefined layers in a diagram, it's best to use this option when you're working with layers that you create.

It's never a good idea to rename a predefined Visio layer. Visio always uses the predefined layers when you add a new shape to the diagram. If you rename an existing layer and then add a new shape for that layer to the diagram, Visio re-creates the layer for you. The diagram now has two layers that effectively point to the same shape type, which makes the layers relatively useless for helping you organize your diagram. The following steps describe how to rename a layer:

1. **Choose View⇨Layer Properties or click Layer Properties on the View toolbar.**

   Visio displays the Layer Properties dialog box.

2. **Select the layer that you want to rename and then click Rename.**

   Visio displays the Rename Layer dialog box.

3. **Type the new name in the Layer Name field and then click OK.**

   Visio adds the new layer name to the list in the Layer Properties dialog box.

4. **Click OK.**

Hiding a layer

One of the big advantages of using layers in a drawing is that you can turn them off when you don't want to display their shapes. Consider the office layout example that was mentioned earlier in the chapter. Suppose that you want to work on the placement of nonmovable furniture in the building. You'll want to display the layers that contain the building walls (that is, Building Envelope, Door, Window, and Walls), but you don't need furniture and other items (Computer, Equipment, Moveable Furnishings, Furniture) cluttering your view.

In another scenario, you might know that some shapes are covering other shapes. Furniture might hide the electrical outlets in a room. You can hide the furniture to see the electrical outlets better. The following steps describe how to hide a layer:

1. **Choose View⇨Layer Properties or click Layer Properties on the View toolbar.**

   The Layer Properties dialog box appears.

2. **Find the name of the layer that you want to hide. Deselect the check box that appears in the Visible column for that layer.**

   The check mark is removed, making the layer invisible.

   To display or hide all layers at the same time, click the word *Visible* at the top of the column. (The column header is also a button.) This toggles every item in the column on or off.

3. **If you want to hide another layer, click Apply and then repeat Step 2.**

4. **When you've finished hiding layers, click OK.**

To redisplay a hidden layer, follow the same steps but select a check box in the Visible column this time.

Assigning Shapes to Layers

When you drag into a drawing a shape that isn't preassigned to a layer, the shape goes unassigned. The same is true when you create a shape using the drawing tools or insert a shape from another file, clip art, or picture. (You can test this by selecting the shape and then choosing Format⇨Layer. The Layer dialog box will show no layers selected for the unassigned shape.) There's certainly nothing wrong with having unassigned shapes, but in many cases, you want to assign the shapes to Visio's preassigned layers or to layers you create. The following steps describe how to add a shape to a layer:

1. **Select the shape to assign.**

If the shape is part of a group, click the group and then click the shape to select it by itself (it displays its own round green handles with an *x* inside).

2. **Choose Format➪Layer.**

The Layer dialog box appears, as shown in Figure 10-4, displaying a list of all layers in the drawing.

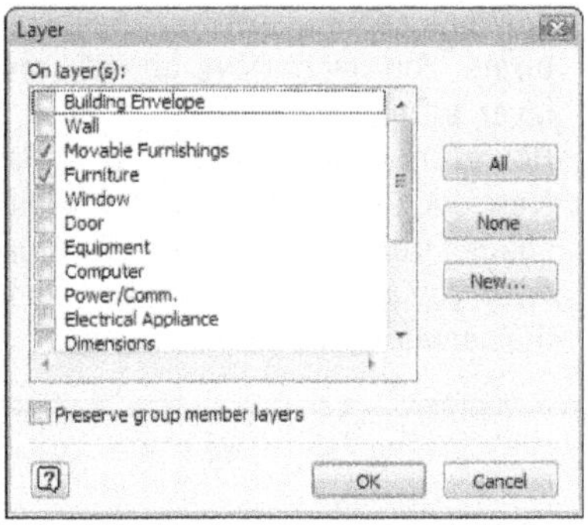

Figure 10-4:
Use the
Layer dialog
box to
assign a
shape to
one or more
layers.

3. **Select the layer (or layers) to which you want to assign the shape.**

Yes, you can select more than one layer. If the layer you want doesn't exist, click New, type a layer name, and then click OK. Visio adds the new layer to the list shown in Figure 10-4.

4. **Select the Preserve Group Member Layers box to retain group layer assignments when the shape you selected is a grouped shape and you've assigned its member shapes to other layers.**

5. **Click OK.**

Visio provides several ways to create a layer, one of which is by clicking New in the Layer dialog box shown in Figure 10-4. Refer also to Figure 10-3 for instructions on adding a layer. Either method works.

Sometimes you want to remove a shape from a particular layer. For example, you might rent a piece of furniture or other equipment for a while, and then decide to purchase it. The furniture no longer belongs to the Rented Furniture layer, so you need to remove it. The following steps describe how to remove a shape from a layer:

1. **Select the shape you want to reassign.**

2. **Choose Format➪Layer.**

The Layer dialog box appears.

3. **Deselect the box next to the layer you want to unassign.**

4. **Click OK.**

Using shapes on many layers

Why would you want a shape to appear on more than one layer? One reason is that a shape might belong to more than one category. Suppose that your drawing is a landscape plan and has many layers, among them, Flowering Plants and Shrubs. A plant you assign to the Shrubs layer might also be a flowering plant, in which case you would assign it to both layers. What's the advantage? You might want to check your plan for consistency of color among the flowering plants, so you would turn off the Shrubs layer and display only the Flowering Plants layer.

Another reason is that you can track a group of shapes on one layer and component shapes on individual layers. For example, suppose that you're diagramming a computer network that contains components from multiple manufacturers. You might have an IBM layer, an HP layer, a Dell layer, a Compaq layer, and so on. However, you would also have a layer called Network Components, which would include shapes from *all* the manufacturer layers. This gives you an easy way to track components in the network or by manufacturer.

Determining which layer a shape is assigned to

After you start using layers, your first question will be, "How do I tell which layer a shape is assigned to?" If it's a preassigned shape, it's not always clear which layer or layers Visio chooses. If you have the Format Shape toolbar displayed (refer to Table 10-1), the layer name appears in the Layer field. When you see Multiple Layers displayed in the Layer field, click the entry to display the Layer dialog box shown in Figure 10-4.

The other way to determine where the shape is assigned is by choosing Format➪Layer. The Layer dialog box appears, with a check mark next to the layer that the shape is assigned to. If the shape is assigned to more than one layer, check marks appear next to multiple layers.

Activating layers

Activating a layer causes Visio to assign all unassigned shapes to the active layer. You can activate a single layer, or you can activate multiple layers. When you activate multiple layers, Visio automatically assigns the unassigned shapes you use in your drawing to *all* active layers. The following steps describe how to activate a layer:

1. **Choose View➪Layer Properties or click Layer Properties on the View toolbar.**

   You see the Layer Properties dialog box.

2. **Select the check box in the Active column for each layer or layers that you want to make active (refer to Figure 10-2).**

3. **Click OK.**

Using Layers on Background Pages

Just as foreground pages can have layers, so too can background pages. To create layers on a background page, you first need to create the background page (refer to Chapter 9). The following steps describe how to create a layer for the background page:

1. **Display your background page by clicking the correct tab at the bottom of the drawing area (such as Background-1 or a specific name).**

2. **Choose View➪Layer Properties or click Layer Properties on the View toolbar.**

3. **Click New to display the New Layer dialog box.**

4. **In the Layer Name box, type a new name and then click OK.**

   Visio adds the name to the Layer Properties list.

5. **If you want to add other layers, click Apply and repeat Steps 3 and 4.**

6. **When you're finished adding layers, click OK.**

7. **Add shapes on the background page to the layers using the method described in the "Assigning Shapes to Layers" section, earlier in this chapter.**

Protecting Layers from Changes

After you go to all the trouble of defining layers and adding shapes to them, nothing is worse than another user (or yourself) accidentally deleting or changing them. You can protect a layer from changes by *locking* it. After you lock a layer, you can't move, change, or delete shapes — you can't even select them. You also can't add shapes to a locked layer. The following steps describe how to lock a layer:

1. **Choose View⇨Layer Properties or click Layer Properties on the View toolbar.**

   Visio displays the Layer Properties dialog box (refer to Figure 10-2).

2. **Locate the layer that you want to lock and then select the Lock check box for that layer.**

   A check mark appears in the column. This shows that the layer as locked.

   If you want to lock all layers at once, click the word *Lock* at the top of the column. (The column header is also a button.) To unlock all layers at the same time, click the Lock button again.

3. **If you want to lock another layer, click Apply and repeat Step 2.**

4. **When you've finished locking layers, click OK.**

When you're ready to work on the layer again, you can unlock it easily by deselecting the check box in the Lock column. The layer will appear again in the Layer dialog box.

You can't lock a layer that's marked as an active layer. Remember that Visio automatically assigns all unassigned shapes to the active layer or layers. If you could lock the active layers, Visio couldn't assign your shapes to any layer. When you try to lock an active layer, Visio automatically makes the layer inactive.

Locking a layer isn't foolproof protection from changes. After all, you can unlock a layer just as easily as you can lock one. Think of a locked layer as an alert or a reminder — to yourself or other users — that shapes on a locked layer *shouldn't* be changed. If you want to protect a file fully from changes, open it or distribute it to other users as a read-only file. For more information on creating read-only files, see Chapter 12.

Assigning a Color to a Layer

Some diagrams become extremely complex after you add enough features to them. Assigning a color to each layer lets you determine quickly which shapes belong to a particular layer. You can also assign a color to all locked layers. This reminds you immediately which shapes you can't alter. When you distribute the drawing to other users for review and comment, you may want to assign a color to the layer that each user may change. The following steps describe how to add a color to a layer:

1. **Choose View↪Layer Properties or click Layer Properties on the View toolbar.**

   Visio displays the Layer Properties dialog box (refer to Figure 10-2).

2. **Find the layer to which you want to assign a color and then select the Color check box for the layer name.**

   A check mark appears in the column.

3. **Make your selection in the Layer Color drop-down list.**

   Visio offers several dozen colors and shades of gray. If these aren't enough options, you can create a custom color using the next set of steps.

4. **Click OK.**

   All shapes on the layer take on the color you chose.

When you assign a color to a layer, it affects the printed copy, if you have a color printer. All layers with a color assigned to them print all shapes in that color, regardless of any other custom color formatting applied to the shape. To restore original colors to shapes on that layer, you must remove the color assignment from the layer. To remove a color from a layer, display the Layer Properties dialog box again and deselect the check box in the Color column.

Removing a color from a layer doesn't remove any custom colors that you created. They are still available in the Color dialog box. The following steps describe how to create a custom color after you open the Layer Properties dialog box and choose a layer to change:

1. **Scroll to the bottom of the Layer Color field list and click More Colors.**

   The Colors dialog box appears, as shown in Figure 10-5.

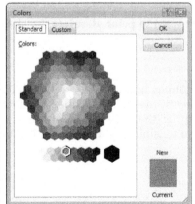

Figure 10-5: Choose from a wider variety of colors on the Standard tab.

2. **If you want to choose a color on the Standard tab, click the color.**

3. **If you instead want to create a color, follow these steps:**

   a. **Click the Custom tab.**

   b. **Click a shade closest to the color you want to create.**

   c. **To change the intensity of the color, move the small, black arrow up and down the vertical slide bar at the right of the dialog box.**

   d. **To adjust the amount of red, green, or blue in a color, enter a number between 0 and 255 in the appropriate box.**

4. **Click OK.**

   Visio returns to the Layer Properties dialog box and shows the custom color you applied to the selected layer. If you click the Layer Color box, you'll see the custom color you created listed just below color number 23.

Selecting Layers to Print

Visio lets you print selected layers, so you can present output in printed form using the same methods you use on-screen. In a building layout, for example, you probably want to print only the Building Envelope (walls) for the building contractor. Employees don't want or need to see the wiring or HVAC layouts but will probably want to see the layers for the walls, cubicle walls, nonmovable furniture, and possibly the electrical outlets. The following steps describe how to select one or more layers for printing:

1. **Choose View⊏▷Layer Properties or click Layer Properties on the View toolbar.**

   Visio displays the Layer Properties dialog box (refer to Figure 10-2).

2. **For the layers that you don't want to print, deselect the check box in the Print column.**

3. **Click OK.**

Don't be deceived by the Visible column in the Layer Properties dialog box! You can't keep a layer from printing by making it invisible. The Print column is the only setting that affects printing; the Visible column affects only what you see on the screen. If a layer isn't visible, but a check mark appears in the Print column, it still prints.

Snap and Glue Options for Layers

If you've followed some of the steps in this chapter, you've seen the Layer Properties dialog box (refer to Figure 10-2), and you're probably wondering about the Snap and Glue columns. You can modify the Snap and Glue options for each layer individually. Refer to Chapter 6 for more information about the Snap and Glue features. The following rules apply to the Snap and Glue options in the Layer Properties dialog box:

✔ **Snap:** When you select Snap for a particular layer, shapes on that layer can snap to shapes on other layers and vice versa. (In other words, Visio enables Snap in both directions.) Deselecting Snap for a particular layer lets shapes on that layer snap to shapes on other layers, but not vice versa.

✔ **Glue:** When you select Glue for a particular layer, shapes on that layer can glue to shapes on other layers and vice versa. Visio enables Glue in both directions. Deselecting Glue for a particular layer lets shapes on that layer glue to shapes on other layers, but not vice versa.

By default, Visio enables Snap and Glue on all layers in a drawing. If you want shapes on other layers to avoid shapes on a particular layer, deselect both options (Snap and Glue) for that layer.

Part III

Taking Your Drawings to the Next Level

The 5th Wave   By Rich Tennant

©RICHTENNANT

FIRED

YOU

"Nifty chart, Frank, but not entirely necessary."

In this part . . .

Now you start to get into the nitty-gritty of Visio — the stuff that'll make you look like a real pro! You position shapes in a drawing with great precision. Then you have fun creating your own shapes with some cool Visio tools and features. You find out how to work with pages in a drawing and how to keep shapes organized by placing them on different layers. Even more fun, you discover how to create your own themes so you can dress up your pages with greater ease. You could get by without knowing these things, but then again, you'd just be getting by.

Chapter 11

Creating Stencils, Master Shapes, and Templates

- -

In This Chapter

▶ Creating and editing stencils

▶ Working with master shapes

▶ Creating and saving custom templates

- -

*Y*ou can use almost any software program as-is successfully without ever taking the time to customize it. However, when you use the program often, customizing can save you valuable time and keystrokes. Like most software programs, Visio has many features you can customize, or personalize, such as stencils, master shapes, and templates. Perhaps it's more accurate to call these *extensions* because you can actually add things to Visio that make it more useful — for *you*.

Working with Stencils

Chapters 1 and 2 cover the basics of opening and using stencils. This chapter goes beyond the basics and tells you about Document Stencils, how to customize existing stencils, and how to create your own.

If the template you're using doesn't contain all the shapes you need and you know the required shape exists in a stencil not provided with the current template, choose File➪Shapes to open additional stencils. Shapes in the Visio Extras folder don't generally appear in any of the templates, so this is the first folder you should check when you know a shape exists, but can't remember which template to associate with the shape.

Using the Stencil toolbar

As you work with stencils, use the buttons on the Stencil toolbar to work faster and with less effort. The buttons and their descriptions appear in Table 11-1. To display the Stencil toolbar, right-click the toolbar area and choose Stencil, or choose View⇨Toolbars⇨Stencil.

Table 11-1		Stencil Toolbar Buttons
Button	**Name**	**What It Does**
	New Stencil	Creates a new stencil.
	Show Document Stencil	Displays the Document Stencil for the current drawing.
	Icons and Names	Displays only icons and names for shapes on the current stencil. This option works best for shapes with short names.
	Names under Icons	Displays the icon with the shape name under the icon. In many cases, such as when working with shapes with long names, this display lets you see the shape name better and uses screen real estate more efficiently.
	Icons Only	Displays only icons for shapes on the current stencil. This option works best when you know the shapes by sight and all of the shapes have a unique appearance — you can generally display more shapes by using icons than you can using names or a combination of icons and names.
	Names Only	Displays only shape names for shapes on the current stencil. This option works best with engineering or other shapes that have unique and descriptive names.
	Icons and Details	Displays only shape icons and details for shapes on the current stencil. This option isn't very helpful for stencils supplied with Visio because many of the details simply tell you to drag the shape onto the form. However, if you provide descriptive details with custom shapes, it can prove helpful. For example, you might include usage requirements or other company-specific information.

As you work with and create drawings, Visio displays the stencil shape icons and names in the Shapes window. (Note that the Icons and Names button on the toolbar is highlighted.) If you don't care about seeing the names of shapes, or if you want to view more shapes in the Shapes window at one time, click the Icons Only button. (Some stencils contain so many shapes that you need to scroll through them.) If you want names without the pictures (icons), choose Names Only. You can also display the ToolTip (the one Visio pops up when you hover over a shape in a stencil) along with the icon and shape name by choosing the Icons and Details button.

An example of each of these stencil options is shown in Figure 11-1. Note that if you have several stencils open, they must all be displayed in the same manner.

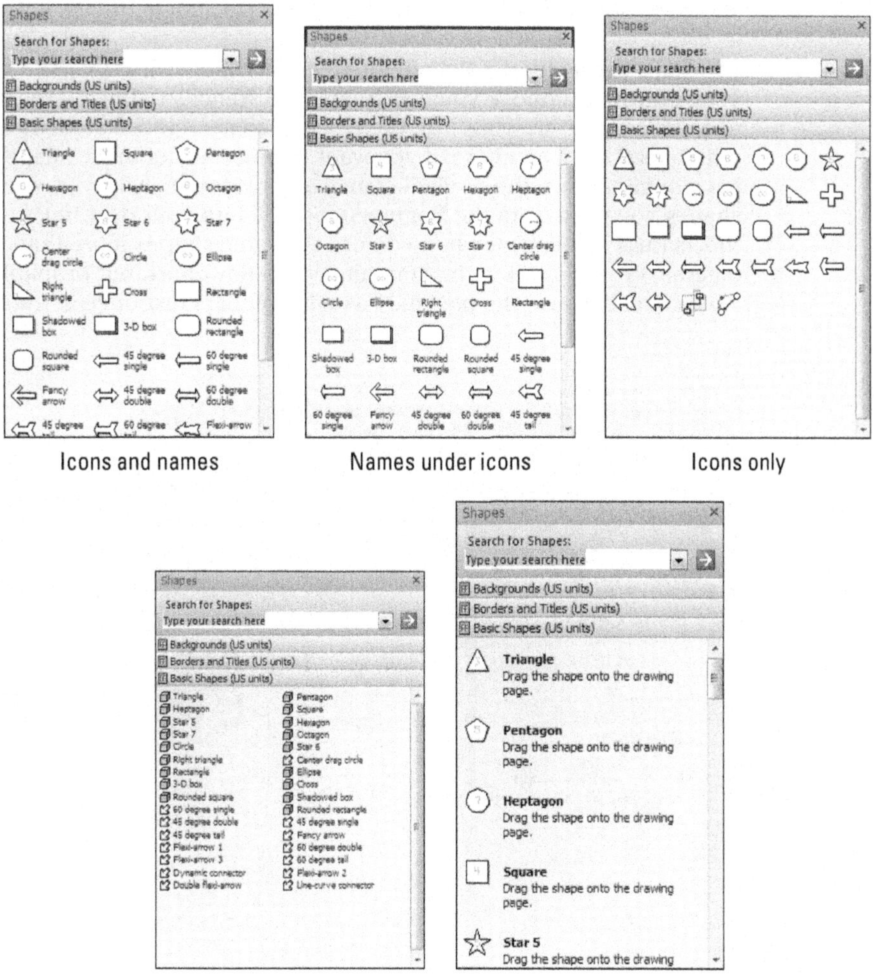

Icons and names — Names under icons — Icons only

Names only — Icons and details

Figure 11-1: Display a stencil in the manner you find most useful.

Using a Document Stencil

When you create a drawing, Visio automatically creates a Document Stencil. You were probably unaware of it until now, unless you discovered it on your own at the bottom of the File➪Shapes menu.

When you're working on an existing drawing, choose File➪Shapes➪Show Document Stencil or click Show Document Stencil on the Stencil toolbar and see what happens. Visio opens a stencil with the title "Document Stencil." (See the lower-left corner of Figure 11-2.) It includes all the shapes that you've used so far in the current drawing. Each time you add a shape from a stencil to your drawing, Visio adds it to the Document Stencil automatically.

So what's the point of a Document Stencil? It acts as a log for the shapes in your drawing. Suppose you had to open 15 stencils to find all the shapes you needed for your drawing. You then closed some of those stencils when you didn't need them anymore. If you want to reuse any of those shapes, you don't have to hunt down the original stencil and reopen it. Instead, you can drag the shapes you need from the Document Stencil into your drawing. Consequently, this feature works best when you use the same shapes more than once in a diagram (you'd use it with something like a flowchart, but probably not with a pie chart because the pie chart usually appears just once in the diagram).

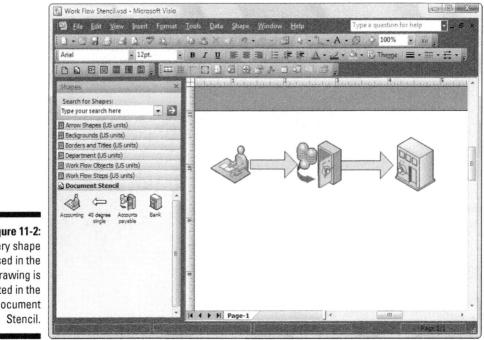

Figure 11-2:
Every shape used in the drawing is listed in the Document Stencil.

To close the Document Stencil, right-click the stencil's title bar and choose Close. Note that Visio always creates a Document Stencil with a drawing, whether or not you display the Document Stencil.

The Document Stencil works just as any other custom stencil does. You can add new shapes to it, remove shapes you no longer need, modify shapes, change shape icons, and define shape properties. You can read about all of these activities in the next section of this chapter. The important difference is that the Document Stencil only affects the current diagram. Any changes you make to this stencil will appear with the current diagram and nowhere else. If you want to create an assortment of modified shapes for use with a number of diagrams, you should create a custom stencil, rather than modify the shapes on the Document Stencil.

Creating a custom stencil

Most people use the same shapes more than once in Visio. For example, you might have a particular set of furniture in a warehouse that you always use to get an office ready for occupancy after a change in owner, repairs, or renovation. If you do use the same shapes more than once or find yourself modifying shapes in the same way for multiple diagrams, you can save time by creating a custom stencil. Using one or more custom stencils means that every stencil you open is customized for your particular needs.

The quickest way to create a custom stencil is to base it on an existing stencil or drawing. The following steps describe how to create a custom stencil by copying an existing stencil or drawing:

1. **Do any of the following:**

    • **Open a drawing that already contains most of the shapes you want to include.**

    Whenever possible, open a diagram that contains the modified shapes you want. Creating a stencil that has the shapes with the required modifications in place saves time and effort modifying them again later. If you don't have a diagram that contains the shapes you want, create a sample drawing and drag all the shapes you want on your custom stencil onto the drawing. (If you make a sample drawing, the order and arrangement of the shapes don't matter. You don't really care about the drawing; it's the stencil you want to save.)

    • **Open a Visio stencil that you want to copy shapes from or open the Document Stencil (choose File⇨Shapes⇨Show Document Stencil). Arrange the stencils on the screen so you can see all of them.**

    • **Create custom shapes that you want to add to a stencil.**

You can use any shape that you draw as input for a stencil. In fact, this is one of the best uses for custom stencils. You only have to draw the shape once to use it as often as you want.

2. **Choose File➪Shapes➪New Stencil or click New Stencil on the Stencil toolbar.**

   A new stencil named Stencil*x*, where *x* is a number, appears on the left side of your screen. Visio increments the number each time you create a new stencil.

3. **Drag a shape onto the custom stencil (see Figure 11-3) using one of these methods:**

   • **From the drawing page,** hold down the Ctrl key (so the shape is copied, not moved) and drag the shape onto the new stencil. (When you hold down the Ctrl key as you drag the shape, you see a plus symbol next to your mouse pointer.) Visio names the shape Master.0 and names subsequent shapes Master.1, Master.2, Master.3, and so on. (You can rename these, as you see in the next section of this chapter.)

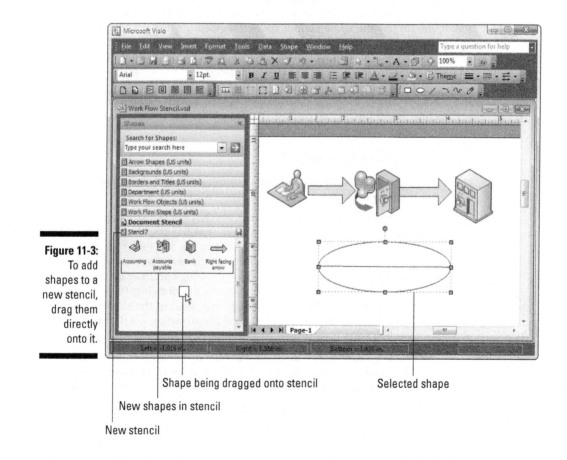

Figure 11-3:
To add shapes to a new stencil, drag them directly onto it.

Shape being dragged onto stencil   Selected shape

New shapes in stencil

New stencil

- **From the Document Stencil or from a Visio stencil,** drag the shape onto the new stencil. (You don't need to hold the Ctrl key because Visio automatically copies the shape instead of moving it.) The shape retains its Visio name (such as Rectangle, or Terminal Server, or External Interactor).

4. **Right-click the stencil's title bar, and then choose Save from the context menu when all the shapes you want are on the custom stencil.**

   Visio displays the Save As dialog box and selects the My Shapes folder, where stencils are stored. This folder already contains a stencil called Favorites, which Visio creates automatically for you.

5. **In the File Name box, type a name for the stencil.**

   In the Save as Type box, Visio automatically chooses Stencil for the file type (*.vss).

6. **Click Save.**

   Visio returns to the drawing screen and the stencil name now appears in the title bar.

Any Document Stencil modification you make appears only in that diagram. A custom stencil that you create is available to any diagram. When you choose File⇨Shapes, your custom stencil appears in the My Shapes category, as shown in Figure 11-4.

Figure 11-4: Custom stencils are listed under Shapes⇨ My Shapes.

Most users have shapes (usually in an existing drawing) that they want to include in a custom stencil, so the preceding steps include adding shapes to the stencil. Adding shapes at this time isn't required, however. You can simply choose File⇨Shapes⇨New Stencil to create a new stencil, and then save it immediately without adding any shapes.

Don't worry about completing your stencil in one try. You can always come back later and add shapes, edit shape properties, and perform other tweaks. Before you can modify an existing custom stencil, you must tell Visio that you want to edit it. Right-click the stencil's title bar and choose Edit Stencil from the context menu to place the stencil in edit mode. The icon changes to display the edit status, and Visio enables editing commands that it normally grays out. Make sure you save your stencil each time you modify it.

Naming master shapes on a custom stencil

Earlier in this chapter, you saw how Visio names shapes on custom stencils Master.0, Master.1, Master.3, and so on as you add them to the stencil. These are temporary names as you create a custom stencil; your shapes really should have more descriptive, permanent names.

When you name a shape, you can also type a *ToolTip* (a description that pops up when you hover over the shape). In addition, you can store keywords with the shape. Keywords help Visio find the shape when you perform a search. Type each keyword on a new line in the Keywords field of the Master Properties dialog box. (Refer to Chapter 4 for help on searching for shapes.) The following steps describe how to rename a stencil:

1. **Display the stencil that contains the shapes you want to rename.**

2. **Right-click the stencil title bar and choose Edit Stencil from the context menu when the stencil isn't already in edit mode.**

   Visio adds a red asterisk to the title bar to indicate that the stencil is in edit mode. In addition, it highlights the Edit Stencil option of the context menu. When you see the red asterisk or the highlight, you know that the stencil is already in edit mode.

3. **Right-click a shape in the stencil and choose Edit Master⇨Master Properties.**

   The Master Properties dialog box appears, as shown in Figure 11-5.

4. **Type a name for the shape in the Name field.**

5. **Type the description or instruction in the Prompt field.**

Generally, you want to provide more information than to tell the user to drag and drop the shape onto the form. Custom shapes require some explanation of use and purpose so that you know why you created it and to act as documentation when you let others use the stencil. Don't make the comment overly large because the ToolTip becomes difficult to see.

6. Choose Tall, Wide, or Double in the Icon Size field when you want an icon size other than Normal.

Use different icon sizes when a shape is oddly shaped or large. If the user can't make out the shape's purpose from the icon, the icon isn't very helpful in identifying the shape. If the automatic icon doesn't help anyone identify the shape, consider creating an icon of your own. See the section "Creating a custom icon," later in this chapter, for details.

7. Choose Left or Right when you don't want to use Center as the alignment for the shape name.

8. Type all the words by which you want to be able to search for this shape in the Keywords field.

Make sure you provide descriptive keywords that you're likely to use in a search; otherwise, the search becomes less useful. Choose words that are too common, and you'll receive too many returns when you perform a search. Use uncommon words, and you'll never find the shape because they're terms that you don't commonly use. In some cases, it's helpful to provide a keyword that identifies the shape as custom. For example, you might type your initials as a keyword to make it easy to locate all of the custom shapes you've created.

9. Click OK.

Visio updates the name of the shape on the stencil.

These steps are the long version for renaming. Use them when you want to edit the prompt and keywords, in addition to changing a shape's name. The following steps describe how to rename a shape when you only want to change the shape's name:

1. **Display the stencil that contains the shape you want to rename.**

2. **Right-click the stencil title bar and choose Edit Stencil from the context menu.**

3. **Right-click a shape in the stencil and choose Rename Master.**

   Visio highlights the current name below the shape in the stencil.

4. **Type a new name for the shape and then press the Enter key or click a blank area of the stencil.**

Adding master shapes to a custom stencil

You can easily add more shapes to a custom stencil after you create and save it. Just drag shapes from a drawing (remember to hold down the Ctrl key so you're copying rather than moving) or from another stencil (no Ctrl key needed) onto the custom stencil. Be sure to save your stencil again by right-clicking the title bar and choosing Save.

If you try to add a shape to a Visio stencil, Visio informs you promptly that you can't perform this action. Generally, you don't want to edit the stencils that come with Visio to ensure that you have a complete collection of baseline shapes to use and customize as needed. After all, if you could add a shape to a Visio stencil, you might just as easily delete a shape.

You can add shapes to a custom stencil without having the custom stencil open. This is a good method to use if you're in the middle of creating a drawing and run across a shape that you know you'll want to use in the future but don't need now. The following steps describe how to add a shape to a custom stencil without opening it first:

1. **Display the stencil that contains the shape you want to save.**

2. **Right-click the shape you want to save and choose Add to My Shapes.**

   A menu listing all custom stencils appears.

3. **Click the name of the stencil that you want to use to save the shape.**

   Visio saves the shape to your custom stencil.

If the custom stencil is open when you add a shape, Visio adds the shape but doesn't save it right away. Visio asks you later (when you close the drawing or close Visio) whether you want to save changes.

Deleting master shapes from a custom stencil

Visio protects its stencils so that you don't accidentally wipe out its shapes. However, you can delete master shapes from a custom stencil anytime you like because you created the stencil yourself. You may find yourself adding and deleting shapes often as your needs change for the types of drawings you create. The following steps describe how to delete a shape from a custom stencil:

1. **Open the custom stencil.**

2. **Right-click the stencil title bar and choose Edit Stencil from the context menu.**

   Visio adds a red asterisk to the title bar to indicate that the stencil is in edit mode.

3. **Right-click the shape you want to delete and choose Delete.**

It's as simple as that. If you change your mind right away, you're in luck because you can choose Edit➪Undo after you delete a shape to bring it back.

Creating a custom icon

In most cases, the icon that Visio automatically generates based on the shape you copy or create works fine. However, some shapes are so complex, large, or oddly shaped that the automatic icon doesn't help the user identify them. When this problem occurs, you need to create a custom icon for your shape. The following steps describe how to perform this task:

1. **Open the custom stencil.**

2. **Right-click the stencil title bar and choose Edit Stencil from the context menu.**

3. **Right-click the shape you want to modify and choose Edit Master➪ Edit Icon Image from the context menu.**

   Visio displays an icon edit window like the one shown in Figure 11-6. The window provides access to colors, including a special Transparent color that lets the background show through. You also have access to a Pencil Tool for changing individual tools, a Bucket Tool you can use to fill areas, a Lasso Tool you use to select irregular areas, and a Selection Net Tool you use to choose rectangular areas.

4. **Perform any required modifications to the icon.**

5. **Click Save and close the window.**

   Visio changes the appearance of the icon to match your changes.

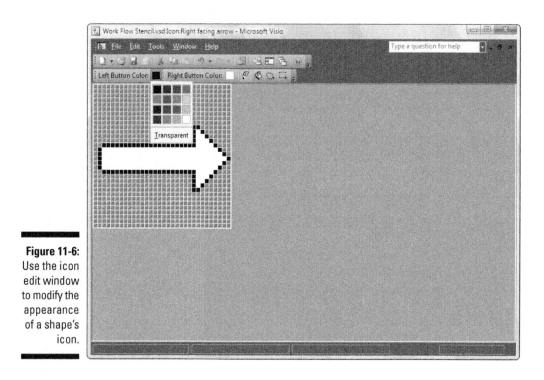

Figure 11-6:
Use the icon edit window to modify the appearance of a shape's icon.

Creating a Custom Template

A *template* is like a model for a drawing: It sets up the page size, orientation, drawing scale, grid, text, and font styles for your drawing area. A template also automatically opens appropriate stencils for the type of drawing that you're creating.

The biggest advantages that templates offer are consistency and efficiency. Companies that rely on Visio often create custom templates that include their name, logo, corporate colors, contact information, and so on. This approach ensures that every drawing created using Visio has the same look and feel. Even if you're not using corporate information, you might want a custom template for a series of related drawings so that they are consistent from first to last.

It's possible that none of the Visio templates meet your needs exactly, but you can create a custom template that does. You can base your custom template on an existing Visio template or drawing and then change it, or you can create a custom template from scratch. The following steps describe how to create a custom template:

1. **Select the drawing type that you want to use.**

   Choose File⇨New⇨Choose Drawing Type. If you want to base your new template on an existing drawing, choose File⇨Open to open your file.

2. **Choose File⇨Shapes to open any stencils that you want to include in your new template.**

3. **Choose File⇨Page Setup.**

   The Page Setup dialog box appears.

4. **Click the Print Setup, Page Size, or Drawing Scale tab, as appropriate, to make changes to the template.**

   Refer to Chapter 3 for help with the settings on these tabs.

5. **Create a background page, when desired, for your template.**

   See Chapter 9 for details.

6. **Choose File⇨Save As.**

   The Save As dialog box appears.

7. **In the Save In box, choose the folder in which you want to save your new template.**

   Choose the Visio Solutions folder if you want the template to appear in the Choose Drawing Type dialog box when you start Visio or when you choose File⇨New⇨Choose Drawing Type.

8. **Type a name for your new template in the File Name field.**

9. **Choose Template in the Save as Type field.**

10. **Click Save.**

    Visio saves your new template.

Where's the style?

Previous versions of Visio included the concept of a style. A *style* let you define the appearance of a particular shape. You might decide that the shape is green and uses an Arial font for text. Visio 2007 doesn't use styles; it uses themes. *Themes* provide an overall look for your diagram as well as individual elements; instead of working with individual shape colors, you choose the color scheme for the entire diagram. Themes are also a lot more flexible and easier to create.

Chapter 4 tells you how to use themes in your diagram. You'll find all of the details on creating theme colors in the "Creating new theme colors" section of Chapter 8. The "Creating new theme effects" section of Chapter 8 tells you how to create theme effects to use in your diagram, and you'll discover how to copy existing themes in the "Copying new themes" section of that chapter. In short, you should consider themes as the new style for Visio 2007.

If you want to create a custom template from scratch, the best way to start is to set up a drawing with all the settings you want the template to have. Choose File⇨Page Setup to set the page size, drawing scale, and page property settings that you want for the new template. And don't forget about background pages (refer to Chapter 9) and layers (refer to Chapter 10). When the drawing is the way you want it, follow Steps 6 through 10 in the preceding procedure.

Chapter 12

Managing Shape Information, Behavior, and Protection

In This Chapter

▶ Storing information in a shape

▶ Creating reports from stored data

▶ Customizing the behavior of a shape

▶ Adding protection to your shapes and drawings

*V*isio is far more sophisticated than it might appear at a quick glance. You might never guess that a Visio diagram or drawing could have all sorts of data stored with it. It might be an even further leap to assume that you could run custom, sorted reports (simple or complex) on that stored data — but you can. In addition, you can *program* Visio shapes to behave or appear in a particular way or to adjust themselves to changes that you make in a drawing. These aren't trivial features. They're part of the functionality built into Visio that greatly enhances your ability to use the program in many creative ways, as you see throughout this chapter.

Storing Data in Visio Shapes

In Visio, shapes are more than what they appear to be. Some are *smart* — their behavior changes depending on the circumstances in which they're used; others have complex geometry rules. Whatever their particular characteristics, *all* shapes can store data.

Why would you want to store data in a shape? Well, you might not if your drawing illustrates a simple workflow process such as Get bills⇨Enter payables⇨ Pay bills⇨Record in register⇨File paperwork. But what if the process is more complex, and costs are associated with each task? You might want to store cost data, the resources required to complete the task, and the duration of time involved in each task.

Now, pretend you're a property manager in charge of distributing and tracking computer equipment for your company. In an office layout plan, you can store inventory numbers and owner information for each computer component shape shown in a drawing. You might want to store additional information, such as serial numbers, acquisition dates, manufacturer names, or model numbers.

You can even create your own data so that you can customize the shape for your own needs. For example, many people who have used Visio for a long time store personal notes in the shapes they use. A presentation is a lot easier when you have notes to use that you create at the time you develop the presentation material. When working with a floor plan, you can store the manufacturer, cost of purchase, condition, purchase date, and color of a piece of furniture. When working with an engineering drawing or an electronic circuit design, you might store a list of part numbers for each component, along with recommended vendors. The data you store in a shape is dependent on what you want to do with the shape. By storing data with a shape, you give the shape a particular personality and make it easier to identify.

Visio calls any type of custom data that you store in a shape *shape data*. Each data item appears as a *custom property* that has a type, language, format, value, and prompt associated with it. The property *type* defines the kind of data, such as a number, calendar entry, or string. The *format* determines how the data appears. For example, you can display a string in uppercase, lowercase, or mixed-case characters. The *prompt* provides additional information about the data. You could tell the person using the shape what kind of information to type, such as an employee's ID number when working with a floor plan.

In addition, you can use lists or duration (a time frame) as a custom property type. You enter the data in a shape's custom property fields. Many Visio shapes have built-in fields for entering custom property data. For example, all office layout shapes include inventory number and owner fields. Flowchart shapes contain fields for recording cost, duration, and resources.

Some Visio shapes don't have shape data fields. Right-click the shape and choose Data➪Shape Data to determine whether a shape has shape data. If the shape contains shape data, Visio displays a Shape Data dialog box like the one shown in Figure 12-1. If the shape doesn't have shape data, a message tells you that no shape data exists and asks whether you would like to define it now.

Even when a shape doesn't have any shape data associated with it, you can always add data. When a shape has too many properties, you can remove the excess properties with equal ease. The next section of this chapter describes how to perform both of these tasks.

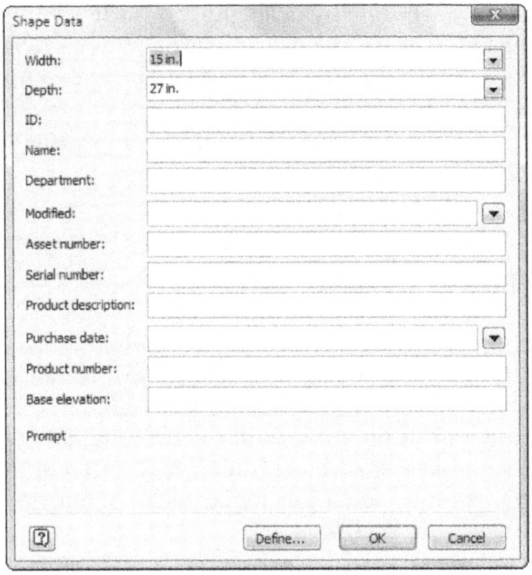

Figure 12-1:
When a
shape has
shape data,
the data
appears
in the
Shape Data
dialog box.

You might remember the Custom Properties dialog box from previous versions of Visio. This dialog box appears as the Shape Data dialog box in Visio 2007. The Custom Properties window has likewise changed to the Shape Data window. Except for the new name, these two elements work much as they did in previous versions of Visio.

Another way to display shape data is with the Shape Data window, which is shown in Figure 12-2. The nice thing about this window is that it stays on the screen, so you can check shape data as you click different shapes in a drawing. Each time you click a shape, Visio displays that shape's data. If a selected shape doesn't contain data, the box simply says "No Shape Data."

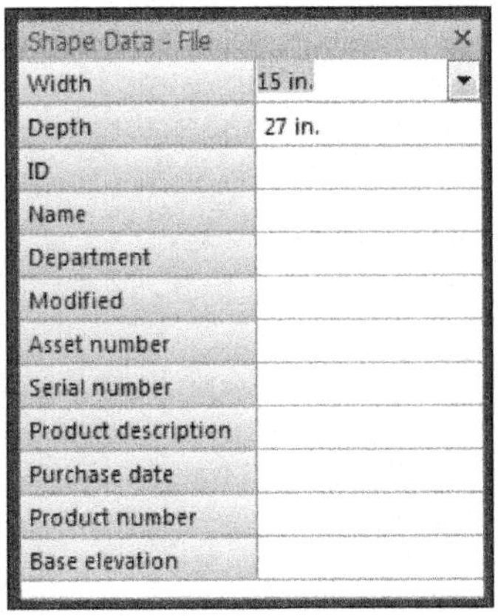

Figure 12-2:
Display the
Shape Data
window to
track or edit
shape data.

You can float the Shape Data window by dragging it anywhere on the screen, or you can dock it along any edge of the drawing area. When docked, the Shape Data window, like the Pan & Zoom window, can be rolled up like a window shade — just click the thumbtack icon and then move the mouse away from the window. To make the window reappear, move the mouse over the title bar. For more details, refer to Chapter 2.

Entering custom shape data

Any Visio shape can contain any data that you need and no more than you need. You accomplish the first goal by adding custom properties to the shape data and the second goal by removing any properties (custom or standard) you don't need. The important issue to consider is that the data you enter should reflect your personal needs. It doesn't matter whether someone at Microsoft felt it was important to add a particular piece of information to a shape; you can have things your own way.

In fact, creating shapes with just the data you need is just one more reason to create custom stencils using the techniques in Chapter 11. You can create shapes that contain the properties you want and then place them in a stencil so that you can use the same properties consistently for all of the diagrams you create. The following steps describe how to add custom properties to a shape. (These steps assume the shape has predefined shape data; see the "Editing custom property fields" section for details on creating your own shape data.)

1. **Open the drawing that contains the shape in which you want to store data.**

2. **Click or right-click the shape, and choose Data⇨Shape Data.**

   A Shape Data dialog box similar to the one in Figure 12-1 appears. All of the properties for the shape appear in the Properties area at the bottom of the dialog box. In Figure 12-1, for example, some of the properties for the selected shape are Width, Depth, ID, Name, and Department (among others). A different shape in the drawing might have different properties such as Diameter, Owner, and Service Date.

3. **Type the data that you want to store in each field.**

4. **Click OK.**

An even quicker way to enter data is by using the Shape Data window (refer to Figure 12-2). It isn't just a display box; you can use it to enter data as well. To enter or change data, click the field you want to change and start typing. Press Tab to move between data fields.

Visio stores the data you enter with the shape. Had someone else entered the data, you probably wouldn't even be aware of it because it doesn't make itself visible — unless you ask for it, or want to run a report on it, as you learn later in this chapter.

Visio 2007 includes a new kind of custom data display called the Data Graphic. The Data Graphic is always visible, and you can use it to implement specific display needs. For example, you can use the Data Graphic to display the owner of every piece of equipment in an office and then print that data as a diagram, rather than as a report. Removing the Data Graphic doesn't change any of the stored data, so you can create and remove a Data Graphic as needs change. The "Using the Data Graphics feature" section of Chapter 14 discusses the Data Graphic in detail.

Editing custom property fields

Suppose you have an office layout drawing that contains office equipment, among other items. You want to store data that defines employee assignments for each piece of equipment, the equipment manufacturer's name, and the location of the equipment, in addition to the fields that already exist. In some cases, you might have to create custom properties — properties that don't exist now — for the shape to accomplish this task.

You can add custom properties to an instance of a shape, a master shape on a custom stencil you create, and a shape in the Document Stencil (making that Document Stencil even more important). The only time you can't add custom data is when working with a Visio stencil. The reason you can't make this change is that Microsoft wants to ensure you always have a complete set of default baseline shapes from which to create your own shapes. This is actually a great policy because it means you can create as many versions of the default shapes as you want without ever touching the default shapes.

The Document Stencil applies only to the current drawing. Custom stencils are those you create with whatever shapes you want and are available to use with any drawing. Refer to Chapter 11 for more information on working with stencils.

Sometimes you also want to remove standard properties from a shape. For example, your organization might not care about the Base Elevation property supplied with many floor plan shapes. You can remove those properties when you don't need them. Simplifying shapes makes them easier to use. Anytime you can simplify a shape, especially in a group setting, you reduce the opportunity for error.

Adding custom properties to an individual shape

Sometimes you have a special shape in a diagram. The shape is unique and has unique data requirements. When you see a unique shape, feel free to add new data fields to just that shape. The following steps describe how to add a custom property field to an individual shape:

1. **Open the drawing that contains the shape you want to modify.**

2. **Select the shape and choose Data⇨Shape Data.**

   When the shape already has shape data, Visio displays the Shape Data dialog box shown in Figure 12-1 (proceed to Step 4). If the shape has no shape data, Visio displays a message box telling you that it doesn't have any data and asking whether you want to add data.

3. **Click Yes when the shape has no shape data.**

   Visio displays the Shape Data dialog box shown in Figure 12-1.

4. **Click Define.**

   The Define Shape Data dialog box appears, as shown in Figure 12-3. If the shape already has shape data defined, the first custom property (such as Height or Depth) appears in the Label box. Visio lists other shape data in the Properties area of the dialog box.

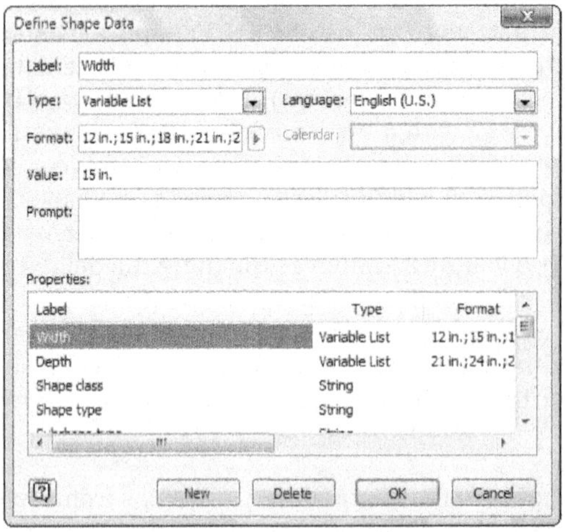

Figure 12-3:
You can
edit, delete,
or create
properties.

5. **Click New.**

   The name in the Label box changes to Property*x,* where *x* is a number. If the shape already has eight properties, for example, Visio uses a property name of Property9. If the shape doesn't have shape data defined yet, the name that appears in the Label box is a placeholder called Property1 (because it's the first property you're defining).

6. **Define your custom property by following these steps:**

   a. **Type a new, descriptive name in the Label field.**

      As you type, the new label appears in the Properties area at the bottom of the dialog box.

   b. **Choose the type of data that the field will hold (String for text, Number for numeric entries, Currency for money, and so on) in the Type field.**

   c. **Choose a format style (such as General, Whole Number, or Fraction) in the Format field. Type the values for a list separated by semicolons when working with a list.**

   d. **Type a description of the input required for this field in the Prompt field.**

      The prompt appears at the bottom of the Shape Data dialog box in the Prompt field. In addition, the prompt appears as a ToolTip when you hover the mouse over a custom property label in the Shape Data window. Always include a prompt with your custom property so that others know how to use it. In addition, the prompt acts as a reminder to you so you know why you created the custom property.

   e. **Type an entry in the Value field if you want to enter a value for the custom property you just created.**

      If you prefer to enter data later, refer to the section "Entering custom shape data," earlier in this chapter.

7. **Click New and repeat Step 6 if you want to create another custom property.**

8. **Click OK.**

   Visio returns to the Shape Data dialog box.

Working with lists requires special information. A fixed list only lets you choose an existing value. You type the acceptable values in the Format field. For example, when a list accepts 1, 2, 3, or 4 as entries, you type **1;2;3;4** in the Format field. Variable lists let you add values using the Value field. To add a new value, type a semicolon and then the value you want to add. To delete a value, you must edit the Format field. See the "Editing existing custom properties" section, later in this chapter, for details. Some items naturally adapt themselves to use with a Variable list. For example, the bookcase shape shown in Figure 12-4 has a list of books that should appear in it.

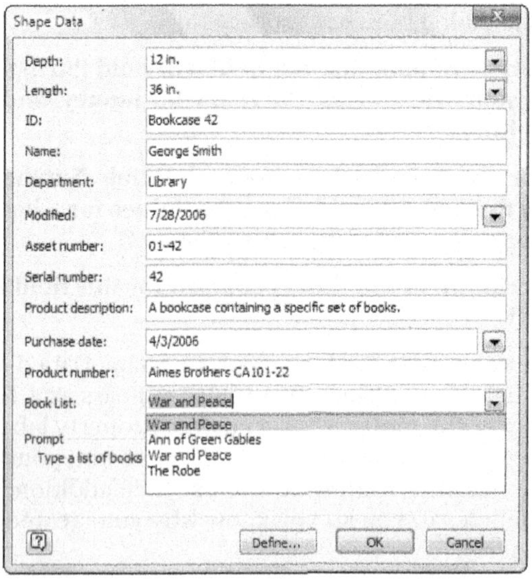

Figure 12-4: Creative use of properties can make a shape unique.

Removing custom properties from an individual shape

You won't need to remove properties from an individual shape very often, but removing a property you don't need can make the shape easier to understand and reports easier to read. For example, all of the floor plan shapes include a Base Elevation property. This property only makes sense for items that you can hang on the wall or mount in some other way. When a piece of furniture sits on the ground all of the time, the Base Elevation property is superfluous. Use the following steps to remove a property:

1. **Open the drawing that contains the shape you want to modify.**

2. **Select the shape and choose Data⇨Shape Data.**

   Visio displays the Shape Data dialog box shown in Figure 12-1.

3. **Click Define.**

   The Define Shape Data dialog box appears, as shown in Figure 12-3.

4. **Select the property you want to remove and then click Delete.**

   Visio removes the property, even when working with standard properties that Visio provides as part of the shape.

5. **Repeat Step 4 when you want to remove other properties.**

6. **Click OK.**

   Visio returns to the Shape Data dialog box.

Adding or removing custom shape properties in stencils

Always add custom properties to a stencil when you can so you don't have to make the same change more than one time. When you make a change to a shape on a stencil, the change applies to every new shape you create using that stencil. Unfortunately, shape data changes aren't retroactive, so changing a shape on a stencil after the fact won't save you from having to make the change on shapes that already exist.

Change the Document Stencil when you intend to use a custom setup only for one diagram. Otherwise, change the shape on a custom stencil you've created. The process for modifying a shape on a stencil is almost the same as modifying an individual shape, but you begin at a different starting point, as described in the following steps:

1. **Open the custom stencil or the Document Stencil that contains the shape for which you want to edit properties.**

2. **Right-click the stencil's title bar and choose Edit Stencil when working with a custom stencil.**

   A small red asterisk appears on the stencil title bar to indicate the stencil is in edit mode.

3. **Copy the shape you want to modify to the drawing area.**

   Visio doesn't let you change the shape properties directly within the stencil; you must modify them outside the stencil and then add the shape back into the stencil.

4. **Modify the shape properties as described in the "Adding custom properties to an individual shape" and "Removing custom properties from an individual shape" sections, earlier in this chapter.**

5. **Select the original shape in the stencil and press Delete to remove it.**

6. **Drag and drop the modified shape onto the stencil.**

   Visio adds the modified shape to the stencil. Remember to press Ctrl if you want to copy the shape, rather than move it from the drawing.

7. **Right-click the stencil's title bar and choose Save when working with a custom stencil.**

At this point, you have a new shape on the stencil that contains precisely the properties you want. However, it's normally a good idea to test whether your custom property fields have really changed. Drag a shape onto your drawing from the stencil you edited. Right-click the shape and choose Data➪Shape Data. The Shape Data dialog box appears, and you see the list of properties you defined.

Editing existing custom properties

Editing properties is something you should do with care because the modified properties won't affect existing shapes unless you change each shape individually. Going back through your diagrams to change what could be thousands of shapes isn't very appealing to anyone. If you modify a property by changing its name, you'll find that reports don't work as they should and you can't find shape data with any ease. When the same datum has different names across shapes, it's very hard to find it. In short, editing custom properties is generally a bad idea. Always add a new property that expresses a new concept, rather than changing an existing property, whenever you can.

Sometimes, you'll find a good reason to change a property. Perhaps you find that using a text data type doesn't work well for a particular shape and you change it to a number instead. Because the name of the property is the same, you can still find it with relative ease. Of course, the differing data types cause problems of their own. The safest property field to change is Prompt. It's extremely unlikely that you'll ever search for a particular prompt, and making the prompt clearer only makes things easier for the user. The following steps describe how to modify an existing property:

1. **Open the drawing that contains the shape for which you want to edit properties.**

2. **Click the shape and choose Data➪Shape Data, or right-click the shape and choose Data➪Shape Data.**

   The Shape Data dialog box appears.

3. **Click Define.**

   The Define Shape Data dialog box appears.

4. **Click the property you want to edit in the Properties area of the dialog box.**

   The property you select appears in the Label box.

5. **Modify any property attributes that require change.**

   Use extreme care in changing the Label field. Changing the Type and Format fields are less hazardous, but consider how the change could affect other diagrams before you make it. A change to the Language and Value fields is relatively safe, but could have unforeseen consequences. The only truly safe change is the Prompt field. Make this change whenever you feel the current prompt is unclear and the person using the property requires additional help.

6. **Click OK.**

   Visio returns to the Shape Data dialog box.

7. **Click OK.**

   Visio returns to your drawing.

Modifying shape data for multiple shapes

You can work with multiple shapes when working with shape data. Simply select the shapes you want to edit and choose Data⇨Shape Data. You'll see the familiar Shape Data dialog box, and you can perform any of the activities described in this section. For example, you can set the name of the person who owns a particular piece of equipment with one edit by selecting all of the pieces the person owns at one time. You can also add and remove common properties from all of the shapes with a single edit.

The only issue you must consider is that Visio only displays common properties. If one shape has a Name field and the other doesn't, you won't see the Name field. In addition, you see the values of the first shape you select. When the first shape has the Name field defined and the second one doesn't, it will appear that both shapes have the Name field defined. Likewise, when the first shape doesn't have the Name field defined, but the second one does, the Shape Data dialog box won't contain any values. Any changes you make to any of the properties affect all of the shapes.

Reporting on Data Stored in Visio Shapes

Data sitting in a shape is of limited use as reference information; it's far more useful when you can report on it. Visio provides the tools you need to generate all kinds of reports on your own, or you can choose from a variety — 22, in fact — of predefined reports.

To generate a report, Visio needs a report definition. The report definition is just a simple set of instructions, specifying the following:

- Which objects you want to report on
- Which shape data you want to display as columns in your report
- Report title
- Subtotals (if applicable)
- Sorting guidelines

When you use one of Visio's predefined reports, you don't need to concern yourself with creating report definitions because they're already created for you. Visio allows you to modify them, though, if you want.

Using a predefined report

You can always access any of the 22 predefined reports that Visio provides, but not all of the reports work in every situation. Consequently, Visio provides an option to display the reports that match your particular diagram. The type and number of predefined reports available to you when you use this filter depend on the type of drawing you create. Some drawings might have just two and others might have eight or more.

Some predefined reports fall into specific categories. For example:

- ✔ **Count and inventory reports** typically count items in a drawing.
- ✔ **Flowchart reports** include information on resources, cost, and duration.
- ✔ **Asset reports** display information about asset type, owner, name, and manufacturer.
- ✔ **Numeric reports** typically run calculations (totals, averages, maximums, minimums, and so on).

Visio makes it easy to use any of the predefined reports. The following steps describe how to select and display a report of your choice:

1. **Open the drawing you want to use.**

2. **Choose Data⇨Reports.**

   The Reports dialog box appears, as shown in Figure 12-5. Predefined reports appear in the Report area. Visio highlights the first report and displays a description of it in the Description area of the dialog box. You can click different reports to display their descriptions, if you want.

Reports

Report	Location
Asset Report	C:\Program Files\Microsof
Door Schedule	C:\Program Files\Microsof
HVAC Duct	C:\Program Files\Microsof
Inventory	C:\Program Files\Microsof
Move	C:\Program Files\Microsof
Space Report	C:\Program Files\Microsof

New...
Modify...
Remove
Browse...

Description
Space Plan: Belongs to, Asset Type, Name, Manufacturer

☑ Show only drawing-specific reports

Run...   Close

3. Deselect the Show Only Drawing-Specific Reports option if you don't see the report you want.

Visio displays the complete list of predefined reports. However, many of these reports won't include fields that your diagram contains, so they may not print or print completely.

If you still don't see the report you want, it might not appear within the directories that Visio searches. Click Browse and locate the VRD file containing the report you want to use.

4. Select the report you want.

5. Click Run.

The Run Report dialog box appears, as shown in Figure 12-6.

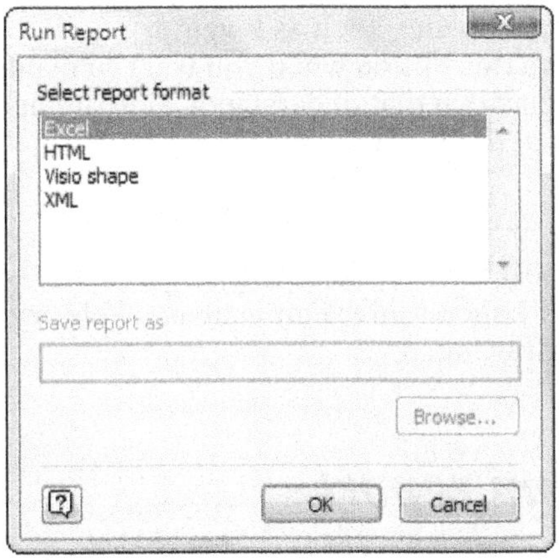

Figure 12-6:
Choose
a report
format for
the output of
your report.

> Run Report
>
> Select report format
>
> Excel
> HTML
> Visio shape
> XML
>
> Save report as
>
> Browse...
>
> OK   Cancel

6. Choose a report format for the results:

- **Excel** generates results in Microsoft Excel. You see a spreadsheet appear and can use the normal spreadsheet functions to manipulate the data. It's possible to save the data later. This option doesn't require any additional input.

- **HTML** saves results in your My Documents folder with the name `Report_x.html` (where *x* is the number of the report beginning with 1 for the first report you generate). Visio then opens the default browser with the report loaded. Visio lets you choose a different destination for the report, and you can choose a better report name, such as Inventory for Bob's Office.

- **Visio Shape** inserts results in the current drawing as a shape. You can choose to create a link to the report or to create a copy of the report in the diagram. Using a link makes your diagram file smaller. However, you must have a copy of the report available to see the data, and links tend to be fragile if you move the diagram. Copying the report makes your diagram file larger, but the diagram loads faster (it doesn't have to locate the report file on disk) and the diagram is more portable.

- **XML** saves results in your My Documents folder with the name `Report_x.xml` (where x is the number of the report beginning with 1 for the first report you generate). Visio then opens the default browser with the report loaded. Of course, the report looks like a standard XML file unless you combine the output with another technology to format the report, such as XSLT. Visio lets you choose a different destination for the report, and you can choose a better report name, such as Inventory for Bob's Office. Generally, you'll use this option when you want to manipulate the data in another application that understands XML or import the data into a database such as SQL Server.

7. **Click OK.**

Choosing the Visio shape report format places the results in the current drawing as a shape. Figure 12-7 shows an example of an inventory report shape in an office floor plan drawing.

Creating a custom report

The predefined reports are simplistic. Microsoft can't possibly guess how you plan to use the diagrams you create, so in most cases, the predefined reports act as a starting point for your own report. You always have two choices; you can branch out on your own and create a report from scratch or modify an existing predefined report. Don't let the idea of creating your own scare you off; the process is simple and will give you exactly the results you want.

Suppose that in an office layout drawing, you want a report that lists only the printers in the drawing, not an entire inventory report. That's straightforward; you're asking for only one simple thing: printers. Therefore, your report definition has only one requirement:

Product Description = printer

Okay, a listing of printers probably isn't a realistic report unless you order supplies or perform maintenance on just the printers in your organization, but it might provide a good starting point — a good test project that won't consume a lot of time to create. In many cases, you'll want something more specific and a little more involved. Maybe there's a recall on a plotter part and you need a count of all the color plotters in the Sales and Marketing departments that were manufactured by ABC Company and have a purchase date of 1999. Generating a report like this requires some simple database-like queries, which you can easily define when you create a custom report. For a report like this, you specify the following:

✓ Department = Marketing

✓ Product Description = color plotter

✓ Manufacturer = ABC Company

✓ Purchase Date = 1999

The simple rule is that whenever you create a custom report, you do three things:

✓ Specify which shapes you want to report on

✓ Choose the custom properties to include in the report

✓ Choose how you want the report sorted and organized

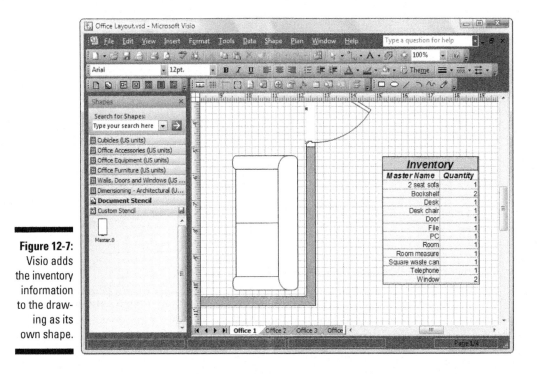

Figure 12-7: Visio adds the inventory information to the drawing as its own shape.

Defining new reports

Visio makes creating a report easy for you by displaying the Report Definition Wizard, which guides you through these choices step by step. The following steps describe how to create a report:

1. **Open the drawing you want to use.**

2. **Choose Data⇨Reports.**

   The Reports dialog box appears.

3. **Click New.**

   The first screen of the Report Definition Wizard dialog box appears, as shown in Figure 12-8. This dialog box lets you choose the source of shapes to use for the report. When your diagram contains multiple pages, you can select the Shapes on All Pages option to choose all of the shapes no matter where they appear. A single page diagram will likely use the Shapes on the Current Page option. You can also use this option when you want to limit the report to a single page of a multipage diagram. The Shapes That Are Selected option is extremely useful because it helps you target just the shape you choose. Finally, the Other option is only enabled for specific diagram types such as an organizational chart. Visio provides special report functionality when you choose this option.

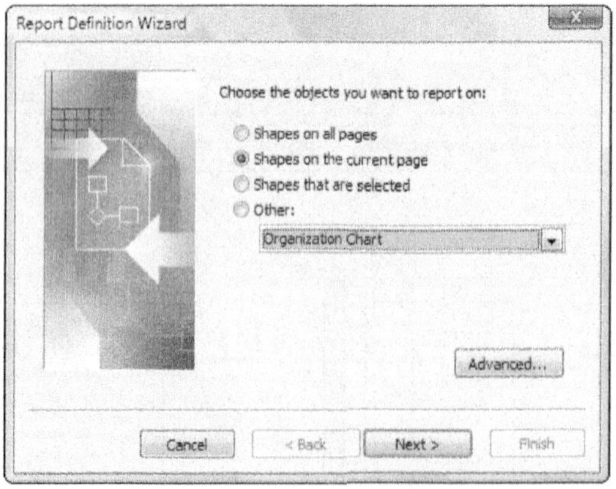

Figure 12-8:
Use the first screen of the Report Definition Wizard to choose the shapes you want to report on.

4. **Choose one of the shape selection options.**

5. **Perform the following steps to define specific criteria (such as the Marketing Department and a purchase date of 1999) to filter the report output. This technique is an especially good way to leverage custom properties you create:**

   a. **Click Advanced.**

      The Advanced dialog box appears, as shown in Figure 12-9.

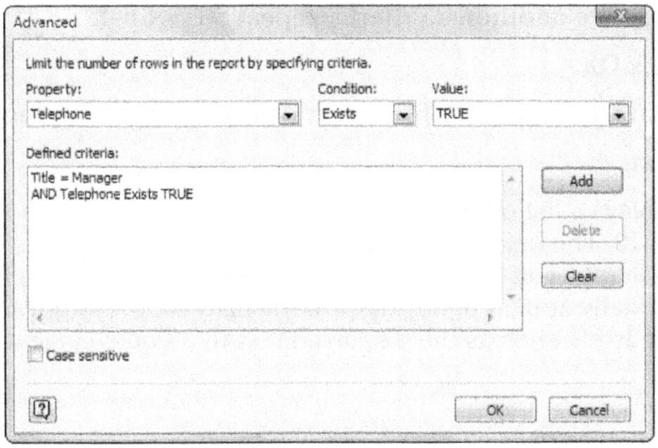

Figure 12-9:
Use the
Advanced
dialog box to
set special
conditions
in the report
definition.

b. **Select a custom property (such as Department) in the Property field.**

c. **Choose a condition (such as =, <, >, <>, <=, >=, or Exists for each custom property you chose in the Condition field.**

For example, if a custom property is Height, you might choose >= as your condition. The special condition, Exists, has a value of TRUE or FALSE. You use Exists to locate shapes that have a specified custom property defined. For example, when choosing from a list of parts, you might want only those parts that don't have a manufacturer defined so that you can assign someone to locate a manufacturer for the part.

d. **Type or select a value for the Property and Condition you selected in Steps 5b and 5c in the Value field.**

For example, enter **6** if you want to find a shape for which the Height property is >=6. Some properties will require that you choose a specific value, rather than type an arbitrary value. For example, a special property, <Layer Name>, requires that you specify one of the existing layers, such as Door. The resulting filter includes only shapes in that layer as part of the report.

e. **Select the Case Sensitive option when you want to create a case-sensitive filter.**

In some cases, case sensitivity is important. For example, when working on an application design, you may want the myValue variable and not the MyValue variable filtered. This option is especially useful in software design, but can provide necessary filtering functionality in any diagram. Case sensitivity applies to all of the filtering criteria or none of it; you can't apply it to one criterion and not to others.

f. **Click Add.**

The condition appears in the Defined Criteria box.

      g. To create additional criteria, repeat Steps 5b–f.

      h. Click OK.

      Visio returns you to the Report Definition Wizard dialog box.

6. Click Next.

    Visio displays a list of properties that you can choose, as shown in Figure 12-10. The default settings display only the properties associated with the shapes you choose. Properties that appear in angle brackets don't normally appear in the shape data. Instead, they appear as part of the shape itself, such as the displayed text that you change using the Text Tool.

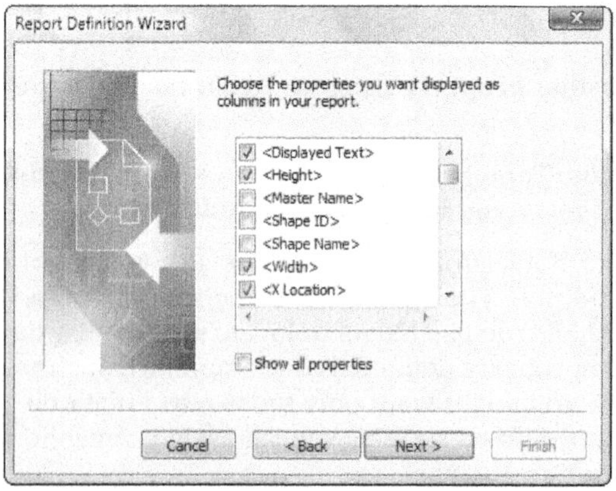

Figure 12-10:
Choose the properties you want to include in the report.

7. Select the Show All Properties check box when you want to display all of the properties, rather than those that Visio selects.

    In some rare cases, you might want to choose properties that could appear with a shape, rather than those that appear in the current diagram. A report doesn't affect just the current diagram. When you create a report, you often create it with multiple diagrams in mind. Consequently, the current diagram may not contain all of the custom properties found in all of the diagrams that the report affects. In this case, selecting the Show All Properties check box lets you choose the properties that appear in other diagrams, but not the current diagram. Generally, the best idea is to locate a diagram that contains all of the properties you want to appear in the report, but sometimes this simply isn't possible.

8. **Select each custom property you want to be displayed in the report (each custom property represents a column in the report), and then click Next.**

   Visio displays the report particulars, such as the title, subtotals, sorting, and the numeric formatting that you want to display, as shown in Figure 12-11.

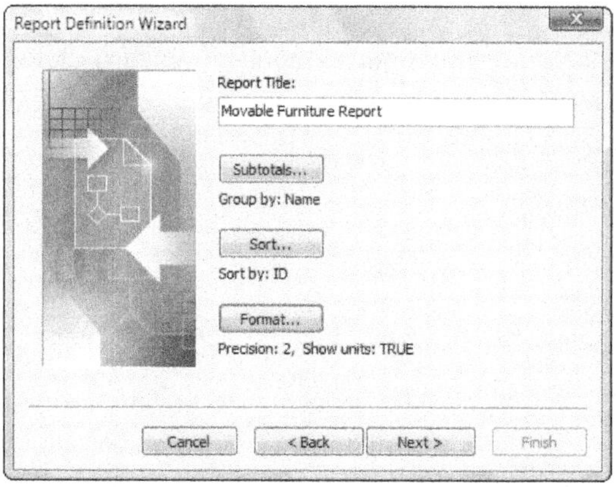

Figure 12-11:
Modify
the report
particulars
such as the
title and
subtotals.

Report Definition Wizard

Report Title:
Movable Furniture Report

Subtotals...
Group by: Name

Sort...
Sort by: ID

Format...
Precision: 2, Show units: TRUE

Cancel   < Back   Next >   Finish

9. **Type a title in the Report Title field.**

10. **Click Subtotals if you want to include subtotals or use grouping in your report.**

    Visio displays the Subtotals dialog box shown in Figure 12-12. It's important to note that you don't have to choose a grouping to use the subtotal feature. The two elements are separate. When you choose a grouping and choose a subtotal value for that group, as shown in Figure 12-12, you obtain a group total. The following steps describe how to create a subtotal:

    a. **Select a property in the Group By field when you want to group items in the report.**

    b. **Click Options to choose grouping options.**

       The grouping options let you eliminate duplicate values in groups. You can also choose to show just the group subtotal, rather than all of the group information. Groups can also include grand totals so that you can see the statistics for each group and for the report as a whole.

c. **Check subtotal options for the report in the Subtotals area.**

Every property enables the subtotal options that work for it. For example, you can't compute the average of a text property, but you can count the number of shapes that have that particular text value. You can create multiple subtotals for each property. For example, you might want to know the maximum, minimum, and average height for all of the furniture in a room.

d. **Click OK.**

Visio returns you to the Report Definition Wizard dialog box.

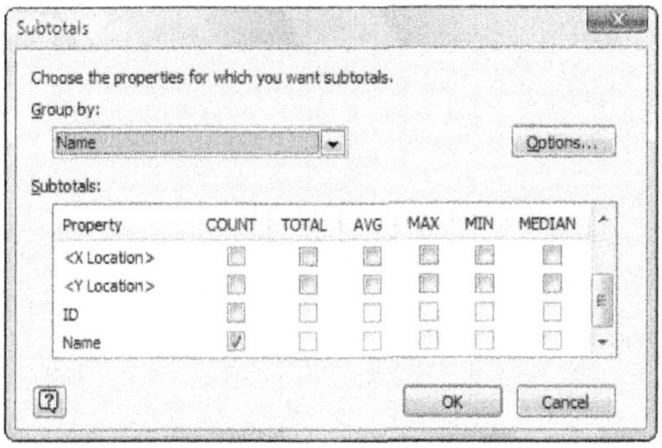

Figure 12-12:
Modify the report particulars such as the title and subtotals.

11. **Click Sort to sort the report by certain criteria and choose the column order.**

Visio displays the Sort dialog box shown in Figure 12-13. You must define a column order or Visio will use the default order shown. Sorting is completely optional, but a sorted report is significantly easier to read. The following steps describe how to sort by specific criteria:

a. **Define a column order for the report by modifying the order of the custom properties in the Column Order list.**

When you see a column you want to move, highlight the column and click Move Up or Move Down as needed to change its order in the list. The top of the list defines the first column in your report.

b. **Choose property names in one or more of the Row Order area drop-down boxes. Select Ascending or Descending depending on the order that you want to use.**

c. **Click OK.**

Visio returns you to the Report Definition Wizard dialog box.

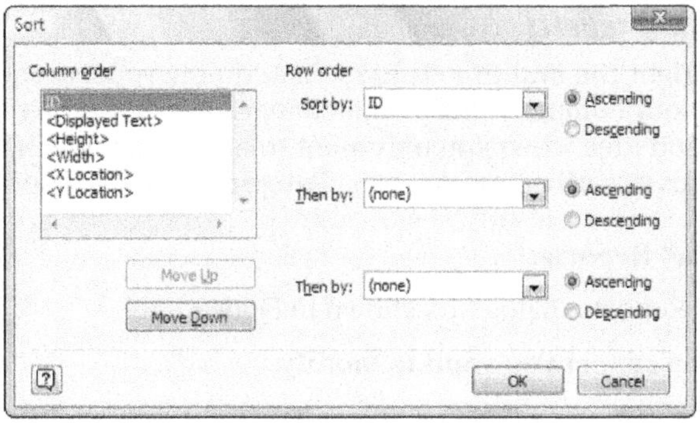

Figure 12-13:
Choose a
sort order
for your
report and
define the
column
order.

12. **Click Format.**

    Visio displays the Format dialog box.

13. **Choose the number of digits of precision you want to use for decimal places (2 is the default). Select the Show Units check box when you want Visio to display units of measure in the report. Click OK.**

    Visio changes the formatting options as specified.

14. **Click Next.**

15. **Type a name for your report in the Name field.**

    The name you type here is the name that you see in the Run Report dialog box when you choose to print a report.

16. **Type a description for your custom report in the Description field.**

17. **Choose a save location for your report.**

    Visio lets you save a report in the diagram or on disk. When you save a report in the diagram, it becomes available to anyone using that diagram, even when you send the diagram to someone else. However, when you save the report on disk, it becomes available to every diagram that uses the template. Save the report to disk when you want to create a global report. You can always send the report to someone else as a separate file when he or she needs it.

18. **Click Finish.**

    Visio returns to the Reports dialog box shown in Figure 12-5. Visio adds your custom report to the list of predefined reports.

Run a custom report just like you do a predefined one: Click Run in the Reports dialog box and then choose the format for your results. If you find errors in your report definition, simply repeat the preceding steps, choosing different options.

Modifying existing reports

Getting a report right the first time is hard. In addition, report requirements often change as your company grows and changes. Creating the report from scratch isn't a good idea when you only want to make a couple of changes. The following steps describe how you can change an existing report as needed:

1. **Choose Data⇨Reports.**

   You see the Reports dialog box shown in Figure 12-5.

2. **Highlight the report you want to modify.**

3. **Click Modify.**

   You see the Report Definition Wizard shown in Figure 12-8.

4. **Follow the steps starting with Step 4 in the previous section to modify the report.**

Updating shape reports

Creating a report as a Visio shape has one distinct advantage. When working with other report types, you must rerun the report from scratch. However, when working with a Visio shape, you only have to right-click the shape and choose Run Report from the context menu to see an update. Visio runs the report in the background and you don't have to make any selections.

When you have made major changes to a report and still want to update the shape within Visio, right-click the shape and choose Update Report from the context menu. Visio displays the Update Report dialog box, where you click Run to perform the update. You can also use this option to choose an entirely different report to fill the shape with data.

Modifying shape reports

Despite your best efforts, the shape report you create might not appear as you anticipated. Perhaps you want to highlight an area of the report or include some additional information. The report contains all of the required data, but it requires a little more pizzazz. Visio lets you perform direct report modification when needed to perform these tasks. Simply double-click the report and the entire Visio display changes, as shown in Figure 12-14.

For those of you familiar with Excel, you'll notice that the Ribbon interface, options, features, and everything about Visio now looks a lot like Excel. In this case, the report was modified to highlight the owner names using a larger font, but any formatting change you can make in Excel, you can also make in Visio. The shape has a hashed border around it now, so you can easily identify which shape has received this special focus.

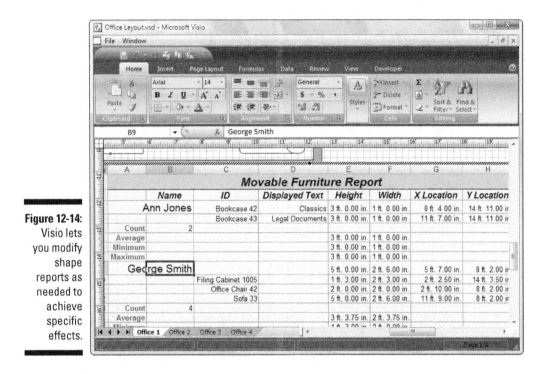

Figure 12-14:
Visio lets
you modify
shape
reports as
needed to
achieve
specific
effects.

As with any Excel spreadsheet, you can add more sheets to this report. That's right, you can hide as much or as little data in the report as you want. You can create charts or graphs based on the report data. Anything you can do with Excel, you can also do with this shape report. At some point, you'll want to stop modifying the report. Simply click anywhere outside of the report and the usual Visio interface will return.

This book doesn't provide you with a complete discussion of Excel. Of course, if you use this Visio feature very much, you'll want to know quite a bit more about how Excel works so you can make maximum use of all of the functionality that Excel provides. Check out *Excel 2007 For Dummies*, by Greg Harvey, PhD (published by Wiley) for more information about Excel.

Any formatting changes you make will stay in place when you update the report using the Run Report option. However, the changes won't stay in place when you use the Update Report option with a modified or different report. Because report elements can easily move during an update, you want to exercise care in making formatting changes — a larger font could suddenly highlight the wrong item if you aren't careful. Always check your report for unexpected changes after you update it.

Customizing Shape Behavior

Most Visio shapes behave in certain ways, depending on the drawing type and the actions you take in a drawing. For example, the 100-square-foot Space shape (on the Wall, Shell, and Structure stencil used in space plan drawings) adjusts and recalculates its square footage automatically if you resize the shape. Double-clicking a shape in an organizational chart lets you edit the displayed text, but double-clicking a report displays the Excel interface shown in Figure 12-14. These are just two examples of smart behavior in Visio shapes. The average user probably doesn't want to change these features without a good reason.

However, you might want to make some simple changes. For example, you might want to convert a 2-D shape to a 1-D shape so that it behaves like a connector. Using this technique would help you create custom arrows or other unusual connectors for your diagrams. You might also want to change the way groups are selected when you click them. In some cases, you might want to change the action that occurs when you double-click a shape. For example, double-click a sofa and nothing happens, even though the default action supposedly lets you type display text for it. When you think about it, creating display text for a sofa isn't a particularly useful action, so you might want to do something else such as display the shape data. These are examples of simple changes that you can make to a single shape in a drawing or to custom shapes on the Document Stencil or a custom stencil.

Changing a shape from 2-D to 1-D

If you were to take the time to hand-draw an arrow like the one shown in Figure 12-15, you'd probably want it to behave as a connector. Instead, it behaves as a 2-D shape because it is a 2-D shape. That is, it has selection handles that allow you to resize the shape's height and width.

In contrast, connectors are 1-D shapes with endpoints that allow you to connect to other shapes, as shown in the lower half of Figure 12-15. To use your hand-drawn shape as a connector, you need to convert it from a 2-D shape to a 1-D shape so that it has endpoints. The following steps describe how to create a 1-D shape:

1. **Create your shape using Visio's drawing tools, or save an existing 2-D shape on a custom stencil.**

2. **Right-click the shape and choose Format⇨Behavior.**

   The Behavior dialog box appears, as shown in Figure 12-16. In the Interaction Style area, the Box (2-Dimensional) option is selected.

3. **Select the Line (1-Dimensional) option in the Interaction Style area.**

4. **Click OK.**

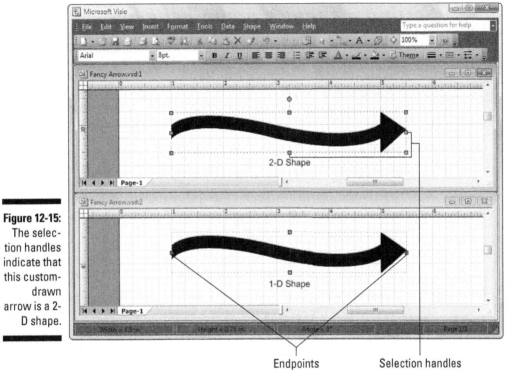

Figure 12-15:
The selec-
tion handles
indicate that
this custom-
drawn
arrow is a 2-
D shape.

Endpoints   Selection handles

Now return to your drawing and select your shape. You see that its selection handles (that allowed you to resize for height and width) are replaced with endpoints. You can connect these endpoints to shapes at connection points. For more information about connecting shapes, refer to Chapter 6.

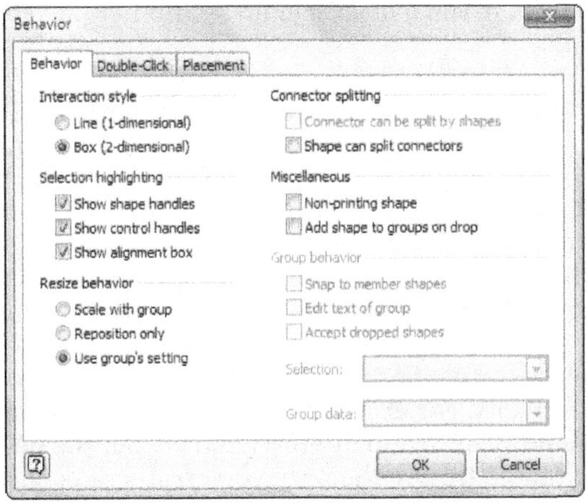

Figure 12-16:
Use the
Behavior
dialog box
to convert
2-D shapes
to 1-D.

Setting a shape's group behavior

A *group* is a set of shapes that behave together as a single unit. Ordinarily when you click a group, Visio selects the group first. If you click a second time, Visio selects an individual shape in the group. However, you can choose to swap this selection order and have individual shapes subselected on the first click, or you can choose to have only the group selected (that is, individual shapes are never subselected). The following steps describe how to change group behavior:

1. **Open the drawing that contains the grouped shape.**
2. **Right-click the group and choose Format➪Behavior.**

   The Behavior dialog box shown in Figure 12-16 appears.
3. **Choose one of the following options in the Selection drop-down list box:**
   - **Group Only:** Prevents the selection of individual shapes in the group.
   - **Group First:** Selects the group with one mouse click and a group component with a second mouse click. This is the default setting.
   - **Members First:** Selects a group component with the first mouse click and the entire group with a second mouse click.
4. **Click OK.**

Setting a shape's double-click behavior

Sometimes you want to change the double-click behavior of a shape. For example, you might want to set a piece of furniture to show its shape data because that action is more practical when working with furniture. By default, a shape's text box opens when you double-click, but Visio provides a wealth of other choices. You can set a shape's double-click behavior to open a grouped shape, display a help screen, run a macro, jump to another page in the drawing, or do nothing at all.

Jumping to another page is a way to create a *drill-down* drawing. Suppose that you're diagramming a worldwide communications network. One page of the drawing, called Corporate, shows a worldwide view of the network set on a background of a world map. Network symbols appear on each continent. Understandably, a diagram of this scope shows very little detail. However, another page of the drawing, called Europe, shows specific locations where network hubs exist, specifically, London, Berlin, Rome, Madrid, and Paris.

The Europe page, however, still doesn't show enough detail, so you create individual pages for each city. For example, you could use a city map of Paris as your background (just to add interest) and lay out the network components on top. (You do this on the page you create for each city.)

Now, the question is, how do you get from the high-level Europe map to the detail? You could search through all the page tabs at the bottom of the screen, but a better solution is to set a shape's double-click behavior to *link* to a specific page. On the Europe page, the network shape for each city is set as the link. (Refer to Chapter 9 for more information about working with pages in a drawing.) The following steps describe how to change a shape's double-click behavior:

1. **Open the drawing that contains the shape you want to change.**

2. **Right-click the shape and choose Format⇨Behavior.**

   The Behavior dialog box shown in Figure 12-16 appears.

3. **Select the Double-Click tab.**

   You see a list of double-click options, as shown in Figure 12-17.

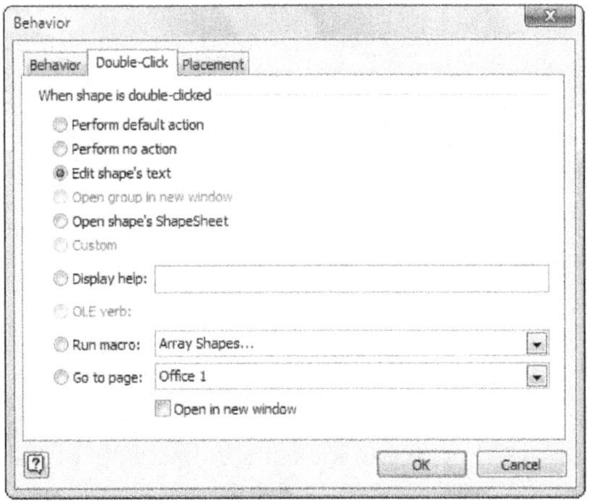

Figure 12-17:
You can set
a shape's
double-click
behavior.

4. **Choose one of the options listed:**

   • If you choose Run Macro, click the down arrow and select a macro from the list. (The topic of macros is beyond the scope of this book.)

   • If you choose Go to Page, click the down arrow and select a drawing page.

5. **Select the Open in New Window check box when you want to see a linked page in a new window or otherwise perform the task in a separate window.**

6. **Click OK.**

Protecting Your Work

When you create drawings that you're going to share with others, you want to protect your work from unwitting destroyers (including yourself). You can protect entire drawings, grouped shapes, individual shapes, or selected aspects of a shape from being changed. The following sections discuss the several methods available for helping you protect your work.

Preventing shapes from being changed

You use the Format⇨Protection command to protect a shape from changes. This command displays the Protection dialog box, which is shown in Figure 12-18.

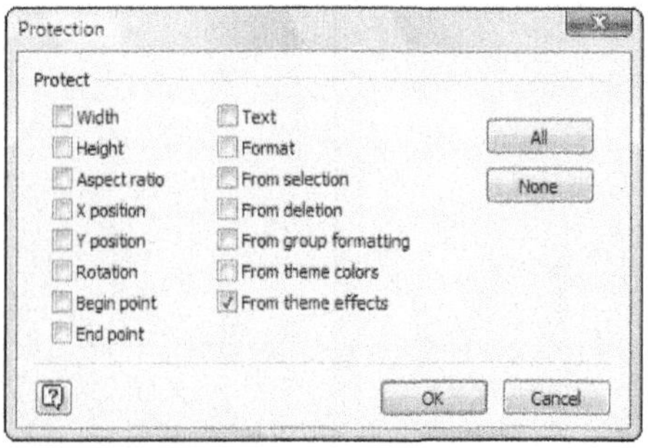

Figure 12-18:
You can choose specific aspects of protection.

As you can see in Figure 12-18, you can lock several aspects of a shape to prevent it from being changed:

- **Width:** Prevents anyone from changing the width of a shape or a grouped shape.

- **Height:** Prevents anyone from changing the height of a shape or a grouped shape.

- **Aspect ratio:** Prevents anyone from changing the ratio between a shape's width and height, such as 1:1.

- **X position:** Prevents anyone from moving the shape from its position on the *x* axis (horizontal). The shape can be moved up or down but not right or left.

✔ **Y position:** Prevents anyone from moving the shape from its position on the *y* axis (vertical). The shape can be moved right or left but not up or down.

✔ **Rotation:** Blocks anyone from rotating the shape or changing its center of rotation.

✔ **Begin point:** Prevents anyone from changing the beginning point of a 1-D shape.

✔ **End point:** Prevents anyone from changing the endpoint of a 1-D shape.

✔ **Text:** Prevents any changes to a shape's or a grouped shape's text box.

✔ **Format:** Blocks changes to any format characteristics.

✔ **From selection:** Makes a shape not selectable (To be effective, this selection requires an additional setting, described in the next section of this chapter.)

✔ **From deletion:** Protects the shape from being deleted.

✔ **From group formatting:** Protects an individual shape within a group from the effects of group formatting.

✔ **From theme colors:** Protects a shape from accepting changes in color due to a change in the theme.

✔ **From theme effects:** Protects a shape from accepting changes in effects, such as line weight, due to a change in theme.

To lock selected aspects of a shape using the Format⇨Protection command, follow these steps:

1. **Open the drawing that contains the shape that you want to protect.**

2. **Select the shape or shapes that you want to protect.**

You can apply protection to more than one shape at a time. To select more than one shape, hold down the Ctrl key as you click each shape.

3. **Choose Format⇨Protection.**

The Protection dialog box appears (refer to Figure 12-18).

4. **Click each shape characteristic that you want to lock.**

5. **Click OK.**

If you want the protection to apply to the shape every time you use it, add the shape to a custom stencil and set the protection there. (See Chapter 11 for more information about creating custom stencils.)

If you use the preceding steps to protect a shape from selection, be aware that the shape can still be selected unless you also protect all shapes using the Drawing Explorer window. (It doesn't make sense, but that's how it works.) This feature is described in the section "Protecting an entire drawing," later in this chapter.

Keeping drawings secure

You have several options for protecting drawings from change. The method you choose depends on the results you want to achieve. All the methods make a drawing readable by others but not changeable (to whatever degree you define).

Locking layers

Locking layers protects parts. If you want other users to be able to edit some layers but not others, *locking layers* is a perfect solution. When you lock a layer, no one can select or change shapes on that layer.

If a user knows how to unlock the layer, shapes on that layer *can* be changed. For more secure protection, see the next section in this chapter. The following steps describe how to lock one or more layers on a drawing:

1. **Open the drawing whose layers you want to protect.**

2. **Right-click the toolbar area and choose View Toolbar.**

3. **Click the Layer Properties button (it looks like a stack of pages) on the View toolbar.**

   The Layer Properties dialog box appears.

4. **Select a check box in the Lock column for each layer you want to lock.**

5. **Click OK.**

Saving files as read-only

To achieve the highest level of protection for a drawing, save it as a read-only file. This action protects every aspect of the file (except viewing) regardless of any other protections that you set. Setting a file as read-only sends a clear message to your viewers that you don't want them making any changes. The following steps describe how to make a drawing read-only:

1. **Open the drawing that you want to save as a read-only file.**

2. **Choose File⇨Save As.**

   The Save As dialog box appears.

3. **Highlight the folder you want to use to save your drawing.**

4. **Type a name for your drawing in the File Name field.**

5. **Click the down arrow next to the Save button (see Figure 12-19) and choose the Read Only option.**

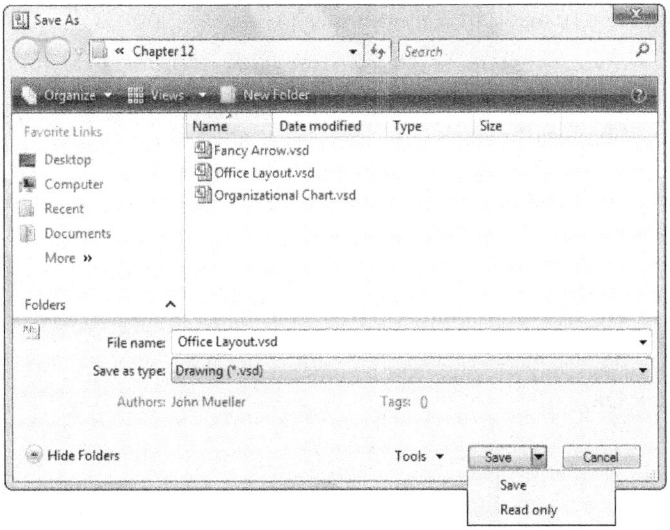

Figure 12-19: You can save a file as read-only.

If users want to change the file, they can choose File➪Save As, save a writable version of the file under a different name, and then work in that file. Your original read-only file is still protected.

Protecting an entire drawing

If you don't want to save a file as read-only, you have one more option. You can set protection for certain aspects of the entire drawing using the Drawing Explorer window. The following steps describe how to perform this task:

1. **Choose View➪Drawing Explorer Window.**

   The Drawing Explorer window appears, as shown in Figure 12-20.

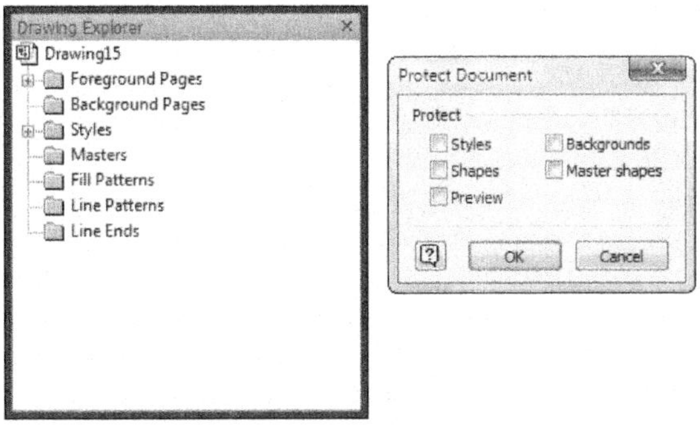

Figure 12-20: You can apply certain protections to an entire drawing.

2. **Right-click the drawing's path name at the top of the window and choose Protect Document.**

   The Protect Document dialog box appears, as shown in Figure 12-20.

3. **Choose any or all of the options shown:**

   - **Style:** Prevents users from changing, creating, or deleting styles but users can still apply styles.

   - **Shapes:** Prevents the selection of shapes when shape protection is set on individual shapes. (See the warning in the "Preventing shapes from being changed" section, earlier in this chapter.)

   - **Preview:** Prevents changes to a drawing's preview image.

   - **Backgrounds:** Prevents changes or deletion to background pages.

   - **Master shapes:** Prevents users from changing, creating, or deleting master shapes.

4. **Click OK.**

Chapter 13

Marking Up Drawings for Review

• •

In This Chapter

▶ Finding out about markup

▶ Adding comments to your drawing

▶ Discovering how markup tracking works

▶ Adding, viewing, incorporating, and deleting markup

▶ Marking a drawing with digital ink

▶ Changing digital ink to text or a shape

• •

*Y*ou'll find many good reasons to mark up your drawings. Reading an article, talking with a friend, or spending time at a seminar might provide ideas that you simply have to include in your drawing. After thinking about the drawing for a while, you might see areas for improvement or might want to include additional details. As with many documents, drawings experience constant change as our view of the real-world object the drawing represents changes. Eventually, the object becomes outdated and the drawing becomes final, but all of the changes in between the beginning and the end of the drawing cycle show a progression of thoughts and ideas.

Getting other people involved with your drawing is an essential part of working with a group. You might pass out rough drafts to several colleagues and ask them to mark up your drawing, and then incorporate those changes into the final version. In some cases, you might simply want peer review and use the markup from several people as ideas for your own changes. A drawing might also require regulatory review, such as a house addition or an engineering design review. Many drawings receive input from others — sometimes as a group and sometimes individually.

Using markup is a traditional way to edit documents. Word processors, such as Microsoft Word, have long had the capability of letting you review and edit on-screen rather than marking up a paper copy of the document. Even though drawings are essentially different in concept and content than word processing documents, many of the reasons for marking a drawing up are the same as those for a word processing document.

Editing, or *annotating,* on-screen has several advantages. First, you can save all of the comments with the file without changing the original. Second, if your colleagues are spread out across the country — or the world — making drawings available electronically saves time and money. Third, electronic editing is orderly and controlled. Fourth, incorporating changes is easy.

In this chapter, you discover the techniques for marking up drawings for two audiences: yourself and others. The markup tools you use are the same regardless of the audience.

Discovering Markup Tools

Markup is just another word for *proposed changes* to a drawing. The process of suggesting changes is called *marking up;* the comments themselves are markup. Visio provides two distinct tools for marking up a drawing:

- Comments
- Digital ink

Comments are notes that you add to a drawing. The notes can serve any purpose that you might imagine; don't limit yourself. Comments appear in a drawing as distinct Visio shapes. Here are a few suggestions for using comments:

- Use as a reminder to perform a task
- Ask a question
- Suggest changes
- Add information

Digital ink is a tool used to mimic handwriting and hand drawing. Even though reviewers are using electronic media, many people feel more comfortable using a pen to make changes. Using digital ink makes it easier to suggest changes in a way that makes people comfortable. Here are some suggestions for using digital ink:

- Circle a shape or draw a new one
- Highlight a title or a text label
- Scribble a handwritten note

Comments and digital ink are bona fide markup tools. A third element, *track markup,* is technically not a tool but rather a feature that helps you review and use proposed changes that others make to a drawing. Visio doesn't require that you use markup tracking for any drawing. However, when you choose to track markup, Visio displays comments and digital ink differently on the screen. You see this difference in the examples provided throughout this chapter.

Adding Comments to a Drawing

You can add a comment anywhere in a drawing using one simple command. Visio saves the comment in a tiny shape that you can place anywhere you like in the drawing. You can open and close the comment when needed. That way, you don't have to worry about the comment cluttering your drawing. The following steps describe how to add a comment to your drawing:

1. **Open the drawing.**

2. **Choose Insert⇨Comment.**

   A comment box appears on the screen with your name and the current date, as shown in Figure 13-1. Visio also displays the Reviewing task pane and the Reviewing toolbar, as shown in the figure (see the "Using the Reviewing toolbar and the task pane" section, later in this chapter, for details on these features). At the upper-left corner of the comment box is a small box with your initials and a comment number, such as JPM4. Visio increments the number with each comment you add. A hidden comment shows only the small box.

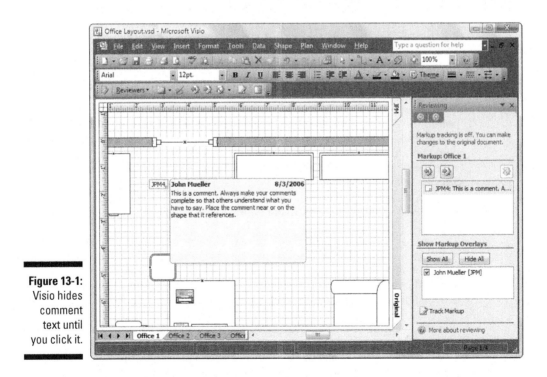

Figure 13-1:
Visio hides comment text until you click it.

3. **Type the text for your comment, and then click anywhere outside the comment box.**

   Visio closes the large comment box and leaves the small shape with your initials in it on the screen.

4. **Drag the comment box to the location in the drawing where it makes the most sense.**

To read a comment, click the small comment shape, and the box opens to display the text of the comment. To edit a comment, *double-click* the shape or choose Edit Comment from the drop-down list box on the Reviewing toolbar. A slightly larger box opens to display the comment so you can edit it.

What *isn't* visible in Figure 13-1 is the color in which the comment appears on the screen. Visio assigns a specific color to each reviewer, and the comment-box outline appears in that color. The next section explains markup tracking in more detail.

How Markup Tracking Works

If you anticipate having one or more people reviewing a drawing, you'll want to use the Track Markup feature in Visio. Using tracking, reviewers can add comments or suggest changes, and each reviewer's comments are distinct from one another. Here's how it works.

To use the Track Markup feature, reviewers must first turn on this feature before they begin reviewing by choosing Tools➪Track Markup or by clicking Track Markup on the Reviewing toolbar. When you turn Track Markup on, the client window border changes to your reviewer color — normally, the border uses the default Windows color. The Reviewing task pane also disables the markup overlays for the diagram. With tracking on, the reviewer can add comments, add new shapes, change the formatting of new shapes, and draw figures or handwritten notes using digital ink.

The reviewer's proposed changes appear on an overlay on the original drawing — nothing in the original drawing is changed. (An *overlay* is similar to a Visio layer, but overlays are *not* placed on separate layers in a drawing. Think of overlays as on-screen layers only.) If several people review the same drawing file, each reviewer's input appears on a separate overlay.

You can see only your own overlay while Track Markup is on. Turn Track Markup off, and you can see all of the overlays again. Visio identifies overlays by colored tabs in the upper-right corner of the drawing window — the original drawing tab appears in the lower-right corner of the drawing. You can see the tabs in Figure 13-2 (although the distinct colors are impossible to see in gray scale). Any additions also appear in the reviewer's color, and you can see each change listed in the Reviewing task pane.

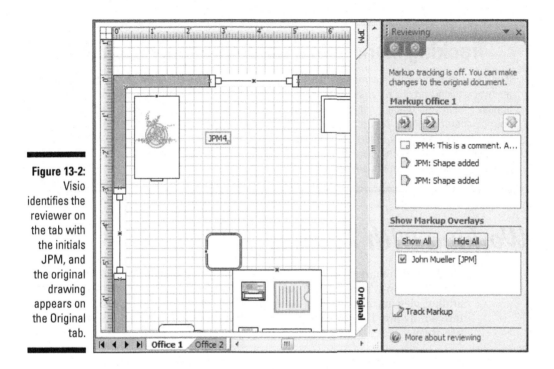

Figure 13-2:
Visio identifies the reviewer on the tab with the initials JPM, and the original drawing appears on the Original tab.

You can ask each reviewer to evaluate a separate copy of the drawing or the original. If reviewers evaluate separate copies, each file will contain your original drawing and one set of reviewer's comments on an overlay. Use separate drawings when asking for comments from peers so that each person provides comments based on his or her own experience, rather than being influenced by others. If all reviewers examine the same file (the original), each reviewer's comments are assigned a different color and appear as multiple overlays in the drawing file. Use the single-file approach in a collaborative work-group scenario so that each reviewer can add to the ideas of other drawing reviewers. You can control whether you see all reviewers' comments or only those of selected reviewers, as you see later in this chapter.

 Even if you, the creator of a drawing, are the only reviewer, you might still want to track markup. Sometimes you're not sure of the changes you want to make right away; you might try out some changes and think about them for a while without altering your original drawing. Markup keeps your original drawing separate from your suggested changes until you incorporate them.

 All changes that a reviewer proposes appear on the screen in the reviewer's assigned color, such as red. Even if the proposed changes include adding text, a shape, or a background in a specific color, all changes appear in the assigned color until you incorporate them into the drawing as permanent changes.

Tracking markup in a networked environment

If you work in a corporate environment, you are almost certainly part of a network, whether you access it from your office computer on-site or your computer at home. A corporate network often includes file servers, where you can store and share a single drawing file with many colleagues. In this environment, anyone who has the proper network permissions can access and review a drawing on the server. Ask your system administrator whether file directories are available for you to use to share drawings with colleagues. This is a great way to take advantage of Visio's tracking tools.

Working with Markup

Working with markup encompasses several activities, starting with displaying the proper on-screen tools. From there you can expand your skills to include adding, viewing, and deleting markup, as well as incorporating markup changes into a drawing. The following sections describe the markup tools and how to use them.

Using the Reviewing toolbar and the task pane

It's a good idea to display the Reviewing toolbar so that all the tracking tools are readily available when you use Visio's tracking feature. See Table 13-1. Some of the tools on the Reviewing toolbar appear in the Reviewing Task Pane as well, which you also need to display when tracking and reviewing markup.

Table 13-1	Reviewing Toolbar Buttons for Marking Up and Reviewing Markup	
Button	**Name**	**What It Does**
	Show/Hide Markup	Toggles the display of markup overlays on and off.
Reviewers ▾	Reviewers	Lists full names of all reviewers.
	Insert Comment	Pops up a new comment box.

Button	Name	What It Does
	Edit Comment	Places the selected comment into edit mode and enlarges the comment box.
	Delete Comment	Removes the selected comment.
	Ink Tool	Displays the Ink toolbar.
	Previous Markup	Selects the markup entry prior to current selection.
	Next Markup	Selects the markup entry after current selection.
	Delete Markup	Deletes current markup. A drop-down list box contains options for deleting all of the markup or specific markups by reviewer.
	Track Markup	Toggles tracking on and off.
	Reviewing Pane	Toggles the display of the Reviewing task pane and off.

Adding markup to a drawing

It's easy to add markup to a drawing; the hard part is remembering to turn tracking on. If you forget, your changes are incorporated into the original drawing (assuming you have permission to change the file).

You know immediately when tracking is turned on because you see a colored border around the drawing area instead of the overlay tabs, which aren't displayed when tracking is turned on. Visio automatically displays the Reviewing Task Pane on the right side of the screen and lists the current reviewer's name. In Figure 13-1, you can see the border around the drawing area and the Reviewing task pane to the right of the drawing area. The following steps describe how to add markup to a drawing:

1. **Open the drawing.**

2. **Click Track Markup on the Reviewing toolbar or choose Tools⇨ Track Markup.**

   The drawing window border color changes. The Reviewing task pane lists your name as the current reviewer.

3. **Make any changes you want to the drawing.**

   Visio displays every change you make (such as text, shapes, and comments) in your reviewing color. However, the Track Markup setting doesn't let you select, delete, or modify any shapes on the original drawing.

4. **Make any of the following suggestions using digital ink (refer to the section "Using Digital Ink," later in this chapter):**

   • Circle or mark areas using pens

   • Highlight areas using highlighters

   • Hand-write notes or draw stick figures using digital ink

5. **Turn Track Markup off when you finish editing the drawing, and save the file.**

If you're the creator of a drawing and distribute it for review, but then decide later to make changes to it yourself, you should also use track markup. This makes your proposed changes to the original drawing, your comments, and your questions visible to reviewers. If you don't turn on Track Markup, your changes alter the original drawing.

Viewing markup in a drawing

If you're the originator of a drawing, it's important to be able to view markup from reviewers. Depending on the situation, reviewing the changes is important to reviewers as well. You want reviewers to see the changes when working in a collaborative environment, but you may not want reviewers to see each other's changes in a peer-review or other individual input environment. If you're a reviewer, your markup is viewable on the screen as you work because Visio creates your personal overlay when you turn on tracking. If others have already reviewed the drawing before you, their markup normally appears on overlays separate from yours. Whether you are a reviewer or the originator of the drawing, you have the choice of viewing or not viewing markup.

Tracking markup and *viewing* markup are two separate things. Tracking turns on the feature of creating an overlay for a reviewer; viewing simply displays overlays. The following steps describe how to view markup:

1. **Open the drawing.**

2. **Choose View⇨task pane or click Reviewing Pane on the Reviewing toolbar to open the Reviewing task pane if it isn't already open.**

   Reviewers' comments appear in the Reviewing task pane.

3. **If you don't see any markup listed in the Reviewing task pane, click Show/Hide Markup on the Reviewing toolbar.**

   Markup entries appear in the Reviewing task pane. Visio identifies each entry with the reviewer's initials and the specific color assigned to him or her.

4. **Click Track Markup on the Reviewing toolbar or choose Tools⇨Track Markup if necessary.**

   When tracking is off, the first line of text in the Reviewing Task Pane is "Markup Tracking is off" and you see overlay tabs with reviewers' initials along the right edge of the drawing page. The Original tab appears at the lower right.

5. **Choose the overlays that you want to display by selecting one or more options in the Show Markup Overlays area of the Reviewing task pane.**

   - Click Show All to display all reviewers' overlays.

   - Click Hide All to turn off the display of all overlays.

   - Select the names of reviewers whose overlays you want to display to view reviewers' comments selectively.

6. **Highlight an entry you want to change in the Markup: Page-# area of the Reviewing task pane ("Markup: Office 1" is shown in Figure 13-2).**

   Visio selects the entity you highlight in the overlay. For example, when you choose a shape entry in the Reviewing task pane, Visio highlights that shape in the reviewer's overlay. Visio groups all markup entries by reviewer (color-coded and preceded by initials).

7. **Click Next Markup in the Markup: Page-# area of the Reviewing task pane or on the Reviewing toolbar to move to the reviewer's next suggestion.**

Incorporating markup changes in a drawing

You might receive many types of suggested changes from reviewers: new or changed text, new or changed shapes, comments, format changes, and more. As the creator of the original drawing, you have control of which proposed changes you incorporate into the drawing.

Visio doesn't provide a method for incorporating markup automatically. Even though the Visio documentation suggests creating each shape you want to incorporate from scratch, copying and pasting the shape from the reviewer's overlay makes more sense because the reviewer might change the shape characteristics or add shape data. The following steps describe a technique for incorporating markup that preserves all of the reviewer changes to the shape, text, comment, or other Visio element:

1. **Open the drawing.**

2. **Choose View➪task pane or click Reviewing Pane on the Reviewing toolbar to display the Reviewing task pane.**

   Visio displays the Reviewing task pane.

3. **Click Show/Hide Markup on the Reviewing toolbar if you don't see any markup in the Reviewing task pane.**

   You see markup for the current drawing.

4. **Select the reviewer markup that you want to view in the Show Markup Overlays area of the Reviewing task pane.**

   Only the reviewer markup you select appears.

5. **Click Track Markup on the Reviewing toolbar or choose Tools➪Track Markup if necessary.**

   You see "Markup Tracking is off" in the Reviewing task pane.

6. **Select one of the markup entries you want to incorporate into the original drawing from the Markup: Page-# area of the Reviewing task pane.**

   Visio highlights the selected entry on the reviewer's overlay.

7. **Click Copy.**

8. **Click the Original tab.**

9. **Click Paste.**

   Visio creates a copy of the markup.

10. **Drag the copy of the markup over the existing markup.**

    The copy now covers the markup.

11. **Click the original markup entry again in the Reviewing task pane.**

12. **Click Delete Markup in the Reviewing task pane or on the Reviewing toolbar.**

    Visio removes the markup, and you can see the copy of the markup on the Original tab. You can tell that the copy is on the Original tab because the entity no longer appears in the reviewer's color.

13. **Repeat Steps 6 through 12 for each entity you want to incorporate into the original document.**

14. **Click the down arrow next to Delete Markup on the Reviewing toolbar when you finish working with this reviewer. Choose Delete Markup and Overlays on Current Page➪Reviewer's Name [Initials].**

Visio removes the overlay for that reviewer, along with any remaining reviewer markup.

15. **Incorporate the next reviewer's markup, as described in Steps 6 through 14, until you have incorporated all of the markups.**

Deleting markup

Eventually you'll want to delete markup that people have added to a drawing even if you don't incorporate the markup into the original drawing. One strategy, as outlined in the preceding section, is to delete markup entries one by one as you incorporate them into your drawing. However, if you prefer, you can delete all markup entries for a specific reviewer using the following steps:

1. **Click Show All in the Show Markup Overlays area of the Reviewing task pane.**

   Visio lists all of the drawing's reviewers.

2. **Click the down arrow next to Delete Markup on the Reviewing toolbar, as shown in Figure 13-3.**

Figure 13-3:
Delete all markup for the current page, current document, or a selected reviewer.

3. **Choose one of the following options from the drop-down list:**

   • **Delete Markup:** Deletes the currently selected markup entry.

   • **Delete Markup Overlays on Current Page:** Deletes all markups on the current page. Or, you can choose a reviewer's name from the drop-down menu and delete all of his or her markups on the current page.

   • **Delete All Markup Overlays in Document:** Deletes all markups on every page of the drawing.

   Visio deletes the markup you selected.

Using Digital Ink

Another great markup tool is called *digital ink*. Digital ink lets you annotate a drawing the same way you would on paper. Using digital ink, you can circle items, scribble notes, draw stick figures, and more. Even if you don't have a graphics tablet or a tablet PC, you can use digital ink with your mouse.

You need to first display the Ink toolbar to use digital ink in a Visio drawing because these tools don't appear anywhere else. Click the Ink Tool button to display the Ink toolbar when the Reviewing toolbar is displayed. If the Reviewing toolbar isn't displayed, right-click the toolbar area and choose Ink from the context menu. Visio displays the Ink toolbar. Table 13-2 lists the tools available on the Ink toolbar.

Table 13-2		Toolbar Buttons for Working with Digital Ink	
Button	**Name**	**Toolbar**	**What It Does**
	Ink Tool	Reviewing	Displays the Ink toolbar.
	1 Ballpoint Pen and 2 Ballpoint Pen	Ink	Lets you draw or write on the screen in two different colors. The default color for 1 Ballpoint Pen is blue and for 2 Ballpoint Pen is black. However, you can change the ink color by clicking Ink Color.
	3 Felt-tip Pen	Ink	Lets you draw or write on the screen.
	4 Highlighter and 5 Highlighter	Ink	Lets you highlight areas in a drawing in two different colors. The default color for 4 Highlighter is yellow and for 5 Highlighter is green. However, you can change the ink color by clicking Ink Color.
	Eraser	Ink	Lets you erase any markups you've made.
	Close Ink Shape	Ink	Closes a selected ink shape.
	Ink Color	Ink	Lets you change the color of ink for any pen or highlighter.
	Ink Thickness	Ink	Lets you adjust the thickness of pens.

Selecting an ink tool

Visio provides several ink tools on the Ink toolbar (refer to Table 13-2). Two ballpoint pens, a felt-tip pen, and two highlighters should provide plenty of choices for you to mark up a drawing. You also have an Eraser tool and options for adjusting the ink color and line thickness.

To select an ink tool, just click it. The mouse pointer changes to a pen-shaped pointer. The only difference between ballpoint and felt-tip is the point thickness: 1 point for the two ballpoint pens and 1¾ points for the felt-tip pen. Highlighters draw at a thickness of 10 points, but they provide a highlight so you can see anything behind the color.

1 point is approximately ½₂ inch.

You can use any of the pen or highlighter tools as-is, or you can click the Ink Color or Ink Thickness button to change the default characteristics. Choose the drawing tools you want to use. Click the drop-down arrow on the Ink Color button to display a color palette and select a new color for that tool. Likewise, the arrow next to the Thickness button drops down a list of thicknesses, and you can choose a new thickness for the selected tool.

You can also change the pen and highlighter characteristics after the fact. Select the markup using the Pointer Tool. Choose the new characteristics using Ink Color or Ink Thickness. Visio makes the changes you request. Nothing is final when you place it on the drawing.

Using ink tools

You can use the pens and highlighters from the Ink toolbar to mark up or point out areas in a drawing, or you can use them to design a shape. If you just want to circle something in a drawing, sketch an arrow to draw attention to an item, highlight an area of the drawing, or hand-write a text message, you can use a pen or highlighter the same way you would if you were drawing on paper. Figure 13-4 shows a drawing that has been marked up with hand-written comments, added shapes, and highlighted areas.

Notice that the diagram shows More? in heavier print. You might think that this text was drawn using 3 Felt-tip Pen, but in reality, a standard pen was used and the characteristics of the markup were changed later. Notice the selection handles around the text. Visio views it as a standard 2-D shape, so you can do anything with this text that you do with any other 2-D shape. The following steps describe how to add digital ink to your drawing:

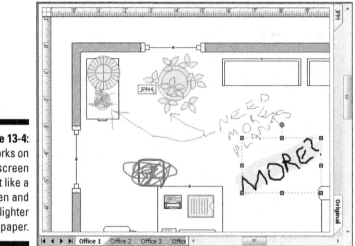

Figure 13-4:
Ink works on
the screen
just like a
pen and
highlighter
on paper.

1. **Open the drawing.**

2. **Right-click the toolbar area and choose Ink.**

   The Ink toolbar appears (refer to Figure 13-4).

3. **Select any of the tools listed in Table 13-2 from the Ink toolbar.**

   The mouse pointer changes to the correct digital-ink pointer.

4. **Draw, write a comment, erase doodles, change ink color or thickness, or perform any other digital ink–related tasks.**

   Note: If you're using a mouse rather than a pen on a tablet, hold the left mouse button down as you draw or write. You *can* lift your pen as you draw or write a comment, but you must do it very quickly! Using the mouse can prove difficult and you may want to use a tablet or stylus instead. A tablet or stylus makes it easier to write clearly.

   If you want to fill a shape that you drew using digital ink, you must draw it using only *one* line segment and be sure to close it by joining the end to the beginning. (Zoom in on the drawing area so that you can see the endpoints clearly.) If you use multiple line segments, Visio doesn't recognize it as a closed shape and therefore can't fill it.

5. **When you finish, lift your pen (or release the mouse button) and pause.**

   After a second or two, Visio draws a dotted blue outline with solid corners around the text or shape that you drew. Visio considers everything, including text, within this border a shape.

6. **To stop using digital ink, click the Pointer Tool (or another tool).**

To erase text or a shape you drew, click the Eraser tool on the Ink toolbar. The mouse pointer changes to an eraser shape. Move the eraser near the text or shape that you want to delete, and it becomes highlighted. Click the mouse button or, if you're using a pen, tap the shape to delete it. The Eraser tool can delete only the entire text or shape, not parts of it. A simpler alternative when working with a mouse is to select the shape as shown in Figure 13-4 and press Delete as you would for any other 2-D shape.

Changing digital ink shapes to geometry

You can convert anything that you draw using digital ink to *geometry*. This means it becomes an actual Visio shape, just as if you had drawn it using a drawing tool.

Why would you want to convert a digital-ink shape to geometry? Because unless you convert it, you can't alter the digital-ink formatting as you would a shape (including line color and style, fill color, transparency, and shadow). You can always change the line thickness and the color using Ink Color and Ink Thickness on the Ink toolbar. It's also possible to assign properties to digital ink, change its behavior (within the limitations of ink), resize it, and change its orientation. Changing the ink to geometry only affects the way you change the ink's appearance. The following steps describe how to change digital ink to geometry:

1. **Click the Pointer Tool on the Standard toolbar.**

2. **Right-click the digital-ink shape you want to convert and choose Convert Ink to Geometry.**

   Visio converts the digital ink to a shape. You might see a small change in the shape appearance, but otherwise, it selects as usual. However, if you try to change the shape characteristics using Ink Color or Ink Thickness, Visio ignores the request. Now you're free to change the characteristics of the shape, such as its line width, line color, fill color, and fill pattern.

 Sometimes when you draw a closed shape and then convert it to geometry, you end up with a 1-D shape instead of a 2-D shape. (This can occur if your beginning point and endpoint don't meet.) If you want the shape to be 2-D, right-click it and choose Format⇨Behavior. On the Behavior tab of the Behavior dialog box, choose the Box (2-Dimensional) option and then click OK. Visio converts the shape to a 2-D shape.

Changing digital-ink shapes to text

Visio can also convert ink to text. If your drawing contains handwritten comments that you created using a tablet PC, you can convert them to text. (Tablet PCs allow you to draw and hand-write text using a stylus.) Drawing text with a mouse also works, but it's less certain because you have less control over the appearance of the digital ink. Text conversion works well with clear text that looks pretty close to printing already. The following steps describe how to convert digital ink to text:

1. **Select the Pointer Tool.**

2. **Select the digital-ink words that you want to convert.**

   If clicking the text doesn't select all of the text, the digital-ink words probably won't convert very well to text. The need to select several pieces of text to form a single word probably spells problems, and you may want to consider retaining the original ink.

3. **Right-click the selected text and choose Convert Ink to Text from the context menu.**

   Visio converts the handwritten words to text, as shown in Figure 13-5. The original text was HI. Obtaining a usable entry required writing and rewriting the text for about a half hour. Figure 13-5 shows the best outcome. Yes, the text converted, but the example still ended up with an extra period at the end of the word.

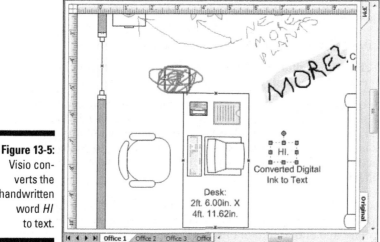

Figure 13-5:
Visio converts the handwritten word *HI* to text.

The conversion of handwriting to text is inaccurate for the most part. Be sure to check the spelling and punctuation of the converted text for errors. The closer the handwriting looks to printing, the more accurate the conversion. If you want to use this technique, be prepared to practice your penmanship a lot.

Chapter 14

Using Visio with Other Programs

*S*ometimes you can get away with using just one computer program to create a document. For example, you only need Visio when you want to create a floor plan or electronic circuit from scratch. However, some diagrams require information from other sources. You might want to base an organization chart on the data stored in another program. A graph might include information from Excel. You might want to use information from SQL Server to create a PivotDiagram based on recent sales. The possibilities for sharing data from other applications are as endless as your imagination.

Sharing data and objects is common with most programs, and Visio is no exception. As a member of the Microsoft Office suite of products, Visio lets you share diagrams and information, and that sharing works in both directions: Think of it as inbound and outbound. For instance, you can use Visio diagrams in other documents (outbound), and you can insert data or images (inbound) into Visio drawings. One inbound feature of Visio is the capability to use data from other programs to generate Visio diagrams. Of course, you also have the option of e-mailing Visio drawings to colleagues, or saving drawings in a format that lets you use them as Web pages.

Using Files from Other Programs in Visio

The most common way to share information from other programs in Visio is to paste the information, insert the information, or open a file of another type. You can paste objects from various sources, as you see later in this chapter in the "Exporting and importing shapes and drawings" section. The following list describes some of the items you can insert into a Visio drawing:

- Picture (from a file, clip art, a scanner, or a digital camera)
- Chart (a simple bar chart you create by entering data)
- Equation symbol
- WordArt
- CAD drawing
- Object

Most of these choices are obvious, except perhaps inserting an object. When you choose the Insert➪Object command, a dialog box appears, displaying a few dozen different objects (such as a media or video clip, a PowerPoint slide, a Microsoft Address Book View, and an Excel worksheet). Simply select the type of object you want and insert an existing file, create one, or display an icon for the object rather than the object itself.

Visio also provides an Insert➪Control command. You use this command to insert controls such as push buttons on a drawing. By adding Visual Basic for Applications (VBA) code to the control, you can define completely new actions for Visio to perform. Working with VBA is outside of the scope of this book. However, *VBA For Dummies, 5th Edition* (by John Paul Mueller, published by Wiley) provides all of the information you need for working with Visio. It even includes a bonus chapter devoted to Visio programming techniques.

If you prefer, you can open a file in Visio. The following list tells you which file types Visio supports directly:

- Drawing, Stencil, Template, and Workspace (all Visio file types)
- Scalable Vector Graphics (`.svg`)
- AutoCAD Drawing (`.dwg` and `.dfx`)
- Compressed Enhanced Metafile (`.emz`)
- Enhanced Metafile (`.emf`)
- Graphics Interchange Format (`.gif`)
- Joint Photographic Experts Group File Interchange Format (`.jpg`)
- Portable Network Graphics (`.png`)

✔ Tagged Image File Format (.tif and .tiff)

✔ Windows Bitmap (.bmp and .dib)

✔ Windows Metafile (.wmf)

These file types appear in the Files of Type box in the Open dialog box. When you choose File➪Open and select a file of one of these listed types, Visio pastes the file in the current drawing.

The file opened by the File➪Open command replaces any existing shapes in the drawing. Consequently, you don't want to use this feature with a drawing that already contains shapes that you want to use. A better solution is to use one of the options on the Insert menu to insert the file.

As an alternative to inserting the file, you can copy the drawing or other data onto the Clipboard and then use the options on the Edit menu to paste it into the drawing. Use Edit➪Paste when you want to perform the default action with the data. Use Edit➪Paste Special to display the Paste Special dialog box to either link (see the "Linking shapes and drawings" section, later in this chapter) or embed (see the "Embedding shapes in drawings" section, later in this chapter) the data. Visio 2007 also offers the new option of hyperlinking to the data. Using a hyperlink opens the data in the original application so that you don't even have to worry about it in Visio. See the "Hyperlinking shapes and drawings" section, later in this chapter, for details.

Generating Drawings from Data Stored in Non-Visio Files

You can save yourself a lot of work by using data stored in files you created with other programs, such as Microsoft Excel, Microsoft Project, a database, or a simple text file. By importing the data into Visio, you can create drawings from your stored data. Here are some good reasons for data reuse:

✔ **You can avoid reentering data.** You might have data in another program, such as Excel. No matter how much or little data the external application provides, using it as is generally saves you time typing it again.

✔ **You can avoid errors and inconsistencies.** Using a single application to store the data means that you avoid typing it multiple times and introducing inconsistencies between the copies. In addition, typing it once not only means you're less likely to make a mistake, but also ensures that mistakes are a lot easier to fix.

✔ **You can enter the data in the program in which you use it most.** Even if your data doesn't already exist, you can usually save time by entering it in the application best suited for that kind of data. A spreadsheet is a much better place to enter numbers and manipulate them than using Visio.

✓ **You can share drawings with other Visio users who may not have the same applications that you use to store and compile data.** Suppose that you're a project manager who relies on Microsoft Project to schedule and track large projects. Your site managers, however, don't have Project but do have Visio. You can use Project to generate a daily or weekly Gantt chart (which maps project tasks on a timeline) in Visio and then e-mail it to your site managers. The managers don't need to have Project or know how to use it. All they need to do is open a Visio drawing.

Whenever you create a drawing using external data, the external data is the *source* file. The output from Visio is the *target* file. The source file acts as input to the target file.

Creating an organization chart from existing data

In a company of any significant size, the information in organization charts — employee names, titles, and reporting managers — is almost surely stored already in a Human Resources database. You don't need to rekey this information just to create an organization chart in Visio; you can use the data you already have.

Obviously, maintaining employee privacy is an issue, but your company's Human Resources department might be willing to provide a subset of non-confidential employee information for you to use. If the Human Resources manager seems unwilling to provide the information directly, schedule a meeting with your Database Administrator (DBA) to determine how best to create an SQL Server View that contains the data you need, but won't expose confidential information. You don't need to change the data; you simply need to read it, so a view works perfectly.

Visio's Organization Chart Wizard is a fantastic tool that makes all this possible. (A *wizard* is a set of scripted questions that you answer so Visio can do the behind-the-scenes work for you.) The wizard looks for employee data in one of several possible file formats:

✓ Microsoft Excel (.xls) format.

✓ Microsoft Outlook format.

✓ Tab-delimited file (.txt file extension). A tab-delimited file includes a tab character between variables, such as first name, last name, and title.

✓ Comma-separated value file (.csv file extension). A comma-separated value file contains a comma character as the separator between variables.

✓ Org Plus text file (.txt).

✓ Open DataBase Connectivity (ODBC)–compliant database, such as Microsoft Access.

✓ Information you add manually using the wizard.

Regardless of the file type, the data must be set up in a format that Visio can work with. For example, the employee data file at a minimum *must* include the following pieces of information (referred to as variables, or *fields*):

✓ A unique identifier for each employee, whether a name or an employee number. An employee name can meet the requirement as a unique identifier if each name is unique.

✓ The unique ID of the person to whom the employee reports.

To leave a field blank, enter a comma (with no spaces) between the two commas used to separate entries. (In an Excel file, leave the cell blank.)

Creating an organization chart from existing data

If you already have the data you need to create the organization chart, you'll want to use it as input to the wizard. The following steps describe how to use existing data as input:

1. **Choose File⇨New⇨Business⇨Organization Chart Wizard.**

   Visio displays the first screen of the wizard shown in Figure 14-1. Visio automatically selects the option to create the organization chart from information already stored in a file or database for you.

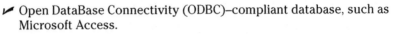

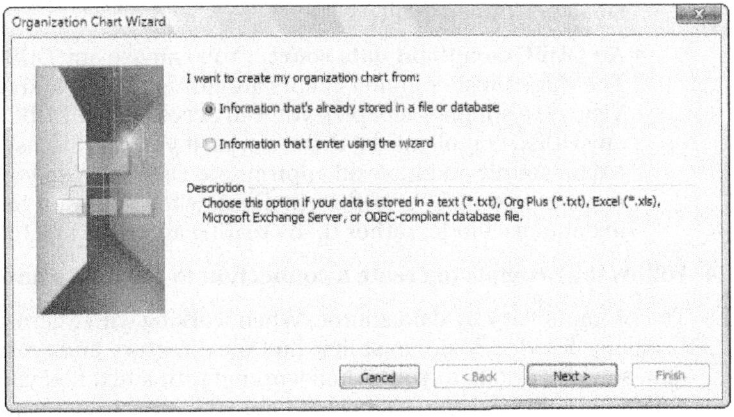

Figure 14-1:
Select a
data entry
option.

2. **Click Next.**

   Visio displays a list of existing data source options, as shown in Figure 14-2.

3. **Choose one of the following sources, and then click Next:**

   - **A Microsoft Exchange Server directory:** Visio automatically scans your system for appropriate directories and presents them to you.

   - **A text, Org Plus (*.txt), or Microsoft Excel (.xls) file:** This could be any text file that contains the appropriate information or an actual spreadsheet file. Use this option with Excel when you want to create an actual link to the file. The benefit of using a link is that you can perform in-place editing should you want to do so. However, the disadvantages include increased Visio file size and a small performance hit.

   - **An ODBC-compliant data source:** You can use any ODBC client. The three most common clients are dBASE, Excel, and Access. Visio also supplies samples you can access using ODBC. However, any ODBC-compliant database works. If you want to use MySQL as a data source and have an appropriate ODBC driver, you can easily use this option. Use ODBC with Excel when you want to use Excel in database mode, rather than creating an actual link to the file.

4. **Follow the prompts to create a connection to the data source.**

   The prompts vary by data source. When working with Microsoft Exchange Service, Visio must first find the directory and present the data-source options to you. When working with a text file, you provide a data file name. When working with an ODBC source, you must first create a connection to that source. Every database uses a different step-by-step procedure to create a new data source.

5. **Choose the fields from your data file that correspond to Name, Reports To, and First Name, and then click Next.**

Visio displays this standard data on the shape as text.

6. **Choose the custom fields you want to include in the organization chart shapes, and then click Next.**

   Visio displays this custom data on the shape as text.

7. **Choose any fields that you want to add to the organization chart shapes as custom property fields, and then click Next.**

   Custom properties contain data stored with a shape (for instance, an employee's telephone number, location, and hire date). For more information about using custom properties, refer to Chapter 13.

8. **Choose whether you want to copy or link to the data when using an ODBC connection, and then click Next.**

   Use the Copy option to create a static snapshot of the data that won't change as you make changes to the database. This option works well when you want to create a historical view of your organization — one that won't change over time. Use the Link option when you want the drawing to update automatically as your database changes. You can also change the database content based on changes you make to the drawing; a link is a two-way conversation with the database. This option works best for most standard organization charts, where you want the chart to keep pace with changes in your organization.

   a. **Click Settings when you choose the Link option.**

      Visio displays the Organization Chart Wizard dialog box shown in Figure 14-3. This dialog box lets you decide how to configure the interaction with the database. For example, you can choose not to allow users to update or delete records by deselecting the appropriate check boxes in the Right Mouse Actions area.

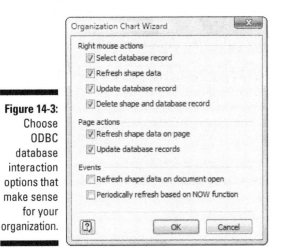

Figure 14-3:
Choose ODBC database interaction options that make sense for your organization.

 b. **Choose the database options you want to use, and then click OK.**

 Visio sets the options for linking to the database. These options never affect a database copy.

 9. **Determine whether you want Visio to break the data into shapes for you automatically or to let you define precisely how the data appears on-screen. When choosing the automatic option, click Finish.**

 When using the Automatic option, Visio creates the organization chart for you automatically.

 10. **Choose how you want to fit information onto the page, and then click Finish.**

 If your organization chart is likely to be larger than one page, you might want to click the option that lets you specify how much data to display on each page. Otherwise, let the wizard decide how to break the chart across pages.

 Visio creates the organization chart based on your data file, the fields that you choose to include, and the format you specify. If the chart has some unexpected results, go back, check the format and content of your input file, and then run the wizard again. Each time you run the wizard, it places the new organization chart output on a new page in the same Visio drawing.

Sometimes when you use a wizard to create an organization chart, the boxes are too small to hold all the text. You don't want to reduce the font size and make it unreadable, but you don't want to resize each box manually, either! Choose View⇨Size & Position to display the Size & Position window. Then select all the boxes you want to resize. (Make sure that you select only the boxes that you want to be the same size.) In the Size & Position window, type new dimensions for Width and Height, and then click anywhere outside the selected shapes. Visio resizes all the selected boxes to the same dimensions.

Creating an organization chart by typing data manually

Your organization might not already have an organization chart to use as input to Visio, but you may want to create one. The manual method provides the advantage of typing the data in using the wizard and then saving the data as an external file. You've performed two tasks at once. Not only do you have a Visio diagram of your organization when you're done, but you also have a data file that you can modify outside of Visio. The following steps describe how to use the manual method:

 1. **Choose File⇨New⇨Business⇨Organization Chart Wizard.**

Visio displays the first screen of the wizard (refer to Figure 14-1). Visio automatically selects the option to create the organization chart from information already stored in a file or database for you.

2. **Select the Information That I Enter Using the Wizard option and click Next.**

   Visio displays a dialog box asking you to choose between an Excel file or a delimited file as output. Use the Excel file option when you have Excel available and plan to use it for editing. This option also works well when you want to work with the data in Word. Use the delimited file option when you want to maintain the data as a text file (editing the text is difficult and error prone) or import the data into a database.

3. **Select a file output option, type a file name, and then click Next.**

   When you choose Excel, Visio actually creates an Excel file for you, fills it with sample data, and opens Excel so you can modify the data. Simply type over the existing data. When you choose delimited text, Visio creates a text file for you, places the sample data in it, and opens Notepad. Using this second approach can be difficult because the data isn't lined up and it's easy to make a mistake.

4. **Type the sample data for your organization chart, save the file, and close the application.**

   Visio displays the next page of the wizard, which asks you how you want to display the data.

5. **Determine whether you want Visio to break the data into shapes for you automatically or to let you define precisely how the data appears on-screen. When choosing the Automatic option, click Finish.**

   When using the Automatic option, Visio creates the organization chart for you automatically.

6. **Choose how you want to fit information onto the page, and then click Finish.**

   If your organization chart is likely to be larger than one page, you might want to click the option that lets you specify how much data to display on each page. Otherwise, let the wizard decide how to break the chart across pages.

   Visio creates the organization chart based on your data file, the fields that you choose to include, and the format you specify. If the chart has some unexpected results, go back, check the format and content of your input file, and then run the wizard again. Each time you run the wizard, it places the new organization chart output on a new page in the same Visio drawing.

Creating a Gantt chart by importing data

A *Gantt chart* is a specific type of diagram used for managing a project. A typical Gantt chart lists the tasks that you need to complete to accomplish a specific goal, the duration of each task, their dependent tasks, and the resources (people and materials) to complete each task. It can also show scheduled dates for beginning and completion, as well as the progress made to date on each task.

If the project data that you want to use exists in a text (.txt) file, you must separate the fields by a tab or a comma. You can also use data from Microsoft Excel (.xls format) or data from Microsoft Project (.mpp or .mpx format), as described later in this chapter. No matter which target file you use, it must include the following information:

- **Unique task number or identifier:** Any number or name that you give to a task to identify it uniquely.

- **Task name:** The name that you give to a task that's part of a project.

- **Duration:** The time allowed to complete a task (for example, days, days/hours, hours, weeks).

- **Start date:** The date when you want a task to begin.

- **Finish date:** The date when you want a task to be completed.

- **Dependency (dependent task):** The task that must be completed before the current task can begin.

- **Resource:** The human resources or materials needed to complete a task.

- **Outline level:** Highest-level tasks are at outline level 1, subordinate tasks (not dependent tasks) are at outline level 2, and so on.

Importing data from a text or Excel file

If you have an Excel or text file that contains the data outlined in the preceding section, you can use it to create a Gantt chart using the Gantt Chart Wizard. The wizard guides you through a series of steps and asks you questions about which file to use, what information you want to include, and how you want the information formatted.

When your project data appears in a Microsoft Excel spreadsheet rather than in a text file, each task appears on a separate spreadsheet row and each piece of information, or *field,* appears in a separate column. The following steps describe how to perform this task:

1. **Choose File➪New➪Schedule➪Gantt Chart.**

   Visio creates a Gantt chart drawing and displays the Gantt Chart Options dialog box. Notice also that the Gantt Chart toolbar is displayed and that the menu bar now contains a Gantt Chart menu (see Figure 14-4).

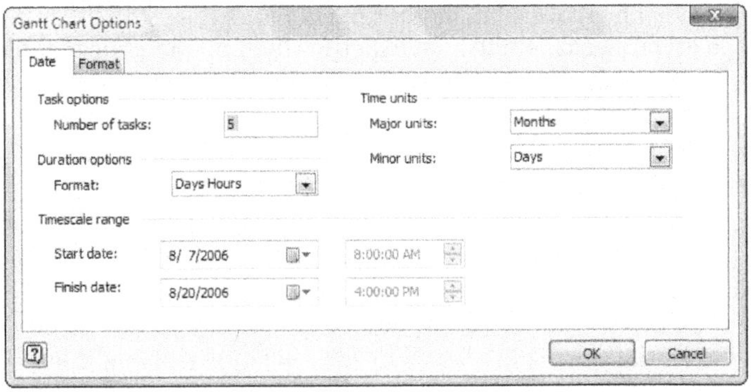

Gantt Chart Options

| Date | Format |

Task options

Number of tasks: 5

Duration options

Format: Days Hours

Timescale range

Start date: 8/ 7/2006   8:00:00 AM

Finish date: 8/20/2006   4:00:00 PM

Time units

Major units: Months

Minor units: Days

OK   Cancel

Figure 14-4: Choose Gantt chart settings for units, duration format, dates, and so on.

2. **Select the options you want (that is, the number of tasks, the units, the duration format, and the start and finish dates), and then click OK.**

   Visio creates the new Gantt chart for you using the options you selected. You also see sample data in the chart that you'll overwrite in the next step.

3. **Choose Gantt Chart⇨Import.**

   Visio displays the first screen of the Gantt Chart Wizard.

4. **Select the Information That's Already Stored in a File option, and then click Next.**

5. **Choose Microsoft Office Excel File or Text File, and then click Next.**

   Visio displays a subset of the data and how it will appear in the Gantt chart. You must perform column mapping to ensure the data appears as expected.

6. **Review the column mapping. Click Change Mapping to change the column mapping when necessary. Click Next.**

   Visio asks you to choose the time intervals for this chart.

7. **Select the time scale and duration options, and then click Next.**

   Visio asks which tasks types you want to include.

   Pay attention to the interval you select for task durations (for example: Days/Hours). The interval used for the Gantt chart must match the interval used in your source file.

8. **Choose the task type options you want include in the Gantt chart, and then click Next.**

   You see a summary of the settings that you've chosen for the Gantt chart.

9. **Click Finish.**

   Visio inserts a new page into your drawing, places a new Gantt chart shape in the new page, and inserts your data. You can delete the initial page by right-clicking the page tab and choosing Delete Page from the context menu.

If, by chance, an error exists in your file, Visio displays an error message for you. The error message tells you exactly which line in your text file the wizard didn't understand. Go back to your text file and check for errors on the suggested line.

Importing data from Microsoft Project

You can also import data from a Microsoft Project file to create a Gantt chart in Visio. Of course, Microsoft Project also provides that capability of creating Gantt charts, so you might wonder why you would use this technique. In most cases, the answer is one of convenience. A colleague might send you (or you might have access to) a Microsoft Project file, but you might not have the program to view the file. In this case, use the steps outlined in the previous section for importing data from a text or Excel file, but specify your Project file as the source file.

Creating data rather than importing

If your data doesn't exist yet and you don't have access to other project management software, you can enter the raw data right into the Gantt Chart Wizard. The wizard creates a text (.txt) file or Excel (.xls) file template for you, opens it, and includes sample data for all the required fields. Just replace the sample data with your data. The following steps describe how to perform this task:

1. **Choose File➪New➪Schedule➪Gantt Chart.**

   Visio creates a Gantt chart drawing and displays the Gantt Chart Options dialog box. Notice also that the Gantt Chart toolbar is displayed and that the menu bar now contains a Gantt Chart menu (refer to Figure 14-4).

2. **Select the options you want (that is, the number of tasks, the units, the duration format, and the start and finish dates), and then click OK.**

   Visio creates the new Gantt chart for you using the options you selected. You also see sample data in the chart that you'll overwrite in the next step.

3. **Choose Gantt Chart➪Import.**

   Visio displays the first screen of the Gantt Chart Wizard.

4. **Select the Information That I Enter Using the Wizard option, and then click Next.**

   Visio displays a dialog box asking which format you want to use to save the data you enter (Excel or text). You also provide a file name for the data.

5. **Choose a data format for the data you want to enter. Type the name of a file to use to save the data. Click Next.**

   Visio asks you how you to format the data on-screen.

6. **Enter the tasks options, duration options, time units, and time-scale range that apply to your project.**

7. **Click Advanced to adjust the start shape, finish shape, left label, right label, inside label, milestones, and summary bars settings.**

   These changes are optional.

8. **Click Next.**

   Visio asks which tasks types you want to include.

9. **Choose the task type options you want to include in the Gantt chart, and then click Next.**

   You see a summary of the settings that you've chosen for the Gantt chart.

10. **Click Finish.**

    Visio inserts a new page into your drawing, places a new Gantt chart shape in the new page, and inserts your data. You can delete the initial page by right-clicking the page tab and choosing Delete Page from the context menu.

Exporting your Gantt chart data

You might find that you've created a Gantt chart for your personal use and everyone wants a copy at some point. In some cases, sending the chart around makes sense, but not everyone has Visio and you don't want to create print-outs that no one can update. The solution to your problem might be exporting your data. You can export the data to an Excel, Microsoft Project, or text file with equal ease. The following steps describe how to perform this task:

1. **Choose Gantt Chart⇨Export.**

   You see the Export Data Wizard.

2. **Select one of the export file formats, and then click Next.**

   You see a summary of the settings you've chosen.

3. **Click Finish.**

   Visio exports the data in the format you requested.

Creating a calendar by importing Outlook appointments

Visio lets you create, edit, and otherwise manipulate calendars. Generally, you use Visio to create an attractive-looking calendar. However, it won't inform you about appointments or past-due tasks. To obtain the full function-ality a calendar program can provide, you need an application such as Outlook or the new Windows Calendar program provided with Vista. Consequently, if you want to ensure that the computer keeps you on track with your appoint-ments, you'll want to start with Outlook or Windows Calendar. However, it's also helpful to import calendars at times because both Outlook and Windows Calendar are spartan. Here are some good reasons to use Visio to modify Outlook and Windows Calendar calendars:

- Reformat the calendar, changing its size, shape, and coloring
- Add special effects such as highlights, shadows, and imported clip art
- Print and distribute the reformatted calendar
- Publish the calendar

Importing a new calendar

Unfortunately, the process is one-way in the current product. You can import a calendar into Visio, but you can't export it. The following steps describe how you can import a new calendar:

1. **Choose File➪New➪Schedule➪Calendar.**

   Visio creates a new Calendar drawing and adds a Calendar menu to the standard menu bar.

2. **Choose Calendar➪Import Outlook Data Wizard.**

   The first screen of the Calendar Wizard appears.

3. **Choose New Visio Calendar. Click Next.**

   The second page of the wizard appears, where you choose calendar dates and times to include.

4. **Choose the starting and ending dates and times for the calendar.**

5. **Click Filter when you want to limit the input you provide. Choose a subject to include in the new calendar, and then click OK.**

6. **Click Next.**

   Visio requests that you provide calendar specifics.

7. **Choose calendar specifics, such as duration, special calendar features such as starting day, and whether you want weekends shaded. Click Next.**

   You see a summary of the calendar specifics.

8. **Click Finish.**

   Visio creates a calendar shape that spans the dates you specified. It includes all appointments scheduled for those dates.

Updating an existing calendar

You'll often find a need to update the static calendars you create with Visio. Rather than repeat the entire process, you can simply open an existing file and update the data in it. You won't have to provide all of the calendar specifics as you do when creating a new calendar. This technique also preserves some of the shape formatting you provide. However, it doesn't preserve embellishments, such as adding graphics to the entries. The following steps describe how to update an existing calendar:

1. **Select the Calendar shape you want to update.**

2. **Choose Calendar⇨Import Outlook Data Wizard.**

   The first screen of the Calendar Wizard appears.

3. **Choose Selected Visio Calendar. Click Next.**

   The second page of the wizard appears, where you choose calendar dates and times to include.

4. **Choose the starting and ending dates and times for the calendar.**

5. **Click Filter when you want to limit the input you provide. Choose a subject to include in the new calendar, and then click OK.**

6. **Click Next.**

   You see a summary of the calendar specifics.

7. **Click Finish.**

   Visio creates a calendar shape that spans the dates you specified. It includes all appointments scheduled for those dates.

Incorporating Visio Shapes and Drawings in Non-Visio Documents

The *Object Linking and Embedding (OLE)* feature of Microsoft Windows makes it possible to share many types of data and graphic images among Windows-compatible applications. A few less-capable applications lack support for OLE. You identify these applications when you find that the Edit⇨Paste command remains grayed out when you copy an object to the Clipboard that the application doesn't support directly. Some applications only support embedding (where the image actually appears as part of the host document file). You identify these applications by the absence of an Edit⇨Paste Special command. Most applications support both embedding and linking (where the host application places a pointer to the file in the document, rather than the actual file).

Linking and embedding produce the same results visually in most cases, but they're different behind the scenes. *Linking* creates a link to the object. This technique ensures that any change you make to the original file also appears in the linked version you create in another document. *Embedding* places a copy of the object into the document. Although this approach increases the file size, it also means that the document is portable. When a program doesn't support OLE, you can *export* Visio drawings or shapes to non-Visio documents.

Visio also supports a new technique called hyperlinking. A *hyperlink* creates an actual HTML-type link in the document. When you Ctrl+Click the link, Visio opens the hyperlinked file in the application that created it. You can also create hyperlinks to Visio documents in other applications.

Linking shapes and drawings

Linking creates a special connection between two files: the *source file* (where the data is created and displayed) and the *destination file* (where the data is displayed only). When you link data to a destination file, the original data stays in the source file where you created it. When you open the destination file using the *host* application (the application that is supporting the Visio drawing), you see a *representation of the data,* like a snapshot, but it isn't really part of the file. Double-clicking the representation normally opens a copy of Visio. Some applications actually host Visio as part of the application frame so it appears as if you haven't left the host application. Other applications open a separate copy of Visio, where you make the required changes. When you finish making the changes, you save the file as usual and close Visio. The host application appears again with the new data. The following steps describe how to create a link to a Visio drawing in another application:

1. **Save the drawing.**

2. **Deselect any shapes you have selected.**

3. **Choose Edit⇨Copy Drawing or press Ctrl+C.**

4. **Open the host application document.**

5. **Choose Edit⇨Paste Special.**

   Visio displays the Paste Special dialog box shown in Figure 14-5.

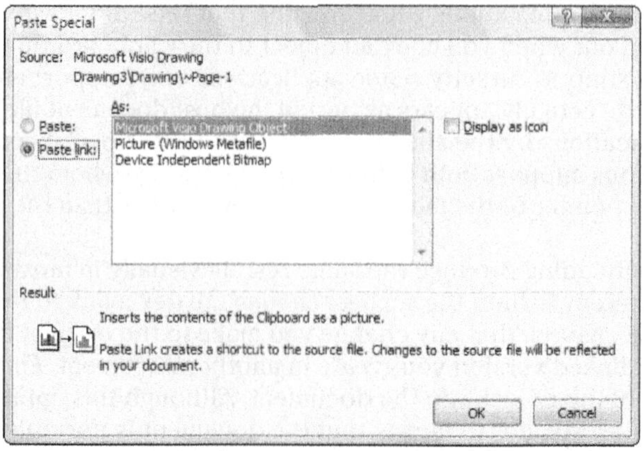

Figure 14-5:
This Paste Special dialog box from Microsoft Word lists several file formats, including Microsoft Visio Drawing Object.

Some programs may use a different command for linking files. For example, when using Word 2007, you choose the Home tab of the Ribbon, click the down arrow next to Paste, and choose Paste Special from the drop-down list box. If this command isn't on your menu, check the online help or user documentation for the program that you're using. In some cases, you can't create a link because the application doesn't support it. Even in these cases, try embedding the drawing by choosing Edit⇨Paste.

6. **Select Paste Link.**

   The As list changes to show the linking options.

7. **Choose Microsoft Visio Drawing Object from the As list box.**

8. **Select the Display as Icon check box when you only want to see a Visio icon, rather than the actual drawing.**

   Many people prefer to display an icon for links so they know that the item is linked, rather than embedded.

9. **Click OK.**

   The drawing or shapes that you linked now appear in the host application's document.

Embedding shapes in drawings

You've probably been embedding objects for years without even knowing it. Every time you cut and paste (or copy and paste) from one program to another, you're embedding objects. Embedding is different from linking because the data you embed becomes part of the destination file. Windows creates a copy of the original object and places it in the host application, so the original Visio drawing and the embedded drawing are completely separate. The following steps describe how to embed an object:

1. **Save the drawing.**

2. **Deselect any shapes you have selected.**

3. **Choose Edit⇨Copy Drawing or press Ctrl+C.**

4. **Open the host application document.**

5. **Choose Edit⇨Paste.**

   The drawing or shapes that you embedded now appear in the host application's document.

Hyperlinking shapes and drawings

One of the new features in Visio lets you create a hyperlink between a host application and Visio. This new option is completely different from the older options that Visio provides because it's more like creating a Web-like connection than a Windows-specific connection. Consequently, this book discusses hyperlinking as a separate and valuable Visio addition. When you add a hyperlink to a Visio drawing in another document, the user presses Ctrl+Click to access the file. The advantage of a hyperlink is that you can see the data just as you normally would, but you always edit it using the original application, so you have more control over the editing process. In addition, unlike other links, you can fix a hyperlink with relative ease.

This feature currently works only in Office products at the moment, including Visio. While you can create a hyperlink to most data, most applications can't create a hyperlink. The following steps describe how to create a hyperlink:

1. **Save the drawing.**

2. **Deselect any shapes you have selected.**

3. **Choose Edit⇨Copy Drawing or press Ctrl+C.**

4. **Open the host application document.**

5. **Choose Edit⇨Paste as Hyperlink or select the Home tab, click the down arrow under Paste, and choose Paste as Hyperlink.**

   Visio creates a hyperlink to the document.

Exporting and importing shapes and drawings

Some computer programs are not OLE compatible; in other words, they don't support Edit⇨Copy and Edit⇨Paste or Edit⇨Paste Special. When you want to use a Visio shape or drawing in a program that doesn't support OLE, you can export the file. *Exporting* converts the data in a Visio file to a non-Visio file format — one that you choose. In the non-Visio program, you then *import* the file as a picture.

The file type that you choose for exporting depends on two things: the program that you want to use the drawing in and how you're going to use the drawing. For example, if you just want to insert the drawing in another file as a picture, use a common graphics format, such as `.bmp`, `.tif`, or `.gif`. If you want to use the drawing in an AutoCAD file, choose the AutoCAD drawing or AutoCAD Interchange format. Here is a list of all the file types that you can use to export a Visio drawing.

XML Drawing (`.vds`)	XML Stencil (`.vsx`)
XML Template (`.vtx`)	Scalable Vector Graphics (`.svg`)
Scalable Vector Graphics — Compressed (`.svgz`)	AutoCAD Drawing (`.dwg`)
AutoCAD Interchange (`.dfx`)	Web Page (`.htm, .html`)
Compressed Enhanced Metafile (`.emz`)	Enhanced Metafile (`.emf`)
Graphics Interchange Format (`.gif`)	JPEG File Interchange Format (`.jpg`)
Portable Network Graphics (`.png`)	Tag Image File Format (`.tif, .tiff`)
Windows Bitmap (`.bmp`)	Windows Metafile (`.wmf`)
XML Paper Specification (`.xps`)	

Exporting a drawing can have unwanted side effects. For example, your lines and text will lose their crisp look when you export to a bitmap format such as TIF, GIF, or BMP. In some cases, the drawing can lose some of the data that defines it. Using a JPG format can result in a loss of data that could reduce color resolution or other features. Consequently, you must export the drawing with care and then view it in the new application to determine whether the drawing quality is still acceptable. The following steps describe how to export a drawing:

1. **Choose File➪Save As to display the Save As dialog box.**
2. **Select the folder you want to use to save the drawing.**
3. **Type a name for the file in the File Name field.**
4. **Choose a file format in the Save as Type drop-down menu.**
5. **Click Save.**

Sending drawings to Outlook

Microsoft Outlook uses the Microsoft Exchange Server format for storing files. If you want to store a drawing in an Outlook folder, you can. Open the Visio drawing and choose File➪Send To➪Exchange Folder. Choose the folder that you want and then click OK. Your drawing is stored as an embedded object in the Outlook folder you chose (such as Drafts). You can open the drawing in Outlook and then send it to someone using File➪Send To.

You have two options for opening the Visio drawing in the other application. The best option is to use the File➪Open command to open the file as you would any other file for that application. In some cases, you might have to convert the Visio drawing from an intermediary common format, such as TIF, to a format the application understands. In this case, use the application's Import command (normally found on the File menu). The reason this second option isn't as acceptable is that you're performing a second conversion with a second potential loss of information from the drawing.

Using Visio Viewer to Share Visio Drawings

Even if some of your colleagues don't have Visio, you can still send them a Visio drawing. To view the drawing, they must download and install Visio Viewer from the Microsoft Download Center:

```
http://office.microsoft.com/downloads
```

When you open a drawing using Visio Viewer, the viewer displays the drawing in a Microsoft Internet Explorer (Version 5.0 or later) window. Note that you can view a drawing created in Visio 2003 only with Visio Viewer 2003. However, you can view drawings created in earlier versions of Visio (Version 5.0, 2000, and 2002) using Visio Viewer 2002, also downloadable from Microsoft's download center.

Saving Visio Drawings for the Web

The Internet contains so much information — and graphics are a huge part of the data flow. Many software companies are making it easier than ever to save files specifically for publishing to the Internet, and Microsoft is no exception. The File menu in Visio contains a Save as Web Page command, which automatically saves your drawing using an .html (HyperText Markup Language) extension. You can save new Visio drawings directly to this format, or save existing Visio drawings in Visio format as well as .html. Your drawings will look as cool on your Web page as they do in Visio. The following steps describe how to perform this task:

1. **Choose File➪Save as Web Page.**

   The Save As dialog box appears.

2. **Choose the folder in which you want to save the file.**

3. **Type a name for the file in the File Name field.**

4. **Click Publish.**

   Visio displays the Save as Web Page dialog box shown in Figure 14-6. This dialog box defines publishing details for your drawing. The General tab shown in the figure defines which pages of your drawing appear in the Web page, the functionality of the Web page, whether you provide supporting files for others to see, and the Web page title. The Advanced tab describes enhanced, such as Vector Markup Language (VML), and common, such as Graphics Interchange Format (GIF), display options for the graphic. You also select the target monitor size, a hosting Web site (so you don't have to copy the files manually), and the style sheet you want to use for formatting.

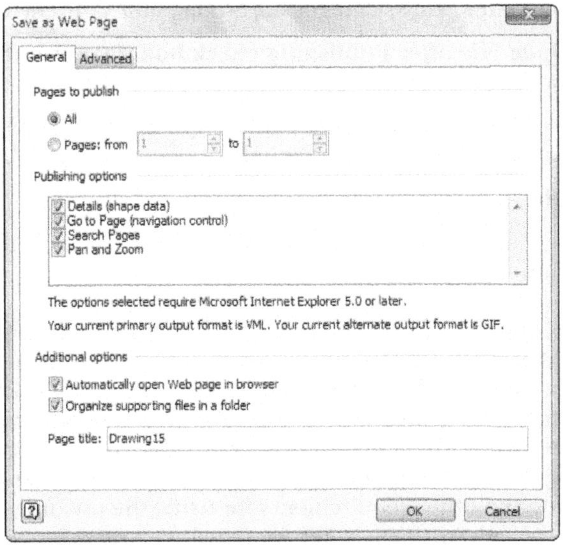

Figure 14-6:
Use the
Save as
Web Page
dialog box
options to
define how
Visio pub-
lishes your
drawing.

5. **Choose all of the Web page output options you want, and then click OK.**

6. **Choose Web Page in the Save as Type field, if it's not already chosen for you.**

7. **Click Save. (To save the file as read-only, click the down arrow next to the Save button and select Read Only.)**

   Visio saves the file and displays it in a browser window when you choose the Automatically Open Web Page in Browser option on the General tab of the Save as Web Page dialog box.

8. **Click the *X* in the upper-right corner, or choose File⇨Close to close the file.**

Publishing Your Drawing in XPS Format

The XML Paper Specification (XPS) file format is a new addition to Office 2007 products, including Visio 2007. This feature lets you publish your Visio drawing in XML format. You can import the document directly into any application that supports the XPS format. The following steps describe how to publish your drawing in XPS format:

1. **Choose File➪Publish as XPS.**

   Visio displays the Publish as XPS dialog box.

2. **Choose the folder in which you want to save the file.**

3. **Type amplifying information about the document in the Title, Subject, Authors, Comments, Tags, Categories, Status, and Content Type fields.**

4. **Select the Open File after Publishing check box if you want to see the results of publishing the file immediately.**

5. **Choose one of the standard optimization options or click Options to select the optimization options manually.**

6. **Click Publish.**

   Visio displays the resulting file when you choose the Open File after Publishing option.

Because XPS is a form of XML, you can also create a special application to read the XML data and import the resulting data into just about any application. It's important to know that the actual XPS file is an archive. Give it a `.zip` extension and you can open it using WinZIP or any other program that reads archive files. Inside you'll find the expected XML file, some relationship (`.rel`) files, `.jpg` files containing your drawings, and a few other files that describe resources and other requirements for using the document. You can read more about this interesting new file format at `http://www.microsoft.com/whdc/xps/default.mspx`.

Creating Data Links to SQL Server and Spreadsheets

Visio provides a powerful new feature that helps you interact with databases and spreadsheets at a new level. Instead of linking, embedding, or hyperlinking data, you can now interact with the spreadsheet or database as a data manager. The data has a new focus. You can create a data link that provides a means of viewing and interpreting data.

Using the Data Link feature

Before you can do much with the new data features of Visio, you must create a data link using the Data Link feature. A *data link* is a live connection to some kind of data on your system. You shouldn't view the Data Link feature in the same light as you would other connection types. It provides a new way to look at data. For example, you can attach data to a shape that normally doesn't provide data. The shape can present visual cues about the data it contains. One possibility is to change the shape color as needed to indicate status. The data need not be of a particular type. You could monitor the status of a system using live links — green might indicate that the component is operating correctly, while red indicates an error condition.

Defining the data link

The first step in using the Data Link feature is to create the connection to the data source. Here is a list of data sources that Visio supports:

Excel	Access
SharePoint Services	SQL Server
OLE-DB data source	ODBC data source

The Excel, Access, SharePoint Services, and SQL Server connections are what you expect: direct connections to a particular application type. The Object Linking and Embedding–Database (OLE-DB) connection requires a special provider. This connection type supports databases such as Access, SQL Server, and Oracle. The Open DataBase Connectivity (ODBC) option lets you work with any database that supports ODBC, such as dBASE, FoxPro, Paradox, MySQL, and specially formatted text such as Comma-Separated Value (CSV) files.

Creating a connection to a data source varies a little by connection type. An Excel connection requires that you choose a file, using Access means selecting a file and a table within the file, SharePoint Services requires that you provide the URL to the service, SQL Server requires a standard database connection, OLE-DB relies on specific provider information, and ODBC means setting up a data source. The following steps describe how to create a typical data link:

1. **Choose Data⇨Link Data to Shapes.**

   Visio displays the Data Selector dialog box, which lists all of the connection types.

2. **Select a data connection type and then click Next.**

   You see the first connection dialog box for your particular connection.

3. **Follow the connection prompts for your particular connection.**

Visio will ask you questions that determine which data from the data source appears as the data link. Eventually, you see the successful import page of the wizard.

4. **Click Finish.**

An External Data window appears.

It's important to check the External Data window to determine whether you obtained the data you actually need. When you see that the data isn't correct, right-click the tab for the data link and choose Remove from the context menu.

Assigning a data link to a graphic

After you have live data to work with, you need to link the data to a shape. You can perform this task using one of several techniques. The easiest and least error-prone method is to drag a row of data to a shape. When you see the shape highlighted, drop the row onto it. Every time you create a new link, you see the link symbol added to that row in the External Data window.

The first link you create displays the Data Graphics task pane. The Data Graphics task pane defines the appearance of the data you drop onto a shape. For example, you can position the text differently or assign it to an element of the shape. Don't worry about this task pane for now; the "Using the Data Graphics feature" section, later in this chapter, discusses this feature.

Assigning data to multiple shapes at once

In some cases, you can save time by assigning data to multiple shapes at once. For example, you might want to use multiple copies of the same shape, but with data for each database element, such as an employee. Begin by selecting the shape you want to use in the Shapes windows. Select the rows you want to use in the External Data window by using the Ctrl+Click method. Drag the rows to the drawing, and you'll find that Visio automatically links the data for you.

Using automatic data assignment

Use automatic data assignment when you already have the shapes you want to use in place. This technique lets you assign data to existing shapes in drawings you created earlier without expending a lot of extra energy. The following steps describe how to use the automatic data assignment technique:

1. **Select the shapes you want to use.**

2. **Choose Data➪Automatically Link.**

You see the Automatic Link Wizard.

3. **Select the All Shapes on This Page option when you plan to link all of the shapes in a drawing to the data or selected shapes. Click Next.**

   Visio asks how you want to link database data to the shape data.

4. **Choose an entry in the Data Column drop-down list box and one from the Shape Field drop-down list box.**

5. **Click Add and perform Step 4 for every link you want to create between the database and the selected shapes.**

6. **Click Next.**

   You see a summary of the automatic link options.

7. **Click Finish.**

   Visio creates the required links for you.

Using the Data Graphics feature

A *Data Graphic* isn't an image for your database data; it defines the appearance of the data. For example, you might want to display a salesperson's name in a certain way or add color to the shape based on a data value. Visio provides a number of Data Graphics for you. However, these data graphics don't generally provide enough flexibility to meet specific needs. The following sections describe how to work with the Data Graphics feature.

Using Data Graphics

Using a Data Graphic is the precisely the same as using a theme (refer to the "Using themes" section of Chapter 4 for details). Simply select the shape (not the data) that you want to change and choose one of the entries in the Data Graphics task pane. Choosing None hides the data from view.

Creating Data Graphics

Most of the Data Graphic designs that Visio supplies display the database data as a callout. This approach works fine when the shape you're using doesn't lend itself to data inside the shape. However, you might want to display the data as part of an organization chart or other drawing type that does work well with data within the shapes. Consequently, you'll often find that you need to create a data graphic of your own. The following steps describe how to create a data graphic of your own:

1. **Click New Data Graphic in the Data Graphics task pane.**

   You see the New Data Graphic dialog box.

2. **Define a Default Position by choosing options in the Horizontal and Vertical fields.**

3. **Select the Show Border around Items at Default Position check box when you want to see a border around the data.**

Even when you don't plan to keep the border for presentation purposes, using a border can make it easier to see where your data could end up within the shape so that you can position it better. When you have the data positioned, you can remove the border. Using this technique assures that future data won't exceed a shape's bounds.

4. **Select the Hide Shape Text When Data Graphic Is Applied check box when you don't want the standard shape text bleeding through the Data Graphic.**

This option is especially important when you work with shapes that normally include text, such as the squares in an organization chart.

5. **Click New Item.**

A list of item options appears, and you have the following choices:

- **Choose Text** when you want to display data as text within or around the shape. Text can include a number of embellishments such as fills, and Visio supports a number of text styles including headings and callouts.

- **Choose Data Bar** when you want to display a data value as a kind of bar graph. Bar graphs aren't always strictly bars. You might decide to display the bar as a series of stars.

- **Choose Icon Set** to display a particular icon when the data meets certain criteria. You can include multiple icons on the set. One icon might indicate that pressure has dropped in a line since the last reading. Another icon may indicate that a component is overheating or that a salesperson has met a particular sales goal. The meaning of the icon depends on how you define it.

- **Choose Color by Value** when you want to change the shape's color depending on a particular condition. As with icons, the meaning of the color depends on how you define this item.

6. **Choose a new item.**

You see the dialog box associated with that item. All of the dialog boxes include common options, such as the data field, and item-specific options, such as the icon assignments for an Icon Set.

7. **Choose values for the Data Field, Callout, and Callout Position fields. Modify any item specific data. Click OK.**

Visio adds the item to the New Data Graphic dialog box.

8. **Perform Steps 5 through 7 for each new item you want to add.**

9. **Click OK to create the new Data Graphic.**

Working with the PivotDiagram feature

The *pivot diagram* is an analysis tool that lets you combine and extract data in ways that show patterns. For example, you might want to know what buying trends are in various regions of the country. A pivot diagram is a kind of table that adds depth to the data in your database. Excel has had the equivalent for quite some time in the form of the pivot table. The Visio pivot diagram is a more graphical version of the pivot table, so if you have worked with one, you have already worked with the other from a conceptual perspective.

The easiest way to create a pivot diagram is to use the PivotDiagram template that Visio provides. However, you can also create a pivot diagram manually. The following steps describe how to use the PivotDiagram template:

1. **Choose File⇨New⇨Business⇨PivotDiagram.**

   Visio creates a new pivot diagram for you and displays the Data Selector Wizard.

2. **Create a connection to your data (refer to the instructions in the "Defining the data link" section, earlier in this chapter, for details).**

   Visio creates a Pivot Node shape that contains the basic information for the pivot diagram. In addition, you see the PivotDiagram window.

3. **Choose a data field from the Category list of the PivotDiagram window.**

   Visio adds all of the entries for that data field to the Pivot Node shape in an organization chart format.

4. **Select an individual data field shape in the drawing, and choose another data field in the Category list for analysis purposes.**

   This is where the pivot diagram becomes most useful because you can perform analysis of each salesperson by quarter (as an example).

5. **Perform Steps 3 and 4 for any other categories you want to add to the pivot diagram.**

6. **Apply Data Graphics (refer to the "Using the Data Graphics feature" section, earlier in this chapter, for details) to the shapes as needed to present the data in the required form.**

Part IV
Advancing Your Knowledge of Visio

The 5th Wave   By Rich Tennant

"Well, shoot! This eggplant chart is just as confusing as the butternut squash chart and the gourd chart. Can't you just make a pie chart like everyone else?"

In this part . . .

This part of the book assumes that you've become confident in your Visio skills. You're probably more than a casual user — but there's still more you can do to become the resident expert. In this part, you uncover the real power of Visio: its programmability. You don't have to be a techie programmer-type to benefit from this feature. However, you do have to be ready to create your own stencils, master shapes, and templates.

You find out how to store data in shapes and discover how storing data lets you generate all types of reports. If you work in a group that shares Visio drawings, you'll find Visio 2007's annotating and reviewing features extremely useful. Then, take advantage of the capability to share Visio drawings with other programs.

Most important for any organization with databases is that Visio 2007 provides a new way to use data in drawings. You can use the data to change the appearance of shapes and even analyze them in Visio. This part helps you make use of this new feature to create impressive drawings that automatically update their information.

Chapter 15

Ten Common Tasks in Visio

*L*et's face it, as you work with any software program, you need to perform plenty of mundane tasks that just don't seem to fit easily in the table of contents or index of the user's manual or don't pop up automatically in online help files when you search. You know that the answer has to be there somewhere — if you could just find it! This chapter covers ten of those tasks.

Rotating Shapes to a Specific Angle

Sometimes you want to rotate a shape to a specific angle, such as 45 degrees. The quickest way to do this is to select the shape, grab the shape's rotation handle, and start rotating the shape right or left. Watch the status bar, which displays the exact angle as you rotate the shape. Rotating counterclockwise produces a positive number; rotating clockwise produces a negative number.

If you prefer to type a specific angle, you can choose View⇨Size & Position Window. Select the object you want to rotate. Enter the angle in the Angle field of the Size & Position window. To rotate the shape in a counterclockwise direction, use a positive number. To rotate the shape clockwise, enter a negative number.

Centering a Drawing before Printing

Centering a drawing before you print it is a simple option that you might miss if you don't happen to be looking at the Shape menu. Whether shapes in the drawing are selected or not, choose Shapes⇨Center Drawing. Visio repositions all the shapes on the page so that they're centered in relation to the page borders.

However, this doesn't necessarily mean that all the shapes are on the page. If your drawing is too large for the page, you can rearrange or resize shapes, change your page size or orientation (choose File⇨Page Setup and then click the Page Setup tab), or scale the drawing (choose File⇨Page Setup and then click the Drawing Scale tab).

Resizing a Page to Fit the Content of a Drawing

If you can't — or don't want to — move, adjust, rearrange, or resize shapes in a drawing to fit on standard-size paper, you can always adjust the page size to fit the content of the drawing. (You can print an odd-sized drawing on multiple pages or by using a large-scale printer or plotter. See the next section.) With the drawing displayed, choose File⇨Page Setup. On the Page Size tab, click the Size to Fit Drawing Contents button, and then click OK. Visio automatically resizes your drawing page.

If you prefer to adjust the drawing page manually, just point your mouse to any edge of the paper near a corner, and then press and hold the Ctrl key. The mouse pointer changes to a double-headed diagonal arrow, which you can drag to resize. (Don't point directly at the corner. If you do, you get a rotation handle, which lets you rotate rather than resize the page.) Release the Ctrl key and mouse button when the page is the size you want it.

Creating a Drawing That Spans Several Pages

This tip and the preceding one are related. If you want to create a large drawing to print on oversized paper or be tiled across several pages, you can set up the drawing in two ways. If you know the paper size, define it up front: Choose File⇨Page Setup, select the Print Setup tab, and set the paper size.

If you're not sure how large the drawing will be, just start creating the drawing and let it evolve. When you think you have the drawing the way you want it, use one of the methods in the preceding tip to size the page to fit the drawing content. Then choose File⇨Page Setup and click the Print Setup tab. Check the preview; it shows you how your drawing size compares to your paper size. Adjust the paper size as necessary

Saving a Company Logo as a Stencil Shape

To save a company logo as a stencil shape, bring your company logo into the current Visio drawing. To do so, choose Insert⇨Picture⇨From File, choose File⇨Open, or copy the logo in a different program and then choose Edit⇨Paste in Visio. Generally, it isn't a good idea to use a hyperlink (Edit⇨Paste as Hyperlink) when you need an aesthetically-appealing picture.

Create a stencil by choosing File⇨Shapes⇨New Stencil, or open an existing custom stencil. Drag the logo that you placed in the drawing onto the stencil. Right-click the shape in the stencil, choose Rename Master, and then type a new name. To make the logo available in any drawing, open the custom stencil whenever you open or create a new drawing.

Creating and Adding a Background Design to a Drawing

You can create a custom background from clip art, photos, or other types of drawings. Paste or insert the object, size it to fit the page, drag it onto a custom stencil to save it, and then give it a name that indicates it is a background shape. Make backgrounds semitransparent so that they don't overpower your drawing. See the next tip to find out how to adjust transparency.

Adding a Visio-created background to a drawing is a simple matter of dragging a shape into the drawing. Choose File➪Shapes➪Visio Extras➪ Backgrounds to open the Backgrounds stencil. Drag a shape onto the drawing. Don't worry about the shape fitting the page; Visio fits the background shape to the page size automatically.

Look at the page tabs at the bottom of the drawing window, and you'll see that the background shape is automatically placed on a new background page. If your drawing had only one page, Visio automatically assigns the background to the only foreground page.

Adjusting the Transparency of Shapes and Text in a Drawing

The fastest way to adjust transparency is to select the shape or text and then click the Transparency button on the Format Shape toolbar. Select a percentage setting from the drop-down list, or click More Transparency Levels to display a dialog box where you can use a slider to select a specific percentage. An alternative to this method is to right-click the shape or text and choose Format➪Fill or Format➪Text to display a dialog box where you can adjust transparency.

Adding the Same Shape or Image to All Pages in a Drawing

When you want to add a shape or an image to all the pages in a drawing, add the shape to a background page. Then choose File➪Page Setup, click the Page Properties tab, and assign the background to each foreground page individually.

Note: If you're creating a drawing, create your background page first and complete it, and then start inserting foreground pages. In the Page Setup/ Page Properties dialog box, the name for the background page pops up automatically as the suggested background, saving you the step of having to assign the background individually to each foreground page.

Unlocking a Shape

A shape that displays gray handles when you select it is locked. Some Visio grouped shapes are made up of many components and are purposely locked so that you don't tamper with them. The entire group or just a component of the group might be locked.

To unlock a shape or a component of a grouped shape, right-click it and choose Format⇨Protection. The Protection dialog box that appears indicates by a check mark all aspects of the shape that are locked. You can unlock aspects individually (such as Width or Rotation) by clicking them to remove the check mark. To unlock all aspects (that is, to protect no aspects), click the None button.

Note that some shapes that appear to be locked (because their selection handles are gray) aren't locked in every aspect. For instance, you might be able to add text but not be able to rotate the shape. Only the Protection dialog box tells you for sure which aspects are locked.

Copying Formatting from One Shape to Another

Sometimes you need to copy formatting from one shape to another. Select the shape or text whose formatting you want to copy, and then click Format Painter on the Standard toolbar. Your mouse pointer changes to a paintbrush. Point to the shape you want to apply the format to and click. Visio copies the format to the shape instantly. Format Painter works for shape formatting (such as color, shadow, and transparency) as well as text formatting (font, size, style, text color, and so on.)

Visio 2007 has reduced the need to copy formatting from one shape to another. Use themes whenever possible to format shapes so that you can obtain a consistent appearance among projects. In addition, themes are faster to use than other formatting techniques. Remember that themes come in two types: Theme Effects (which change the font, style, and so on) and Theme Colors (which adjust every color aspect of the shape).

Chapter 16

Ten Web Sites Devoted to Visio

*T*he Internet moves faster every day. Someone has an idea that a second person improves and a third person proves as the best way to accomplish the task. Of course, the fame only lasts a short time because someone else comes along with another idea. It's this constant exchange of ideas, theories, resources, and even links to yet other Web sites that should have you running to your nearest Web site today. A book helps teach principles and techniques that don't change quickly. Web sites serve an entirely different purpose by helping you implement the principles and techniques that you learn from the book. The following sections provide a quick overview of ten Web sites that can help you implement the principles and techniques you discovered in this book.

VisioCafe

`http://www.visiocafe.com/`

VisioCafe is a great place to go when you need the latest news. The tabbed interface makes it incredibly easy to locate just what you need. The topics include news, resources, Frequently Asked Questions (FAQs), links, and stencils.

However, the real value of this Web site lies in the Visio collections. Here you'll find a robust assortment of stencils of all types. I actually had to look up a few of the stencil types to even know what they are, but if you're in the right profession, you know already. If you're looking for a stencil for a particular discipline and haven't found it on Microsoft's Web site (see the next section), this is a great place to look.

Microsoft Visio

`http://www.mvps.org/visio/`

One of the most valuable resources of the Microsoft Visio Web site is its listing of download sites for hard-to-find templates and stencils. This is a generic Web site, rather than one devoted to a specific occupation, so the templates aren't for a specific occupation. All you need to do is click Visio Download Sites to see this impressive listing. You'll find many expected topics, such as chemistry, electrical, and industrial automation. However, less expected topics also appear, including household, hobbies (including games), and music.

The Web site also provides an array of other resources. Click Information Sites and you'll see everything from tutorials to a list of books written about Visio. The General Topics page is one of the more informational (rather than URL-specific) pages on the Web site. For example, you'll find a list of command-line switches for Visio, which comes in handy for overloading commands. The Web page describes the entire process for you.

Design-Drawing

`http://www.design-drawing.com/`

Design-Drawing provides a wealth of articles and tutorials about Visio (`http://www.design-drawing.com/visio/`). Some of the topics are complex. For example, if you're wondering how Visio compares to AutoCAD, you can discover the differences here.

Most of the articles you find on Design-Drawing are practical. Many people have two monitors attached to their machines today. However, the question is how best to use them to make your computing experience better. You'll find an article on Design-Drawing that discusses this very topic. Chapter 14 discusses the problem of getting your Visio drawings into other applications. Design-Drawing provides instructions for transferring your Visio drawings to Actrix 2000.

Visio The Blog

http://msmvps.com/blogs/visio/default.aspx

Visio The Blog is someone's blog. The Blog contains the author's recent experiences with Visio and helps you get more out of the product. Unlike a static Web site, blogs can provide a human touch. You can comment about what the author wrote and read the entries by other people. In the latest entry as of this writing (http://msmvps.com/blogs/visio/archive/2006/04/23/92232.aspx), the author describes the code behind borders and title pages that stretch to fit the page. It's truly interesting reading if you want a better understanding of how Visio performs all of the work that it does.

Cisco Systems

http://www.cisco.com/en/US/products/prod_visio_icon_list.html

Even though the Cisco Systems Web site isn't completely devoted to Visio, it's an important place to visit if you use Cisco's products. This one Web page contains a considerable number of Visio stencils that provide everything you need for Cisco Systems products.

Dell

http://www.dell.com/content/topics/topic.aspx/global/products/pvaul/topics/en/visio

Cisco Systems isn't the end of the line when it comes to vendor-specific offerings. Many vendors offer Visio stencils. For example, you can find Dell product stencils at this site. You can save considerable time and effort by obtaining the stencils from the vendor, rather than drawing them yourself.

Microsoft Visio Home Page

`http://office.microsoft.com/visio/`

The Microsoft Visio Home Page provides you with access to all of the Microsoft-supported materials, including the latest news, updates, stencils, templates (`http://office.microsoft.com/en-us/templates/default.aspx`), and other resources. This Web site also includes tutorials (`http://office.microsoft.com/en-us/training/default.aspx`), a developer center (`http://msdn.microsoft.com/office/program/visio/default.aspx`), and a link to Visio experts (`http://office.microsoft.com/en-us/assistance/HA012125731033.aspx`). Make sure you also check out the large list of third-party products and resources (`http://directory.partners.extranet.microsoft.com/advsearchresults.aspx?productscsv=15`).

Nick Finck

`http://www.nickfinck.com/`

Some people overlook personal Web sites, but that would be a mistake when it comes to Visio. Personal Web sites such as Nick Finck's often have well-crafted stencils and templates that you can use for specific purposes. In this case, you'll find the Visio stencils for information architects at `http://www.nickfinck.com/stencils.html`. This Web page also has a number of links to other Web sites, the vast majority of which are personal. One of the best features of Nick's Web site is the obvious care he took in creating his stencils and the obvious pride he has in presenting them.

ConceptDraw

`http://www.conceptdraw.com/en/scripts/loadvisioconv.php`

ConceptDraw is a Visio competitor, so you might not expect to see its Web site listed in this chapter. However, ConceptDraw isn't one of the export options that Visio supports. Consequently, if you need to exchange drawings with a ConceptDraw user, you might be out of luck unless you know about the converter. This converter allows conversions both ways. Consequently, your friend who uses ConceptDraw can send you drawings as well, and you can easily convert them into Visio format. It's interesting to note that there are a number of these conversion Web sites, so you can probably find a converter somewhere for most major drawing packages.

ABC Amber Conversion and Merging Software

http://www.processtext.com/abcvisio.html

You might need to share Visio drawings with a lot of different people, all of whom have different drawing programs. ABC Amber Visio Converter supports an amazing number of formats that you won't commonly find anywhere else. The free download means that you can try this product before you buy it. The conversions that grabbed my attention most, however, are the CHM and HLP help file formats. Using this utility means that you can create help files using Visio. Given that Visio supports all of the required elements, such as linking to other pages natively, you should be able to create some impressive help files with this product.

Actually, this entire Web site is devoted to converting one file format to another. Not only can you find a number of converters, but you'll also find a wealth of advice in obtaining a good conversion. This is a great Web site to visit if you work with a large number of clients who might send you data in just about any format imaginable.

Part V
The Part of Tens

The 5th Wave   By Rich Tennant

In this part . . .

Ah, the "Part of Tens" — a mysterious title that hints that you're going to discover at least ten things about *something.* It's a curious yet helpful part of all *For Dummies* books. *Curious* because there really isn't any standard thing you'll find here. *Helpful* because you find some helpful hints, tips, tricks, and trivia that you won't find anywhere else in the book!

This book's "Part of Tens" section contains answers to ten "How do I . . .?" questions, as well as some downright practical tips for working with Visio. Finally, I point you to some online Visio resources, where you can find sample drawings, tutorials, advice from pros, and Microsoft Visio resources. Most importantly, most of these Web sites provide additional templates and stencils that you can use for specialty tasks.

Index

BUSINESS, CAREERS & PERSONAL FINANCE

0-7645-5307-0

0-7645-5331-3 *†

Also available:
- Accounting For Dummies †
  0-7645-5314-3
- Business Plans Kit For Dummies †
  0-7645-5365-8
- Cover Letters For Dummies
  0-7645-5224-4
- Frugal Living For Dummies
  0-7645-5403-4
- Leadership For Dummies
  0-7645-5176-0
- Managing For Dummies
  0-7645-1771-6

- Marketing For Dummies
  0-7645-5600-2
- Personal Finance For Dummies *
  0-7645-2590-5
- Project Management For Dummies
  0-7645-5283-X
- Resumes For Dummies †
  0-7645-5471-9
- Selling For Dummies
  0-7645-5363-1
- Small Business Kit For Dummies *†
  0-7645-5093-4

HOME & BUSINESS COMPUTER BASICS

0-7645-4074-2

0-7645-3758-X

Also available:
- ACT! 6 For Dummies
  0-7645-2645-6
- iLife '04 All-in-One Desk Reference
  For Dummies
  0-7645-7347-0
- iPAQ For Dummies
  0-7645-6769-1
- Mac OS X Panther Timesaving
  Techniques For Dummies
  0-7645-5812-9
- Macs For Dummies
  0-7645-5656-8

- Microsoft Money 2004 For Dummies
  0-7645-4195-1
- Office 2003 All-in-One Desk Reference
  For Dummies
  0-7645-3883-7
- Outlook 2003 For Dummies
  0-7645-3759-8
- PCs For Dummies
  0-7645-4074-2
- TiVo For Dummies
  0-7645-6923-6
- Upgrading and Fixing PCs For Dummies
  0-7645-1665-5
- Windows XP Timesaving Techniques
  For Dummies
  0-7645-3748-2

FOOD, HOME, GARDEN, HOBBIES, MUSIC & PETS

0-7645-5295-3

0-7645-5232-5

Also available:
- Bass Guitar For Dummies
  0-7645-2487-9
- Diabetes Cookbook For Dummies
  0-7645-5230-9
- Gardening For Dummies *
  0-7645-5130-2
- Guitar For Dummies
  0-7645-5106-X
- Holiday Decorating For Dummies
  0-7645-2570-0
- Home Improvement All-in-One
  For Dummies
  0-7645-5680-0

- Knitting For Dummies
  0-7645-5395-X
- Piano For Dummies
  0-7645-5105-1
- Puppies For Dummies
  0-7645-5255-4
- Scrapbooking For Dummies
  0-7645-7208-3
- Senior Dogs For Dummies
  0-7645-5818-8
- Singing For Dummies
  0-7645-2475-5
- 30-Minute Meals For Dummies
  0-7645-2589-1

INTERNET & DIGITAL MEDIA

0-7645-1664-7

0-7645-6924-4

Also available:
- 2005 Online Shopping Directory
  For Dummies
  0-7645-7495-7
- CD & DVD Recording For Dummies
  0-7645-5956-7
- eBay For Dummies
  0-7645-5654-1
- Fighting Spam For Dummies
  0-7645-5965-6
- Genealogy Online For Dummies
  0-7645-5964-8
- Google For Dummies
  0-7645-4420-9

- Home Recording For Musicians
  For Dummies
  0-7645-1634-5
- The Internet For Dummies
  0-7645-4173-0
- iPod & iTunes For Dummies
  0-7645-7772-7
- Preventing Identity Theft For Dummies
  0-7645-7336-5
- Pro Tools All-in-One Desk Reference
  For Dummies
  0-7645-5714-9
- Roxio Easy Media Creator For Dummies
  0-7645-7131-1

* Separate Canadian edition also available
† Separate U.K. edition also available

Available wherever books are sold. For more information or to order direct: U.S. customers visit www.dummies.com or call 1-877-762-2974.
U.K. customers visit www.wileyeurope.com or call 0800 243407. Canadian customers visit www.wiley.ca or call 1-800-567-4797.

⊛WILEY

SPORTS, FITNESS, PARENTING, RELIGION & SPIRITUALITY

0-7645-5146-9

0-7645-5418-2

Also available:
- Adoption For Dummies
  0-7645-5488-3
- Basketball For Dummies
  0-7645-5248-1
- The Bible For Dummies
  0-7645-5296-1
- Buddhism For Dummies
  0-7645-5359-3
- Catholicism For Dummies
  0-7645-5391-7
- Hockey For Dummies
  0-7645-5228-7

- Judaism For Dummies
  0-7645-5299-6
- Martial Arts For Dummies
  0-7645-5358-5
- Pilates For Dummies
  0-7645-5397-6
- Religion For Dummies
  0-7645-5264-3
- Teaching Kids to Read For Dummies
  0-7645-4043-2
- Weight Training For Dummies
  0-7645-5168-X
- Yoga For Dummies
  0-7645-5117-5

TRAVEL

0-7645-5438-7

0-7645-5453-0

Also available:
- Alaska For Dummies
  0-7645-1761-9
- Arizona For Dummies
  0-7645-6938-4
- Cancún and the Yucatán For Dummies
  0-7645-2437-2
- Cruise Vacations For Dummies
  0-7645-6941-4
- Europe For Dummies
  0-7645-5456-5
- Ireland For Dummies
  0-7645-5455-7

- Las Vegas For Dummies
  0-7645-5448-4
- London For Dummies
  0-7645-4277-X
- New York City For Dummies
  0-7645-6945-7
- Paris For Dummies
  0-7645-5494-8
- RV Vacations For Dummies
  0-7645-5443-3
- Walt Disney World & Orlando For Dummies
  0-7645-6943-0

GRAPHICS, DESIGN & WEB DEVELOPMENT

0-7645-4345-8

0-7645-5589-8

Also available:
- Adobe Acrobat 6 PDF For Dummies
  0-7645-3760-1
- Building a Web Site For Dummies
  0-7645-7144-3
- Dreamweaver MX 2004 For Dummies
  0-7645-4342-3
- FrontPage 2003 For Dummies
  0-7645-3882-9
- HTML 4 For Dummies
  0-7645-1995-6
- Illustrator cs For Dummies
  0-7645-4084-X

- Macromedia Flash MX 2004 For Dummies
  0-7645-4358-X
- Photoshop 7 All-in-One Desk Reference For Dummies
  0-7645-1667-1
- Photoshop cs Timesaving Techniques For Dummies
  0-7645-6782-9
- PHP 5 For Dummies
  0-7645-4166-8
- PowerPoint 2003 For Dummies
  0-7645-3908-6
- QuarkXPress 6 For Dummies
  0-7645-2593-X

NETWORKING, SECURITY, PROGRAMMING & DATABASES

0-7645-6852-3

0-7645-5784-X

Also available:
- A+ Certification For Dummies
  0-7645-4187-0
- Access 2003 All-in-One Desk Reference For Dummies
  0-7645-3988-4
- Beginning Programming For Dummies
  0-7645-4997-9
- C For Dummies
  0-7645-7068-4
- Firewalls For Dummies
  0-7645-4048-3
- Home Networking For Dummies
  0-7645-42796

- Network Security For Dummies
  0-7645-1679-5
- Networking For Dummies
  0-7645-1677-9
- TCP/IP For Dummies
  0-7645-1760-0
- VBA For Dummies
  0-7645-3989-2
- Wireless All In-One Desk Reference For Dummies
  0-7645-7496-5
- Wireless Home Networking For Dummies
  0-7645-3910-8

HEALTH & SELF-HELP

0-7645-6820-5 *†   0-7645-2566-2

Also available:

Alzheimer's For Dummies
0-7645-3899-3
Asthma For Dummies
0-7645-4233-8
Controlling Cholesterol For Dummies
0-7645-5440-9
Depression For Dummies
0-7645-3900-0
Dieting For Dummies
0-7645-4149-8
Fertility For Dummies
0-7645-2549-2

Fibromyalgia For Dummies
0-7645-5441-7
Improving Your Memory For Dummies
0-7645-5435-2
Pregnancy For Dummies †
0-7645-4483-7
Quitting Smoking For Dummies
0-7645-2629-4
Relationships For Dummies
0-7645-5384-4
Thyroid For Dummies
0-7645-5385-2

EDUCATION, HISTORY, REFERENCE & TEST PREPARATION

0-7645-5194-9   0-7645-4186-2

Also available:

Algebra For Dummies
0-7645-5325-9
British History For Dummies
0-7645-7021-8
Calculus For Dummies
0-7645-2498-4
English Grammar For Dummies
0-7645-5322-4
Forensics For Dummies
0-7645-5580-4
The GMAT For Dummies
0-7645-5251-1
Inglés Para Dummies
0-7645-5427-1

Italian For Dummies
0-7645-5196-5
Latin For Dummies
0-7645-5431-X
Lewis & Clark For Dummies
0-7645-2545-X
Research Papers For Dummies
0-7645-5426-3
The SAT I For Dummies
0-7645-7193-1
Science Fair Projects For Dummies
0-7645-5460-3
U.S. History For Dummies
0-7645-5249-X

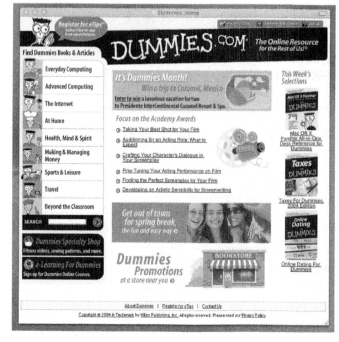

Get smart @ dummies.com®

- **Find a full list of Dummies titles**
- **Look into loads of FREE on-site articles**
- **Sign up for FREE eTips e-mailed to you weekly**
- **See what other products carry the Dummies name**
- **Shop directly from the Dummies bookstore**
- **Enter to win new prizes every month!**

* **Separate Canadian edition also available**
† **Separate U.K. edition also available**

Available wherever books are sold. For more information or to order direct: U.S. customers visit www.dummies.com or call 1-877-762-2974.
U.K. customers visit www.wileyeurope.com or call 0800 243407. Canadian customers visit www.wiley.ca or call 1-800-567-4797.